W9-BZT-616

47th EDITION

Warman's®

Antiques&
Collectibles
2014

NOAH FLEISHER

Published by

Krause Publications, a division of F+W Media, Inc.
700 East State Street • Iola, WI 54990-0001
715-445-2214 • 888-457-2873
www.krausebooks.com

To order books or other products call toll-free 1-800-258-0929
or visit us online at www.krausebooks.com.

ISBN-13: 978-1-4402-3462-0
ISBN-10: 1-4402-3462-0

Cover Design by Jim Butch
Designed by Sharon Bartsch, Lanae Besch, Megan Merkel and Jana Tappa
Edited by Mary Sieber

Printed in China

On the cover, clockwise from upper left:

Tiffany flower form vase, **$1,725;** *chaise longue, Tommi Parzinger design,* **$7,500;** *Chinese double gourd covered jar,* **$37,375;** *"Late Moon Rising (Wild Horse Creek)" by Birger Sandzén,* **$262,900.**

On the back cover:

Handel peacock floor lamp, **$23,575;** *Neil Armstrong NASA lithograph print,* **$5,078;** *Bing Steam Vis-À-Vis,* **$18,880.**

Contents

Introduction

BY NOAH FLEISHER

The overall world of antiques and collectibles, in its totality, is wonderfully, maddeningly diverse, interesting and inexhaustible. As tastes vary, so does opinion.

I've been around the business for a little while now – coming up on 15 years – though not nearly as long as the very best, most of it spent as an editor at various antiques publications and, more recently, in the world of public relations. In this time I've gotten a world class education from some of the best in the business and made more than a few good friends. In writing this piece, I have gone back to some of these friendships. Rather than take a traditional approach to an overview of the market by consulting dealers, auctioneers and experts – whose brilliance is sprinkled liberally throughout this edition – I thought I'd turn to those who generally create those overviews: antiques editors.

Noah Fleisher

The four editors who contributed to this piece – Scudder Smith, publisher and editor of *Antiques and The Arts Weekly* (also known as The Bee); Lita Solis-Cohen, senior editor of *Maine Antiques Digest*; Catherine Saunders-Watson, editor, *Auction Central News*; and Karen Knapstein, print editor, *Antique Trader* – are spread across the country and cover distinctly separate types of markets, though their obvious expertise and experience in the business tie them and their opinions together.

The publications these fine journalists work for are the respective bibles of their erudite audiences and, as you will read, their assessments reflect the diversity of their experiences and personalities. They are in the trenches, day in and day out, and they see all sides of what happens across the world of antiques. I can't thank each of them enough for their time, energy and forthright honesty in answering the questions.

That said, then, let's turn it over to them and see what they have to say about the state of the antiques and collectibles market in the coming year:

What is your general assessment of the overall health of the antiques and collectibles market right now?

- **SCUDDER SMITH:** The overall health of the business varies from dealer to dealer, with those who have built a bank of rich clients doing well as long as they can provide top-of-the-line antiques. Most of the dealers I know, and some I just see at shows, are saying that business is off and expect a good eight to 10 years before things are right again. One of the big failings of the business is that there are no young people, ages 20-45, showing any interest in collecting.
- **LITA SOLIS-COHEN:** The "best" – the highest quality in every field – is healthy. The rest is languishing in every field.

NOAH FLEISHER *received his Bachelor of Fine Arts degree from New York University and brings more than a decade of newspaper, magazine, book, antiques and art experience to his position as Public Relations Director of Heritage Auctions, one of the country's foremost auction houses. He is the former editor of Antique Trader, New England Antiques Journal and Northeast Antiques Journal, is the author of Warman's Modern Furniture, and has been a longtime contributor to Warman's Antiques and Collectibles.*

- **CATHERINE SAUNDERS-WATSON:** Auction houses that are particular about what they sell are doing extremely well; there are auction records set just about every week, but those records are being set by houses that are smart, aggressive and tuned into what collectors want. This is a profit-driven business, and consignors want maximum financial return for their collections. If every step of an auctioneer's business model isn't geared toward profit, they'll very quickly find themselves unable to compete for business against other houses that have big ad and promotional budgets. Dealers – no matter what they sell – must be diversified. I know from having been a dealer for years that you have to have a number of revenue streams working for you all the time. You have to hustle. You have to stay aware of trends and be smart about what you buy for resale.
- **KAREN KNAPSTEIN:** Top tier categories are still faring remarkably well, as should always be the case given the finite number of superlative examples for investment. The balance of the collecting markets continues to be challenged. Dealers and auctioneers need to diversify not only their inventories and services, but also their marketing strategies; they can't rest back on their heels and do what they've always done. Becoming active and visible to potential new markets via social media is going to be crucial for business survival, whether it is for networking purposes, acquiring new consignments or finding new bidders and buyers.

Taking the long view and looking back a decade or two, where is the business now compared to then? What subsets of the market have remained strong? Weak?

- **SMITH:** Twenty years ago things were great, all manner of antiques were selling, the good and the bad, and the business was booming. I've seen dealers at some shows – mostly the outdoor flea markets such as those run by Russell Carrell – buy something, sell it to another dealer after taking only a few steps, and that dealer, in turn, sells it again before returning to their booth. Objects have sold as many as five times before being offered to the retail public. That is very rare today and pre-show selling between dealers has fallen off for most of them. Again, the best will sell and the best folk art, which is my prime interest, continues to sell.
- **SOLIS-COHEN:** The market has shrunk; fewer collectors in all fields. The Tiffany market is strong but not as deep. The market for 20th century design is healthy. Good design sells; there is no market for bad design. This is true of every segment of the market. Condition is important. Original surface is still a factor in every field, even though in Federal and Classical furniture old surfaces are refreshed. We have been reporting how brown furniture has dropped dramatically in price. The best still brings big prices; the rest is really affordable, cheaper than new furniture in many cases. The old mantra "buy the best you can afford and in the best condition" is still the way to go. Run-of-the-mill Victorian furniture is a hard sell and Arts and Crafts is affordable. For those furnishing Prairie Style houses, prices are well below the top of the market a decade ago. The best art pottery is strong while the rest is more affordable than it once was. The secondary market for good studio pottery, glass, metalwork, and modernist jewelry is alive with, again, the best examples selling well.

- **SAUNDERS-WATSON:** Obviously, the biggest change has been collectors and auction houses coming together through Internet live bidding. Ten years ago I knew many people who didn't have the slightest idea how auctions of any kind worked. They were intimidated by the whole process. Now they bid and buy with regularity via the Internet. They like the shield of anonymity that the Internet provides for them and, of course, they have a smorgasbord of antiques and art available to them because they can bid in auction houses all over the world. On LiveAuctioneers.com, alone, you can bid in sales from 1,300+ auction houses. Where auctions have remained strong, shows have lost market share. So many great shows have passed into history or just aren't what they used to be, which is a shame.

- **KNAPSTEIN:** There's been a shift from the show floor to the auction floor; auctions are growing while antiques shows are contracting – there aren't as many and they aren't as big. Many buyers who are looking for quality (both design and construction) are savvy enough to head to the sources where dealers get their inventory, allowing them to buy better quality with a limited budget. Choice vintage advertising, posters, fine jewelry and watches, select American art pottery in excellent condition, and fine and original illustration art all remain strong. Furniture prices remain weak, unless it's by superlative mid-century designers and makers. It's definitely a buyer's market in nostalgic categories like Depression and pressed glass, formal dinnerware, vintage toys, and costume jewelry. Items made to be collectible – such as plates and commemoratives – are quite possibly all-time lows.

What is the most surprising development relating to the business that you've seen in recent years?

- **SMITH:** Auctions are becoming the way to sell, not dealers, and most auction houses have seen an increase in business, from what they tell me. One auctioneer told me he has enough merchandise, and really good things, to carry him through 2013, with things still coming in. Asian material has also come on strong in the past few years.

- **SOLIS-COHEN:** Private sales by auction houses and the huge amount of Internet business. Christie's is launching an Internet platform. Sotheby's failed more than a decade ago; they got into it too soon. Now Sotheby's and Christie's online auctions are really well done with more and more people watching the sales, even if they are bidding by phone. Fewer people than ever come to the salesrooms.

- **SAUNDERS-WATSON:** I can't really say it was surprising to me, personally, but I think many found it surprising that so many newly affluent Chinese would become interested in buying back their heritage and now had the money to do so. This happened in Russia as well. A lot of high-end dealers and auction houses were waiting for the opportunity to cultivate a wealthy new clientele in Russia and China, in particular.

- **KNAPSTEIN:** I'm surprised at how long it's taking some auctioneers and dealers to include online components in their businesses. In order to be successful in any retail situation, you want to remove as many obstacles between a buyer and seller as possible. In not presenting inventory to the world on the web, it's being kept a secret from countless potential buyers.

Victorian pink glass cabinet vase with applied gilt and floral enamel decoration, circa 1900, 3 1/2" high. **$191**

What areas, going into the coming year, do you think will be hot?

- **SMITH:** I have noticed the word "mid-century" popping up frequently, and I think that is where lots of people are going, especially the younger ones. Shows are heading that way, such as The Metro Show in NYC, and dealers are bringing more to the other shows – and it's selling. I think Asian will continue on for a few years, and modern art seems to be finding its place among the hot areas of collecting.

- **SOLIS-COHEN:** Unless the economy recovers, nothing will go crazy like contemporary art, which is bought and sold as a commodity. Most art is not collected for investment. American paintings have held up but, again, at the top of the market. Hudson River School paintings are well off their high, but get a great one and it will soar. The same goes for the Pennsylvania Impressionists.

- **SAUNDERS-WATSON:** Modern and contemporary art, rare gold and silver coins, Golden Age comic books, rare sports memorabilia with impeccable provenance from Hall of Famers (especially baseball and basketball, but watch for hockey to make a big splash), cast-iron mechanical banks, certain types of antique toys. Entertainment memorabilia related to Marilyn Monroe, Elvis Presley and, to a lesser extent, James Dean will continue to fascinate collectors. Tiffany Studios' productions can do no wrong. Neither can Georg Jensen silver or Chanel costume jewelry and couture. Those companies' designs are classics and will continue to be viewed as such by collectors.

- **KNAPSTEIN:** Mid-century design is timeless; buyers are motivated by quality designs from Nakashima, Charles and Ray Eames, Maloof, Bertoia and Wright, to name a few. Results for early American painted furniture and outstanding folk art examples also seem to be on an upswing.

What areas have gone cold?

- **SMITH:** Furniture, brown stuff, is stone cold and dealers are taking fewer pieces to shows as a result. Game boards, quilts, baskets, etc., have all had their day, and now they have to be great to make the grade.

- **SOLIS-COHEN:** Baseball cards and collectibles. Dolls are down but good ones sell. Silver is not easy to sell. Much of it brings more as melt value. Tiffany silver does better than other makers.

- **SAUNDERS-WATSON:** I would not want to have a large collection of granny glass, brown furniture, or anything that was created expressly as a "collectible." Remember Beanie Babies? For that matter, I would not want any type of antique that is moderately to very common.

- **KNAPSTEIN:** "Limited edition" collectibles like plates and figurines, ordinary-looking furniture, and production glass are all bringing soft results. Anything in lukewarm markets (carnival glass, china sets, common books) with condition issues is going to be a losing proposition, unless it is truly rare.

With the advent of the Internet, "Antiques Roadshow," and the slew of antiques-related TV shows now on the air, is it possible anymore to find a one-in-a-million item for $1 at a garage sale?

- **SMITH:** "Roadshow" and other shows related to antiques still have an audience, but others have fallen away, such as the last Keno Brothers venture. I think more of them will end unless the interest spurs them on. I know people who watch them all the time, but only to see what things bring; they have no interest in going out looking – in fact their houses are void of antiques. It's just entertainment and does nothing for the business. However, some good finds are still at tag sales, etc., but few and far between.

- **SOLIS-COHEN:** Discoveries are still made. We just reported on an American Indian Navajo blanket that came from a trailer in the desert of California. The owner saw one like it on "Roadshow" and sent it to auction. It brought $1.8 million. The owner knows where to take it now.
- **SAUNDERS-WATSON:** I'd like to think so. It's the reason why I brake for yard sales. I don't know that I've found a one-in-a-million item that way, but I did find a circa-1830 ship diorama that the owner thought was a step above firewood, bought it for a dollar, and resold it for $2,900.
- **KNAPSTEIN:** We report regularly of some phenomenal finds at flea markets, yard sales, and thrift stores. Our latest "Favorite Finds" contest included the tale of a $1 flea market lamp that turned out to be a genuine Tiffany Studios piece; it sold for $2,000. Genuine gemstone jewelry mixed in with dime-store costume jewelry is an all-too-common mistake that sellers make and buyers cash in on. The antiques-reality entertainment genre has definitely raised the awareness of the possibility of amazing discoveries. However, when an executor (oftentimes a relative with a busy life of his or her own) is faced with the enormous task of cleaning out a property and making sure everyone gets a share, he may take shortcuts and do what's easiest, not necessarily what's most profitable for the family in the long run – leading to some outrageous buys at estate sales.

Is the antiques show, antiques fair, or country auction alive and well? If not, what has replaced it? If so, what evidence are you seeing to support this?

- **SMITH:** Too many shows are going by the wayside, and those coming along are having trouble attracting dealers. Shows are not what they were years ago. However, there are some shows that continue to bring in the crowds, such as the New Hampshire Dealers Antiques Show, the extra large Baltimore Antiques Show, the ADA Show in Deerfield and, of course, the Winter Show. Auctions on site, especially out in the country, still draw, as do single-owner sales, though the one-owner collection has been out of circulation for a good number of years.
- **SOLIS-COHEN:** Some say in five years most of the business will be done on the Internet and only a few shows will survive. Some say the illustrated catalog will be a thing of the past. Photography has improved. Close-up and details tell more than the eye can see and now you can see it all on a mobile device. Nevertheless, people still want to hold what they buy. Conservators are sent to previews to look things over for those who cannot get there. There used to be well-attended forums and lectures; no more (or they are dumbed down). A few remain but not as many as the old days. Education is important to build a collecting base.
- **KNAPSTEIN:** Country and estate auctions are not going away; as long as there are homes filled with lifetime acquisitions, there will be estate auctions. (As one local auctioneer replied when asked, "How's the auction business?" – "People are dying to have auctions with me.") Ownership is temporary; our heirs determine if they have a strong enough sentimental bond with our things to keep them, or if those items will be sold to a new owner. As far as the antiques show goes, in order to survive it will have to offer much more than just booth after booth of dealers lining up their inventory. It also will have to be about the experience. Even if a show-goer doesn't make a purchase, they should still walk away with something to ensure they come back to the next show: information they didn't have before, pleasant memories, dealer contacts that may lead to a future purchase, networking with like-minded collectors, and so on.

What is one area of antiques and collectibles you think will prove to be a "sleeper" in the next few years?

- **SMITH:** I think mid-century will do well. Whatever makes it into any sleeper grouping has to be of quality; I think people are tired of buying lesser things, which was okay when money was more plentiful. Now spending is given careful thought and the best things continue to sell. If I had to guess, besides modern things, jewelry might do better, as well as sports memorabilia, which is already popular, but there's room for more.

- **SOLIS-COHEN:** If I knew what the next hot corner of the market was going to be I would corner it; I've been thinking about wine! Jewelry seems to have a broad market, but it has to be well designed or melt it for the gold value. All the auctions have reported good jewelry sales, and show dealers who have a case of jewelry along with their silver or furniture or paintings say it pays their booth rents. I don't know the jewelry market well enough to know which corner will be hot, but I hear pearls are coming back.

James D. Julia, Inc.

Coral carving, 19th century, Japan, figure of Jurojin with children, signed, 4 3/4" high overall. **$2,875**

  Find out what is on the radar for museum exhibitions. The market for sculpture has some life and some very good dealers. I think contemporary American Indian art is as strong as the American Indian historical material, which has been a quiet corner of the market for the last few years. Charles Montgomery said, "Behind every great collection is a great dealer." But it has to be a dealer with an unerring eye.

- **SAUNDERS-WATSON:** Modern technology items. We've already seen that original Apple computers can make a quarter of a million dollars at auction. Just as collectors of the past 15-20 years sought out early Atari and video games, collectors of the Internet generation will be looking for the now-quaint-looking technological devices. I still have my first cell phone. It looks like an antique with its pull-up antenna that had a range of about five miles. I find it amusing. When I look at it, it reminds me of the day an ISP started up in the rural area of New Hampshire where I was living. The connection was so slow, I couldn't even send an attachment without the e-mail freezing up, but it was the dawning of a new era. Significant tech items from the last quarter of the 20th century will all be museum worthy someday.

- **KNAPSTEIN:** My opinion may be affected by my own affinity, but I think the ebook explosion by publishers will lead to a wider appreciation for early, finely crafted books. You don't get the same tactile satisfaction holding an e-reader that you do holding a tooled leather-bound classic. Overall, I think that American folk art is underappreciated and undervalued when compared to other art forms. Each piece is truly unique; it's just a matter of time before it's recognized as an effective way to express our individuality, connect with our nation's past, and – hopefully – pad our portfolios.

Warman's—Who We Are

Edwin G. Warman was an entrepreneur in Uniontown, Pa. He dabbled in several ventures, including ownership of a radio station. He was also an avid antiques collector who published his price listings in response to requests from friends and fellow collectors. The first modest price guide was published in 1948 as *Warman's Antiques and Their Current Prices*. It was a bold move. Until then, antiques were sold primarily through dealers, antiques shops and at auctions. The sellers and buyers negotiated prices and were forced to do their own research to determine fair prices. Under Warman's care, the price guide changed all that forever. Warman also published some specialized price guides for pattern glass and milk glass, as well as his "Oddities and Curiosities" editions, under the banner of the E.G. Warman Publishing Co.

Although the name varied slightly over the years, *Warman's Antiques and Their Current Prices* covered such collectible areas as mechanical banks, furniture and silver, just like the Warman's of today. His pages consisted of a brief statement about the topic, either relating to the history or perhaps the "collectibility" of the category. A listing of current prices was included, often containing a black and white photograph.

E.G. Warman died in 1979. His widow, Pat Warman, continued the tradition and completed work on the 15th edition after his death. The estate sold the E.G. Warman Publishing Co. to Stanley and Katherine Greene of Elkins Park, Pa., in 1981. Chilton Books bought the Warman Publishing Co. in the fall of 1989. With the 24th edition, Warman's was published under the Wallace-Homestead imprint. Krause Publications purchased both the Warman's and Wallace-Homestead imprints in 1997.

We are proud to continue the rich tradition started some 65 years ago by Mr. Warman, a man driven by his love of antiques and collectibles and by a thirst for sharing his knowledge.

The Warman's Advantage

The Warman's Advantage manifests itself in several important ways in the 2013 edition. As we reviewed past volumes, we wanted to make this book as easy to use as possible. To that end, we've consolidated and reorganized how we present several key categories. Our new mantra is, "What is it first?"

For instance, an antique clock may also have an advertising component, an ethnic element (like black memorabilia), reflect a specific design theme (like Art Deco) and be made of cast iron. But first and foremost, it's a clock, and that's where you'll find it listed, even though there are other collecting areas involved.

There are a few categories that remain iconic in the collecting world. Coca-Cola collectibles cross many interests, as do folk art, Asian antiques and Tiffany designs, to name just a few. These still have their own broad sections.

In addition to space memorabilia and John Wayne collectibles, newly expanded sections include ceramics, jewelry, toys, illustration art, books, and glass.

Prices

The prices in this book have been established using the results of auction sales across the country, and by tapping the resources of knowledgeable dealers and collectors. These values reflect not only current collector trends, but also the wider economy. The adage that "an antique (or collectible) is worth what someone will pay for it" still holds. A price guide measures value, but it also captures a moment in time, and sometimes that moment can pass very quickly.

Beginners should follow the same advice that all seasoned collectors will share: Make mistakes and learn from them; talk with other collectors and dealers; find reputable resources (including books and websites), and learn to invest wisely, buying the best examples you can afford.

Words of Thanks

This 47th edition of the Warman's guide would not be possible without the help of countless others. Dozens of auction houses have generously shared their resources, but a few deserve special recognition: Heritage Auctions Inc., Dallas; Backstage Auctions, Houston; Woody Auction, Douglass, Kan.; Greg Belhorn, Belhorn Auction Services LLC, Columbus, Ohio; Andrew Truman, James D. Julia Auctioneers, Fairfield, Maine; Anthony Barnes at Rago Arts and Auction Center, Lambertville, N.J.; Karen Skinner at Skinner Inc., Boston; Morphy Auctions, Denver, Pa.; Susan Pinnell at Jeffrey S. Evans & Associates, Mount Crawford, Va.; Rebecca Weiss at Swann Auction Galleries, New York; and Leslie Hindman Auctioneers, Chicago. And, as always, special thanks to Catherine Saunders-Watson for her many contributions and continued support.

Bonhams

Antique turquoise and diamond locket pendant, circa 1880, gross weight approximately 34.4 g., mounted in 18 karat gold, 2 1/4" long. **$1,500**

Read All About It

There are many fine publications that collectors and dealers may consult about antiques and collectibles in general. Space does not permit listing all of the national and regional publications in the antiques and collectibles field; this is a sampling:

- *Antique Trader*, published by Krause Publications, 700 E. State St., Iola, WI, 54990 – www.antiquetrader.com
- *Antique & The Arts Weekly*, 5 Church Hill Road, Newton, CT 06470 – www.antiquesandthearts.com
- *AntiqueWeek*, P.O. Box 90, Knightstown, IN 46148 – www.antiqueweek.com
- *Maine Antique Digest*, P.O. Box 358, Waldoboro, ME 04572 – www.maineantiquedigest.com
- *New England Antiques Journal*, 24 Water St., Palmer, MA 01069 – www.antiquesjournal.com
- *The Journal of Antiques and Collectibles*, P.O. Box 950, Sturbridge, MA 01566 – www.journalofantiques.com
- *Southeastern Antiquing & Collecting* magazine, P.O. Box 510, Acworth, GA 30101 – www.go-star.com/antiquing

Let Us Know What You Think

We're always eager to hear what you think about this book and how we can improve it. Contact:

Paul Kennedy
Editorial Director, Antiques & Collectibles Books
Krause Publications
700 E. State St., Iola, WI 54990-0001
715-445-2214, Ext. 13470
Paul.Kennedy@fwmedia.com

Visit an Antiques Show

One of the best ways to enjoy the world of antiques and collectibles is to take the time to really explore an antiques show. Some areas, like Brimfield, Mass., and Manchester, N.H., turn into antiques meccas for a few days each summer when dealers and collectors come for both specialized and general antiques shows, plus auctions.

Here are a few of our favorites:
- Brimfield, Mass., shows, held three times a year in May, July and September, www.brimfield.com
- Round Top, Texas, antiques shows, held spring and fall, www.roundtop.com/antique1.htm
- Antiques Week in and around Manchester, N.H., held every August, www.antiquesweeknh.com
- Palmer/Wirfs Antique & Collectible Shows, including the Portland, Ore., Expos, www.palmerwirfs.com
- The Original Miami Beach Antique Show, www.dmgantiqueshows.com
- Merchandise Mart International Antiques Fair, Chicago, www.merchandisemartantiques.com
- High Noon Western Americana Show and Auction, Phoenix, www.highnoon.com

Ask an Expert

Many contributors have proved invaluable in sharing their expertise during the compilation of the 47th edition of the Warman's guide. For more information on their specialties, call or visit their websites.

Caroline Ashleigh
Caroline Ashleigh Associates LLC
1000 S. Old Woodward, Suite 105
Birmingham, MI 48009-6734
248-792-2929
www.auctionyourart.com
Vintage clothing, couture and accessories, textiles, western wear

Tim Chambers
Missouri Plain Folk
501 Hunter Ave.
Sikeston, MO 63801-2115
573-471-6949
E-mail: plainfolk@charter.net
Folk art

Noah Fleisher
E-mail: noah.fleisher@yahoo.com
Modernism

Reyne Haines
Reyne Gallery
4747 Research Forest Dr. #180-274
The Woodlands, TX 77381
513-504-8159
www.reyne.com
E-mail: reyne@reyne.com
20th century decorative arts, lighting, fine jewelry, wristwatches

Ted Hake
Hake's Americana & Collectibles Auctions
P.O. Box 1444
York, PA 17405
717-848-1333
E-mail: auction@hakes.com
Pop culture, Disneyana, political

Leslie Holms
Antique Purse Club of California
55 Ellenwood Ave.
Los Gatos, CA 95030
408-354-1626
E-mail: cree56@comcast.net
Antique handbags of all kinds

Mark Ledenbach
www.halloweencollector.com
E-mail: marlede@sbcglobal.net
Vintage Halloween collectibles

Mary P. Manion
Landmarks Gallery & Restoration Studio
231 N. 76th St.
Milwaukee, WI 53213
800-352-8892
www.landmarksgallery.com
Fine art and restoration

Suzanne Perrault
Perrault Rago Gallery
333 N. Main St.
Lambertville, NJ 08530
609-397-1802
www.ragoarts.com
E-mail: suzanne@ragoarts.com
Ceramics

Michael Polak
www.bottlebible.com
E-mail: bottleking@earthlink.net
Vintage bottles

David Rago
Rago Arts and Auction Center
333 N. Main St.
Lambertville, NJ 08530
609-397-9374
www.ragoarts.com
Art pottery, Arts & Crafts

**Dennis Raleigh Antiques
& Folk Art**
P.O. Box 745
Wiscasset, ME 04578
207-882-7821
3327 Cones Ct.
Midland, MI 48640
989-631-2603
www.dennisraleighantiques.com
E-mail: dgraleigh@verizon.net
Decoys, silhouettes, portrait miniatures

Henry A. Taron
Tradewinds Antiques
P.O. Box 249
Manchester-By-The-Sea, MA 01944-0249
(978) 526-4085
www.tradewindsantiques.com
Canes

Andrew Truman
James D. Julia, Inc.
P.O. Box 830
Fairfield, ME 04937
207-453-7125
www.juliaauctions.net
E-mail: atruman@jamesdjulia.com
Toys, dolls, advertising

David J. Wagner, Ph.D.
President, David J. Wagner, L.L.C.
www.davidjwagnerllc.com
davidjwagnerllc@yahoo.com
414-221-6878
American wildlife art

Auction Houses

Sanford Alderfer Auction & Appraisal
501 Fairgrounds Rd.
Hatfield, PA 19440
215-393-3000
www.alderferauction.com
Full service

American Bottle Auctions
2523 J St., Suite 203
Sacramento, CA 95816
800-806-7722
www.americanbottle.com
Antique bottles, jars

American Pottery Auction
Waasdorp Inc.
P.O. Box 434
Clarence, NY 14031
716-759-2361
www.antiques-stoneware.com
Stoneware, redware

American Sampler
P.O. 371
Barnesville, MD 20838
301-972-6250
www.castirononline.com
Cast-iron bookends, doorstops

Antiques and Estate Auctioneers
44777 St. Route 18 E.
Wellington, OH 44090
440-647-4007
Fax: 440-647-4006
www.estateauctioneers.com
Full service

Auctions Neapolitan
1100 First Ave. S.
Naples, FL 34102
239-262-7333
www.auctionsneapolitan.com
Full service

Belhorn Auction Services, LLC
P.O. Box 20211
Columbus, Ohio 43220
614-921-9441
www.belhorn.com
Full service, American art pottery

Backstage Auctions
448 West 19th St., Suite 163
Houston, TX 77008
713-862-1200
www.backstageauctions.com
Rock 'n' roll collectibles and memorabilia

Bertoia Auctions
2141 DeMarco Dr.
Vineland, NJ 08360
856-692-1881
www.bertoiaauctions.com
Toys, banks, holiday, doorstops

Bonhams
101 New Bond St.
London, England W1S 1SR
44-0-20-7447-7447
www.bonhams.com
Fine art and antiques

Brian Lebel's Old West Auction
451 E. 58th Ave.
Denver, CO 80216
480-779-9378
www.codyoldwest.com
Western collectibles and memorabilia

Brunk Auctions
P.O. Box 2135
Asheville, NC 28802
828-254-6846
www.brunkauctions.com
Full service

Caroline Ashleigh Associates, LLC
1000 S. Old Woodward, Suite 105
Birmingham, MI 48009-6734
248-792-2929
www.auctionyourart.com
Full service, vintage clothing, couture and accessories, textiles, western wear

Clars Auction Gallery
5644 Telegraph Ave.
Oakland, CA 94609
888-339-7600
www.clars.com
Full service

Coeur d'Alene Art Auction
8836 Hess St.
Hayden Lake, ID 83835
www.cdaartauction.com
*19th and 20th century
Western and American art*

Cowan's
6270 Este Ave.
Cincinnati, OH 45232
513-871-1670
www.cowanauctions.com
*Full service, historic Americana,
Native American objects*

Cyr Auction Co.
P.O. Box 1238
Gray, ME 04039
207-657-5253
www.cyrauction.com
Full service

Early Auction Co., LLC.
123 Main St.
Milford, OH 45150
513-831-4833
www.earlyauctionco.com
Art glass

Elder's Antiques
901 Tamiami Trail (US 41) S.
Nokomis, FL 34275
941-488-1005
www.eldersantiques.com
Full service

Greg Martin Auctions
660 Third St., Suite 100
San Francisco, CA 94107
800-509-1988
www.gregmartinauctions.com
*Firearms, edged weapons, armor,
Native American objects*

Grey Flannel
8 Moniebogue Ln.
Westhampton Beach, NY 11978
631-288-7800
www.greyflannel.com
Sports jerseys, memorabilia

Guernsey's
108 E. 73rd St.
New York, NY 10021
212-794-2280
www.guernseys.com
Art, historical items, pop culture

Guyette Schmidt & Deeter
P.O. Box 1170
24718 Beverly Road
St. Michaels, MD 21663
410-745-0485
www.guyetteandschmidt.com
Antique decoys

**Hake's Americana
& Collectibles Auctions**
P.O. Box 1444
York, PA 17405
717-848-1333
www.hakes.com
Character collectibles, pop culture

Heritage Auctions, Inc.
3500 Maple Ave., 17th Floor
Dallas, TX 75219-3941
800-872-6467
www.ha.com
Full service, coins, pop culture

Humler & Nolan
28 W. 4th St., Suite A-5
Cincinnati, OH 45202
513-381-2041 or 513-381-2015
www.humlernolan.com
*Antique American and European
art pottery and art glass*

iGavel, Inc.
229 E. 120th St.
New York, NY 10035
866-iGavel6 or 212-289-5588
igavelauctions.com
Online auction, arts, antiques and collectibles

Ivey-Selkirk
7447 Forsyth Blvd.
Saint Louis, MO 63105
314-726-5515
www.iveyselkirk.com
Full service

**Jackson's International Auctioneers
and Appraisers**
2229 Lincoln St.
Cedar Falls, IA 50613
319-277-2256
www.jacksonsauction.com
*Full service, religious and Russian objects,
postcards*

James D. Julia, Inc.
P.O. Box 830
Fairfield, ME 04937
207-453-7125
www.juliaauctions.net
Full service, toys, glass, lighting, firearms

Jeffrey S. Evans & Associates
2177 Green Valley Ln.
Mount Crawford, VA 22841
540-434-3939
www.jeffreysevans.com
Full service, glass, lighting, Americana

John Moran Auctioneers, Inc.
735 W. Woodbury Rd.
Altadena, CA 91001
626-793-1833
www.johnmoran.com
Full service, California art

Keno Auctions
127 E. 69th St.
New York, NY 10021
212-734-2381
www.kenoauctions.com
Fine antiques, decorative arts

Lang's Sporting Collectibles
663 Pleasant Valley Rd.
Waterville, NY 13480
315-841-4623
www.langsauction.com
Antique fishing tackle and memorabilia

Leslie Hindman Auctioneers
1338 W. Lake St.
Chicago, Il 60607
312-280-1212
www.lesliehindman.com
Full service

McMasters Harris Auction Co.
5855 John Glenn Hwy
P.O. Box 1755
Cambridge, OH 43725
740-432-7400
www.mcmastersharris.com
Dolls and accessories

Michaan's Auctions
2751 Todd St.
Alameda, CA 94501
800-380-9822
www.michaans.com
Antiques, fine art

Michael Ivankovich Auction Co.
P.O. Box 1536
Doylestown, PA 18901
215-345-6094
www.wnutting.com
Wallace Nutting objects

**Leland Little Auctions
& Estate Sales, Ltd.**
246 S. Nash St.
Hillsborough, NC 27278
919-644-1243
www.llauctions.com
Full service

Litchfield County Auctions, Inc.
425 Bantam Road (Route 202)
Litchfield, CT 06759
860-567-4661
212-724-0156
www.litchfieldcountyauctions.com
Full service

Morphy Auctions
2000 N. Reading Rd.
Denver, PA 17517
717-335-3435
www.morphyauctions.com
Toys, banks, advertising, pop culture

Mosby & Co. Auctions
905 West 7th St., #228
Frederick, MD 21701
301-304-0352
www.mosbyauctions.com
Mail, phone, Internet sales

Neal Auction Co.
4038 Magazine St.
New Orleans, LA 70115
504-899-5329
800-467-5329
www.nealauction.com
Art, furniture, pottery, silver, decorative arts

New Orleans Auction Galleries, Inc.
801 Magazine St.
New Orleans, LA 70130
800-501-0277
www.neworleansauction.com
Full service, Victorian

Noel Barrett Vintage Toys @ Auction
P.O. Box 300
Carversville, PA 18913
215-297 5109
www.noelbarrett.com
Toys, banks, holiday, advertising

Old Town Auctions
P.O. Box 91
Boonsboro, MD 21713
240-291-0114
301-416-2854
www.oldtownauctions.com
Toys, advertising, Americana; no Internet sales

Old Toy Soldier Auctions USA
P.O. Box 13324
Pittsburgh, PA 15243
Ray Haradin
412-343-8733
800-349-8009
www.oldtoysoldierauctions.com
Toy soldiers

Old World Auctions
2155 W. Hwy 89A, Suite 206
Sedona, AZ 86336
800-664-7757
www.oldworldauctions.com
Maps, documents

Past Tyme Pleasures
39 California Ave., Suite 105
Pleasanton, CA 94566
925-484-6442
www.pasttyme1.com
Internet catalog auctions

Philip Weiss Auctions
1 Neil Ct.
Oceanside, NY 11572
516-594-0731
www.prwauctions.com
Full service, comic art

Pook & Pook, Inc.
463 East Lancaster Ave.
Downingtown, PA 19335
610-629-0695
www.pookandpook.com
Full service, Americana

**Professional Appraisers
& Liquidators, LLC**
16 Lemington Ct.
Homosassa, FL 34446
800-542-3877
www.charliefudge.com
Full service

**Quinn's Auction Galleries
& Waverly Rare Books**
431 N. Maple Ave.
Falls Church, VA 22046
703-532-5632
www.quinnsauction.com
www.waverlyauctions.com
Full service, rare books and prints

Rago Arts and Auction Center
333 N. Main St.
Lambertville, NJ 08530
609-397-9374
www.ragoarts.com
Arts & Crafts, modernism, fine art

Red Baron's Antiques, Inc.
6450 Roswell Rd.
Atlanta, GA 30328
404-252-3770
www.redbaronsantiques.com
Full service, Victorian, architectural objects

Rich Penn Auctions
P.O. Box 1355
Waterloo, IA 50704
319-291-6688
www.richpennauctions.com
Advertising and country-store objects

Richard D. Hatch & Associates
913 Upward Rd.
Flat Rock, NC 28731
828-696-3440
www.richardhatchauctions.com
Full service

Robert Edward Auctions, LLC
P.O. Box 7256
Watchung, NJ 07069
908-226-9900
www.robertedwardauctions.com
Baseball, sports memorabilia

Rock Island Auction Co.
4507 49th Ave.
Moline, IL 61265-7578
800-238-8022
www.rockislandauction.com
Firearms, edged weapons and accessories

St. Charles Gallery, Inc.
1330 St. Charles Ave.
New Orleans, LA 70130
504-586-8733
www.stcharlesgallery.com
Full service, Victorian

Samuel T. Freeman & Co.
1808 Chestnut St.
Philadelphia, PA 19103
215-563-9275
www.freemansauction.com
Full service, Americana

Seeck Auctions
P.O. Box 377
Mason City, IA 50402
641-424-1116
www.seeckauction.com
Full service, carnival glass

Skinner, Inc.
357 Main St.
Bolton, MA 01740
978-779-6241
www.skinnerinc.com
Full service, Americana

Sloans & Kenyon
7034 Wisconsin Ave.
Chevy Chase, MD 20815
301-634-2344
www.sloansandkenyon.com
Full service

Slotin Folk Art/Folk Fest Inc.
5619 Ridgetop Dr.
Gainesville, GA 30504
770-532-1115
www.slotinfolkart.com
Naïve and outsider art

Sotheby's
1334 York Ave.
New York, NY 10021
212-606-7000
www.sothebys.com
Fine art, jewelry, historical items

Strawser Auctions
P.O. Box 332, 200 N. Main
Wolcottville, IN 46795
260-854-2859
www.strawserauctions.com
Full service, majolica, Fiestaware

Swann Galleries, Inc.
104 E. 25th St.
New York, NY 10010
212-254-4710
www.swanngalleries.com
Rare books, prints, photographs, posters

Theriault's
P.O. Box 151
Annapolis, MD 21404
800-638-0422
www.theriaults.com
Dolls and accessories

Tom Harris Auction Center
203 S. 18th Ave.
Marshalltown, IA 50158
641-754-4890
www.tomharrisauctions.com
Full service, clocks, watches

Tradewinds Antiques
P.O. Box 249
Manchester-By-The-Sea, MA 01944-0249
978-526-4085
www.tradewindsantiques.com
Canes

Treadway Gallery
2029 Madison Rd.
Cincinnati, OH 45208
513-321-6742
and
John Toomey Gallery
818 North Blvd.
Oak Park, IL 60301
708-383-5234
www.treadwaygallery.com
Arts & Crafts, modernism, fine art

Woody Auction
P.O. Box 618
317 S. Forrest
Douglass, KS 67039
316-747-2694
www.woodyauction.com
Glass

CONTRIBUTORS
Tom Bartsch
Eric Bradley
Brent Frankenhoff
Kyle Husfloen
Paul Kennedy
Karen Knapstein
Mark B. Ledenbach
Kristine Manty
Michael Polak
Ellen T. Schroy
Susan Sliwicki
David Wagner
Martin Willis

Advertising

BY NOAH FLEISHER

The enduring appeal of antique advertising is not hard to understand. The graphics are great, they hearken back to a simpler time and a distinct American identity and – perhaps best of all – are available across all price levels. That means buyers from all tax brackets and walks of life.

"It's like anything in collectibles and antiques," said Dan Matthews, president and owner of Matthew's Auction in Moline, Illinois, one of the nation's top auctioneers of petroliana and the author of *The Fine Art of Collecting and Displaying Petroliana*. "The best stuff, the very top, sells no matter what. Right now the medium market is doing okay and the lower continues to drag a bit behind."

The most reliable value in Matthews' market continues to be top-of-the-line petroliana – names like Harbo Petrolium, Keller Springs, Quiver, or Must-go can command tens of thousands of dollars – but there is a definite hierarchy at play and, if you are thinking of expanding your collecting horizons to include antique signage, you would do well to know the market.

Noah Fleisher

Seasoned collectors will warn, with good reason, that money should not be the motivating factor in the hobby, so it may be somewhat deceptive to start this discussion with the idea of monetary value. The true value of antique advertising signs, from gas stations to country stores to soda pop, lies in the context of their production and the nostalgia they evoke of that time.

The best antique advertising evokes the meat of the first half of the 20th century, when signs were the most effective ways to catch the eyes of car culture consumers. The signs and symbols evolved to reflect the values and styles of the regions where they were posted and the products they reflected. A sign with bold color, great graphics, and a catchy slogan can transport a collector back decades in an instant. Collectors feel a rapport with a piece; they don't see dollar signs.

"Buy it because you like it," said Matthews, "because you can live it with it and it means something to you. Never get into something because you think you'll make money."

Look at one of the most collectible and popular markets: Coca-Cola. Fifteen years ago the best Coke pieces in the middle market could reliably command several thousand dollars. Coca-Cola manufactured hundreds of thousands of signs and related ephemera, millions even, and they began to come out of the woodwork. There is little more evocative of classic Americana than the red and white of Coke, but as everybody sold their pieces and everybody acquired their bit of nostalgia, the market cooled and prices went down significantly. Pieces that had routinely brought $500-$1,000 could suddenly be had for significantly less, and people stopped selling.

Now, however, with several years of very quiet action in the books, the cycle seems to be turning around. New collectors have entered the market and older collectors are leaving. Those collections are finding new owners at a decent price.

"Coca-Cola does seem to be coming back," said Matthews. "It's been stagnant for the past five years, but good clean signs are finding good homes at good prices."

As with any category, the very best antique advertising will bring top dollar no matter what, as a look through the recent advertising sales database of prices realized at an auction house like Morphy's will attest to. In those sales it can be seen that that the rarest of Coca-Cola paper and tin routinely bring tens of thousands of dollars.

Embossed tin Luden's Cough Drops sign, excellent condition, framed 36 1/2" x 20 1/2". **$660**

Morphy Auctions

That said, then, let's talk money. Antique advertising provides a tangible place for collectors to put real money. Looking through recent prices realized at the top auction venues – like Matthews, Morphy Auctions, and William Morford – it's obvious that top dollar can be had for the true rarities in the business and that the middle market provides a solid outlet for design-minded collectors as opposed to those who collect to amass a sizable grouping.

There are opportunities everywhere for the educated collector – from the country auction to the flea market. Going head to head, out of the blocks, with the top collectors in the business at the top auctions can result in frustration. Rather, if you're just getting your feet wet, research online, email experts and ask for resources, do your due diligence in seeing what the market is bringing and, then, take those skills to unlikely places and see what turns up.

"All the fields we deal in seem to be doing quite well right now," said Matthews. "Gas and oil, which there's more of than anything else, keeps going up more and more. The best thing to do is buy from reputable auction houses and dealers, from people who guarantee your product."

Barring the finds you can make at small antiques shows, shops and markets, expect to go into an auction ready to spend an average of $500 for a quality piece of petroliana, for pieces like rare oil and gas cans. A sharp and patient buyer can grab a steal for $10 or a masterpiece for a $1,000. As with anything else, a seasoned and practical eye comes with practice. The prices broaden greatly when the market is expanded to include country store advertising and specific brand advertising, like Campbell's Soup.

"Like most kinds of collectibles, everybody starts out buying middle grade stuff and graduates to the higher stuff," said Matthews. "Collectors in this hobby are very dedicated; prices on the best stuff haven't peaked yet, that's for sure."

A lot of the steadiness in the market is coming from the exposure antique advertising is getting in places like cable television, via shows like "American Pickers" and "Pawn Stars," where a premium is placed on supreme objects.

"These kinds of shows are only helping the hobby get bigger," Matthews added. "Take Ford Oil cans, for instance. Before these shows, the market was dominated by a handful of players. The prices ran way up. Those guys all got out, cans went down to $500 or so from $1,000 or more. Then these shows premiered, oil cans got some attention, and now a lot more collectors are back in at $1,000."

Factor in the pop culture value, as blue collar treasures are increasingly regarded as art , and the horizon is bright for this working-man's collectible.

"I see younger generations continuing to get into this hobby more and more," said Matthews. "As long as we have to put gas in our cars and food in our mouths, people will collect this stuff."

NOAH FLEISHER *received his Bachelor of Fine Arts degree from New York University and brings more than a decade of newspaper, magazine, book, antiques and art experience to his position as Public Relations Director of Heritage Auctions, one of the country's foremost auction houses. He is the former editor of* Antique Trader, New England Antiques Journal *and* Northeast Antiques Journal, *is the author of* Warman's Modern Furniture, *and has been a longtime contributor to* Warman's Antiques & Collectibles.

Morphy Auctions

Aero and Columbia two-gallon motor oil cans, light wear to the Columbia can and light-to-medium wear on the Aero can with minor wear and scratches, each 11" tall. **$60**

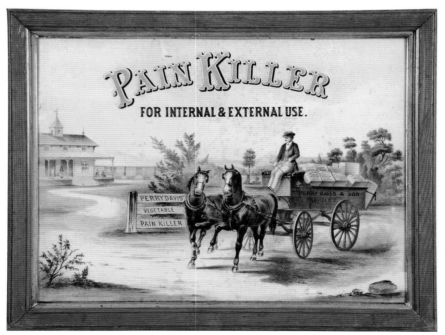

Morphy Auctions

Early tin Davis Pain Killer sign, circa 1880s, framed without glass, rare, wonderful remaining color and image areas, a few short scratches and minor stains; otherwise, minor tone differences and light surface marks, framed 27 3/4" x 21 1/4". **$12,600**

Morphy Auctions

Sinclair H-C Gasoline globe, circa 1930s to 1940s, clean and bright with little wear, milk glass body with two lenses, both with some interior staining and soiling, 16 1/2" tall. **$780**

Morphy Auctions

Two embossed tin Moxie signs, circa 1930s, one bright and clean with only minor surface rubs and a few small marks, the other sign has more advanced rubs, chips, and wear, each 8 1/4" diameter. **$180**

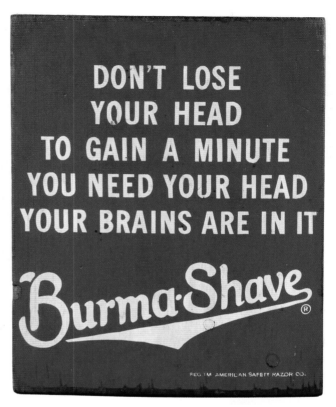

Morphy Auctions

Wooden Burma-Shave advertising sign, "Don't lose your head/ to gain a minute/you need your head/your brains are in it." **$360**

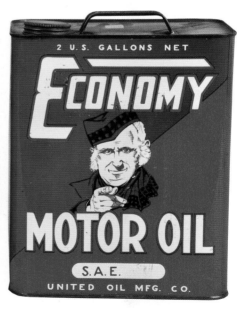

Morphy Auctions

Double Eagle and Economy two-gallon motor oil cans, nice graphics and colors, moderate marks and wear, each 11 1/2" tall. **$150**

Morphy Auctions

*Tomahawk and Uncas two-gallon motor oil cans, medium to heavy overall wear, largest 11 3/4"
tall.* **$180**

Morphy Auctions

*Early embossed tin
Butter-Krust Bread sign
with whimsical graphics,
central image is in great
condition, one scratch at
top center field and head
area of child, a few minor
surface marks, shallow
dents and crimps.* **$7,200**

Morphy Auctions

Two orange Hygrade light globes with old and likely original bases, general overall wear and staining with color loss. **$240**

Morphy Auctions

Ten miniature oil can savings banks, circa 1940s to 1950s, light to moderate wear and soiling on average, largest 3 1/4" tall. **$270**

Oertels '92 Beer back advertising figure, circa 1940s, plaster, excellent condition, 16 1/2" tall. **$150**

Morphy Auctions

Morphy Auctions

Cherry Smash label under glass syrup bottle, clean, bright, colorful label with minor surface marks and light surface scratch to left side, 12 1/2" tall. **$3,000**

Morphy Auctions

Jackie Coogan Peanut Butter pail, original lid, excellent condition, 3 1/2" tall. **$420**

Morphy Auctions

Neon three-color Planters Peanuts sign, circa 1980s, acrylic, appears to be handmade, near mint condition, 30 1/4" x 27 1/4". **$1,020**

Morphy Auctions

Embossed tin Coca-Cola sign, circa 1910 to 1912, framed without glass, shows detail of a straight-sided bottle on left insert, shallow dents, crimps, medium surface wear with scratches, paint chips, and a small amount of missing metal in right corners and side, framed 12 1/2" x 35 1/2". **$1,320**

Morphy Auctions

One-piece Texaco gas globe, heavily embossed, clean and bright with little overall wear, strong paint remains on both sides, 17 1/2" tall. **$3,300**

Morphy Auctions

Tin Sweet Orr & Co. overalls sign, circa 1890s, early frame without glass, lithography by C.W. Shonk; colors are bright and unfaded, a few small surface scratches, minor scuffs, and rubs. **$13,800**

Morphy Auctions

Cast iron Planters Mr. Peanut Hamilton scale, one-cent operation, all original paint with medium to heavy expected wear and minor rust, original wheel mounts for rolling in and out of a store, one wheel is missing and one is broken, original condition. **$19,800**

Morphy Auctions

Standard Oil Company glass bottle and stopper, petite size with outstanding label, one or two hairline closed cracks around top border with a few edge nicks on label, ground glass stopper has one small closed crack, 6 1/2" tall. **$1,080**

Morphy Auctions

Hires large paper poster, circa 1940-1950, new old stock heavy paper, almost no wear or marks, 34" x 58". **$150**

Wooden Moon's Feeds sign, circa 1930s to 1940s, handmade, overall appearance is nice with proper crazing present on the lettering, construction is made of individual horizontal boards secured by metal straps on the back, mild to medium wear with slight weathering. **$420**

Morphy Auctions

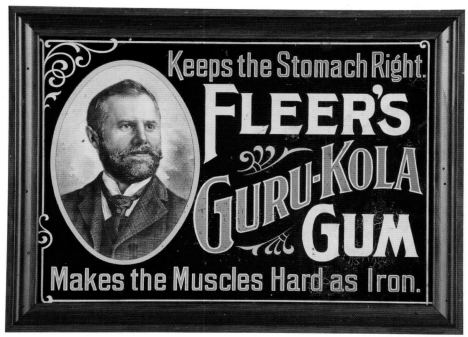

Morphy Auctions

Tin Fleer's Guru-Kola Gum sign, circa 1905 to 1910, made by Sentenne & Green, great graphics and design. Minor marks, light surface rust, active crazing, lifting, and flaking, framed 15 1/4" x 11 1/2". **$1,800**

Morphy Auctions

Tin Shoe Lace Service Station display, image of man driving a shoe on wheels, image on all three sides, excellent to near mint condition, 13 3/4" x 11 1/4" x 11". **$5,400**

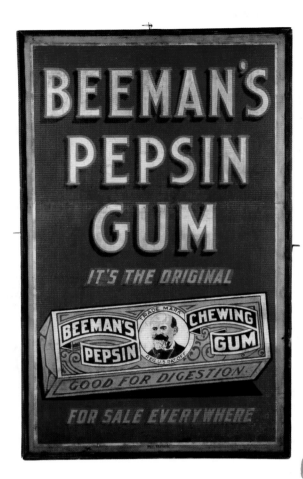

Morphy Auctions

Tin Beeman's Pepsin Gum sign, circa 1905, handmade, tin, with old (if not original) wooden framework, stamped "Mr. Brook" at bottom, light staining, medium soiling, wear and minor marks. **$16,800**

Morphy Auctions

Antique Bourbon trade figure, circa 1950s to 1960s, fiberglass construction with medium overall marks, wear, and soiling, 45" tall. **$210**

Morphy Auctions

Coca-Cola window display, 1937, very rare, beautiful overall condition, top banner piece and two separate standup cardboard cutouts, top piece slides into two slots at the top of the background. **$16,200**

Morphy Auctions

Rare embossed tin Modox sign, circa 1900 to 1905, framed without glass, outstanding graphics of Indian in full headdress, light to medium overall wear with some minor chips and nicks that mostly impact background colors and border areas. **$7,200**

Morphy Auctions

Tin Amalie Motor Oil sign, 1955, new old stock with a few short scratches near the center and minor edge wear, 53 1/2" long. **$720**

Morphy Auctions

Tin Stein Club sign, circa 1910, scarce, strong colors and great overall condition, three or four small surface crimps are visible when viewed at certain angles, a few minor spots and small surface scratches as well, framed 30 1/2" x 22 1/2". **$8,400**

Americana

BY NOAH FLEISHER

The collecting field of historical Americana is so broad and diverse, so infinitely parsible, that entering it with confidence can prove a daunting task to both neophyte and experienced collectors alike. For the purposes of this introduction and this section, we've chosen to keep the focus on historical Americana as it applies to key figures in American history – presidents, politicians and assorted prominent thinkers; artifacts that are, in this writer's estimation, easily identifiable and therefore easier to relate to.

For Tom Slater, formerly of Slater's Americana and currently the director of Americana Auctions at Heritage Auctions, there is a conflict in the Americana market currently between an abundance of good material and a lack of erudition among "new" collectors.

"You don't see new collectors getting into Americana the same way that you see it in categories like comics or sports, which are more in-tune with current pop culture trends," he said. "New generations in these types of categories are being created by osmosis, inheriting their love of collecting – and often parts of their collections – from family members and friends, being influenced by what's clicking in the popular imagination and current public zeitgeist. When you get into more esoteric subjects, they require more commitment to develop working knowledge to be an effective collector."

Noah Fleisher

Key trends in historical Americana are easy to read: signatures, ephemera, and artifacts directly related to early popular American figures – think George Washington, Thomas Jefferson and Abe Lincoln – will always command solid prices; a search through the prices realized anywhere from independent dealers, eBay and a variety of auction houses will confirm this.

A little deeper into the market, and a little further into the roster of historical figures from whom artifacts can be found and acquired, and the story begins to play out a little differently.

"At a certain point and a certain level, you can't tell what's going to sell or at what price," said Slater. "In the last five to 10 years we've seen a somewhat weaker, leaner and meaner stripe of collector emerge than we used to have. They're simply more discriminating now in how they spend and what they spend on. They're looking for the right pieces and the right values."

While that might necessarily mean that you're going to have serious competition and have to dig a little deeper into your bank account to acquire that George Washington compass, book plate or signed letter, it also means that – if you do your homework and know what you are looking for – there is tremendous opportunity.

"Quality is key at whatever level you are collecting," said Slater. "Spend on quality, on what you love, and you'll never be disappointed with how much you enjoy something, what you pay for it or what it may bring when the time comes to sell it."

In terms of the broader market, there's a plethora of good material available, which may be a factor in the current price pause seen. The fact is that – though Americans love their history and have always actively coveted pieces of it – there is relatively little "brand new" material being found, unlike newer specialty categories like comics, sports and entertainment memorabilia. Twenty and 30 years ago, dealers and collectors alike were pulling significant pieces of historical Americana out of shows, shacks, attics and yard sales at incredible rates. Those glory days are done and picked over for the most part. You're not likely to find a William Stone lithograph of The Declaration of Independence in a garage sale anymore.

Heritage Auctions, Inc.

George Washington personally owned compass used as a young surveyor in the wilds of Virginia, before he became the father of his country. Well-made and substantial, the upper portion of brass; very good condition, it shows clear indications of extensive use; 5" long. Sold by the heirs of George Washington, John Augustine Washington, and Bushrod Washington, and accompanied by a letter of provenance from the family. **$59,750**

"When you get into areas where there aren't constantly new discoveries being made, you need to have a much deeper sense of going on," said Slater. "It seems there's a direct relationship between that and attracting new people, which is not necessarily the case in Americana right now."

Say you have done your research, read your history and have developed a fascination with the Founding Fathers. You'll have to look far and wide, and spend a pretty penny, for pieces that come directly from Washington, Adams, Jefferson, Madison or Monroe. If you know what you like, however, there is plenty to be had from those that surrounded those men, their families and their lives. Context becomes all important, as does understanding what you're looking at when it looks at you.

"Attention spans are decreasing, which means fewer collectors are willing to undergo what can be a long and steep learning curve," said Slater. "The categories that are thriving are the ones that are more easily accessible. That, however, means greater competition down the line. For collectors willing to put in the time, the reward can be significant."

What is influencing the market right now? An aging collector population, for one, and a somewhat jaded collector base at the very top of the market, for another.

Collectors who have been in the market for 40 or 50 years are aging out of active buying and are selling off their core collections. In many cases they simply have no heirs that are following them in their pursuit or they have too much in their collections for their families to efficiently and profitably disperse.

We are also living in a much more disposable culture these days. As subsequent generations come of age in an increasingly paperless society, less appreciation is created for the material culture of the past. A prime is example is the current cooling in the realm of John F. Kennedy and Camelot collecting.

"Kennedy had been a touchstone for almost three generations," said Slater. "Now those collectors, those people who were born and raised on Camelot and its attendant glamour, are aging out and the polish has faded somewhat on the perspective of those times. This has created, simultaneously, a leveling off in prices for JFK memorabilia and a golden opportunity for smart collectors willing to hold on to something for the duration. If history has taught us anything, it's that eventually everything comes around again and is eventually seen as being new."

Do your homework, learn what's scarce and what's in demand and know a treasure when it's in front of you. Be patient with your purchases and diligent in your pursuit of the material you want. Right now your purchases – be they with a major auction house or a reputable dealer – may have an air more of stewardship than of investment, but the popularity of television shows and books on antiques and collectibles points to an increased awareness in the potential value of historical material, if not its inherent value simply as a piece of history.

"That wider recognition of value that seems to be dawning in the general public is the thing that is encouraging," said Slater. "The smart, educated collector that will endure the vagaries of the market will, in time, realize the full potential not only of their investment but also of their passion for the subject."

NOAH FLEISHER *received his Bachelor of Fine Arts degree from New York University and brings more than a decade of newspaper, magazine, book, antiques and art experience to his position as Public Relations Director of Heritage Auctions, one of the country's foremost auction houses. He is the former editor of* Antique Trader, New England Antiques Journal *and* Northeast Antiques Journal, *is the author of* Warman's Modern Furniture, *and has been a longtime contributor to* Warman's Antiques & Collectibles.

Heritage Auctions, Inc.

George Washington: U.S. patent signed "Go: Washington" as president for "new machinery called the Cotton Gin" issued to Hodgen Holmes, not Eli Whitney. The patent is countersigned by Timothy Pickering as secretary of state and Charles Lee as attorney general. One vellum partly printed page, 12.5" x 15", "City of Philadelphia," May 12, 1796. By signing this, Washington – America's icon of independence – unwittingly signs away the freedom of future generations of African-American men and women. The invention transformed America, expanding the cotton culture in the South and spreading it westward, breathing new life into slavery, the institution that many had hoped would die a natural death. **$179,250**

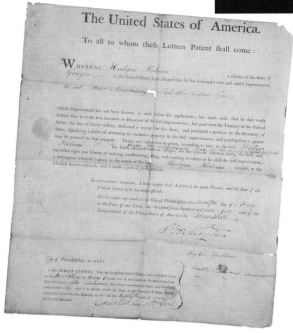

Heritage Auctions, Inc.

Theodore Roosevelt-themed classic, large "Gone With The Wind" style lamp. This scarce lamp has always been one of the most sought after of Roosevelt's three-dimensional display items. Great condition, 25" tall. **$7,768**

Heritage Auctions, Inc.

George Washington signed book from his library bearing his bookplate, A View of the History of Great-Britain During the Administration of Lord North, to the Second Session of the Fifteenth Parliament, in Two Parts, with Statements of the Public Expenditure in that Period. London: Printed for G. Wilkie, 1782. George Washington has placed his illustrious signature at the upper right corner of the title page: "Go: Washington." 8vo, ii, 411 pages. Of note is the existence of an authentic personal bookplate of General Washington's, measuring 2.5" x 3.75", affixed to the front pastedown endpaper. **$101,575**

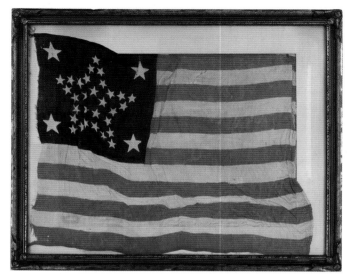

Pook & Pook, Inc.

Thirty-four star American flag, circa 1860, 15" x 17 1/4". **$4,131**

Heritage Auctions, Inc.

George Washington centennial saucer with flags, 5.25" dish celebrating Washington's centennial, near fine condition. **$39**

Heritage Auctions, Inc.

President John Adams and Major General Alexander Hamilton: Period Manuscript Copy of Orders Regarding the Death of George Washington and the Military's Funeral Arrangements for their "Patron and Father." Four pages, 8" x 12.75", blank laid paper with "1802" watermark (likely the approximate date of origin), the date and location listed as December 21, 1799, Philadelphia at top of page one, and December 24, 1799, New York at the end of page four, "signed" by William North (adjutant general of the army) at the close. **$3,884**

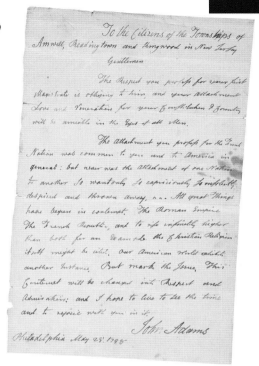

Heritage Auctions, Inc.

Heritage Auctions, Inc.

Abraham Lincoln, large gem albumen mourning badge, the black ribbon indicating it was used at the time of Lincoln's assassination. The copper frame is 1" x 1 1/4" size; eagle retains most of its original silvered and stickpin attachment. A clean example and quite scarce. **$478**

John Adams autograph letter signed as the second President to the citizens of three townships in New Jersey. One page, 8" x 12.75", May 25, 1798. In this document, Adams, only a year into his only presidential term, replies to "the Citizens of the Townships of Amwell, Readingtown and Kingwood in New Jersey" concerning the defining issue of his presidency: the diplomatic crisis with France. Overall near fine condition. **$28,680**

Heritage Auctions, Inc.

John Adams, unique bridle rosette from his 1797 inauguration. The front of this keepsake from Adams' inauguration is made of wood, with a high relief dome painted a reddish color. The back is leather and bears an inscription that has been applied by tapping something along the lines of an awl to make deep, pinhead sized impressions that form the lettering "John Adams M. 4, 1797." **$9,560**

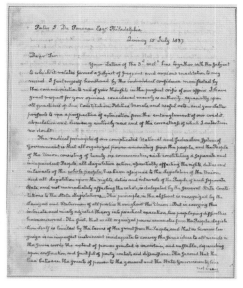

Heritage Auctions, Inc.

John Quincy Adams autograph letter signed "J.Q. Adams." Four pages, 8" x 10", Quincy, MA, July 15, 1837. Among the finest known Adam-signed letters, it discusses the United States Constitution as it related to the finances of the government and evokes such names as Martin Van Buren, Andrew Jackson and John Marshall. Fine condition. **$26,290**

Heritage Auctions, Inc.

Thomas Jefferson, parallel rule drafting instrument. While this tool at first glance connotes Jefferson's architectural accomplishments, it also speaks to the scientific and intellectual interests common to learned men of his class and standing. This technical instrument assisted the study of mathematics and science, including but not limited to astronomy, geometry, engineering, architecture and land surveying. **$16,730**

Heritage Auctions, Inc.

Thomas Jefferson, brass diameter measure drafting tool. With no markings of maker or measurement, this tool's precise functionality and origin remain a mystery, though there is no disputing it was Jefferson's. 3.25" x 2.5" when fully extended, the brass tool is comprised of three crescent-shaped arms radiating from a central sphere. Fine condition. **$11,950**

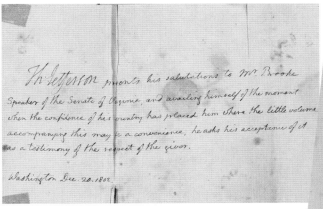

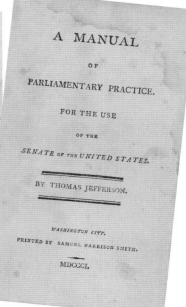

Heritage Auctions, Inc.

Thomas Jefferson, presentation copy of A Manual of Parliamentary Practice with holographic edits and an autograph letter signed transmitting the book to Francis T. Brooke. The first American publication on parliamentary procedure, published at the end of Jefferson's stint as the Senate's presiding officer (as vice president of the United States) between 1797 and 1801. The rules set forth by Jefferson in the book are still in use today.
$113,525

Heritage Auctions, Inc.

Abraham Lincoln, supremely rare and important portrait campaign flag from 1860. Among categories of collectible political campaign novelties, flag-format banners are among the most highly prized. Within this subcategory, 1860 and 1864 Lincoln flags carrying the candidate's portrait are the most sought after of all. 17.5" x 10.75", custom-framed to an overall 20" x 14". **$33,460**

Heritage Auctions, Inc.

A pair of spectacles that belonged to Abraham Lincoln, zinc-colored metal, adjustable frames, open loop terminals on the bow ends; stamped "18" on each bow. Analysis has shown that, judging by these, Lincoln was mildly far-sighted, a characteristic shared by the two pairs given to the Library of Congress by his granddaughter in 1937. Excellent condition. **$179,250**

Heritage Auctions, Inc.

Abraham Lincoln, lock of hair, part of a larger one from the legendary Oliver R. Barrett collection, sold at Parke-Bernet Galleries in 1952. Strands from a lock taken from Lincoln's head shortly after his assassination, upwards of 50 individual strands. **$21,510**

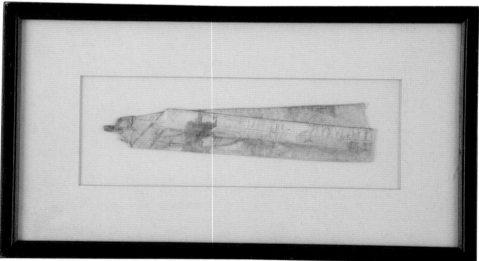

Heritage Auctions, Inc.

Bloodstained half of Abraham Lincoln's shirt collar from the night of April 14, 1865. Doubled-over piece of white cloth, about 1.5" x 8", considerably soiled and bloodstained, with one particularly sizeable brownish-red bloodstain at one side. The detachable collar fell off as Dr. Charles A. Leale, the first physician to reach him, struggled to remove the president's shirt and find his wound. Not long afterward, Lt. Newton Ferree of the 157th Ohio entered the box and discovered the collar. Possibly the finest single Lincoln "blood relic" that exists. **$65,725**

Heritage Auctions, Inc.

Abraham Lincoln, John Wilkes Booth assassination broadside. A "Booth Reward Broadside" constitutes a Holy Grail for Lincoln aficionados. Like the Charleston Mercury "The Union is Dissolved!" broadside and Ford's Theatre playbills, it is widely sought after. Measures approximately 13" x 24" and has been professionally backed with rice paper to repair a few small tears. A key relic of the Civil War and the final chapter in the saga of Abraham Lincoln. **$47,800**

Heritage Auctions, Inc.

Abraham Lincoln's circular wooden inkstand, made from a single block of wood tapered in the middle and flaring out at top and bottom to about 5.5" in diameter. Two glass inkwells, of about 1" and 1.75" diameter, are inserted in the top, which also has five small round holes drilled into it to hold pens. The lacquered body of the inkstand bears the remnants of its original gilt ornamentation, the most discernible bit of which is a spread eagle. **$80,663**

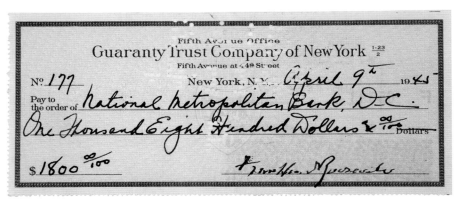

Heritage Auctions, Inc.

Franklin D. Roosevelt's final check register and the last check he ever signed; an archive of 47 checks signed by FDR along with his final check register. A black leather Guaranty Trust Company of New York check register book that begins with check number 44 and ends with check number 189. In addition, there are two blank checks that would have been check numbers 190 and 191. **$23,900**

Heritage Auctions, Inc.

Franklin Roosevelt pocket watch, a high-quality repeater watch with his engraved initials "FDR" and a portrait of Eleanor in the back case. **$18,400**

Heritage Auctions, Inc.

Theodore Roosevelt letter to Secretary of the Treasury Leslie M. Shaw, Dec. 27, 1904. Roosevelt's famous letter decrying the "atrocious hideousness" of America's coinage and suggesting Augustus St. Gaudens redesign the nation's gold coins. Called the "Genesis Letter" in numismatics, it led to the creation of some of the most sought-after gold coins ever struck. **$94,000**

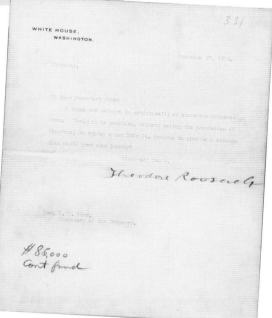

Heritage Auctions, Inc.

Franklin Roosevelt, personal presidential flag used during World War II. This design was adopted in 1916 at the order of Woodrow Wilson and incorporates the eagle from the presidential seal on a deep blue field with a white star in each corner. The flag itself is made of wool with the design elements embroidered. Possibly displayed in the president's office or possibly flown on a vehicle in which he rode. This style flag remained in use through 1945, when President Truman ordered an extensive redesign. **$23,900**

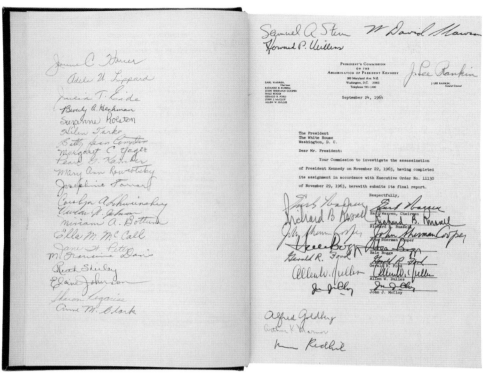

Heritage Auctions, Inc.

John F. Kennedy assassination-related, Warren Commission Report, signed by all seven commission members, including Chairman Earl Warren, plus the general counsel, four assistant counsel members, two staff members, and 33 aides; 47 signatures in all. **$19,120**

Heritage Auctions, Inc.

John F. Kennedy signed photograph with a humorous inscription to Barry Goldwater. This black-and-white 8" x 10" image is an original photograph taken by Goldwater. Across the bottom JFK wrote: "For Barry Goldwater – Whom I urge to follow the career for which he has shown such talent – photography! – from his friend – John Kennedy." Near mint condition. **$17,925**

Heritage Auctions, Inc.

John F. Kennedy, birthday cake side decoration from May 19, 1962, the night Marilyn Monroe sang "Happy Birthday, Mr. President" to JFK, just a few months before her death. At the conclusion of her performance, a large birthday cake was carried into the hall. A police officer retrieved the decoration as a souvenir. **$6,573**

Heritage Auctions, Inc.

John F. Kennedy, perhaps the only existing Kennedy rocking chair with ironclad authentication from the Kennedy family. Over the years Kennedy would use approximately 14 such chairs, making sure that one was available anywhere he spent a considerable amount of time. The Kennedy family affixed a brass plaque declaring it to be the late president's own chair, accompanied by a 2000 letter from Edward Kennedy, confirming that the chair was actually used by JFK, the only one ever authenticated by the family. **$65,725**

Heritage Auctions, Inc.

Richard M. Nixon's original White House presidential flag, from the latter part of Nixon's term in office. 70.5" x 57" including fringe, carefully sewn down to archival backing and custom framed. **$19,120**

Heritage Auctions, Inc.

Bill Clinton's Fleetwood Mac-signed saxophone, one of the saxophones signed by Fleetwood Mac, who performed at his 1993 inauguration. In excellent condition with a few small dings and scratches. **$8,963**

Pook & Pook, Inc.

Large Pennsylvania Uncle Sam cookie cutter, 19th century, 15 1/4" high. **$2,133**

Heritage Auctions, Inc.

Reagan Reagan single signed baseball, 1984. Reagan-signed balls are desirable in any condition, but this oddity was included in a dozen baseballs the president signed to a GOP donor. From the latter part of his second term. **$5,975**

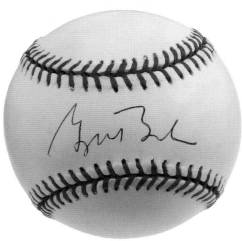

Heritage Auctions, Inc.

George W. Bush single signed baseball. Before his career in politics, which included being governor of Texas, George W. Bush ruled as part owner and managing general partner for the American League's Texas Rangers. **$1,315**

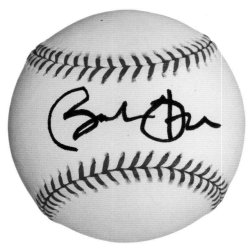

Heritage Auctions, Inc.

Barack Obama single signed baseball, 2008, PSA Mint 9, official 2007 World Series baseball, before he was president. **$2,032**

Art

Original Comic and Comic Strip Art

BY NOAH FLEISHER

"Original comic book and comic strip art is a market that's driven in large part by nostalgia," according to Todd Hignite, vice president of Heritage Auctions and a leading authority on the market for comic art. "You have collectors that buy it because they love it, because it takes them to a specific place and time in their lives."

Hignite is quick to relate, however, that the market for original book and strip art is undergoing something of a change in recent years, that the art is performing different functions, and a new generation of buyers is entering the market at the very moment that another generation is starting to get out.

The result?

"You have a group of younger buyers, in their 40s and 50s, who have always wanted the comic books they've seen growing up," said Hignite. "The early Spider-Man, X-Men, Fantastic Four, Hulk comics. Only now they see that the original art from these books is available. Suddenly they don't have to have just one of the copies of a book that is out there, they can actually get the original art. It's largely focused on Silver Age comic books."

At the same time, the older generation of collectors – the ones that completed their comic book pursuits decades ago, graduating to the pursuit of the original Golden Age art from the books they grew up on – are beginning to liquidate their collections and slow down their purchasing. This has created relatively predictable prices across Golden

Noah Fleisher

Age comic art, anywhere from $100 up to $100,000 and beyond for the truly iconic cover art of DC greats like Joe Kubert, Jerry Robinson, Jack Kirby, and Mac Raboy.

As an aside, the Holy Grails of Golden Age comic art would easily be the covers for *Action Comics* #1 or *Detective Comics* #27, the first appearances of Superman and Batman, respectively. That artwork, along with all the art from those books, is considered to have disappeared long ago.

One of the most interesting things to consider when looking at this shift toward higher prices for Silver Age and even Modern Age work is to look at the sheer magnitude of the prices realized for the work of Silver Age and especially Modern masters – see the $400K+ paid for the Dark Knight Splash Page, the $657,250 for Todd McFarlane's original cover art for 1990's *Spider-Man* #328, or the $155,350 paid for Jack Kirby's iconic 1960s Silver Surfer page from *Fantastic Four* #55.

"These are prices that were unthinkable a decade ago, or even five years ago," said Hignite. "Now, however, for a variety of reasons, key artwork that is little more than 20 years old is steadily commanding six figures at auction while regular pages, which you could pick up for a song a few years back, are routinely bringing a few hundred apiece. It's a very good return."

The shift is generational, in one sense, but also symbolic in another. The collectors coming into money and time to gather the Modern and Silver Age material right now are making a statement with their collecting. The great pieces of the 1970s, 1980s and 1990s are among the last pieces of comic art done the old fashioned way: with black and white drawings, penciled, inked and colored on board and sent to a press for printing. Digital technology has taken over the business of comic art, so the choicest nuggets from what could be the last great age of original hand-drawn comic art are commanding prices that, more and more, are in line with traditional fine art.

What about original comic strip art? What has the market brought in recent years for the masters of the daily, and what has the decline of the newspaper done to collectors and prices?

"There are certain names that are evergreen original comic strip art – all the big guys of the heyday of daily and Sunday strips," said Hignite. "Names like Charles Schulz, Gary Larson, George Herriman, Hal Foster, Winsor McCay, and Alex Raymond, they've consistently drawn strong prices and look to continue doing so."

What does that mean in the rest of the market? What about the masses of other strips from the 1920s to the 1990s? Looking at prices at auction over the last several years, it seems to mean that there are a lot of opportunities for those titles, along with their contemporaries, for the collectors whose fancy they tickle. In other words:

"In original comic strip art, unless you're spending $5,000 to $50,000 on one of the top names," said Hignite, "you should buy it because you love it and it appeals to you. If you want to live with it, then it's the right piece, at whatever level you're buying."

Which opens up another avenue for original strip art – as well as interior page original art from more general and mid-run comic books – that of original comic art as design.

"Bought, framed and hung, the original art from daily strips and comics is more and more appealing for the sheer design elements they bring," said Hignite. "They're great conversation pieces, yet they aren't so big or ostentatious that they dominate a room. We see more and more that these original pieces are being acquired at very fair prices and used to very good effect hung on a wall."

So where can you find prime examples of original comic strip and book art? At any reputable dealer, at any reputable auction house, and at almost any reputable antiques and/or collectibles show. The operative word here is "reputable," which means doing your homework, not being afraid to ask questions and buying with confidence once you are sure what piece you want and what price you are willing to spend.

"Always do your research," said Hignite. "You may pull a gem out of a dusty bin at an antiques festival or you may pounce on an overlooked treasure for nothing in an auction. The thing is to recognize the opportunity and to be ready and willing when it comes."

NOAH FLEISHER *received his Bachelor of Fine Arts degree from New York University and brings more than a decade of newspaper, magazine, book, antiques and art experience to his position as Public Relations Director of Heritage Auctions, one of the country's foremost auction houses. He is the former editor of* Antique Trader, New England Antiques Journal *and* Northeast Antiques Journal, *is the author of* Warman's Modern Furniture, *and has been a longtime contributor to* Warman's Antiques & Collectibles.

Todd McFarlane, The Amazing Spider-Man #328 cover original art (Marvel, 1990). Spidey demonstrates his powers on the Hulk in this cover illustration by Todd McFarlane; includes original logo and masthead paste-up copy, 10" x 15". This art is currently the world record holder for the highest price ever realized for a piece of original comic art. Provenance: Shamus Modern Masterworks Collection. **$657,250**

Frank Miller and Klaus Janson, Batman: The Dark Knight #3, Batman and Robin iconic splash page 10 original art (DC, 1986). Frank Miller's The Dark Knight Returns defined the best of 1980s comics and has since been universally acknowledged as one of the most important and influential stories ever published. 11 1/2" x 17 3/4". **$448,125**

Heritage Auctions, Inc.

Todd McFarlane, Spider-Man #1 cover original art (Marvel, 1990). Single biggest-selling comic book of all time to that point in terms of dollars generated. Initial press run was 2.35 million copies, a number not seen in comics since the 1950s, and Marvel had to print hundreds of thousands more to meet demand. 9 3/4" x 15". Provenance: Shamus Modern Masterworks Collection. **$358,500**

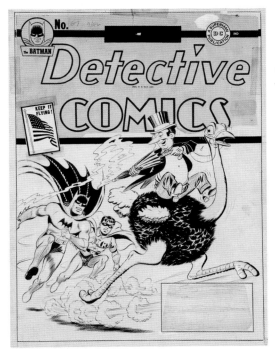

Heritage Auctions, Inc.

Jerry Robinson, Detective Comics #67, first Penguin cover original art (DC, 1942). Batman and Robin have Penguin on the run in this WWII-era cover. Jerry Robinson penciled and inked this cover art, original paper Detective Comics masthead and "Keep It Flying" photostat, missing "Crime's Early Bird"-type blurb. 12 1/2" x 17". Provenance: Robinson Collection. **$239,000**

Heritage Auctions, Inc.

*Norman Mingo, Mad #30
front and back cover, Alfred
E. Neuman painting original
art group (EC, 1956). Norman
Mingo illustrates write-in
candidate for president, Alfred
E. Neuman, in this cover
painting from 1956, Alfred
E. Neuman's first full cover
appearance. 17" x 21" with a
13" x 17" image area.* **$203,150**

Heritage Auctions, Inc.

*Fred Ray and Jerry Robinson,
Batman #11 cover original art
(DC, 1942). Earliest Batman,
Robin, and Joker cover ever
offered for public sale. 12 1/2" x
17 1/4".* **$195,500**

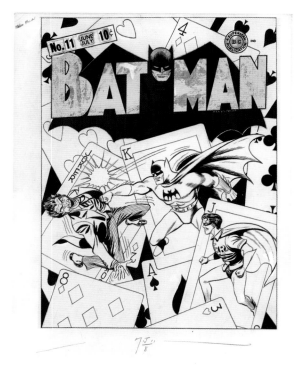

©2005 HeritageComics.com

Heritage Auctions, Inc.

Jack Kirby and Joe Sinnott, Fantastic Four #55 Spectacular Silver Surfer half-splash page 3 original art (Marvel, 1966). From the classic "When Strikes the Surfer" hails the legendary Stan Lee-Jack Kirby collaboration, with Silver Age inks by "King" Kirby brush-man, Joe Sinnott. 12 1/2" x 18 1/2". **$155,350**

Heritage Auctions, Inc.

Jack Kirby and Joe Simon, Adventure Comics #73 Manhunter cover original art (DC, 1942). Adventure Comics #73 is tied with Star Spangled Comics #7 as the first Simon & Kirby cover for DC. Noted as one of Overstreet's 100 most valuable Golden Age books. Image area 12 1/2" x 17". Provenance: Robinson Collection. **$119,500**

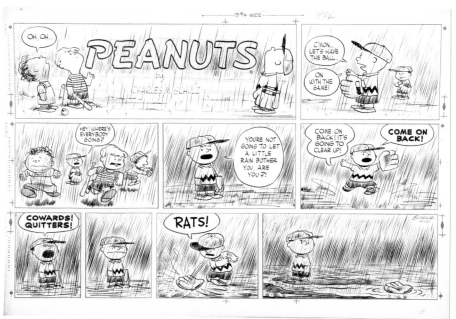

Heritage Auctions, Inc.

Charles Schulz, Peanuts Sunday comic strip original art, dated 4-10-55 (United Feature Syndicate, 1955). Features most of the early Peanuts cast of boys, Pigpen, Schroeder, and Shermy. 22 3/4" x 15 1/4". **$113,525**

Heritage Auctions, Inc.

Bill Watterson, Calvin and Hobbes 1989-1990 calendar cover watercolor illustration original art (circa 1988). Few pieces of original art are as scarce and sought after as a Calvin and Hobbes original by the characters' creator Bill Watterson. Only a small handful of originals have ever come onto the market. 13" x 10". **$107,550**

Heritage Auctions, Inc.

Fred Ray, Action Comics #46 Superman cover original art (DC, 1942). Cover sets the stage for Man of Tomorrow's battle with Domino in amusement park. 12 1/2" x 17 1/4". Provenance: Robinson Collection.
$101,575

Heritage Auctions, Inc.

Robert Crumb, Mr. Natural #1 cover original art (San Francisco Comic Book Co./Apex, 1970). In Underground Comix, there are few characters as beloved as Robert Crumb's Mr. Natural. 10" x 14". **$101,575**

Heritage Auctions, Inc.

Charles Schulz, Peanuts Sunday comic strip original art, dated 9-8-57 (United Features Syndicate, 1957). When Linus tickled Snoopy, a Peanuts classic was born. 22 1/2" x 15". **$101,575**

Heritage Auctions, Inc.

Frank Miller, Daredevil #188 Black Widow cover original art (Marvel, 1982). Black Widow has a grasp on Matt Murdock in this cover illustration by Frank Miller from his groundbreaking run on the series that thrust him into Marvel superstardom. 9 3/4" x 15". **$101,575**

Heritage Auctions, Inc.

Frank Frazetta, original cover art for Famous Funnies #213 (Eastern Color, 1953). One of eight covers done for Famous Funnies, featuring Buck Rogers and his companion confronting a creature intruding upon their existence. Image area 17 1/4" x 14 1/2". **$100,625**

Heritage Auctions, Inc.

Joe Kubert, The Brave and the Bold #34, the landmark first Silver Age Hawkman cover original art (DC, 1961), spotlighting the Winged Wonders as they mix it up with the Creature of a Thousand Shapes that helped launch a space-age "new frontier." 12 1/2" x 18". **$89,625.**

Heritage Auctions, Inc.

Alex Raymond, Flash Gordon with Matching Jungle Jim Topper Sunday comic strip original art, dated 7-21-35 (King Features Syndicate, 1935). 25 1/2" x 34". Provenance: Don Vernon Collection. **$77,675**

Heritage Auctions, Inc.

Ub Iwerks and Win Smith, Mickey Mouse Daily #15 comic strip original art (King Features, 1930). Most famous mouse in the world as he appeared in Hearst newspapers on Jan. 29, 1930. One of few originals from this era still known to exist. 23" x 6". **$74,750**

Heritage Auctions, Inc.

Kevin Eastman and Peter Laird, first-ever drawing of the Teenage Mutant Ninja Turtles (1983). Reprinted many times over the years, this drawing was sent out in the original press release package in 1984 and found its way into much early press coverage. It was also shown in the First Comics graphic novel in 1986, a special edition reprint of the first issue from 1992, and as a pin-up in some of the Mirage black and white issues. 8 1/2" x 11". Provenance: Collection of Kevin Eastman. **$71,700**

Heritage Auctions, Inc.

*John Byrne and Terry Austin,
X-Men #137, page 44 original art
(Marvel, 1980). Death of Phoenix
is remembered by anyone who read
comics in the 1980s. Jean Grey's life
ended on the next page. 10" x 15".*
$65,725

Heritage Auctions, Inc.

*Dave Cockrum, X-Men #102 cover
original art (Marvel, 1976). "If
Colossus Should Fall – Who Shall
Stop The Juggernaut?" was the cover
blurb that accompanied this battle
cover. 11 1/2" x 17 1/2".* **$65,725**

Heritage Auctions, Inc.

Wally Wood, Weird Science #14 cover original art (EC, 1952). Wood's science fiction covers remain among the best the genre has ever produced. 13" x 19". **$56,350**

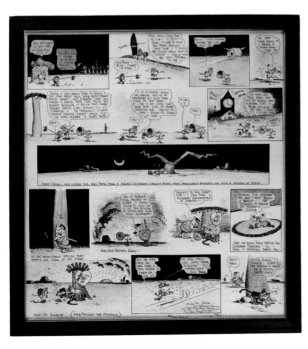

Heritage Auctions, Inc.

George Herriman, hand-colored Krazy Kat Sunday comic strip original art dated 6-25-22 (King Features Syndicate, 1922). Spotlights four of the major Krazy Kat characters: Ignatz Mouse, Bum Bill Bee, Offisa Bull Pupp, and Krazy Kat herself. 18 1/2" x 21 1/2". **$53,775**

Heritage Auctions, Inc.

Alex Ross, Superman, 20th century painting original art (1998). Superman takes to the skies in this Alex Ross painting used to create a limited edition lithograph for Warner Bros. and a series of signed giclee prints, as well as a large regular edition poster run, all of which have sold out. 15 1/2" x 22". **$52,282**

Heritage Auctions, Inc.

Carmine Infantino and Murphy Anderson, The Flash #146 Mirror Master cover original art (DC, 1964). Prime-time, vintage Silver Age footrace featuring the Scarlet Speedster and one of his oldest foes, the Mirror Master. Original Infantino and Anderson Flash covers rarely surface. 12 1/2" x 18 1/2". **$44,813**

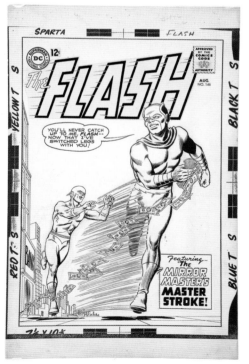

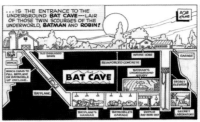

Heritage Auctions, Inc.

Bob Kane, original comic strip art for Batman dated 10/29/43 (Detective Comics, Inc./McClure Newspaper Syndicate, 1943). Rare, this is the fifth from the introductory week of this historic strip, which includes a detailed cutaway view of the Batcave. Rendered in pen and ink and blue pencil (to indicate shading). 22 3/4" x 5 3/4". **$43,700**

Heritage Auctions, Inc.

Wally Wood, Mad #4 "Superduperman" title page 1 original art (EC, 1953). The title page from the superhero lampoon secured the future of MAD and EC. First issue of MAD to sell well and it was also the first time MAD satirized something other than an EC comic. 13" x 18". **$43,319**

Heritage Auctions, Inc.

Winsor McCay, Little Nemo in Slumberland (featuring the first appearance of Flip) partial Sunday comic strip original art, dated 3-4-06 (New York Herald, 1906). Debut of Flip is showcased in this Sunday comic. 21 1/2" x 23 1/2". **$40,250**

Heritage Auctions, Inc.

Milton Caniff, historic first introducing Terry and the Pirates daily comic strip original art (Chicago Tribune, 1934). 20" x 6". **$38,828**

Heritage Auctions, Inc.

Steve Ditko, The Amazing Spider-Man #12 Doctor Octopus Battle page 17 original art (Marvel, 1964). Few originals are more sought after than a Spider-Man page drawn by Sturdy Steve Ditko. 12 1/2" x 18 1/2". **$38,838**

Heritage Auctions, Inc.

Carmine Infantino, original cover art for Superman #199 (DC, 1967). Cover is legendary in scope and design, drawn by Infantino, one of the artists who defined the Silver Age of comics. 12" x 18 1/2". **$33,925**

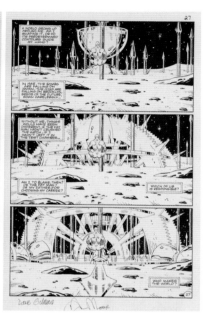

Heritage Auctions, Inc.

Dave Gibbons, Watchmen #4 "Watchmaker" Doctor Manhattan Raises His City on Mars, pages 26 and 27 original art (DC, 1986). Double-page spread features the watershed moment when Doctor Manhattan designs and raises a city on Mars. Combined image area 21" x 16". **$26,290**

Heritage Auctions, Inc.

Hal Foster, Prince Valiant Sunday comic strip #724 original art dated 12-24-50 (King Features Syndicate, 1950). From "The Missionaries" story arc, a Prince Valiant and Hal Foster classic. 23 1/2" x 34". **$21,510**

Heritage Auctions, Inc.

Chic Young, the second Blondie daily comic strip original art, dated 9-16-30 (King Features Syndicate, 1930). Young Blondie Boopadoop gets grilled by her fiancee's father, Mr. Bumstead, in this early Blondie daily, the second strip appearance ever. 18" x 4". **$20,913**

Heritage Auctions, Inc.

Gary Larson, The Far Side daily comic strip original art dated 2-12-83 (Chronicle Features, 1983). Cartoonist Larson pays a sly tribute to Walt Disney's classic animated feature Pinocchio in this panel featuring a "field cricket" preserved in alcohol. 6 1/4" x 8". **$20,315**

Burne Hogarth, Tarzan Sunday comic strip #523, "Peril from the Sea" original art dated 3-16-41 (United Feature Syndicate, 1941). Episode pits the Lord of the Jungle against the sea. 19 1/2" x 26 1/2". **$13,145.**

Joe Shuster and Jerry Siegel, George Roussos Sketchbook Batman and Superman illustration original art (circa 1942). Superman's creators pay homage to George Roussos with this signed sketch. 9" x 11 3/4". **$11,651**

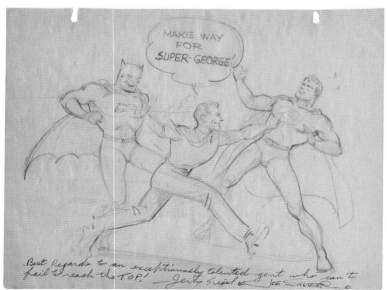

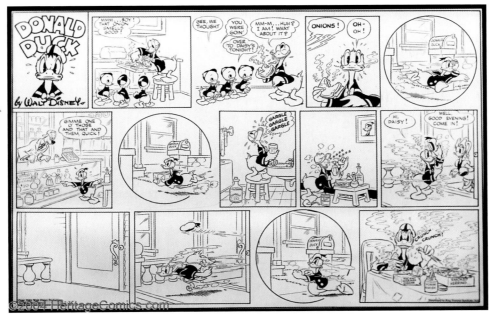

Heritage Auctions, Inc.

Al Taliaferro, original comic strip art for Donald Duck, Sunday dated 2-23-40 (Walt Disney Productions/ King Features Syndicate, 1940). Donald, Daisy and Donald's nephews Huey, Dewey, and Louie, try to combat a odiferous problem. 23 1/2" x 15 1/2". **$11,500**

Heritage Auctions, Inc.

Murphy Anderson, Overstreet Comic Book Price Guide #31 cover featuring Batman original art (2001). Cover illustration by Murphy Anderson is a re-creation of Detective Comics #31, featuring Batman vs. the Monk. 16" x 21". **$8,963**

Heritage Auctions, Inc.

George Perez, Star Trek #1 cover original art (DC, 1984). Kirk, Bones, Scotty, Uhura, Sulu, and Saavik lead the crew of the U.S.S. Enterprise in search of the Klingons in "The Wormhole Connection." 10" x 15".
$7,469

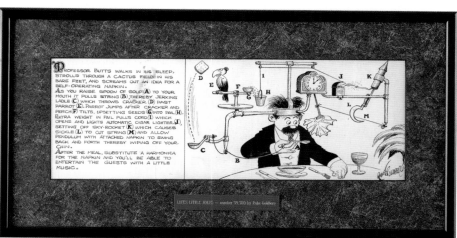

Heritage Auctions, Inc.

Rube Goldberg, Life's Little Jokes #59,380 daily comic strip original art (undated). Example explains Professor Lucifer Butts's need for a self-operating napkin. 17" x 6". From the estate of Bruce Hamilton.
$6,573.

Heritage Auctions, Inc.

Jaime Hernandez, Love and Rockets #14 "Locas en las Cabezas" page 4 original art (Fantagraphics, 1985). Classic mid-1980s page featuring Maggie and Hopey. 10" x 13". **$3,585**

Heritage Auctions, Inc.

Elzie Segar, Popeye "Sindbad the Sailor" specialty illustration original art and movie window card (1936). Max Fleisher's first color cartoon starring Segar's popular star of the Thimble Theatre comic strip, and was twice as long as most cartoons of its day. 12 3/4" x 14 3/4. Provenance: Estate of Bruce Hamilton. **$6,573**

Heritage Auctions, Inc.

Three Caballeros book cover original art (Walt Disney/ Random House, 1944). Original cover image to the first book adaptation to Walt Disney's South-of-the-Border favorite, Three Caballeros. 10 1/2" x 11 1/4". **$2,151**

Heritage Auctions, Inc.

Tom Lyle, Spider-Man #50 cover original art (Marvel, 1994). Son of Kraven the Hunter has come for the man he believes tarnished his family's good name, Spider-Man. This scene was used to create a holographic foil cover for "Son of the Hunter." 10" x 15". **$1,912**

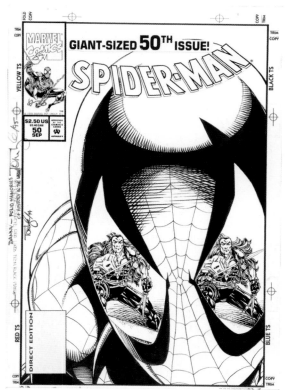

Heritage Auctions, Inc.

Marge Buell, Little Lulu panel page original art (Saturday Evening Post, undated). Children's comic strips were rarely as funny and charming as those by Lulu's creator, Marge. 8 1/4" x 8 3/4". Provenance: Random House Archives. **$1,380**

Heritage Auctions, Inc.

Sidney Smith, Santa Claus' Night in Chicago comic strip original art (undated). Yuletide classic. 19" x 25 1/2". **$777**

Heritage Auctions, Inc.

Ashley Wood and Jim Daly, Ghost Rider 2099 #16 Page 6 original art (Marvel, 1995). Organic page from "Dangerous Curve." 10 1/2" x 15 1/2". **$56**

Heritage Auctions, Inc.

The Simpsons, "Mr. Burns" preliminary animation drawing original art, group of three (undated). Tireless pursuer of ever greater wealth and power through the exploitation of his hapless workers, Charles Montgomery Burns is portrayed in these three animation sketches. 10 1/2" x 12 1/2" each. **$31**

Heritage Auctions, Inc.

Donald Duck children's book illustration page 18 original art (Disney, undated). Painted in mixed media illustration on board. 10" x 5". **$56**

Brad Anderson, Marmaduke daily comic strip original art (John F. Dille Co., 1959). **$40**

Yogi Bear and Boo Boo illustration original art (undated). "Hey there Boo Boo!" 10" x 5". **$29**

Fine Art

Fine art, created for aesthetic purposes and judged by its beauty rather than its utility, includes original painting and sculpture, drawing, watercolor, and graphics. It is appreciated primarily for its imaginative, aesthetic, or intellectual content.

Today's fine art market is a global one, currently estimated to be worth $56.5 billion. After being dominated by Chinese and Asian buyers in 2010 and 2011, the 2012 fine art market recorded the entrance of major buyers from Russia and the Middle East.

Fine art remains a solid investment as well. Christie's, the world's largest seller of fine artworks, recorded record sales in 2012. Edvard Munch's "The Scream" sold for $120 million in May 2012, the priciest artwork ever sold at auction.

"Late Moon Rising (Wild Horse Creek)," 1923, oil on canvas, Birger Sandzén (American, 1871-1954), signed and dated lower right: "Birger Sandzén / 1923"; important motif of Wild Horse Creek, which ran through land owned by Sandzén's in-laws near Bogue, Kansas; 36 1/4" x 48 1/4". Provenance: Acquired from a former art student. **$262,900**

"St Francis" stone sculpture, Beniamino Benvenuto Bufano (American, 1898-1970), St. Francis of Assisi, 29 3/4" x 17 1/2" x 50" without base. **$20,000**

"Fishing for Frogs," William Adolphe Bouguereau (French, 1825-1905), oil on canvas, signed and dated lower right: "W. Bouguereau 1882," 54" x 42". Provenance: Luckett Collection, Westchester, New York; private collection. **$1,762,500**

"The Family Dog," 1860, oil on board laid on board, Conrad Wise Chapman (American, 1842-1910), inscribed and dated lower left: "Roma 1860," 9" x 14". **$16,250**

Skinner, Inc.

"Apollo and Marsyas," oil on canvas, Italian School, 19th century, unsigned, 33 1/2" x 26 3/4", framed. **$18,960**

Skinner, Inc.

Greek icon depicting Saints Cosmos and Damian, 17th century, tempera and gilt on panel depicting the two physician saints, with affixed label to back reading "Parke Bernet Gallery 2/17/48," 8 1/2" high x 6 7/8" wide. **$2,726**

Skinner, Inc.

Russian icon of St. George slaying the dragon, Palekh school, 19th century, the kovcheg panel with Christ blessing from the clouds above and light brown border, 10 1/4" x 8 1/2".
$1,304

Skinner, Inc.

Russian icon of St. Theodore the Recruit, 19th century, the kovcheg panel with two figures adorned with riza halos amid cloudwork in the upper corners, brown border, 13 7/8" x 11 7/8".
$2,552

Coeur d'Alene Art Auction

"Autumn Day," 1883, oil on canvasboard, Norton Bush (1834-1894), signed lower right, 24" x 29".
$9,360

Coeur d'Alene Art Auction

"A Roll to Loo'Ard," 1956, oil on canvas, Montague Dawson (1895-1973), signed lower left, 24" x 36".
$87,750

Coeur d'Alene Art Auction

"Gatun Lake – Panama," 1874, oil on canvas, Norton Bush (1834-1894), signed lower right, 30" x 50".
$58,500

Coeur d'Alene Art Auction

"Cowboys Roping the Bear," oil on canvas laid on board, Frank Tenney Johnson (1874-1939), signed lower right, 26 1/4" x 36 1/4". **$921,000**

Coeur d'Alene Art Auction

"The Sutter Creek Stage," 1932, oil on canvas, Frank Tenney Johnson (1874-1939), signed and dated lower left, 36" x 46". **$409,500**

Heritage Auctions, Inc.

*"October Morning,"
1940, oil on board,
Maynard Dixon
(American, 1875-
1946), signed and
dated lower right:
"Maynard Dixon,
1940," inscribed
verso: "771, October
Morning, Maynard
Dixon, Tucson,
Ariz.," 19 1/2" x 15".*
$68,500

Heritage Auctions, Inc.

*"The Foothills of
California, Tejon
Ranch," circa 1929,
oil on canvas, John
Bond Francisco
(American, 1863-
1931), signed lower
right: "J. Bond
Francisco," inscribed
verso: "The Foothills
of California, Tejon
Ranch," original
gold-leaf exhibition
frame by Carrig-
Rohane, 33 1/2" x
45".* **$62,500**

Heritage Auctions, Inc.

"Self-Portrait," oil on canvas, Helena Adele M. Dunlap (American, 1876-1955), signed lower right: "H. Dunlap," 21 1/4" x 17 1/4". **$15,000**

Heritage Auctions, Inc.

"Still Life with Grapes," 1900, oil on canvas, Edith White (American, 1855-1946), signed and dated lower left: "Edith White 1900," 12" x 15". **$1,850**

Heritage Auctions, Inc.

"Le Port de Saint-Tropez," oil on canvas, Pierre-Auguste Renoir (French, 1841-1919), signed lower right: "Renoir," 6 3/4" x 10 1/2". **$242,500**

Heritage Auctions, Inc.

"The Proposal," 1891, oil on canvas, Wladislaw Czachorski (Polish, 1850-1911), signed and dated upper right: "Czachorski / 1891," 36" x 22". **$116,500**

Heritage Auctions, Inc.

"Winter," oil on board, Guy Carleton Wiggins (American, 1883-1962), signed lower left: "Guy Wiggins N.A.," titled and signed verso: "WINTER / 5th AVE. AT 42nd ST. / Guy Wiggins N.A.," accompanied by copy of letter of authenticity from Guy A. Wiggins, Jr., 22" x 18". **$43,750**

Heritage Auctions, Inc.

"Cherokee Roses in a Glass Vase," circa 1883-1888, oil on canvas, Martin Johnson Heade (American, 1819-1904), signed lower right: "M.J. Heade," 19" x 12". **$170,500**

Heritage Auctions, Inc.

"Young Shepherdess," 1878, oil on canvas, Victor Charles Thirion (French, 1833-1878), signed and dated lower left: "V. Thirion / 1878," 54" x 30". **$50,000**

Heritage Auctions, Inc.

"Youth, No. 766," oil on canvas, Hovsep Pushman (American, 1877-1966), signed lower left: "Pushman," 36" x 28 1/2". **$56,250**

Heritage Auctions, Inc.

"Cherries," 1879, oil on canvas, Jules Emile Santin (French, 1829-1894), signed and dated lower left: "Emile Jules Saintin / 1879," 22" x 18". **$25,000**

Heritage Auctions, Inc.

"L' amour Fraternel," oil on canvas, Leon Jean Basile Perrault (French, 1832-1908), signed upper right: "L. Perrault," 22" x 18". **$25,000**

Heritage Auctions, Inc.

"Pickin' Cotton," oil on board, William Aiken Walker (American, 1838-1921), signed lower left: "WAWalker," inscribed in pencil verso: "Man," 12 1/4" x 6 1/4". **$11,875**

Pook & Pook, Inc.

Portrait of Napoleon on horseback, oil on canvas, 19th century, 48 1/4" x 40 1/2". **$4,029**

Heritage Auctions, Inc.

"Hidden Treasure," 1901, oil on canvas, Adam Emory Albright (American, 1862-1957), signed and dated lower right: "Adam Emory Albright / 1901," 24" x 16". **$6,250**

Heritage Auctions, Inc.

"Morning Light," 1922, oil on board, Henry Clarence Pitz (American, 1895-1976), signed and dated lower right: "Pitz / 1922," 11 3/4" x 9 3/4". **$2,500**

Heritage Auctions, Inc.

"Curiosity and the Butterfly," oil on wood panel, Julius Adam (German, 1852-1913), signed upper right: "Jul Adams," original panel, European, 19th century, applied ornament with inner gilded filet and linen mat, Louis style frame, 11" x 8 1/2". **$5,000**

Heritage Auctions, Inc.

"Playing Cards," oil on cradled wood panel, Carl Reichert (Austrian, 1836-1918), signed by the artist with his pseudonym lower right: "J. Hartung," 10" x 12 1/2". **$1,625**

Heritage Auctions, Inc.

"Oklahoma," illustration for Country Gentleman Magazine, *1926, oil on canvas, Frank Earle Schoonover (American, 1877-1972), signed and dated lower right, 24" x 36".* **$27,500**

Pook & Pook, Inc.

Seascape with sailboats, circa 1940, oil on canvas, signed lower right "M.G. Friedrich," 24" x 36". **$3,318**

Dog Art

From the humble folk art picture of the family pet to the professionally commissioned portrait, man's best friend has been depicted in art for centuries. Whether an art enthusiast's tastes lean toward loyal lap dogs or hunting hounds, realistic interpretations of canines in art – whether fine or folk – is at an all-time high, which is high enough for major auction houses like Bonhams (held annually after the Westminster Dog Show) to hold sales attributed solely to dog-themed art. For more on dog art, major exhibitions are held at New York's Metropolitan Museum of Art and the Morgan Library & Museum. The William Secord Gallery in Manhattan and the American Kennel Club's Museum of the Dog, also in New York, are both dedicated solely to dog art.

Pook & Pook, Inc.

Portrait of spaniel, oil on canvas, 20th century, signed Steve Rogers lower left, 24" x 30". **$652**

Heritage Auctions, Inc.

"The Duke of Marlborough, Portrait of a Puppy," oil on panel, James Carroll Beckwith (American, 1852-1917), inscribed, signed and dated: "His Grace The Duke of Marlborough," 13 3/4" x 10". **$3,906**

Pook & Pook, Inc.

Portrait of dog, oil on board, Eva Webster Russell (American, 20th century), 4 1/2" x 7 1/4". **$533**

Heritage Auctions, Inc.

*"Two Setters on Point," oil on canvas, Edmund Henry Osthaus (American, 1858-1928), signed lower left:
"Edm. H. Osthaus," 20" x 40".* **$10,000**

Pook & Pook, Inc.

Two King Charles spaniels, oil on board, signed lower right: "F. Crosby 1928," 13 1/2" x 19 1/2". **$533**

Pook & Pook, Inc.

Pair of portraits of King Charles spaniels, oil on board, 19th century, 5 3/4" x 7 1/2". **$830**

Bronze Statuary

Bronze is an alloy of copper, tin, and traces of other metals. It has been used since Biblical times not only for art objects but also for utilitarian wares. After a slump in the Middle Ages, the use of bronze was revived in the 17th century and continued to be popular until the early 20th century.

A signed bronze commands a higher market price than an unsigned one.

Bonhams

Patinated bronze figure of a skeleton, after a model by Carl Kauba (Austrian-American, 1865-1922), late 19th/early 20th century, depicted as holding a skull and standing on a volume inscribed "Hippocrates" in Greek letters, inscribed on reverse of hip bone "C. Kauba," dark green marble base, 17". **$22,500**

Heritage Auction Galleries

Bronze statue of a World War I Italian soldier throwing a grenade, signed "L. Coti" and marked "Mozzanica" (a town in the Lombardy region of Italy where the bronze was likely cast). Soldier wears Adrian-style helmet, throwing stick-type grenade, his other hand clutching at his chest. 16 1/2" high. **$1,046**

Leslie Hindman Auctioneers

Russian bronze figural group, Vasilii Grachev (1831-1905), depicting a Cossack farewell kiss, signed in Cyrillic with Woerffel foundry mark, set on marble plinth, bronze 9 1/8" high. **$1,100**

Coeur d'Alene Art Auction

"The Mustanger," bronze, Daro Flood (b. 1954), AP 2/3, stamped in base: "© - AP 2/3," 25" high. **$8,190**

Skinner, Inc.

Gilt-bronze "Thousand-Arm Kuan Yin," China, with 11 heads at five levels facing in three directions, standing on a lotus throne, hands holding different items including bow and arrow, necklace, mirror, flower branch and bottle, 42". **$3,000**

Coeur d'Alene Art Auction

"The Broncho Buster," bronze, Frederic Remington (1861-1909), Henry-Bonnard Bronze Co. Casting No. 37, stamped under base: "[Casting No.] 37"; stamped in base: "Cast by the Henry-Bonnard Bronze Co. N-Y. 1898"; 23" high. **$222,300**

Skinner, Inc.

"Pair of Women Dressed as a Hen and a Rooster," Alfred Grevin (1827-1892) and Friedrich Beer (1846-1912), hen with basket of eggs and rooster with riding crop, each with dark brown and copper-colored patina, circular bases incised "A. Grevin et Beer" and "E. TASSEL fondeur Ed^n," *13" h.* **$1,422**

Skinner, Inc.

"Industry Rewarded," Edouard Felicien Alexis Pepin (French, b. 1853), late 19th/early 20th century, female figure holding cornucopia and placing laurel wreath on laborer's head while he sits surrounded by tools and plans, chocolate brown patina, base incised "E. PEPIN," without foundry mark, detached circular revolving bronze base, total 39 1/2" high, cornucopia unattached. **$5,629**

Michaan's Auctions

"Star Maiden" bronze with green patina, Alexander Stirling Calder (American, 1870-1945), signed on the base of globe "Stirling Calder," dated verso "MCMXV," inscribed on right side of base "Copyright 1914, Panama Pacific International Exposition Co."; commissioned for the 1915 Panama Pacific Exposition, San Francisco, 54" x 19 1/2" x 13 1/2". **$20,000**

Illustration Art

BY BRENT FRANKENHOFF & MAGGIE THOMPSON, COMICS BUYER'S GUIDE

Collectors, whether looking for a distinctive decoration for a living room or seeking a rewarding long-term investment, will find something to fit their fancy — and their budget — when they turn to illustration art.

Pieces of representational art — often, art that tells some sort of story — are produced in a variety of forms, each appealing in a different way. They are created as the source material for political cartoons, magazine covers, posters, story illustrations, comic books and strips, animated cartoons, calendars, and book jackets. They may be in color or in black and white. Collectible forms include:

Maggie Thompson and Brent Frankenhoff

• **Mass-market printed reproductions.** These can range from art prints and movie posters to engravings, clipped advertising art, and bookplates. While this may be the least-expensive art to hang on your wall, a few rare items can bring record prices. Heritage Auction Galleries, for example, commanded a price of $334,600 for a Universal 1935 Bride of Frankenstein poster (artist unidentified).

• **Limited-run reproductions.** These range from signed, numbered lithographs to numbered prints.

• **Tangential items.** These are hard-to-define, oddball pieces. One example is printing plates (some in actual lead; some in plastic fused to lightweight metal) used by newspapers and comic-book printers to reproduce the art.

• **Unique original art.** These pieces have the widest range of all, from amateur sketches to finished paintings. The term "original art" includes color roughs produced by a painter as a preliminary test for a work to be produced, finished oil paintings, animation cels for commercials as well as feature films, and black-and-white inked pages of comic books and strips. They may be signed and identifiable or unsigned and generic. "Illustration art" is often differentiated from "fine art," but its very pop-culture nature may increase the pool of would-be purchasers. Alberto Vargas (1896-1982) and Gil Elvgren (1914-1980) bring high prices for pin-up art; Norman Rockwell (1894-1978), James Montgomery Flagg (1877-1960), and J.C. Leyendecker (1874-1951) were masters of mainstream illustration; and Margaret Brunda ge (1900-1976) and Virgil Finlay (1914-1971) are highly regarded pulp artists.

BRENT FRANKENHOFF *is the editor of* Comics Buyer's Guide, *the longest-running U.S. magazine about comic books. A lifelong collector (he got his first comics when he was three and still has them), he's been following the comics market for more than 20 years. The award-winning* **MAGGIE THOMPSON** *was among the pioneering amateurs who formed the foundation in the 1960s of today's international anarchy of comic-book collecting. With her late husband, Don, she edited* Comics Buyer's Guide *and is, today, Senior Editor of that publication, also remaining active as collector and essayist.*

Heritage Auctions, Inc.

"Skirting the Issue (Breezing Up)," 1956, oil on canvas, Gil Elvgren (American, 1914-1980), signed lower left, 30" x 24". Provenance: Estate of Charles Martignette. **$176,500**

Heritage Auctions, Inc.

"American Beauties (I Hope He Mrs. Me)," 1949, oil on canvas, Gil Elvgren (American, 1914-1980), 30" x 24". Provenance: Estate of Charles Martignette. **$68,500**

Heritage Auctions, Inc.

"Surprised?" 1952, oil on canvas, Gil Elvgren (American, 1914-1980), signed lower center, 30" x 24". Provenance: Estate of Charles Martignette. **$43,750**

Heritage Auctions, Inc.

"Time to Go! Everyone's Waiting for Schrafft's," Schrafft's Chocolate advertisement, oil on canvas, Walter Beach Humphrey (American, 1892-1966), signed lower right, 41" x 30". Provenance: Estate of Charles Martignette. **$27,500**

Heritage Auctions, Inc.

"Rockets to Nowhere," book cover, 1954, acrylic on board, Alex Schomburg (American, 1905-1998), signed lower left, 24" x 20". This painting was published as the dust jacket artwork for the juvenile novel Rockets to Nowhere *by Phillip St. John (Lester Del Rey), John C. Winston (1954).* **$15,000**

Heritage Auctions, Inc.

"Two Blues Please," Tattle Tales *pulp cover, oil on canvas, Hugh Joseph Ward (American, 1909-1945), signed lower right, 30" x 21". Provenance: Estate of Charles Martignette.* **$15,000**

"Refreshment on the Beach," Coca-Cola advertisement, gouache on board, Pete Hawley (American, 20th century), 26" x 20". **$27,500**

"Backyard Campers," Saturday Evening Post *cover, Sept. 5, 1953, gouache on board, Amos Sewell (American, 1901-1983), 28 1/4" x 21 3/4".* **$27,500**

Heritage Auctions, Inc.

"Swords of Mars," preliminary book cover, mixed media on board, J. Allen St. John (American, 1872-1957), not signed, 11 3/4" x 19". **$15,000**

Heritage Auctions, Inc.

"Little Fur Family," Garth Williams (American, 1912-1996), group of four: page 8, 18, 22, and 25 illustrations, 1946, pen, watercolor, and gouache on board, not signed, 5 1/2" x 3 1/2" (largest). Provenance: Estate of Garth Williams. **$15,000**

"The Roadblock," preliminary drawing for the Saturday Evening Post *cover, July 9, 1949, pencil and charcoal on paper, Norman Rockwell (American, 1894-1978), signed and inscribed to the artist's goddaughter, 24" x 19".* **$32,500**

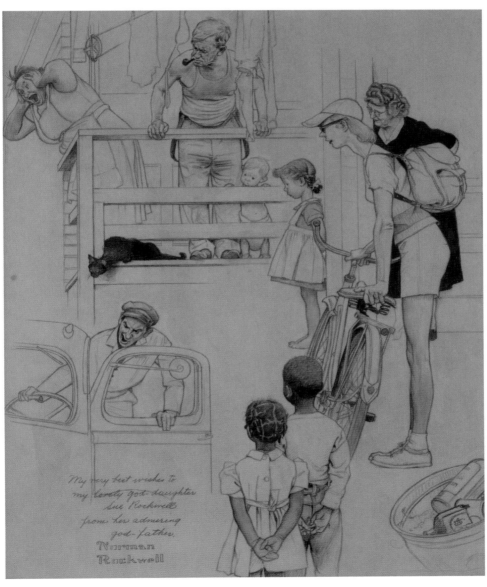

Heritage Auctions, Inc.

"Returning Fire," 1920, oil on canvas, Frank Spradling (American, 1885-1972), signed lower right, 40" x 27". Provenance: Provenance: Estate of Charles Martignette. **$11,250**

Heritage Auctions, Inc.

"Say Hires!", Hires Root Beer advertisement, circa 1904, oil on canvas, not signed, 17" x 13", with original Hires serving tray. **$3,131**

"Day in the Life of a Little Boy," study for the Saturday Evening Post *cover, May 24, 1952, pencil with highlights on board, Norman Rockwell (American, 1894-1978), 11" x 10 1/2".* **$46,875**

Wildlife Art

BY ERIC BRADLEY

Americans' love affair with wildlife art began long before there was a United States.

Sir Walter Raleigh, planning his first expedition to the new world, requested artist John White to accompany the trip as a vital crewmate and fellow history maker. If he could show all of England the wonderful and profitable beasts and flowers to be found in the New World, Raleigh knew future trips would be all but certain. Images of flora and fauna equaled fame and fortune.

White's lifelike watercolors of brown pelicans, land crabs and loggerhead turtles delivered beyond Raleigh's wildest dreams. Those early works from the late 1500s are the start of a genre of art uniquely American in subject, artistry and political power. American wildlife art has inspired kings, presidents and the public.

David J. Wagner, Ph.D.

In the last 20 years, American wildlife art has established itself as a legitimate genre in both antique and postmodern art. A genre that had been taken for granted for so long has come into its own as a form of art both respectable and politically powerful. The market for wildlife art is surging. A single hand-colored engraving by John James Audubon, arguably the biggest name in American wildlife art, sold for $105,000 by the Neal Auction Company while the Julius Bien reissue folio of Audubon's The Birds of America sold for $230,000.

American Wildlife Art *by David J. Wagner*

Although Audubon's name has become synonymous with American wildlife (he portrayed some 2,000 birds and hundreds of animals and plants), his work was built on nearly 200 years' worth of his predecessors' endeavors. The demand for wildlife art was solidified during the Age of Enlightenment, when collectors themselves funded expeditions for new discoveries.

"This was the age of discovery and enlightenment," said David Wagner, author of the groundbreaking book *American Wildlife Art* (Marquand Books, 2008). "A time when big science was interested in collecting and collecting information: data, words, pictures and numbers."

This pursuit sparked a tsunami of immigration that rushed to document all the unique living things to be found in the new world. Sadly, one price was to be paid by the creatures themselves, as in the case of the American passenger pigeon, of which Audubon himself marveled: "The air was literally filled with Pigeons; the light of noon-day was obscured as by an eclipse."

"The art certainly presented wildlife as a means to drive economic investment in the New World," Wagner said. "And art did play a role in the demise in what had been." Wagner's book documents for the first time the history and contemporary impact of American wildlife art. Its manuscript grew out of his 1992 PhD dissertation, and its 395 pages represents but one-third of his total research on the topic. He shows that up until the 1850s, wildlife art had largely been something of a pursuit for the wealthy.

In the 1850s, cheaper printing methods made the art accessible to the middle class. Wildlife art became less about scholarly illustration and more about depicting the average hunting camp. That's when a 39-year-old New York publisher, Nathaniel Currier, hired his brother-in-law, James Ives, to launch a company advertised as "Print-Makers to the American People." At first the Currier & Ives Company focused on sporting and hunting art in subscription form. The hardscrabble life of the early American was easing, and hunting and fishing took on less of an importance for survival than it did for sport and leisure.

In this era, artists such as Arthur Fitzwilliam Tait (1819-1905), William Ranney (1813-1857) and William Harnett (1848-1892) celebrated the outdoors as a resource to be relished. One sculptor in particular, Edward Kemeys (1843-1907), has the distinction of being the first major figure in American wildlife art to be born in the United States. Kemeys found patrons for his sculptures of mountain lions for New York's Central Park and the iconic lions guarding the entry to Chicago's Art Institute.

By the dawn of the 20th century, artist Carl Rungius (1869-1959) had begun honing a unique approach to depicting big game and sporting scenes. "After Audubon, who was larger than life, no one emerged to take his place," Wagner said. "There was a vacuum. Tait was hugely popular, as was Currier & Ives. With Rungius, his images had the subject of sportsmen but rendered from the perspective of an artist. America was just learning about Impressionism and Modernism. Rungius' paintings were large and he used color to achieve his Impressionism. It was chunkier and used different types of color."

The style of Louis Agassiz Fuertes, a contemporary of Rungius, is steeped in Audubon's scientific rendering with a mix of human-like emotions to his subjects. "His wood ducks almost smile at you in a folksy way. He wanted to know the inner self of the animal," Wagner said.

Rungius' and Fuertes' work modernized American wildlife painting and established it as a legitimate profession. It also created a standard of excellence throughout the 20th century, according to Wagner.

The 20th century exploded with a proliferation of wildlife art. From the National Wildlife Federation to the Federal Duck Stamp Competition, the oversupply of limited edition collectible prints to car companies naming products after the Cougar, the Mustang and the Ram, wildlife art touches every aspect of our collective modern popular culture.

By the late 20th century, painter Robert Bateman had become America's most influential living wildlife artist, Wagner said, because his aesthetic was purposefully integrated with ecological ideology and the enterprise of publishing. His painting "Mossy Branches – Spotted Owl" was released as a limited edition print in 1990 by Mill Pond Press. The edition of 4,500 prints sold out within a month of its release – during the height of an effort to preserve land in the Pacific Northwest to protect the endangered spotted owl.

What does the future of American wildlife art hold?

"I can make one prediction," Wagner said. "New heroes will jump out and will become icons in their own right," he said. "It won't be a one-shot phenomenon. It's going to be an artist with a whole body of work. Someone will come out and be the next James Audubon or Robert Bateman, someone with a signature style."

ERIC BRADLEY is public relations associate at Heritage Auctions, the world's third largest auction house. He is former editor of Antique Trader magazine and is the author of Antique Trader 2013 Antiques and Collectibles Price Guide, America's no. 1-selling guide to the antiques and collectibles market. An award-winning investigative journalist with a degree in economics, Bradley has written hundreds of articles about antiques and collectibles and has made several media appearances as an expert on the antiques market at MoneyShow San Francisco, on MSN Money, Nasdaq.com and on AdvisorOne.com. His work has received press from The New York Times and The Philadelphia Inquirer.

Guernsey's

"Two Ducks," gouache, watercolor, pencil and ink on board with overlay, Roger Tory Peterson, cover art for World of Birds, 1964; 13" x 13". Provenance: Estate of Roger Tory Peterson and Virginia Marie Peterson. **$4,000**

Guernsey's

"Downy Woodpecker," ink, gouache on heavy paper, early work of Roger Tory Peterson, "RTP" inked in upper right corner; 4" x 6". Provenance: Estate of Roger Tory Peterson and Virginia Marie Peterson. **$700**

Guernsey's

*"Turkey, Pheasant, Grouse,"
gouache, watercolor, pencil and ink
on board with overlay, Roger Tory
Peterson,* Field Guide to Eastern
Birds, *1980. Also page 121 in* Field
Guide to the Birds of Eastern and
Central North America, *2002; 15"
x 9". Provenance: Estate of Roger
Tory Peterson and Virginia Marie
Peterson.* **$2,250**

Guernsey's

*"Cardinal, Grosbeaks," gouache,
watercolor, pencil and ink on board
with overlay, Roger Tory Peterson,
cover art for* Field Guide to Eastern
Birds, *1980; 3" x 6" on 10" x 10"
board. Provenance: Estate of Roger
Tory Peterson and Virginia Marie
Peterson.* **$3,000**

Guernsey's

*"Two American Wigeons on the
Wing," oil on canvas in wood
frame, Roger Tory Peterson's
first oil painting, executed in
Chautaugua, New York; 12" x
16". Provenance: The estates of
Roger Tory Peterson and Virginia
Marie Peterson. Reference:*
Roger Tory Peterson: The Art
and Photography of the World's
Foremost Birder, *Rizzoli, NY:
1994, page 15.* **$8,000**

Guernsey's

"California Condor," gouache, watercolor, pencil and ink on board with overlay, Roger Tory Peterson, page 187, Plate 3 from Eagles, Hawks and Falcons of the World, *1968, Vol. I; 17" x 13". Provenance: Estate of Roger Tory Peterson and Virginia Marie Peterson.* **$8,000**

Guernsey's

"Canada Lynx," Plate 16, John James Audobon (1785-1851), lithograph with original hand color. First Imperial Folio Edition by J. T. Bowen, paper: 21" x 27". Text above image: "No. 4," left, and "PLATE, XVI," right. Text below image: "Drawn from Nature by J.J. Audubon F.R.S. F.L.S.," left, and "Lith, Printed and Col'd by J.T. Bowen. Philid's," right. Plate legend text: "LYNX CANADENSIS, GEOFF./ CANADA LYNX./ 3/4 Natural Size/ Male"; no variants. **$22,000**

Guernsey's

"Common American Swan," Plate 411, John James Audobon (1785-1851), Havell Edition (1827-1838), plate prepared (1838), printed, and colored by Robert Havell Jr. (1793-1898). Plate dimension format: large, paper dimensions: 26 1/2" x 39". Text above image: "No 83," left, and "PLATE CCCCXI," right. Text below image: "Drawn from Nature by J.J. Audubon F.R.S. F.L.S.," left, and "Engraved Printed and Coloured by Robt Havell 1838," right. Plate legend text: "Common American Swan, / CYGNUS AMERICANUS, Sharpless. / Nymphea flava. - Leitner"; no variants. **$80,000**

Guernsey's

"Common American Wildcat," Plate 1, John James Audubon (1785-1851) and John Bachman (1790-1874), Viviparous Quadrupeds of North America, *First Imperial Folio Edition, lithograph with original hand color. Paper size: 21" x 27", framed size: 35" x 41". Text above image: "No. 1," left, and "PLATE, I," right. Text below image: "Drawn from Nature by J.J. Audubon F.R.S. F.L.S.," left, and "Lith, Printed and Col'd by J.T. Bowen. Phila. 1842," right. Plate legend text: "LYNX RUFUS.GULDENSTAED/ Common American Wildcat/ 3/4 Natural Size/ Male." In the 1830s, as the final plates were being completed for Audubon's monumental "Birds of America" series, the artist began to gather material for his second and equally ambitious undertaking. Planning to complete the definitive study of American wildlife, Audubon set out to document the animals of North America and to present them in a format as impressive and sweeping as what he used for his birds. The result of the artist/naturalist's years of field research, travel, and seemingly endless study was the* Viviparous Quadrupeds of North America. **$18,000**

Guernsey's

"Monarch," Danaus plexippus, North America, photograph printed from a negative from the Roger Tory Peterson Estate taken by Peterson himself; bears estate stamp and numbered 1/1, printed image area 13" x 19" and overall mat size 20" x 24". **$300**

Guernsey's

"American Black Bear," Plate 141, John James Audubon (1785-1851) and John Bachman (1790-1874), Viviparous Quadrupeds of North America, *First Imperial Folio Edition, lithograph with original hand color. Paper dimensions: 22" x 28". Text above image: "No. 29," left, and "PLATE, CXLI," right. Text below image: "Drawn from Nature by J.W. Audubon," left, and "Lith, Printed and Col'd by J.T. Bowen. Philid. 1848," right. Plate legend text: "URSUS AMERICANUS, PALLAS./ AMERICAN BLACK BEAR./ Male and Female"; no variants.* **$9,500**

Coeur d'Alene Art Auction

"Autumn Sorcery – Mallards," oil on board, Harry Adamson (b. 1916), 26" x 36", signed lower left. **$43,875**

Coeur d'Alene Art Auction

"In the Presence of a Mighty King" (2012), oil on canvas, John Banovich (b. 1964), 30" x 45", signed lower right. **$22,000**

Coeur d'Alene Art Auction

"Elephants' Playtime" (1984), oil on canvas, David Shepherd (b. 1931), 23 1/2" x 42", signed and dated lower right. **$55,575**

"Coyote" (1991), acrylic on board, 8" x 10", signed and dated lower right; "Golden Eagle" (1985), acrylic on board, 8" x 10", signed and dated lower right; "Mountain Goat" (1988), acrylic on board, 8" x 10", signed and dated lower right; all by Robert Bateman (b. 1930). **$43,875 set of three**

"Sunset Over the Plains" or "Deer in a Sunset Landscape" (circa 1887), oil on canvas, Albert Bierstadt (1830-1902), 21 1/2" x 29", signed lower left. **$514,800**

Coeur d'Alene Art Auction

"Lioness & Impala," bronze, Kenneth Bunn (b. 1935), 21" high, stamped in base: "© Bunn AP/7." **$4,680**

Coeur d'Alene Art Auction

"Dense Cover," oil on board, Ken Carlson (b. 1937), 13" x 18", signed lower right. **$17,550**

Coeur d'Alene Art Auction

"Rocky Retreat," oil on canvas, John Clymer (1907-1989), 36" x 40", signed lower left. **$58,500**

Coeur d'Alene Art Auction

*"Catching the Scent,"
oil on canvas laid
on board, Michael
Coleman (b. 1946),
30" x 40", signed
lower right.* **$9,945**

Coeur d'Alene Art Auction

*"Elk at Jackson
Lake, Wyoming," oil
on canvas, John Fery
(1859-1934), 18" x
28", signed lower
left.* **$7,020**

Coeur d'Alene Art Auction

*"High Plains Drifter,"
(2012), acrylic on
board, Daniel Smith
(b. 1954), 18" x 28",
signed and dated
lower left.* **$9,360**

Coeur d'Alene Art Auction

"The Gift," oil on canvas, Bonnie Marris (b. 1951), 32" x 24", signed lower right. **$15,210**

Coeur d'Alene Art Auction

"The Leopard," acrylic on board, Bob Kuhn (1920-2007), 24" x 36", signed lower right. **$117,000**

Coeur d'Alene Art Auction

"Border Patrol" (1985), acrylic on board, Bob Kuhn (1920-2007), 8" x 12", signed lower right. **$29,250**

Coeur d'Alene Art Auction

"Prelude to Battle," acrylic on board, Bob Kuhn (1920-2007), 20" x 30", signed lower left. **$70,200**

Coeur d'Alene Art Auction

"An Enemy That Warns" (1921), bronze, Charles M. Russell (1864-1926), 6" high, stamped in base: "C.M. Russell / Roman Bronze Works, N.Y." **$292,500**

Coeur d'Alene Art Auction

"The Range Father," bronze, Charles M. Russell (1864-1926), 6" high, stamped in base: "CM Russell / Roman Bronze Works N.Y." **$46,800**

Asian

Art and antiques from Asia have fascinated collectors for centuries because they are linked with the rich culture and fascinating history of the Far East. Their beauty, artistry and fine craftsmanship have lured collectors through the ages.

The category is vast and includes objects ranging from jade carvings to cloisonné to porcelain, the best known of these being porcelain.

Large quantities of porcelain have been made in China for export to America from the 1780s. A major source of this porcelain was Ching-te-Chen in the Kiangsi province, but the wares were also made elsewhere. The largest quantities were blue and white.

Prices for Asian antiques and art fluctuate considerably depending on age, condition, decoration, etc.

James D. Julia, Inc.

Rare pair of hardwood Chinese framed embroideries, 19th century, circa 1870, China, carved and pierced rosewood frames, foo dog feet, enclosing embroidered panels of 100 birds, overall: 74" high x 46 1/2" wide x 20" deep. Frame: 53 1/2" high x 38 1/4" wide. Embroidery: 43 1/2" high x 29" wide. **$86,250**

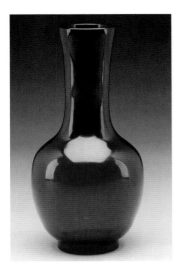

James D. Julia, Inc.

Peking glass vase, 18th century, China, rare hand cut and polished example in transparent amber, 14 3/8" high.
$2,472

James D. Julia, Inc.

Jeweled silver box, 19th century, Nepal, central plaque of jade inlaid with coral and carnelian, filigreed silver surface inset with cabochons of turquoise, garnet, jade, opal and glass in form of Makala masks and figures of various Buddhist divinities, 5" high x 7 1/4" diameter. **$1,380**

James D. Julia, Inc.

Rhinoceros horn cup, Kang Hsi Period (1662-1722), China, red amber color, surface carved in high relief with flowering prunus branch against simulated rock work, interior similarly carved and pierced with molded edge and sloping sides, base recessed, fitted to a later pierce carved rosewood stand, 182 grams, 2 1/2" high overall; mouth: 4 3/4" long x 4" wide. Foot: 1 3/4" diameter. **$34,500**

James D. Julia, Inc.

Peking glass vase, Tao Quang mark and probably of the period (1821-1850), China, cobalt blue bottle vase with high foot rim, 8 1/4" high.
$4,025

James D. Julia, Inc.

Jade carving, 19th century, China, figural group of a Mandarin on horseback with groom, grayish white jade, 5 1/3" high x 4 1/2" long overall. **$5,175**

James D. Julia, Inc.

Bronze image of Padma Pani, 19th century, Nepal, high copper content, posed with ornate headdress and with swirling trains, floral sprig from left arm on double lotus plinth, 29 3/4" high. **$1,610**

James D. Julia, Inc.

Chinese Export Mandarin pitcher, mid-19th century, China, sides with oval reserves of domestic scenes, front decorated with a large reserve of Mandarins in palace scenes, all set within an ivory glaze decorated with butterflies and flowers with gilt highlights, 9 1/2" high. **$2,645**

James D. Julia, Inc.

Pair of polychrome decorated phoenixes, late Ming or Qing Dynasty, China, each pottery bird posed on rockwork in opposing directions with rich coloration, 19 1/2" high. **$20,000-$30,000**

James D. Julia, Inc.

Rare cinnabar seal paste box, early Ming Period, 15th century, surface deeply carved as stylized lotus, 3" diameter. **$6,900**

James D. Julia, Inc.

Ivory carving of the god of longevity, China, Ming Period (1368-1644), possibly earlier, figure holding a ling chih scepter, surrounded by attendants, offered with a carved ivory stand, 14 1/2" high including stand. **$1,380**

James D. Julia, Inc.

Hanging scroll, China, Wang Yuanqi (1642-1715), ink on paper depicting, in the style of Huang Gongwang, a recluse in a pavilion in a mountainous landscape with pines and rivers, inscribed, signed, dated summer in bingzi year, with eight seals, colophon by Lu Hui (1851-1920), with two seals, 36" x 16 1/4". Provenance: Formerly in the Fritzsche Collection; purchased from Sotheby's New York, April 1985; formerly in the Chinese painting collection by Pang Laichen (1864 -1949). **$24,150**

James D. Julia, Inc.

Bronze tiger, Meiji Period (1868-1912), Japan. modeled as a stalking tiger with open mouth, founder's mark on base, museum or identification number etched in belly, 6 1/2" high x 16 1/2" long. **$3,680**

James D. Julia, Inc.

Carved jade incense box, 19th century or earlier, China, white stone with conforming lid carved overall with floral sprigs and carved carnelian knop, lid with Mughal style scrolling floral vinery, 1" high x 2 1/4" diameter. **$13,800**

James D. Julia, Inc.

Carved rosewood and ivory figure of an immortal, China, Ming Period (1368-1644), base of rosewood carved with rocks in bamboo with figure of Taoist immortal, 9 1/2" high overall. **$24,150**

James D. Julia, Inc.

Blue and white ginger jar, Kang Hsi Period (1662-1722), designs of reserves of 100 antiques on prunus strewn ice ground, old label Cheong Kee & Co. (The Curios House) established 1918 Coleman Street, 1st Floor, Corner of Hill Street Singapore/ No "9" (written in pen) "Blue and white ginger jar" (written in pen), 8" high x 7 1/2" diameter, cover absent. **$1,840**

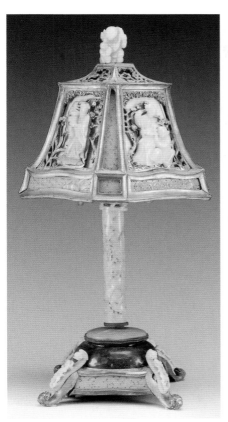

James D. Julia, Inc.

Rare jade composition lamp attributed to Edward I. Farmer, 1920-30, New York. Jade elements, 18th/19th century, China, shade composed of four white jades in the form of immortals, additionally set with eight carved and pierced floral panels, all set within gilt carved scrolling floral framework, mounted to base with figural jade finial of child and adult. Base designed with a white jade perfume cylinder and cover forming the shaft. Platform base made from jade bowl of spinach color beneath a white jade disc, scrolled gilt legs, each capped with a white jade buckle alternating with four carved and pierced panels, all set in carved gilt wood, 28" high. Provenance: Ex-collection of Edsel Ford; acquired from a gallery in Detroit, circa 1946, by descent through the family of current owner. **$69,000**

James D. Julia, Inc.

Carved ivory jar with cover, 19th century, China, four-character Cheng Hua mark on base, surface carved in high relief with lotus flowers, floral scrolls, jui-i borders and lion mask jump rings, central panels depicting figures in palace scenes, fitted cover carved with dragons and pearls, with three figures in a pine grove beneath a scholar's stone, fitted with a wood stand. Jar: 21" high. **$7,475**

James D. Julia, Inc.

Loose painting, China, Xie Zhiliu (1910-1997), ink and light color on paper depicting a lotus pond with three seals, 27" x 17 3/4". Provenance: Previous owner received directly from artist. **$3,450**

James D. Julia, Inc.

Chinese porcelain garden barrel, 19th century, China, unusual jar shaped form, sided and top pierced with cash coins in Famille Rose palette decorated with exotic birds and butterflies within floral cartouche, shoulder with green vinery on yellow ground, 17 1/2" high x 14" diameter. **$2,587**

James D. Julia, Inc.

Coral carving, 19th century, Japan, figure of Jurojin with children, signed, 4 3/4" high overall. **$2,875**

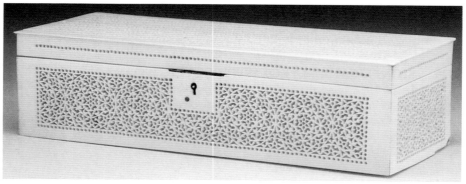

James D. Julia, Inc.

Carved and pierced ivory box, mid-19th century, northern India, finely carved overall with pierced arabesques within a pointillated border, 2 1/4" high x 8 1/2" long x 3 1/4" deep. **$1,610**

James D. Julia, Inc.

Hanging scroll, China, Huang Junbi (1898-1991), ink and light color on paper, depicting a mountainous landscape with cottages and waterfall, dedicated to Mr. Shanqing (son of P.Y. Wang) and Ms. Qilan (daughter-in-law of P.Y. Wang; daughter of Eu Tong Sen and Jenny Eu), inscribed with "Quan qing song la bai yu zhong," signed "Huang Junbi," with two seals of the artist "Nanhai Huang Shi" and "Junbi," 22 1/4" x 11 3/4". Provenance: Ex: P.Y. Wang Collection. **$28,750**

James D. Julia, Inc.

Peking glass vase, Ch'ien Lung mark and possibly of the period (1735-1796), bottle shaped vase, cameo cut red to snowflake depicting a battle scene, 9 1/4" high. **$4,600**

James D. Julia, Inc.

Gilt bronze Shakyamuni Buddha, 18th century or earlier, depicted in double lotus position with hands in the "earth-touching" (Bhumisparsha mudra) pose, with six-character seal mark impressed in rear of statue, fitted hardwood stand, 11 3/4" high overall. **$5,750**

James D. Julia, Inc.

Stoneware teapot, China, signed Jiang Rong b. 1919 with a seal and signed Huang Lung Shan Yuan Kuang Tsu Sha, Yi Hsing ware carved as sections of bamboo with foliage, cicada finial, 3 1/4" high. Provenance: Purchased directly from the artist in YiXing during late 1970s by the current owner's mother when she was a design department's professor in Wuxi Light Industrial Institution. **$2,587**

James D. Julia, Inc.

Pair of carved ivory urns with covers, late 19th/early 20th century, China, each with seal mark on base and with foo dog mask handles, surface carved with figures in relief in floral designs, each offered with hardwood stand, 24 1/2" high, 27" high overall. **$14,950**

James D. Julia, Inc.

Relief tapestry of sacred white peacock of India, mid-20th century, India. Silk work tapestry with gold and silver threads depicts three-dimensional image of peacock perched on a tree branch with green variegated foliage in a water landscape, against a black sky within an arabesque floral border in lavender repeating blooms accented with gold thread in a red frame, center of each flower mounted with alternating ruby (40 total) and opal (39 total) cabochons. Tail plumage set with 72 large emerald cabochons of varying size and coloration, totaling approximately 3,000 carats. 63" x 26 1/2", frame: 73" x 38". **$40,000-$60,000**

James D. Julia, Inc.

Silver covered bowl, 18th century, Japan, engraved with Tokugawa crests amongst dense scrolling foliate vinery on a nanako ground, conforming lid with chrysanthemum finial, 4 1/4" high x 6" diameter. Provenance: Consigned by the granddaughter of Gen. and Mrs. William Crane; originally belonging to Lois Whitin Crane and Brig. Gen. William C. Crane of Leesburg, Virginia, who were collectors of Japanese art and antiques. **$3,450**

James D. Julia, Inc.

Pewter wine pot, early 20th century, moon-shaped, engraved on one side with a figure beneath conifers, the opposing side with a poem, jade handle, spout and finial, interior base with impressed seal mark, 4" high x 6" long. Provenance: Consigned by the granddaughter of Gen. and Mrs. William Crane, originally belonging to Lois Whitin Crane and Brig. Gen. William C. Crane of Leesburg, Virginia, who were collectors of Japanese art and antiques. **$4,887**

James D. Julia, Inc.

Peking glass censer, Hsien feng seal mark on base, possibly of the period (1851-1861), translucent green glass with tripod footed base, 2 3/4" high x 4" diameter. **$3,737**

James D. Julia, Inc.

Carved wood kylin, 19th century, China, gold gilt and red lacquered example, 10" high x 14 1/4" long. **$2,530**

James D. Julia, Inc.

Large cloisonné censer, early 20th century, China, with four-character mark on base, ruyi shaped handles and animal form gilded feet, conforming lid has large pierced foliate gilt finial, decorated with the eight precious emblems within stylized lotus scrolling on pale turquoise ground, 27" high x 12" wide x 17 1/2" long. **$4,025**

James D. Julia, Inc.

Pair of cloisonné vases, early 20th century, Japan, wireless decoration of iris flowers on pale yellow ground, signed Ando, 9 1/2" high. **$1,725**

James D. Julia, Inc.

Rare carved dragon and flower coconut shell brush pot, Qing Dynasty, Yongzheng Period, China, exterior carved in low relief with floral scrolling vinery terminating in dragon heads, interior lined in gold paper, 6 1/2" high x 5 3/4" deep. **$16,675**

Autographs

BY ZAC BISSONNETTE

In *The Meaning and Beauty of Autographs*, first published in 1935 and translated from the German by David H. Lowenherz of Lion Heart Autographs, Inc. in 1995, Stefan Zweig explains that to love a manuscript, we must first love the human being "whose characteristics are immortalized in them." When we do, then "a single page with a few lines can contain the highest expression of human happiness, and … the expression of deepest human sadness. To those who have eyes to look at such pages correctly, eyes not only in the head, but also in the soul, they will not receive less of an impression from these plain signs than from the obvious beauty of pictures and books."

John M. Reznikoff, founder and president of University Archives, has been a leading dealer and authority on historical letters and artifacts for 32 years. He described the current market for autographs as "very, very strong on many fronts. Possibly because of people being afraid to invest in the market and in real estate, we are seeing investment in autographs that seems to parallel gold and silver."

Reznikoff suspects that Civil War items peaked after Ken Burns' series but that Revolutionary War documents, including those by signers of the Declaration of Independence and the Constitution, are still undervalued and can be purchased for under $500.

Currently, space is in high demand, especially Apollo 11. Pop culture, previously looked at as secondary by people who dealt in Washingtons and Lincolns, has come into its own. Reznikoff anticipates continued growth in memorabilia that includes music, television, movies and sports. Babe Ruth, Lou Gehrig, Ty Cobb and Tiger Woods are still good investments but Reznikoff warns that authentication is much more of a concern in sports than in any other field.

The Internet allows for a lot of disinformation and this is a significant issue with autographs. There are two widely accepted authentication services: Professional Sports Authenticator (PSA/DNA) and James Spence Authentication (JSA). A dealer's reliability can be evaluated by seeing whether he is a member of one or more of the major organizations in the field: the Antique Booksellers Association of America, UACC Registered Dealers Program and the National Professional Autograph Dealers Association (NPADA), which Reznikoff founded.

There is an additional caveat to remember and it is true for all collectibles: rarity. The value of an autograph is often determined less by the prominence of the signer than by the number of autographs he signed.

ZAC BISSONNETTE *is a consignment director for Heritage Auctions and has been featured on The Today Show, The Suze Orman Show, CNN, and National Public Radio. In addition to his work in the antiques field, he has served as a financial journalist for* Glamour, The Daily Beast, The New York Times, The Huffington Post, *and* AOL Money & Finance. *He has a degree in art history from the University of Massachusetts.*

Apple Computer contract and dissolution of contract, signed by Steve Jobs, Steve Wozniak and Ronald Wayne. Includes three documents: two typed documents signed by "Stephen G. Wozniak," "steven p. jobs," "Ronald G. Wayne"; Apple Computer Company Partnership Agreement, dated 1 April 1976, three pages, 8 1/2" x 11", with small staple holes and crease in upper left corners; with an amendment dated 12 April 1976, one page, with erasure and minor corrections to text, registrant's copy of County of Santa Clara Statement of Withdrawal signed by "Ronald G. Wayne," one page. **$1,594,500**

Autograph sketchleaf of Wolfgang Amadeus Mozart, including sketches for the canons "Difficile Lecto Mihi Mars," K. 559, and "Bona Nox! Bist a Rechta Ox," K. 561, the contents of the leaf notated in various brown inks, framed and glazed, no place or date [Vienna, circa 1788]. **$561,816**

Heritage Auctions, Inc.

Neil Armstrong signed 8" x 10" color NASA lithographed print of him in his iconic white suit, boldly signed in blue felt tip: "Neil Armstrong." **$5,078**

NEIL A. ARMSTRONG

Heritage Auctions, Inc.

George Washington autograph document signed "G Washington," with a William Fairfax autograph letter signed and addressed to Washington. The document in Washington's hand is a survey description and plat for 140 acres "of Escheat land" in Prince William County, Virginia, for the future owner George Byrne. William Fairfax's letter assigns the young surveyor to make "an accurate Survey . . . and a Plat." **$101,575**

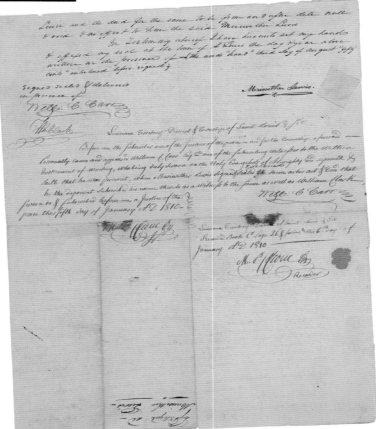

Heritage Auctions, Inc.

The only known document bearing the signatures of both legendary explorers Meriwether Lewis and William Clark, a land indenture signed "Meriwether Lewis" and "Wm. Clark"; two pages, St. Louis, Aug. 23, 1809, 12 1/2" x 15 3/4". **$110,000**

Heritage Auctions, Inc.

Franklin D. and Eleanor Roosevelt signed 1941 Christmas photo, Eleanor posed knitting alongside Franklin at a table with books, signed "Franklin D. Roosevelt" and "Eleanor Roosevelt," 9 1/4" x 7 1/2" (sight), matted, overall 14" x 13". **$2,270**

Heritage Auctions, Inc.

Winston S. Churchill photograph signed "Winston S. Churchill/1943" as British prime minister, 6" x 8" three-quarter length black and white photograph, mounted, 7 1/2" x 10 1/2". **$4,780**

Heritage Auctions, Inc.

Signed personal check of American aviator and polar explorer Richard E. Byrd, 1888-1957. **$225**

Heritage Auctions, Inc.

Inscribed oversized portrait of Albert Einstein taken during his first visit to America, showing the physicist shortly after he decided to let his graying hair grow longer. Einstein inscribed below the photo in blue ink in German, "Something to remember us by, dedicated in friendship to an ardent awakener of the Jewish soul and one who successfully fought for our university. Albert Einstein May 1921." In 1921, Einstein visited America and while in New York City, the April 3 New York Times reported that "he looked like an artist." Sometime near that date he had this photograph taken by Herman Mishkin's photography studio (stamped "Mishkin N.Y." in lower right); 10" x 12". **$26,290**

Heritage Auctions, Inc.

Marilyn Monroe signed black and white photograph, 14" x 11", circa 1956, original print with matte finish, blue fountain pen ink inscription on the right side reads, "To Roy, Love & Kisses and – thanks for keeping me out of the clink! Marilyn Monroe." "Roy" was Beverly Hills police officer Roy Garrett, who had a habit of asking movie stars to send him an autographed photo, and evidently let Marilyn go without a ticket, as he received this from her a few days later. **$31,250**

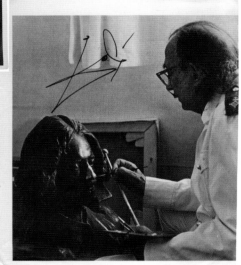

Heritage Auctions, Inc.

Black and white photograph of an older Salvador Dali working on a bronze sculpture of a man with a pointed beard, signed "Salvador Dali," 9 3/4" x 11 3/4". **$209**

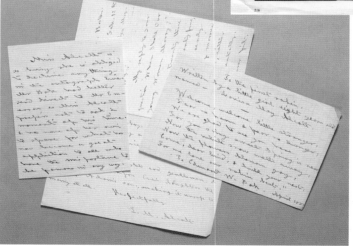

Sotheby's

Group of three Louisa May Alcott items including two autograph letters signed and an autograph manuscript poem, various dates, all to Edward Bok, both in his capacity as autograph seeker and later as editor of Brooklyn Magazine. **$6,250**

Heritage Auctions, Inc.

Signed photograph of Eddie Rickenbacker, American World War I fighter ace, 3 3/4" x 5", matted with a larger printed image, includes COA from R&R Enterprises. **$375**

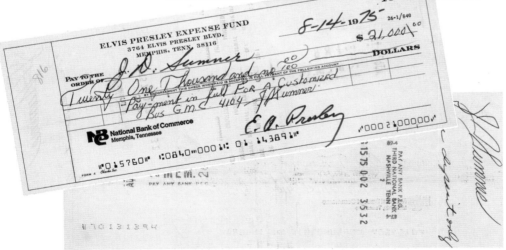

Heritage Auctions, Inc.

Elvis Presley-signed check to J. D. Sumner, dated 1975, written to J. D. Sumner for the purchase of a customized GMC bus and signed in bold blue ink by "E. A. Presley." The bonus is the signature on the back of the check of Sumner, Elvis' friend and the leader of the Stamps Quartet, who performed regularly with Elvis in the 1970s. **$4,602**

Heritage Auctions, Inc.

Gloria Swanson autographed 1950 Sunset Boulevard half-sheet poster, 22" x 28". The large, bold signature reads: "To Richard Moore, Greetings and Joy, Gloria Swanson, 1980." **$3,585**

Heritage Auctions, Inc.

Pink Floyd-signed guitar, red finish Squier Tele by Fender, serial number CY98126435. David Gilmour and Richard Wright signed in blue felt tip on the pickguard; Roger Waters and Nick Mason signed on the body with Mason adding his stylized "Pink Floyd." Originally purchased at a Christie's London auction in 2006; comes with copies of the catalog page and invoice. Fender gigbag included. **$3,000**

Heritage Auctions, Inc.

John Lennon autographed Imagine poster showing him at his white piano, rare, signed, "To Gail, Love from John Lennon," dated 1971, the year the Imagine album was released. The story is that "Gail" was the daughter of one of the recording engineers or crew. Professionally matted and framed with UV3 preservation glass to an overall 29 1/2" x 29 1/2", top third folded back for better display. **$21,250**

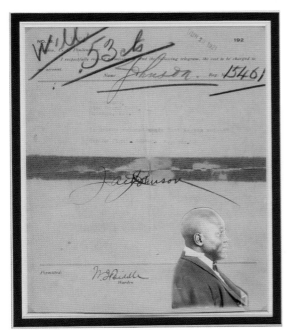

Heritage Auctions, Inc.

Former Heavyweight Champion Jack Johnson-signed telegram sent from Leavenworth Prison in 1921. It is believed this is the first and only document from Johnson's year of incarceration. Beneath text instructing that "Warden, U.S. Penitentiary" charge the cost of transmission to his prison account, Johnson's typed message to a Chicago recipient inquires about a future opponent: "Is Grover colored. What weight. Can he fight. Regards." Johnson's black fountain pen signature appears at the close, 7 1/2 x 9". Document is professionally matted and framed to 17 1/2 x 19". **$11,950**

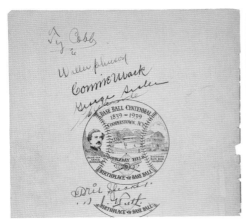

Heritage Auctions, Inc.

1939 Inaugural Hall of Fame Induction Class-signed program. Autograph display of the personnel represented on the June 12, 1939 opening of the Baseball Hall of Fame in Cooperstown, New York. Signatures are on rear inside cover of the Doubleday Field program, from top to bottom: Ty Cobb, Walter Johnson, Connie Mack, George Sisler, G.C. Alexander, Tris Speaker, Babe Ruth, Cy Young, J. Honus Wagner, Larry Lajoie. **$41,825**

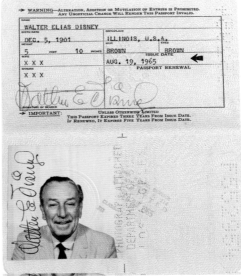

Heritage Auctions, Inc.

Walt Disney's United States passport, dated Aug. 19, 1965, issued to the legendary animator shortly after the success of Mary Poppins (1964) and 16 months before his death (Dec. 15, 1966). Disney signed the passport twice in blue ink, as "Walter E. Disney," including once along the edge of his photo. It bears one set of visa stamps for a trip to and from London. **$28,680**

Heritage Auctions, Inc.

Legendary Scot Old Tom Morris-signed cabinet photograph, 4" x 5 1/2", on a St. Mary's Studio, St. Andrews mount. At the base of the mount is the Morris signature and date Sept. 27, 1901, in his own hand. The photo comes with provenance indicating it was found in a private home called Wemyss House, a dwelling within feet of the Old Course at St. Andrews. The owner of the home was a member of the Royal & Ancient at the time and was given this photo as a gift from Morris in 1901. **$11,950**

Banks

BY ERIC BRADLEY

Banks that display some form of action while accepting a coin are considered mechanical banks. Mechanical banks date back to ancient Greece and Rome, but the majority of collectors are interested in those made between 1867 and 1928 in Germany, England, and the United States. More than 80 percent of all cast-iron mechanical banks produced between 1869 and 1928 were made by J. & E. Stevens Company of Cromwell, Connecticut. Tin banks are usually of German origin.

Eric Bradley

The mechanical bank hobby continues to catch headlines for the longtime collections coming to market. A few thousand mechanical banks change hands every year, with more than 1,500 selling at auction in 2012. This amount appears to be increasing as well-known collectors offer their treasures to a new generation of collectors.

The sale of a circa-1890 Santa with tree mechanical bank reached a record $22,050 during a July 2012 RSL Auction Company sale in Timonium, Md. In September 2012, the Al Winick collection of 100 fine mechanical banks was the center of the bank-collecting universe. Offered by Morphy Auctions of Denver, Pennsylvania, more than 100 bidders showed up – in person – for the chance to buy some of the rarest banks to come to market since the Stephen and Marilyn Steckbeck sale of 2007. The Winick collection held a rare blue variant of Kyser & Rex's circa-1886 Mikado mechanical bank, which claimed top-lot honors with an astonishing $198,000 selling price. A beautiful example in near mint condition, the cast iron depiction of a magician performing a sleight-of-hand shell game trick had been estimated at $100,000-$150,000.

With crossover appeal to black Americana collectors, an 1880 Freedman's Bank was in enviable near mint condition and came with provenance from both the Tudor and Steckbeck collections. It cashed out at $138,000.

Other Kyser & Rex cast iron mechanical banks that finished in the top 10 included a merry-go-round, ex-Steckbeck collection, for $126,000 and a roller skating bank depicting an old-fashioned skating rink with skaters for $84,000. Also finishing well in the money were two desirable productions by J. & E. Stevens: a football-theme calamity bank in superb condition for $38,400 and an 1880 chimpanzee bank for $37,200.

You don't need to own a bank to start collecting toy and mechanical banks. Auctions abound with more affordable character banks and premium banks from the mid-20th century. Designs are as varied as your imagination and cover a number of historical events, political figures, and landmarks. Unlike other collecting areas, many rare forms of mechanical and still banks (banks with no mechanical action) are highly valued, even if it they are not in perfect condition. Record-setting banks that lead the market are those that are of a rare form and retain at least 90% of their original paint.

Popeye tin litho dime register bank set. First piece has 1929 "King Feat Synd." copyright with image of Popeye at deposit window on front and side images of Olive Oyl and Wimpy. Next two pieces are old store stock color varieties, one brown, one yellow, copyright 1956 KFS Inc. Tops feature image of Popeye juggling coins, sides feature illustrations of Olive Oyl with Oscar, Wimpy with Rough House, and Sweet Pea. Each still sealed in original header bag with 2" x 4" header card noting original sale price of 29¢ and maker Kalon Mfg. Corp., 5" x 2 1/2" x 3/4" each. Provenance: Carl Lobel Collection. **$1,530**

Dark green figural glass 3.5 oz. jar depicting a circus elephant with "Jumbo Peanut Butter" blanket on back, circa 1930s, Frank Tea & Spice Company, complete with original tin screw-on lid at bottom, coin slot in lid; in addition to Jumbo name and company information, text reads "Write For New Peanut Butter Recipes," 3 1/2". **$417**

Cast iron Mikado mechanical bank by Kyser & Rex, blue variation, 6 3/4" tall. **$198,000**

ERIC BRADLEY is public relations associate at Heritage Auctions, the world's third largest auction house. He is former editor of Antique Trader magazine and is the author of Antique Trader 2013 Antiques and Collectibles Price Guide, America's no. 1-selling guide to the antiques and collectibles market. An award-winning investigative journalist with a degree in economics, Bradley has written hundreds of articles about antiques and collectibles and has made several media appearances as an expert on the antiques market at MoneyShow San Francisco, on MSN Money, Nasdaq.com and on AdvisorOne.com. His work has received press from The New York Times and The Philadelphia Inquirer.

Hakes Americana & Collectibles

Donald Duck toy telephone bank, circa mid-1930s, by N.N. Hill Brass Company, which produced a number of different Disney telephone toys including several color and style variations of Donald Duck and Mickey Mouse telephones. Tall pressed steel with thick die-cut cardboard Donald figure attachment, rotary dial works and rings, original fabric cord, bank box attachment on bank, designated coin slots for pennies, nickels and dimes, 4 3/4". **$575**

Morphy Auctions

Cast iron rollerskating mechanical bank by Kyser & Rex, 9" long. **$84,000**

Hakes Americana & Collectibles

Nickel-plated cast iron beehive bank designed by Arthur Golton, elaborate design with high relief text and scrollwork, store sold version (most are from specific actual banks and have their imprint cast on one side), 7 1/8" long rod with rectangular opening on one end for use as key, bank functions by turning beehive until coin drops into predetermined slots 1, 2, 3 or 4, interior of bank contains original cardboard containers to hold coins, 6 3/4" x 6 3/4" x 6 3/4" tall overall. **$560**

Hakes Americana & Collectibles

Painted cast iron bank with large head, full figure man standing next to carpetbag atop base, titled in relief on front "Stump Speaker" with word "Bank" in relief on two sides, patented 1886 by Shepard Hardware Company. When coin is placed in figure's hand and lever is pressed, he lowers his hand and drops coin into carpetbag, which has opened; upon releasing lever, his jaw moves up and down and bag closes; 3 7/8" x 4 7/8" x 9 7/8" tall overall. **$1,018**

Hakes Americana & Collectibles

Organ monkey bank, patent #D-259,403, June 13, 1882, made by Kyser & Rex Company, Frankford, Pennsylvania. Place coin in tray, turn handle, and monkey lowers coin into organ while he tips his hat and cat and dog revolve, 4" x 5 1/4" x 7 1/4" tall overall. **$420**

Morphy Auctions

Cast iron watchdog safe mechanical bank by J. & E. Stevens, 6" tall. Provenance: Manlove, Steckbeck. **$26,400**

Hakes Americana & Collectibles

Standing full figure rooster still bank with coin slot at top of back by A.C. Williams, circa 1920s, 4 3/4" tall. **$143**

Morphy Auctions

Cast iron Uncle Remus mechanical bank by Kyser & Rex. **$31,200**

Hakes Americana & Collectibles

Painted cast iron Oregon battleship bank by J. & E. Stevens, 1896-1906, 1 3/4" x 5" x 4" tall. Battleship became famous after taking part in the destruction of the Spanish fleet at Santiago, Cuba, during the Spanish American War. **$316**

Morphy Auctions

Cast iron mason mechanical bank by Shepard Hardware Company, 7" tall. **$5,100**

Morphy Auctions

Cast iron Santa at chimney mechanical bank, gray coat variation, 6" tall. **$1,320**

Morphy Auctions

Freedman's mechanical bank, early bank with figure that has been redressed, 10 1/2" tall. Provenance: Tudor, Steckbeck. **$138,000**

Morphy Auctions

Cast iron rooster mechanical bank by Kyser & Rex, highlights to base, 6" tall. **$2,700**

Morphy Auctions

Cast iron carnival mechanical bank, original working condition, 8 1/4" tall. Provenance: Griffith. **$12,000**

Morphy Auctions

Cast iron chimpanzee mechanical bank by Kyser & Rex. **$37,200**

Books

Collecting early books is a popular segment of the antiques marketplace. Collectors of early books are rewarded with interesting titles and exquisite illustrations, as well as fascinating information and stories. The author, printer, and publisher, as well as the date of the printing, can increase the value of an early book.

Heritage Auctions, Inc.

Rare first English edition of Sir Isaac Newton's landmark, The Mathematical Principles of Natural Philosophy, *translated into English by Andrew Motte. Two octavo volumes, approximately 7 3/4" x 4 1/2". Engraved frontispiece after and by A. Motte in each volume, 47 folding engraved plates, two folding letterpress tables, three engraved headpieces by Motte, and numerous woodcut head- and tail-pieces. Contemporary full calf, spines rebacked to style in matching brown calf. Covers double-ruled in gilt, spines elaborately tooled in gilt in compartments, five raised bands, burgundy and olive gilt morocco lettering labels.* **$40,625**

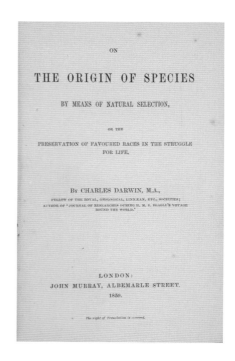

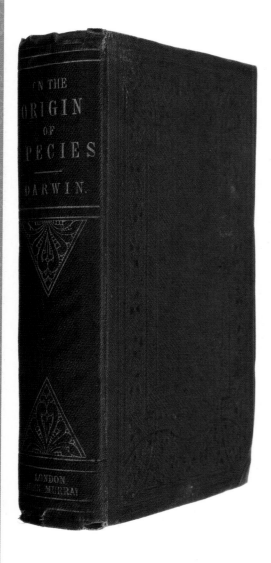

Heritage Auctions, Inc.

On the Origin of Species by Means of Natural Selection, or The Preztion of Favored Races in the Struggle for Life *by Charles Darwin, first edition of the most influential scientific work of the 19th century. London: John Murray, 1859. Original green ripple-grained cloth with covers stamped in blind and spine in gilt. Original brown coated endpapers. Housed in a green quarter leather and cloth clamshell case.* **$83,500**

The Corsair of Lord Byron. *Milan:
The Typographical Society of Italian
Classicks, 1826; 8vo, 9 1/4" x 6".
Printed on vellum, illuminated with 10
full-page miniatures within decorated
borders, six illuminated headpieces and
three tailpieces by Giambattista Gigola,
signed and dated March 1828. Full
straight-grain red morocco by Lodisiani,
cathedral-style panel decoration in
blind within a double-filleted gilt
border, spine in six diced compartments
with raised gilt bands, elaborate gilt
dentelles, sky blue silk moiré guards
similarly stamped in gilt, blue silk
markers. Contemporary brown morocco
solander case paneled in blind and gilt,
sky blue silk moiré lining.* **$37,500**

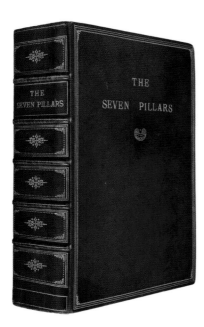

Seven Pillars of Wisdom *by T.E. Lawrence. London: For the
Author by Manning Pike and H. J. Hodgson, 1926. Extremely
scarce privately printed edition, one of only 170 complete
copies, so initialed by Lawrence at page xix: "Complete
copy i.xii.26 T. E. S." Quarto. Approximately 10" x 7 1/4".
Illustrated with 65 lithographic plates (61 bound at rear).
Bound in contemporary full green crushed levant morocco,
covers triple-ruled in gilt, front cover lettered in gilt with gilt
central Arabian motif, spine tooled, ruled, and lettered in
gilt in compartments, five raised bands, gilt board edges and
turn-ins, top edge gilt, others in gilt on the rough.* **$62,500**

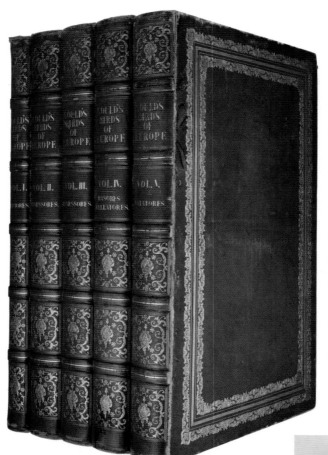

Heritage Auctions, Inc.

The Birds of Europe *by British ornithological master John Gould. London: Richard and John E. Taylor, 1832-1837. Five imperial folio volumes measuring 21 1/2" x 14 1/4" each, 449 hand-colored illustrations on 448 lithographed plates printed by Charles Hullmandel. Majority of the plates by Elizabeth Gould from sketches by Gould, with the remainder by Edward Lear. With all title pages, dedication page, preface, introduction, and subscriber's list present. Bound in contemporary full green morocco with gilt-stamped ornamentation and borders by Hering with his stamp. Spine in six compartments with gilt-stamped borders, decorations, and titles. Gilt-rolled edges and rich inner dentelles. All edges gilt.* **$80,500**

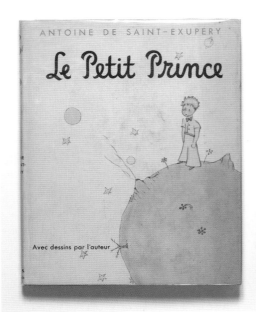
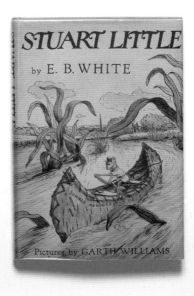

Sotheby's

Le Petit Prince *by Antoine de Saint-Exupery and* Stuart Little *by E.B. White.* Le Petit Prince, *first edition in French: New York, Reynal & Hitchcock, 1943; square 8vo, 8 3/4" x 7", illustrated by the author, publisher's brown-stamped illustrated tan cloth in pictorial dust jacket;* Stuart Little: *New York, Harpers, 1945, 8vo, 8" x 5 1/2", illustrated by Garth Williams, publisher's illustrated tan cloth in Williams pictorial dust jacket; first edition, first issue with 10-5 and IU on copyright page.* **$1,625**

Sotheby's

Quotations from Chairman Mao *(Chinese title) by Mao Tse-Tung. Beijing: by the Central Intelligence Bureau of the Chinese People's Liberation Army, 1964, 6mo, 5 7/16" x 4", 250 pages, half-title printed in red, title page printed in red and green within a double green border, lithograph portrait of Mao, rare facsimile of Lin Biao's calligraphic endorsement of Mao's writings; a few Chinese characters effaced from half-title, manuscript notes in blue ink on final page and facing fly leaf, red vinyl plastic covers with printed errata slip in pocket of inside back cover.* **$13,750**

WINSTON S. CHURCHILL

THE SECOND WORLD WAR

VOLUME I

The Gathering Storm

Heritage Auctions, Inc.

Association copy of Winston S. Churchill's The Second World War. London: Cassell & Company Ltd., (1948-1954). First British edition, first printings, with note, "Inscribed for Commander L. A. Burt by Winston S. Churchill, 1949" in Volume II. Complete in six octavo volumes, illustrated with maps and diagrams, bound in full black cloth with gilt spine titles, top edges stained red, dust jackets. **$4,375**

Sotheby's

The Tale of Peter Rabbit *by Beatrix Potter. Frederick Warne and Company, 1902 or 1903; 16mo, first trade edition, third or fourth issue, 31 colored illustrations, leaf endpapers, original olive-green boards, pictorial label on upper cover, contemporary inscription to front fixed endpaper, bookseller's embossed stamp to front free endpaper.* **$5,430**

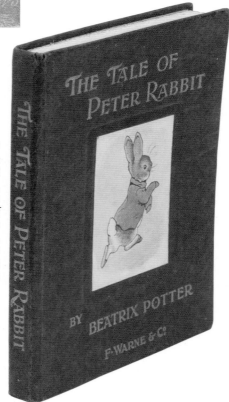

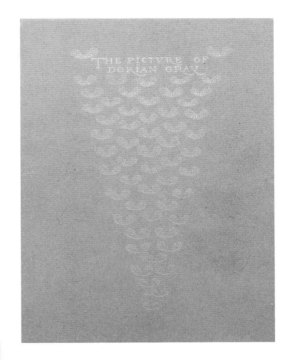

The Picture of Dorian Gray *by Oscar Wilde. London: Ward Lock and Company, 1891; 4to, 8 7/8" x 7 3/8". Dutch handmade paper, original parchment-backed gray bevelled boards, gilt lettering and gilt butterfly designs by Charles Ricketts, top edges gilt, others uncut, gray cloth clamshell case.* **$17,500**

Adventures of Huckleberry Finn *by Mark Twain. New York: Charles L. Webster, 1885, 8 1/2" x 6 1/2". Frontispiece and 173 text illustrations by E. W. Kemble, photogravure plate of a portrait bust by Karl Gerhardt (BAL state 1), title-leaf is a cancel with copyright notice on verso dated 1884 (BAL state 2); leaf 1.8 with tiny hole in the lower margin, misprinted page number on page 155 lightly circled in pencil. Publisher's green pictorial cloth stamped in gilt and black, pale peach endpapers; slight rubbing to corners, head and foot of spine, and bottom board edges, green cloth slipcase, chemise.* **$12,500**

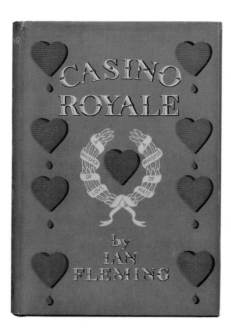

Heritage Auctions, Inc.

Casino Royale, *first edition of the first James Bond book by Ian Fleming; London: Jonathan Cape, 1953. Inscribed by Fleming on the front free endpaper, alluding to the enigmatic head of the British Secret Service: "To M. These pages from my memoirs! Ian." Octavo, 218 pages. Black cloth with front and spine stamped in red, housed in custom clamshell box by The Dragonfly Bindery. The box front reproduces an image of bleeding hearts from front panel of jacket in multicolored leathers.* **$50,787**

Heritage Auctions, Inc.

The Doors: Jim Morrison signed poetry book, The Lords and The New Creatures. Hardcover, 141 pages, published in 1970 by Simon and Schuster, New York. Signed and inscribed on the second blank page in felt pen, "For Vicki, J. Morrison." Accompanied by a letter from Vicki Anderson, who received the book from Jim in the mail when she wrote him that she was working on a term paper on the Doors. **$4,406**

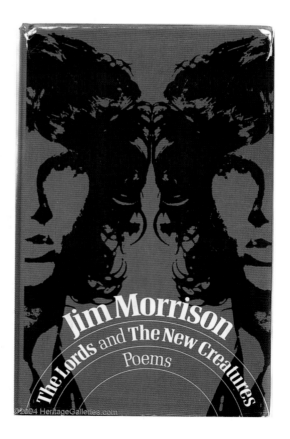

Paperbacks

The first mass-market, pocket-sized paperback book printed in the United States was an edition of Pearl Buck's *The Good Earth*, produced by Pocket Books in late 1938 and sold in New York City.

Paperbacks at first consisted entirely of reprints, but publishers soon began publishing original works. Genre categories began to emerge, and mass-market book covers reflected those categories. Mass-market paperbacks had an impact on slick magazines (slicks) and pulp magazines. The market for cheap magazines diminished when buyers went to cheap books instead. Authors also turned from magazines and began writing for the paperback market. Many pulp magazine cover artists were hired by paperback publishers to entice readers with their alluring artwork. Several well-known authors were published in paperback, including Arthur Miller and John Steinbeck, and some, like Dashiell Hammett, were published as paperback originals.

For more information on vintage paperbacks and details on condition grades, consult *Antique Trader Collectible Paperbacks Price Guide* by Gary Lovisi, or visit www.gryphonbooks. com.

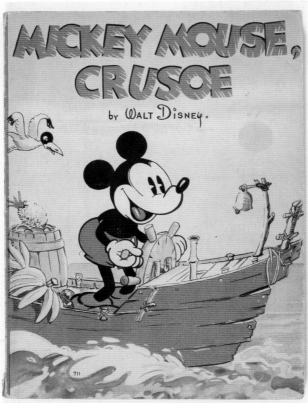

Heritage Auctions, Inc.

Mickey Mouse, Crusoe *paperback storybook, Whitman, 1936, square-bound 78-page book with cardboard covers. Approximately 7" x 9 1/2".* **$101**

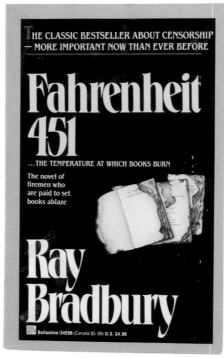

Heritage Auctions, Inc.

Fahrenheit 451 *by Ray Bradbury. New York: Del Rey, 1991. Mass market paperback, 179 pages, later printing, signed by Bradbury, publisher's printed wraps.* **$119**

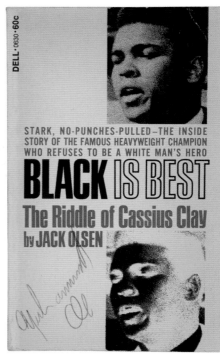

Heritage Auctions, Inc.

Black is Best – The Riddle of Cassius Clay *by Muhammad Ali, 1967, features a near mint blue ballpoint signature from Ali.* **$286**

Heritage Auctions, Inc.

Edgar Rice Burroughs' Big Little Book edition of Tarzan Twins. Racine, Wisconsin: Whitman Publishing Company, 1935, 47 pages, staple-bound with pictorial card stock covers, approximately 5 1/2" x 3 1/2". This is a Big Little Book reprint of the Burroughs story originally published in 1927. **$1,195**

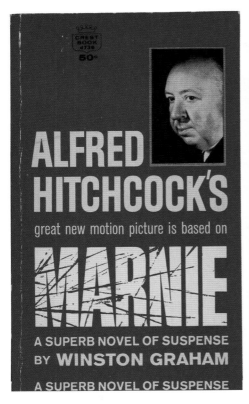

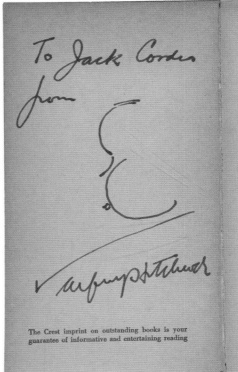

Marnie *signed by Alfred Hitchcock, along with a doodle of his profile, in black ink on the front endpaper.* **$718**

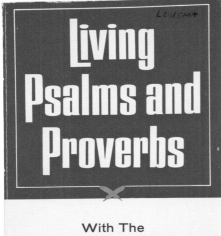

Living Psalms and Proverbs With the Major Prophets Paraphrased. *Wheaton Illinois: Tyndale House Publishers, 1971, 10th printing, 4 1/4" x 6 3/4", 745 pages.* **$1,015**

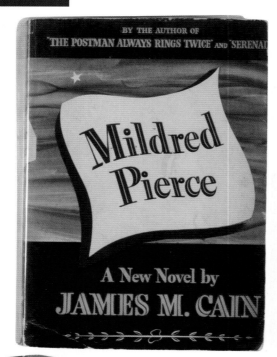

Mildred Pierce *by James M. Cain. New York: Knopf, 1941. First edition, advance review copy. Octavo. Softcover, 387 pages. Original wrappers, with $2.50 price.* **$286**

Descriptive Catalogue of Kodascope Library: Motion Pictures, *Kodascope Library, Inc., 1932. This fifth edition book catalogs the films available for rental in the Kodascope Libraries across the United States, 212 pages, 6" x 8 1/2". With brief descriptions of each film, the book also includes images from the movies, listings of film rental fees, and a listing of prominent stars such as John Barrymore, Adolphe Menjou, and Mary Astor that are featured in Kodascope Library pictures.* **$262**

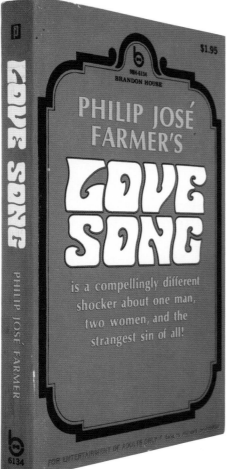

First edition paperback of Love Song *by Philip Jose Farmer. North Hollywood, California: Brandon House, 1970. Farmer's scarcest title, 192 pages, illustrated wrappers, 16mo, 4 1/4" x 6 3/4".* **$179**

Set of four high-grade paperbacks including The Moon Pool *and* Seven Footprints to Satan *by A. Merritt, and* Europa *(two copies) by Robert Briffault. Avon Paperback Books Group, Avon, 1950-1951. Classic covers.* **$334**

Solar Lottery *by Philip K. Dick. New York: Ace Books, 1955. First edition, 188 pages, illustrated wrappers, pocket paperback, 4 1/2" x 6 1/2". This is the first-ever appearance of* Solar Lottery *in any form, which was Dick's first published novel, signed "Philip K. Dick" on title page.* **$507**

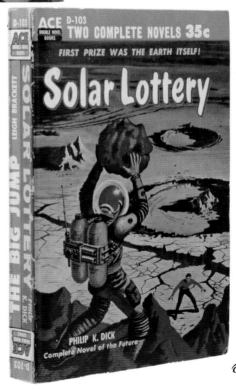

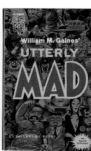

Heritage Auctions, Inc.

"Mad" and "Humbug" first edition paperback group of five books, Ballantine Books, 1954-1957. **$657**

Heritage Auctions, Inc.

Famous Monsters paperback lot including The Best From Famous Monsters of Filmland, Son of Famous Monsters, *and* Famous Monsters Strike Back! *Warren, 1964-1965.* **$286**

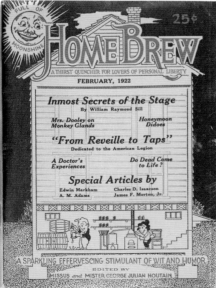

Heritage Auctions, Inc.

Home Brew, *Vol. No. 1, E. D. Houtain, February 1922, featuring H.P. Lovecraft's first published professional fiction. Described as "Grewsome Tales by Howard P. Lovecraft," it contains "From the Dark," which is part one of the six-part story known as Herbert West - Reanimator, which also spawned the successful 1985 film, "Re-Animator."* **$661**

Bottles

BY MICHAEL POLAK

Interest in bottle collecting is strong and continues to grow, with new bottle clubs forming throughout the United States and Europe.

Collectors spend their free time digging through old dumps and foraging through ghost towns, digging out old outhouses, exploring abandoned mine shafts, and searching their favorite bottle or antique shows, swap meets, flea markets, and garage sales. In addition, the Internet offers collectors opportunities and resources without ever leaving the house.

Most collectors look beyond the type and value of a bottle to its origin and history. Researching the history of bottles can be as interesting as finding the bottle itself.

Barber bottle, 7 3/4", medium cranberry, rib-pattern, blue and white enamel floral decoration, bell shape, pontil-scarred base, tooled top, American 1885-1920. **$200-$225**

Ale and gin bottle, London Jockey – Club House Gin, bright almond straw yellow, applied top, American 1865-1875. **$6,500-$7,000**

Bitters bottle, Russ-St. Domingo Bitters – New York, brilliant medium olive green, 9 7/8", smooth base, applied tapered collar top, 1865-1875. **$5,500-$6,000**

MICHAEL POLAK *has collected more than 3,000 bottles since entering the hobby in 1976. He is a regular contributor to a variety of antiques publications and is the author of* Antique Trader Bottles Identification & Price Guide.

Cosmetic/hair restorer bottle, Dodge Brothers – Melanine Hair Tonic, 7 1/4", red amber, applied top, 1875-1885. **$1,200-$1,300**

Cobalt blue medicine bottle, Bennet's Magic Cure, deep cobalt blue, 5 1/8", applied top, 1876-1885. **$1,300-1,500**

Beer bottle, Golden Gate Bottling Works – Chas. Roschmann – San Francisco – This Bottle Never Sold, light amber, one-half pint (split), tooled top, 1890-1910. **$300-$325**

Blown three-mold decanter, medium olive green, 8 1/2", barrel shape, pontil-scarred base, applied tapered collar top, 1815-1830. **$1,600-$1,700**

Fruit jar, Mason's (Keystone) – Patent – Nov 30th – 1858, yellow amber, pint, ground lip, American 1875-1895. **$1,200-$1,400**

Fancy palmetto and acanthus cologne bottle, medium cobalt blue, 5 5/8", American 1840-1860. **$1,000-$1,100**

Figural "man in the moon" decanter, straw yellow figural moon, original red and black paint, ground glass stopper, polished top, base is grass green with original metal connector and rack, American 1890-1915. **$500-$600**

Hutchinson bottle, City Ice – Bottling Wks – Georgetown – Texas, bright green, 7 1/8", American 1895-1905. **$400-$425**

Flask, G.E. Crowley Wine Merchant –18 South Main St. – Butte, Mont., clear glass, half-pint, tooled top, American 1885-1895. **$450-$500**

Fire grenade, "Star (Inside a Star) – Harden Hand Grenade – Fire Extinguisher, medium olive green, quart, sheared and ground lip, American 1875-1895. **$800-$900**

Mineral water bottle, Victoria Springs – A. Frelichsburg – Canada, blue aqua, quart, smooth base, Canadian 1865-1875. **$1,100-$1,200**

Pattern molded bottle, chestnut flask, deep cobalt blue, 4 3/4", 26-broken-rib pattern swirled to right, American 1815-1835. **$450-$500**

Hawaiian bottle, Hawaiian Soda Works – Honolulu, H.I., 1899. **$1,700-$4,600**

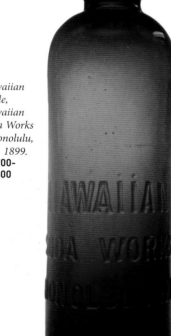

Umbrella ink bottle, Baltimore Star, light sapphire blue, 2 1/2", eight concave panels, open pontil, rolled lip, American 1840-1860. **$1,100-$1,200**

Patriotic bottle, Liberty
eagle, Willington
Glass Cmpany,
West Willington,
Connecticut, quart,
American 1855-1865.
$400-$700

Willington cathedral pickle jar,
medium blue green,
11 1/2", iron pontil, applied lip,
American 1850-1860. **$2,600-
$2,800**

Poison bottle, The J.F. Hartz Co. –
Limited – Toronto, deep cobalt blue,
7 7/8", Canadian 1890-1910, rare in
large size. **$600-$650**

Target ball, IRA Paines Filled Ball Oct 23. 1877, cobalt
blue, 2 5/8" diameter, American 1877-1895. **$2,000-$2,100**

Handled whiskey bottle, Wharton's – Whiskey – 1850 – Chestnut Grove – Whitney Glass Works – Glassboro NJ, medium amber, 10 1/8", American 1860-1870. **$900-$1,000**

Milk bottle, One Quart – Liquid – Carrigan's – Niagara Dairy Co. – Reed, bright green, quart, 9 3/8", American 1920-1930. **$375-$450**

Black glass pancake onion or ship bottle, dark amber, 9 1/4" x 7 1/4" diameter, Scotland 1820-1840. **$550-$650**

Soda bottle, McKay & Clark – No. 130 – Franklin St. – Balt., medium blue green, 8 1/2", 10-pin shape, American 1855-1865. **$1,300-$1,400**

Ceramics

American

Fiesta

The Homer Laughlin China Company originated with a two-kiln pottery on the banks of the Ohio River in East Liverpool, Ohio. Built in 1873-'74 by Homer Laughlin and his brother, Shakespeare, the firm was first known as the Ohio Valley Pottery, and later Laughlin Bros. Pottery. It was one of the first white-ware plants in the country.

After a tentative beginning, the company was awarded a prize for having the best white-ware at the 1876 Centennial Exposition in Philadelphia.

Three years later, Shakespeare sold his interest in the business to Homer, who continued on until 1897. At that time, Homer Laughlin sold his interest in the newly incorporated firm to a group of investors, including Charles, Louis, and Marcus Aaron and the company bookkeeper, William E. Wells.

Under new ownership in 1907, the headquarters and a new 30-kiln plant were built across the Ohio River in Newell, West Virginia, the present manufacturing and headquarters location.

In the 1920s, two additions to the Homer Laughlin staff set the stage for the company's greatest success: the Fiesta line.

Dr. Albert V. Bleininger was hired in 1920. A scientist, author, and educator, he oversaw the conversion from bottle kilns to the more efficient tunnel kilns.

In 1927, the company hired designer Frederick Hurten Rhead, a member of a distinguished family of English ceramists. Having previously worked at Weller Pottery and Roseville Pottery, Rhead began to develop the artistic quality of the company's wares, and to experiment with shapes and glazes. In 1935, this work culminated in his designs for the Fiesta line.

For more information on Fiesta, see Warman's Fiesta Identification and Price Guide by Glen Victorey.

Fiesta Colors

From 1936 to 1972, Fiesta was produced in 14 colors (other than special promotions). These colors are usually divided into the "original colors" of cobalt blue, light green, ivory, red, turquoise, and yellow (cobalt blue, light green, red, and yellow only on the Kitchen Kraft line, introduced in 1939); the "1950s colors" of chartreuse, forest green, gray, and rose (introduced in 1951); medium green (introduced in 1959); plus the later additions of Casuals, Amberstone, Fiesta Ironstone, and Casualstone ("Coventry") in antique gold, mango red, and turf green; and the striped, decal, and Lustre pieces. No Fiesta was produced from 1973 to 1985. The colors that make up the "original" and "1950s" groups are sometimes referred to as "the standard 11."

In many pieces, medium green is the hardest to find and the most expensive Fiesta color.

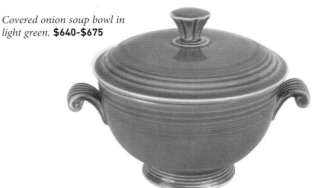

Covered onion soup bowl in light green. **$640-$675**

Fiesta Colors and Years of Production to 1972

Antique Gold—dark butterscotch . . . . (1969-1972)

Chartreuse—yellowish green. . . . . (1951-1959)

Cobalt Blue—dark or "royal" blue . . . . (1936-1951)

Forest Green—dark "hunter" green . . . . (1951-1959)

Gray—light or ash gray . . . . (1951-1959)

Green—often called light green when comparing it
   to other green glazes; also called "Original" green . . . . . . (1936-1951)

Ivory—creamy, slightly yellowed . . . . (1936-1951)

Mango Red—same as original red . . . . (1970-1972)

Medium Green—bright rich green. . . . . (1959-1969)

Red—reddish orange . . . . (1936-1944 and 1959-1972)

Rose—dusty, dark rose . . . . (1951-1959)

Turf Green—olive . . . . (1969-1972)

Turquoise—sky blue, like the stone . . . . (1937-1969)

Yellow—golden yellow . . . . (1936-1969)

Ashtray in yellow. **$39-$45**

Cream soup cups in ivory, **$52-$62**, *turquoise,* **$43-$49**, *and red,* **$58-$70.**

Footed salad bowl in cobalt blue. **$410-$460**

Dessert bowls in turquoise, **$35-$45**, *light green,* **$36-$42**, *and red,* **$42-$52.**

5 1/2" fruit bowls in turquoise, **$23-$30**, *ivory,* **$27-$34**, *and light green,* **$24-$31.**

Carafe in cobalt blue. **$300-$345**

8 1/2" nappy in medium green. **$170-$185**

Nested mixing bowls:
Yellow #7. **$449-$589**
Cobalt blue #6. **$285-$332**
Ivory #5. **$225-$265**
Turquoise #4. **$130-$157**
Red #3. **$135-$158**
Cobalt blue #2. **$118-$147**
Turquoise #1. **$275-$299**

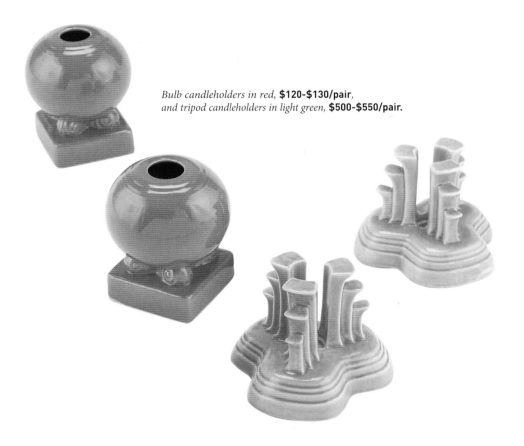

Bulb candleholders in red, **$120-$130/pair**,
and tripod candleholders in light green, **$500-$550/pair.**

Covered casserole in red, **$235-$279**, *and yellow,* **$145-$160.**

Comport in ivory. **$170-$190**

Teacup and saucer in gray. **$36-$43/set**

Sweets comports in yellow, **$70-$79**, *and light green,* **$80-$85.**

Demitasse coffeepot in turquoise, **$650-$695**, *and red,* **$595-$650.**

Covered sugar bowl in yellow, **$48-$57**, *ring-handle creamer in light green,* **$26-$29**, *and stick handle creamer in red,* **$65-$72.**

Covered mustard in ivory, **$335-$350**, *with marmalade jar in light green,* **$325-$375.**

Two-pint jug in light green, **$90-$95**, *with ice pitcher in ivory,* **$140-$160.**

Place setting with 6", 7", and 9" plates and teacup and saucer in chartreuse. **$88-$100/set**

Disk water pitcher in rose. **$245-$285**

10 1/2" compartment plate in red, **$65-$75**, *and 12" compartment plate in light green,* **$58-$65.**

Salt and pepper shakers in yellow. **$25-$29/pair**

7" plates (top to bottom): yellow, **$9-$10**; *turquoise,* **$9-$10**; *red,* **$12-$15**; *forest green,* **$15-$17**; *light green,* **$10-$11**; *chartreuse,* **$14-$16**; *cobalt blue,* **$10-$12**; *rose,* **$15-$17**; *and ivory,* **$10-$12.**

Medium teapot in rose. **$275-$295**

Utility tray in turquoise. **$48-$53**

Sauceboat and underplate in red. **$75-$89 sauceboat only**

Large teapot in yellow. **$290-$300**

Water tumblers in light green, **$65-$68**, *yellow,* **$67-$70,** *and red,* **$75-$85.**

Group of vases: 12" vase in light green, **$1,100-$1,200**; *10" vase in light green,* **$900-$975;** *8" vase in ivory,* **$740-$780**; *8" vase in yellow,* **$570-$640**; *bud vase in red,* **$100-$130**; *and bud vase in cobalt blue,* **$100-$130.**

Fulper

The firm that became Fulper Pottery Company of Flemington, N.J., originally made stoneware pottery and utilitarian wares beginning in the early 1800s. Fulper made art pottery from about 1909 to 1935.

The company's earliest artware was called the Vase-Kraft line (1910-1915). Its middle period (1915-1925) included some of the earlier shapes, but they also incorporated Oriental forms. Their glazing at this time was less consistent but more diverse. The last period (1925-1935) was characterized by Art Deco forms.

FULPER in a rectangle is known as the "ink mark" and dates from 1910-1915. The second mark, which dates from 1915-1925, was incised or in black ink. The final mark, FULPER, die-stamped, dates from about 1925 to 1935.

Treadway Gallery

Vase, double handled shape, brown matte glaze, stamped PRANG mark on base, 6" wide x 4 1/2" high. **$175**

Dirk Soulis Auctions

Bowl vase with three high handles, Fulper marked base, 4" x 5 1/2". **$190**

Dirk Soulis Auctions

Pottery vase with blue crystalline glaze, impressed mark of Fulper, 6 1/2" x 9". **$300**

Treadway Gallery

Sculpture, reclining cat, tan, brown and blue glaze, marked, applied felt pads to base, 9 1/2" wide x 6" high. **$1,000**

Treadway Gallery

Vase, large form with five handles, turquoise glaze with crystalline highlights, marked, 10 1/2" wide x 10" high. **$500**

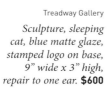

Treadway Gallery

Vase, double handled and bulbous shape, green and red matte glaze, stamped logo on base, 6" wide x 7 1/2" high. **$250**

Treadway Gallery

Sculpture, sleeping cat, blue matte glaze, stamped logo on base, 9" wide x 3" high, repair to one ear. **$600**

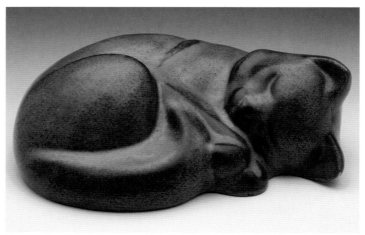

Grueby

William Grueby was active in the ceramic industry for several years before he developed his own method of producing matte-glazed pottery and founded the Grueby Faience Company of Boston in 1897.

The art pottery was hand thrown in natural shapes, hand molded and hand tooled. A variety of colored glazes, singly or in combinations, was produced, but green was the most popular. In 1908, the firm was divided into the Grueby Pottery Company and the Grueby Faience and Tile Company. The Grueby Faience and Tile Company made art tile until 1917; its pottery production was phased out about 1910.

Fontaines Auction Gallery

Low bowl carved with six leaves around the body, matte green finish, signed on bottom, small chip on rim, 2 1/2" high x 6" diameter. **$800**

Skinner, Inc.

Pottery decorated vase, flared rim on tapered form in thick green glaze with tooled broad leaves alternating with yellow buds, circa 1904, impressed Grueby Pottery, Boston, USA and numbered 254, with glaze mark, possibly artist's initials, 10" high. **$25,000**

Treadway Gallery

Vase, bulbous shape with carved and applied leaf and bud design, covered in green matte glaze, impressed logo and artist's initials on base, 4 1/2" wide x 5 1/4" high, five major hairline cracks, one partially restored. **$475**

Rago Arts and Auction Center

Rare advertising tile with candle, brown ground, circa 1910, 6" x 4 1/2", small flake to one corner. **$8,000**

Heritage Auction Galleries

Art pottery vase, yellow glazed with leaf-form pattern to body, circa 1900, marks: (effaced), 5 3/4" high, 1" hairline fraction to upper rim. **$1,875**

CRN Auctions, Inc.

Blue lion and green serpent in blue circle, dark green leaves in each corner, die stamped 677, 6" square, 1" thick. **$800**

Hull Pottery

In 1905, Addis E. Hull purchased the Acme Pottery Company of Crooksville, Ohio. In 1917, the A.E. Hull Pottery Company began making art pottery, novelties, stoneware and kitchenware, later including the famous Little Red Riding Hood line. Most items had a matte finish, with shades of pink and blue or brown predominating.

After a flood and fire in 1950, the factory reopened in 1952 as the Hull Pottery Company. New pieces, mostly with a glossy finish, were produced. The firm closed in 1985.

Pre-1950 vases are marked "Hull USA" or "Hull Art USA" on the bottom. Many also retain their paper labels. Post-1950 pieces are marked "Hull" in large script or "HULL" in block letters.

Each pattern has a distinctive letter or number, e.g., Wildflower has a "W" and a number; Water Lily, "L" and number; Poppy, numbers in the 600s; Orchid, in the 300s. Early stoneware pieces are marked with an "H."

For more information on Hull Pottery, see *Warman's Hull Pottery Identification and Price Guide* by David Doyle.

This 13" Little Red Riding Hood cookie jar is one of the few legitimate Hull Red Riding Hood pieces and the one that started the Red Riding Hood art pottery craze. Notice that the basket is shaped much like a taco shell. This is characteristic of a legitimate Hull cookie jar. Similar Regal Little Red Riding Hood cookie jars have baskets of a different shape.
$500-$700

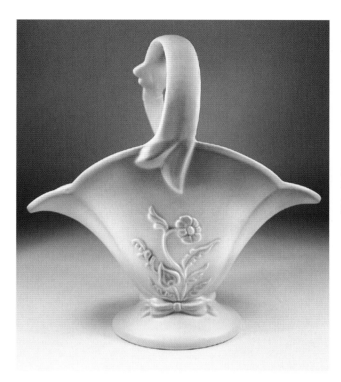

*B-12 Bow-
Knot basket,
10 1/2".*
$750-$1,000

F482 Imperial fish gurgling ewer, 11".
$75-$100

*Ebb Tide, like most of Hull's art pottery lines, came in
multiple color schemes. E-10 ewer, 14".* **$200-$250**

No. 7 Tokay fruit bowl, 9 1/2". **$150-$200**

This 10 1/2" pink and blue Wildflower basket is one of the more sought after "W" series items. It is marked "Hull Art USA W-16-10 1/2"." **$250-$350**

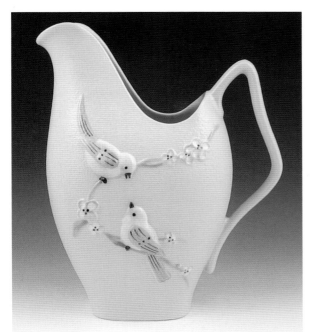

S21 Serenade pitcher, 10 1/2" tall. **$200-$250**

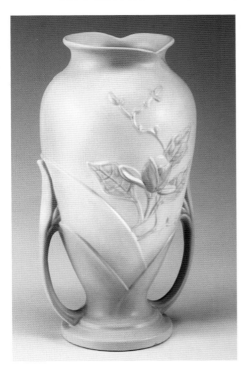

Different decorations front and rear, as well as a variety of colors, were features of the Magnolia and many other Hull lines. No. 16 vase, 15" tall. **$425-$500**

L-16 Water Lily vase, 12 1/2" tall. **$350-$450**

McCoy Pottery

The first McCoy with clay under his fingernails was W. Nelson McCoy. With his uncle, W.F. McCoy, he founded a pottery works in Putnam, Ohio, in 1848, making stoneware crocks and jugs.

That same year, W. Nelson's son, James W., was born in Zanesville, Ohio. James established the J.W. McCoy Pottery Company in Roseville, Ohio, in the fall of 1899. The J.W. McCoy plant was destroyed by fire in 1903 and was rebuilt two years later.

It was at this time that the first examples of Loy-Nel-Art wares were produced. The line's distinctive title came from the names of James McCoy's three sons, Lloyd, Nelson, and Arthur. Like other "standard" glazed pieces produced at this time by several Ohio potteries, Loy-Nel-Art has a glossy finish on a dark brown-black body, but Loy-Nel-Art featured a splash of green color on the front and a burnt-orange splash on the back.

George Brush became general manager of J.W. McCoy Pottery Company in 1909. The company became Brush-McCoy Pottery Company in 1911, and in 1925 the name was shortened to Brush Pottery Company. This firm remained in business until 1982.

Separately, in 1910, Nelson McCoy Sr. founded the Nelson McCoy Sanitary and Stoneware Company, also in Roseville. By the early 1930s, production had shifted from utilitarian wares to art pottery, and the company name was changed to Nelson McCoy Pottery.

Designer Sydney Cope was hired in 1934, and was joined by his son, Leslie, in 1936. The Copes' influence on McCoy wares continued until Sydney's death in 1966. That same year, Leslie opened a gallery devoted to his family's design heritage and featuring his own original art.

Nelson McCoy Sr. died in 1945, and was succeeded as company president by his nephew, Nelson McCoy Melick.

A fire destroyed the plant in 1950, but company officials—including Nelson McCoy Jr., then 29—decided to rebuild, and the new Nelson McCoy Pottery Company was up and running in just six months.

Nelson Melick died in 1954. Nelson Jr. became company president, and oversaw the company's continued growth. In 1967, the operation was sold to entrepreneur David Chase. At this time, the words "Mt. Clemens Pottery" were added to the company marks. In 1974, Chase sold the company to Lancaster Colony Corp., and the company marks included a stylized "LCC" logo. Nelson Jr. and his wife, Billie, who had served as a products supervisor, left the company in 1981.

In 1985, the company was sold again, this time to Designer Accents. The McCoy pottery factory closed in 1990.

For more information on McCoy pottery, see *Warman's McCoy Pottery, 2nd edition*, by Mark F. Moran.

Cherries and Leaves serving bowl, two individual salad bowls, and two cups, all in glossy aqua, mid-1930s, unmarked, all very rare. Serving bowl, 9" diameter, **$450-$550**
Salad bowls, 5" diameter, **$225-$275 each**
Cups, 2-7/8" high, **$90-$110 each**

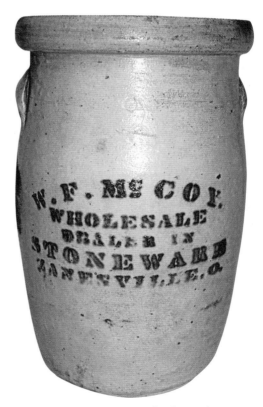

J.W. McCoy jardinière and pedestal in a Carnelian glaze, circa 1905, unmarked, overall 20 1/2" high. **$400+**

W.F. McCoy Stoneware two-gallon butter churn, 1850s, rare. No established value.

*Ball pitcher with ice lip and four goblet-style tumblers in glossy burgundy, 1940s, unmarked. Pitcher, 8 1/2" high, **$50-$60**. Tumblers, 5" high, **$25-$30 each***

*J.W. McCoy squat vase in a blended glaze, circa 1905, unmarked, 6" high. **$150+***

Cucumber and "Mango" salt and pepper shakers with cork stoppers, 1950s, McCoy USA mark,
5 1/4" high. **$90-$110/pair**

Pot and saucer (detached) in glossy burgundy, 1940s, unmarked, 9 1/2" high.
$125-$150

Shoulder bowl in a windowpane pattern, 1920s, with shield mark and #4, 11". **$100-$125**

Two square-bottom Ring ware mixing bowls in green and yellow, 1930s, shield mark with size inside (8" and 9", though they may actually be up to a half inch larger in diameter), also a pattern number (2, indicating the ring pattern). **$150-$175 each**

Carriage with umbrella planter in traditional colors, cold paint in excellent condition, mid-1950s, McCoy USA mark, 9" high. **$200+**

Large fish planter in pink, green and white, 1950s, McCoy USA mark, 12" long. **$1,200+**

Three pigeon or dove flower holders (called "ladder pieces," so named because they were pictured in an early McCoy guide on a drying rack that was tiered like the steps of a ladder), 1940s, USA mark, 3 1/2" high. **$100-$125 each**

Two pitcher flower holders, 1940s, NM USA mark, hand-painted in coral, 3 1/4" high. **$150-$200 each**

Triple bulb bowl in pink and black, 1950s, McCoy mark, 8" wide. **$165-$185**

Cactus flower planter, three pieces, 1950s, marked 677 USA, 7" wide. **$50+**

Hunting dog planter in hard-to-find chartreuse glaze with black dog, 1954 McCoy mark,
12" wide x 8 1/2" high. **$350-$450**

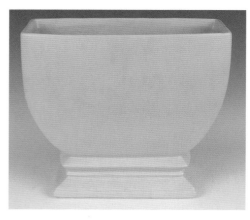

Garden Club vase in matte yellow, late 1950s, McCoy USA mark, 9 1/2" high. **$150-$175**

Lily Bud pillow vase in glossy rose/ pink, 1940s, NM USA mark, 7" high. **$90-$110**

Leaves and Berries vase in matte brown and green, unmarked, 7" high. **$80-$90**

Arrow Leaf vase in rustic glaze, McCoy mark, 10" high. **$125-$150**

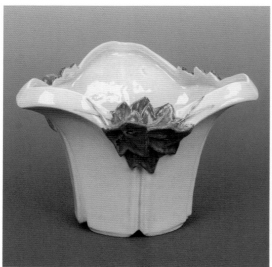

Three-sided ivy planter, 1950s, McCoy USA mark, hard to find, 6" high. **$400-$500**

Butterfly cylinder vase with under-glaze decoration, 1940s, NM mark, 8" high. **$350-$450**
(In typical colors of coral, yellow, blue, or green, **$60-$90**.)

Pine Cone teapot, creamer and sugar, 1950s, McCoy mark. **$125-$150 set**

Jardinière in a majolica glaze, stoneware, early 1920s, 9 1/2" high, 10 3/4" diameter. **$150+**

Red Wing Pottery

Various potteries operated in Red Wing, Minnesota, starting in 1868, the most successful being the Red Wing Stoneware Company, organized in 1877. Merged with other local potteries through the years, it became known as Red Wing Union Stoneware Company in 1906 and was one of the largest producers of utilitarian stoneware items in the United States.

After a decline in the popularity of stoneware products, an art pottery line was introduced to compensate for the loss. This was reflected in a new name for the company, Red Wing Potteries, Inc., in 1936. Stoneware production ceased entirely in 1947, but vases, planters, cookie jars, and dinnerware of art pottery quality continued in production until 1967, when the pottery ceased operation altogether.

For more information on Red Wing pottery, see *Warman's Red Wing Pottery Identification and Price Guide* by Mark F. Moran.

Stoneware

Transitional three-gallon churn with long-stem leaf, in a zinc glaze, 14 3/4" tall with original cover. **$4,000-$5,000**

Five-gallon crock with 6" wing, no oval, also with double trim line and a stamped "5" on base; base also shows a firing ring from the smaller crock it sat on in the kiln, 13" tall. **$250+**

Five-gallon churn-form store advertisement with "elephant ears," with lid adapted from a churn cover with button handle, 16 3/4" tall. **$10,000+**

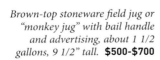

Brown-top stoneware field jug or "monkey jug" with bail handle and advertising, about 1 1/2 gallons, 9 1/2" tall. **$500-$700**

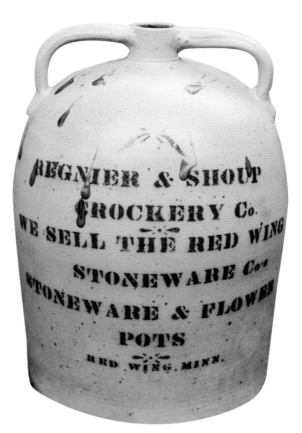

Large and rare advertising stoneware two-handled jug, circa 1890, 15-gallon salt-glazed, promoting "Regnier & Shoup Crockery Co. — 'We sell the Red Wing Stoneware Co.'s Stoneware and Flower Pots' — Red Wing, Minn.," with glaze drips on body (called "turkey droppings"), cracks around mouth, overall excellent condition. No established value.

Four-gallon salt-glaze water cooler with cobalt decoration sometimes referred to as "lazy 8" and "target with tail," circa 1890, with original cover, 11" tall without lid, unmarked. **$3,000+**

Four-gallon salt-glaze "beehive" jug with cobalt decoration referred to as "ribcage" and "target," circa 1890, 15" tall, unmarked. **$2,500+**

Unusual white stoneware ice bucket with cobalt trim, with the same general shape as a 20-pound butter crock, 6" tall, 10" diameter. No established value

Five-gallon ball-lock jar with single wing, 18 1/2" tall with locking device but no handle, found in several sizes, and with gallon number and oval. **$1,000**
Common jar with full marks **$200+**

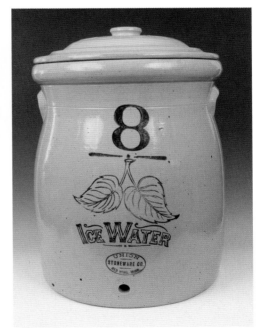

Eight-gallon ice water cooler with "elephant ears" and correct lid, 19" tall with lid. **$6,000-$7,000 if perfect**

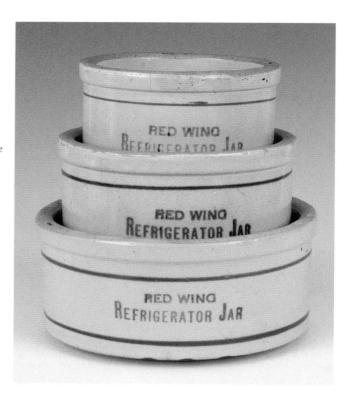

White stoneware refrigerator jars, three sizes, with cobalt trim, each has a raised, footed base so that the same size jars could be stacked, seen here in diameters of 4 3/4", 5 3/4", and 6 3/4". **$250-$350 each**

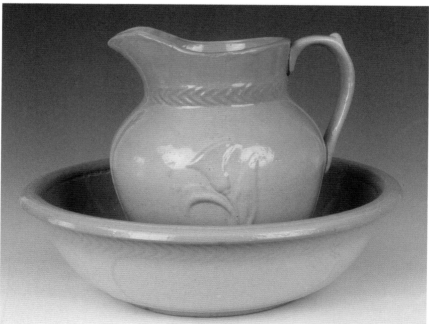

Blue and white stoneware pitcher and basin with raised lily; pitcher, 10 1/2" tall; basin, 15 1/2" diameter, unmarked. **$1,200+ set**

Sponge-decorated umbrella stand, 17 3/4" tall, unmarked. **$1,800-$2,200**

Two sponge-decorated spittoons 4 1/2" and 5 1/2" tall, unmarked. **$500-$700 each**

Mustard jar with bail handle, original lid and Nebraska advertising in blue (commonly found in black), otherwise unmarked, 6 1/4" tall with handle down. **$750+ because of blue advertising**

Stoneware lion doorstop with salt-glaze surface, circa 1890, found in Red Wing, tail broken, unsigned, 12" tall, 17" long. **$20,000+**

Chamber pot with bail handle and blue sponge decoration, unusual crock-form handles on sides, possibly a prototype, 11 1/2". **$1,000 if perfect**

Art Pottery

Belle Kogan planter called "The Nymphs," No. B2500, part of the "Deluxe Line," 16 1/2" wide x 6 3/4" tall.
$180+

Rooster vases in Fleck Zephyr Pink, two sizes, No. 1438 (also found marked No. M1438), designed by Charles Murphy, 9 3/4" and 14" tall. **$200+ each**

Floor vase No. 145, in a glaze called "Ripe Wheat," 15" tall. **$550+**

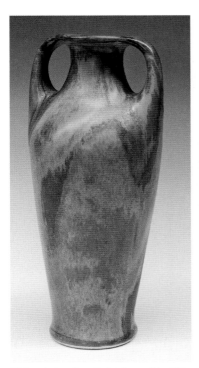

Nokomis two-handled tall vase No. 199, 9 3/4" tall, ink-stamped, "Red Wing Art Pottery." **$500+**

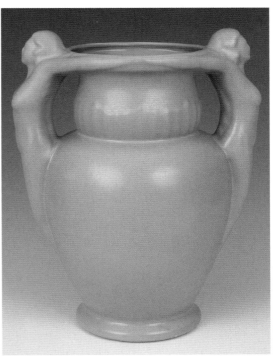

"Double nudes" vase No. 249 in Apple Blossom, 11 3/4" tall, found unmarked or ink-stamped, "Red Wing Art Pottery." **$2,500+**

"6000 Series" flared bowl, late 1940s, No. 6002, 14" diameter, also impressed mark, "Red Wing USA." **$550+**

Dinnerware/Kitchenware

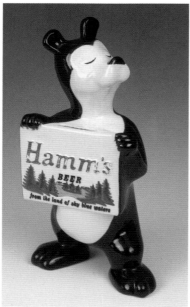

Hamm's Bear bank, late 1950s, 12" tall, unmarked, this example with raised letters, also found with decal. **$400+**

Barrel (spongeware) cookie jar with stepped profile by Red Wing, stoneware, 8 1/4" tall, 1930s, unmarked. **$400+**

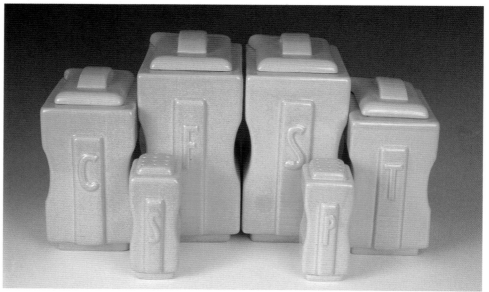

Complete canister set plus salt and pepper shakers, 1938, part of the Gypsy Trail line; flour and sugar, 9" tall; coffee and tea, 7 1/2" tall; salt and pepper, 5" tall, impressed mark, "Red Wing USA." **$500+ set**

Pair of Provincial line candleholders, 1941,
accessories for Ardennes, Brittany, Normandy or
Orleans patterns, each 7 1/4" long, unmarked.
$100+ pair

Delta Blue two-gallon water jar with ceramic
base, 1951, part of the Village Green line, 17"
tall overall. **$500+**

Round-Up two-gallon water jar with
ceramic base, 1955, part of the Casual
line, 17" tall overall. **$500+**

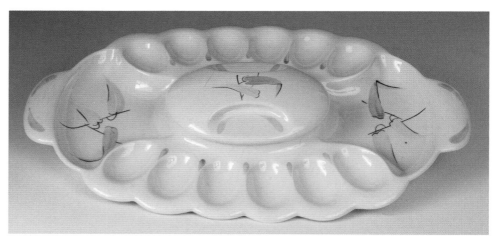

Willow Wind (pink) egg tray with covered central section, 1941, part of the Concord line, 16" wide. **$125+**

Saffron Ware cookie jar with lozenge-shaped panel on front, 9 1/2" diameter, ink-stamped, "Red Wing Saffron Ware." **$300-$500**

Jack Frost cookie jars by Red Wing, 8 1/4" tall and 12" tall, early 1960s, both unmarked.
Short version **$600+**
Tall version **$700+**

Rookwood Pottery

Maria Longworth Nichols founded Rookwood Pottery in 1880. The name, she later reported, paid homage to the many crows (rooks) on her father's estate and was also designed to remind customers of Wedgwood. Production began on Thanksgiving Day 1880 when the first kiln was drawn.

Rookwood's earliest productions demonstrated a continued reliance on European precedents and the Japanese aesthetic. Although the firm offered a variety of wares (Dull Glaze, Cameo, and Limoges for example), it lacked a clearly defined artistic identity. With the introduction of what became known as its "standard glaze" in 1884, Rookwood inaugurated a period in which the company won consistent recognition for its artistic merit and technical innovation.

Rookwood's first decade ended on a high note when the company was awarded two gold medals: one at the Exhibition of American Art Industry in Philadelphia and another later in the year at the Exposition Universelle in Paris. Significant, too, was Maria Longworth Nichols' decision to transfer her interest in the company to William W. Taylor, who had been the firm's manager since 1883. In May 1890, the board of a newly reorganized Rookwood Pottery Company purchased "the real estate, personal property, goodwill, patents, trade-marks... now the sole property of William W. Taylor" for $40,000.

Under Taylor's leadership, Rookwood was transformed from a fledgling startup to successful business that expanded throughout the following decades to meet rising demand.

Throughout the 1890s, Rookwood continued to attract critical notice as it kept the tradition of innovation alive. Taylor rolled out three new glaze lines—Iris, Sea Green and Aerial Blue— from late 1894 into early 1895.

At the Paris Exposition in 1900, Rookwood cemented its reputation by winning the Grand Prix, a feat largely due to the favorable reception of the new Iris glaze and its variants.

Over the next several years, Rookwood's record of achievement at domestic and international exhibitions remained unmatched.

Throughout the 1910s, Rookwood continued in a similar vein and began to more thoroughly embrace the simplified aesthetic promoted by many Arts and Crafts figures. Production of the Iris line, which had been instrumental in the firm's success at the Paris Exposition in 1900, ceased around 1912. Not only did the company abandon its older, fussier underglaze wares, but the newer lines the pottery introduced also trended toward simplicity.

Unfortunately, the collapse of the stock market in October 1929 and ensuing economic depression dealt Rookwood a blow from which it did not recover. The Great Depression took a toll on the company and eventually led to bankruptcy in April 1941.

Rookwood's history might have ended there were it not for the purchase of the firm by a group of investors led by automobile dealer Walter E. Schott and his wife, Margaret. Production started once again. In the years that followed, Rookwood changed hands a number of times before being moved to Starkville, Mississippi, in 1960. It finally closed its doors there in 1967.

For more information on Rookwood, see *Warman's Rookwood Pottery Identification and Price Guide* by Denise Rago and Jonathan Clancy.

Early Wares

Rare pitcher decorated by Laura Fry with incised fronds covered in indigo and dark green glaze, 1882, stamped ROOKWOOD 1882, incised Cincinnati Pottery Club, LAF, 7" x 5". **$1,500-$2,500**
(Laura Fry was a member of the Women's Pottery Club of Cincinnati, a china-painting group, along with Clara Chipman Newton and Mary Louise McLaughlin, before joining the first generation of decorators at Rookwood. During her 10-year stay at the pottery, she developed and patented the atomizer for glazing purposes. From Rookwood, she moved on to the Lonhuda Pottery in Steubenville, Ohio.)

Cameo potpourri jar by A. R. Valentien with a bird on a branch, 1886, stamped ROOKWOOD 1886/Y/27 A.R.V., 7 1/2" x 6". **$1,000-$1,500**

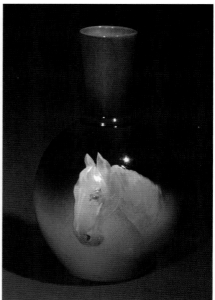

Standard Glaze bulbous bud vase painted by Daniel Cook, 1894, with a white horse's head against a green-to-brown ground, 6 1/4" x 3 1/2". **$1,250-$2,250**

Three Standard Glaze vessels: tall ewer by A.M. Valentien, ovoid vase by C.F. Baker, and bud vase by Irene Bishop, all marked, ewer: 11 1/2". **$400-$800 each**

Sea Green pillow vase with crescent rim, decorated by Edward Diers, 1899, with tall stems and leaves in green against a blue and celadon ground, wrapped in a bronze overlay of iris blossoms, 4 1/2" x 4". **$17,500-$25,000**

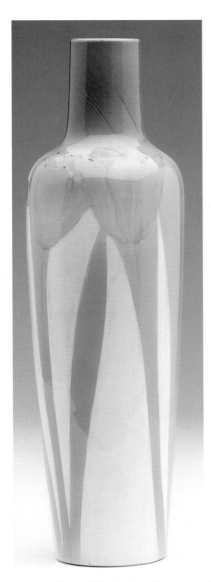

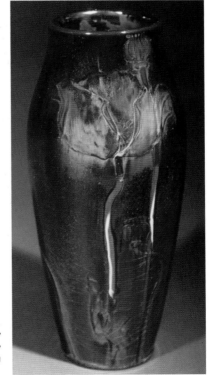

Fine Iris Glaze tall bottle-shaped vase carved and slip-painted with golden tulips and long celadon leaves on white ground, 1900; it appears to be the work of Sara Sax though a factory label covers the artist's mark, purchased from the famous 1942 B. Altman's sale, flame mark/S1656/W, 13 1/4" x 4". **$10,000-$15,000**

Tiger Eye vase, probably by Kitaro Shirayamadani, carved with full-length russet poppies on a silky brown, green and gold ground, mark obscured by glaze, 9 1/4" x 3 3/4". **$4,500-$6,500**

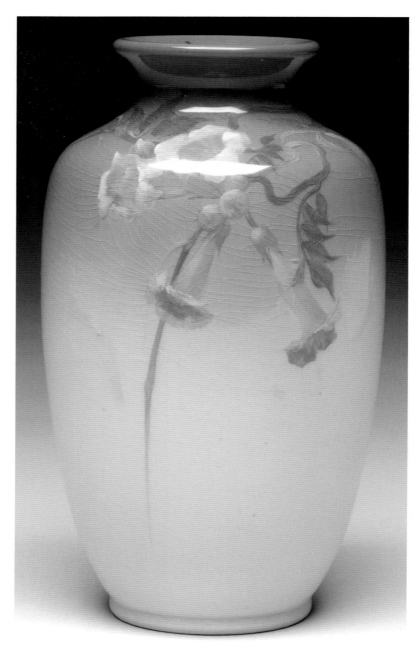

James D. Julia, Inc.

Iris Glaze vase decorated with soft pink flowers, green stems and leaves against a green shading to cream background, marked on underside with Rookwood flame mark dated 1902 with artist initials "FR" for Frederick Rothenbusch, bottom is also marked with an "X," 8". **$413**

Silver-overlaid Standard Glaze two-handled vase by Kitaro Shirayamadani, 1898, painted with orange and golden yellow chrysanthemums and green leaves, and covered in Gorham silver with whiplash strands, 12" x 6 1/2". **$10,000-$15,000**

Silver-overlaid Standard Glaze cylindrical vase, "Edelweiss," painted by Bruce Horsfall with a golden-haired maiden dropping blossoms, 1893, half the vase covered in GORHAM floral silver overlay, flame mark/B-/Edelweiss/589C W, 12 3/4" x 3 3/4". **$17,500-$25,000**

Black Iris vase painted by Sara Sax
with red-hot pokers, 1905, flame
mark/V/982C/artist's cipher/X, 11 3/4".
$4,500-$6,500

Vase by Kitaro Shirayamadani,
1899, painted with a heron
spreading its wings amidst tall
grasses, the bottom wrapped
in a bronze overlay of flowers
and large leaves, 12 1/2" x 5".
$35,000-$45,000

Ceramics **C**

Mat Glazes

Painted Mat vase by Harriet Wilcox embossed with large amber chrysanthemums on a mottled indigo ground, 1901, flame mark/I/386Z/HEW, 8 1/2" x 3 1/2". **$4,500-$5,500**

Vellum flaring vase painted by Ed Diers with pink poppies, 1927, flame mark/XXVII/1369D/V/ED, 9 1/4" x 5". **$4,000-$6,000**

Antiques & Collectibles | *Warman's*   229

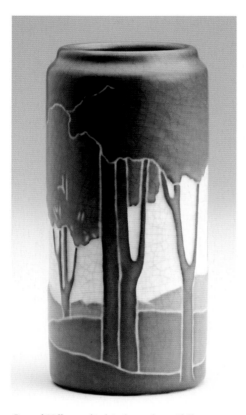

Carved Vellum cylindrical vase beautifully decorated in the Arts & Crafts style by Sara Sax with an abstracted landscape of silhouetted trees and mountains in blue-grays and ivory, 1908, purchased from the famous 1942 B. Altman's sale, flame mark/VIII/952E/artist cipher/V, 7 1/2" x 3 1/2". **$15,000-$25,000**

Incised Mat vase by William Hentschel with blue pods on a partially hammered green ground, 1910, flame mark/X/950C/WEH, 10 1/2" x 4 1/2". **$1,750-$2,250**

Fine and unusual Vellum ovoid vase by Elizabeth McDermott, 1916, with one large tree by a pond in greens and peach, light crazing, flame mark/ XVI/2033E/VE/EHM. 8 1/2" x 3 3/4". **$3,500-$5,500**

Vellum ovoid vase finely painted by Lenore Asbury with blue and red blossoms on a shaded purple-to-mint green ground, 1925, flame mark/XXV/1121C/ L.A., 10" x 4 1/4". **$4,000-$5,000**

Three Incised Mat vases by Albert Pons, Sally Toohey, and William McDonald, all marked, tallest, 7". **$600-$1,000 each**

Incised Mat baluster vase by C.S. Todd with a wreath of stylized leaves in blue, orange and yellow on cobalt ground, 1917, flame mark/ XVII/945/CST, 9 1/2" x 6 1/2". **$750-$1,250**

Incised Mat floor vase by Elizabeth
Lincoln with fleshy pink poppies and
green foliage on an indigo-to-pink
butterfat ground, 1919, flame mark
XIX/264A/V/LNL, 22 1/2" x 9".
$2,000-$3,000

Large banded Vellum bulbous vase by Fred
Rothenbusch, 1917, decorated with snowy winter
landscape on a brown ground, flame mark/
XVII/139B/V/FR/X, 18" x 10". **$5,000-$7,000**

Green Vellum candlestick by Sara
Sax, 1908, with teal blue irises,
flame mark/VIII/822C/G.V./
artist's cipher/X, 8". **$600-$900**

Incised Mat bulbous vase by Rose Fechheimer with a band of pine cones on a brown and red ground, 1906, flame mark/VI/881D/R.F., 6" x 5". **$1,500-$2,500**

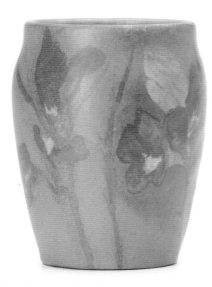

Painted Mat vase by Sallie Toohey with red and yellow blossoms, 1901, flame mark/I/2?52/ST, 5 1/4" x 4". **$2,000-$3,000**

Modeled Mat vase by William Hentschel with deeply mottled poppies and curvilinear stems in flowing light green on a maroon ground, 1912, flame mark/XII/907B/artist's cipher, 17 1/2" x 7". **$4,500-$6,500**

New Porcelain Body

Jewel Porcelain ovoid vase painted by Jens Jensen with Art Deco flowers in brown, pink and indigo Butterfat Glaze on ivory ground, 1932, flame mark/XXXII/S/ artist's cipher, 7 3/4" x 3 3/4". **$3,500-$4,500**

Decorated Mat lobed flaring vase painted by Elizabeth Lincoln with panels of red stylized flowers against pink and red butterfat ground, 1923, flame mark/ XXIII/LNL, 7" x 3". **$1,500-$2,000**

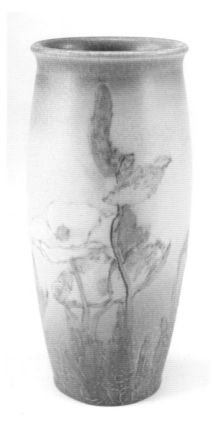

Decorated Mat vase painted by Sally Coyne with pink and red poppies on a yellow-to-green butterfat ground, 1928, flame mark, 7 3/4" x 3 1/2". **$1,250-$2,000**

Wax Mat vase decorated by Loretta Holtkamp with black palm trees on an ivory ground, 1953, flame mark/LIII/LH/S, 8" x 3 3/4". **$1,000-$1,500**

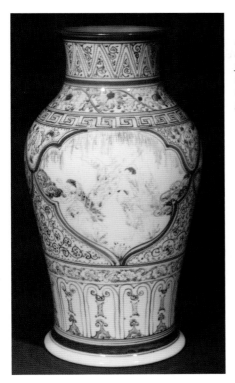

Jewel Porcelain Persian vase by William Hentschel, 1922, painted with Asian figural scenes in cartouches framed by alternating floral and arabesque patterns in mauve, blue and brown on an ivory ground, 13" x 8". **$6,500-$9,500**

Jewel Porcelain scenic vase by Arthur Conant, 1919, with outlined mountains and pagoda and silhouetted trees in white and green, accented by small pink and blue flowers amidst large green leaves on a light blue and lavender ground, 9" x 4". **$3,000-$5,000**

Black Opal vase carved and decorated by Kitaro Shirayamadani, 1925, with large modeled fish swimming through purple and brown seaweed and grasses on a cobalt, celadon, brown, and purple ground, uncrazed, 9 3/4" x 6". **$8,000-$12,000**

Decorated Mat squat vase painted by Louise Abel with a wreath of jewel toned flowers on purple ground, 1923, flame mark/XXIII/1929/artist's cipher, 4 1/4" x 7". **$1,250-$1,750**

Later Mat/Mat Moderne vase by William Hentschel with a nude, antelopes and geese, covered in matte brown and white glaze, 1929, flame mark/ XXIX/6080/WEH, 13 1/2" x 11". **$5,000-$7,000**

Porcelain hemispherical vase painted by Lorinda Epply with Art Deco blossoms in brown and indigo on a chartreuse green ground, 1926, flame mark/XXVI/2254E/LE, 4 1/2" x 5 1/2". **$800-$1,200**

Decorated Mat vase painted by M.H. McDonald with pink leaves on a turquoise butterfat ground, 1928, flame mark/ XXVII/2182/MHM, 5 1/4" x 4". **$900-$1,300**

Production Ware

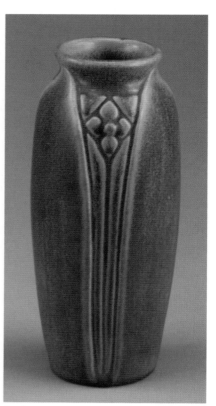

Production ovoid vase, 1923, embossed with berries and leaves under a grape purple matte glaze, a crisp and bright example of this form, flame mark, 5 1/4".
$450-$650

Production vase, 1916, embossed with quatrefoils, covered in a speckled brown, indigo, green, and amber matte glaze, marked, 7 1/2". **$600-$900**

Production low bowl impressed with peacock feathers under a fine matte green-to-rose glaze, 1915, 8" diameter.
$300-$400

Pair of Production bookends, 1928, with baskets of flowers in polychrome glazes, flame mark/XXVIII/2837, 6 1/2" x 5 1/2". **$350-$500**

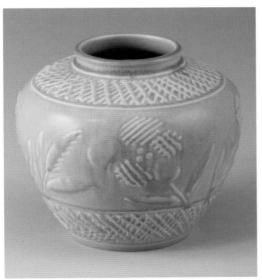

Production bulbous vase, 1942, embossed with stylized flowers and basket-weave design, covered in a light blue matte glaze, flame mark, 6 1/2". **$250-$350**

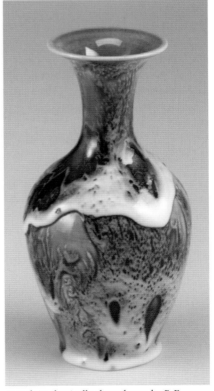

Porcelain classically shaped vase by R.E. Menzel, 1951, covered in a dripping sheer umber and frothy white glaze, flame mark LI/S/REM, 8 3/4" x 4". **$350-$550**

Roseville Pottery

Roseville is one of the most widely recognizable of potteries across the United States. Having been sold in flower shops and drugstores around the country, its art and production wares became a staple in American homes through the time Roseville closed in the 1950s.

The Roseville Pottery Company, located in Roseville, Ohio, was incorporated on Jan. 4, 1892, with George F. Young as general manager. The company had been producing stoneware since 1890, when it purchased the J. B. Owens Pottery, also of Roseville.

The popularity of Roseville Pottery's original lines of stoneware continued to grow. The company acquired new plants in 1892 and 1898, and production started to shift to Zanesville, just a few miles away. By about 1910, all of the work was centered in Zanesville, but the company name was unchanged.

Young hired Ross C. Purdy as artistic designer in 1900, and Purdy created Rozane—a contraction of the words "Roseville" and "Zanesville." The first Roseville artwork pieces were marked either Rozane or RPCO, either impressed or ink-stamped on the bottom.

In 1902, a line was developed called Azurean. Some pieces were marked Azurean, but often RPCO. In 1904 at the St. Louis Exposition, Roseville's Rozane Mongol, a high-gloss oxblood red line, captured first prize, gaining recognition for the firm and its creator, John Herold.

Many Roseville lines were a response to the innovations of Weller Pottery, and in 1904 Frederick Rhead was hired away from Weller as artistic director. He created the Olympic and Della Robbia lines for Roseville. His brother Harry took over as artistic director in 1908, and in 1915 he introduced the popular Donatello line.

By 1908, all handcrafting ended except for Rozane Royal. Roseville was the first pottery in Ohio to install a tunnel kiln, which increased its production capacity.

Frank Ferrell, who was a top decorator at the Weller Pottery by 1904, was Roseville's artistic director from 1917 until 1954. This Zanesville native created many of the most popular lines, including Pine Cone, which had scores of individual pieces.

Many collectors believe Roseville's circa 1925 glazes were the best of any Zanesville pottery. George Krause, who had become Roseville's technical supervisor, responsible for glaze in 1915, remained with Roseville until the 1950s.

Company sales declined after World War II, especially in the early 1950s when cheap Japanese imports began to replace American wares, and a simpler, more modern style made many of Roseville's elaborate floral designs seem old-fashioned.

In the late 1940s, Roseville began to issue lines with glossy glazes. Roseville tried to offset its flagging artware sales by launching a dinnerware line—Raymor—in 1953. The line was a commercial failure.

Roseville issued its last new designs in 1953. On Nov. 29, 1954, the facilities of Roseville were sold to the Mosaic Tile Company.

For more information on Roseville, see *Warman's Roseville Pottery Identification and Price Guide, 2nd edition*, by Denise Rago.

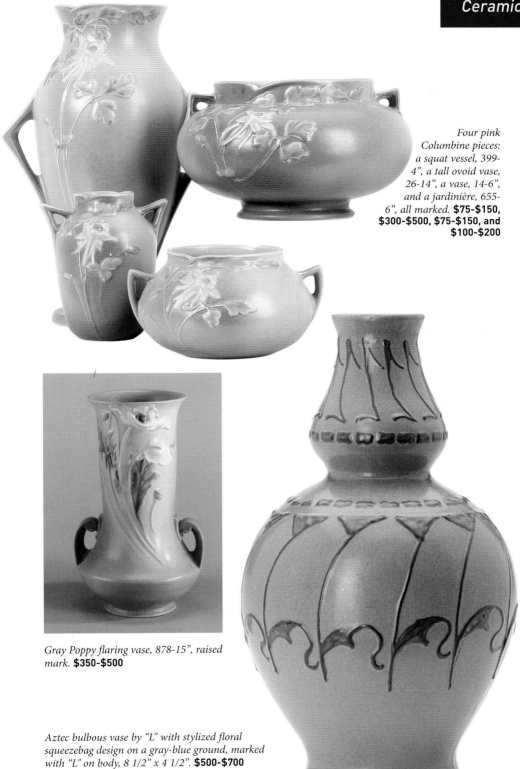

Four pink Columbine pieces: a squat vessel, 399-4", a tall ovoid vase, 26-14", a vase, 14-6", and a jardinière, 655-6", all marked. **$75-$150, $300-$500, $75-$150, and $100-$200**

Gray Poppy flaring vase, 878-15", raised mark. **$350-$500**

Aztec bulbous vase by "L" with stylized floral squeezebag design on a gray-blue ground, marked with "L" on body, 8 1/2" x 4 1/2". **$500-$700**

Pair of green Baneda candlesticks, 1087-5", foil labels. **$450-$650**

Blackberry hanging basket, 348-5", unmarked, 5" x 7". **$850-$1,250**

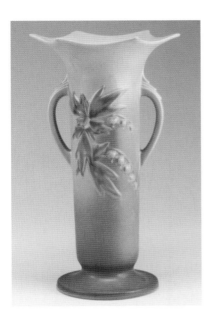

Bleeding Heart pink floor vase, 977-18",
raised mark. **$500-$750**

Blue Apple Blossom basket, 310-10", raised mark.
$150-$250

Artwood Ikebana vase with cypress tree,
1052-8", covered in a glossy yellow and
brown glaze, raised mark. **$250-$300**

Carnelian II rare spherical vase or lamp base covered
in a fine frothy pink, green, and purple glaze, 441-8",
unmarked, 8 1/2" x 8 1/2". **$850-$1,250**

Pink Cremona four-sided vase with blue blossoms and leaves, unmarked, 10 1/4" x 3 1/4". **$250-$350**

Blue Cosmos basket, 358-12", foil label to body and faint impressed mark. **$250-$400**

Brown Bushberry umbrella stand, 779-20", raised mark. **$750-$1,000**

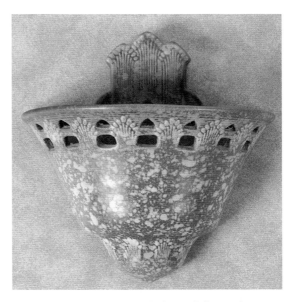

Red Ferella wall pocket, unmarked, 6 3/4". **$1,500-$2,500**

Dahlrose jardinière and pedestal set, unmarked, three sizes available. **$850-$1,500**

Brown Cherry Blossom planter, 239-5", unmarked, 4" x 6". **$250-$400**

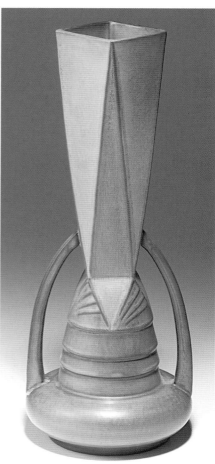

Green Laurel flaring vase, unmarked, 8" x 7".
$350-$500

Rare Futura "Arches" vase in brown and orange, 411-14",
paper label, 14 1/4" x 5 1/2". **$1,750-$2,500**

Fuchsia flower pots, 646-5", one brown with an underplate, and one blue without, all marked.
$200-$300 each

Green Morning Glory double wall pocket, unmarked, 8 1/2". **$550-$750**

Fine and rare Imperial II bowl embossed with banded snail-like design around body, covered in a pale dripping green glaze over a pink ground, 202-6", a very fine example of this form, unmarked, 4 1/2". **$2,250-$3,250**

Exceptional Rozane Royal Light tapering vase with three handles around rim, painted by W. Myers with sweet pea flowers in pink, purple, and ivory, artist's signature, 19" x 6". **$2,000-$3,000**

Green Pine Cone pitcher, 415-9", raised mark.
$300-$400

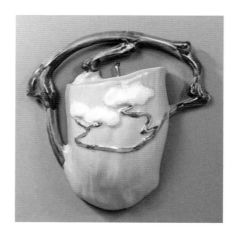

Ming Tree blue wall pocket, 566-8", raised mark.
$150-$200

Pair of green Luffa candlesticks, foil labels, 5" each.
$300-$500

Mock Orange yellow coffee/tea set, 971-T, 971-S, 971-C, 971-P, raised marks. **$750-$850/set**

Green Freesia teapot, 6-T, sugar, 6-S, and a creamer, 6-C, raised marks. **$200-$400**

Montacello bulbous vase covered in an unusual mottled blue glaze, unmarked, 7 1/2" x 6 1/2". **$500-$700**

Blue Pine Cone centerpiece, 324-6", impressed mark. **$500-$750**

Rosecraft Vintage rectangular window box, Rv ink mark, 5 3/4" x 11 1/2". **$600-$800**

Green Magnolia basket, 384-8", raised mark. **$100-$150**

Orian vase with a squat base, the exterior covered in bright red glaze, unmarked, 6 1/2" x 8 1/2". **$150-$200**

Blue Moss planter, 637-5", impressed mark. **$150-$250**

Mostique jardinière and pedestal set, unmarked, 29" overall height. **$650-$950**

Orange Russco triple cornucopia vase, unmarked, 8" x 12". **$200-$300**

Blue Wisteria gourd-shaped bud vase, 631-6", unmarked, 6 1/4" x 4 1/4". **$450-$650**

Silhouette red vase decorated with a nude in the forest, 787-10", raised mark. **$400-$600**

Brown Falline low bowl, 244-8", foil label. **$300-$400**

Brown Water Lily basket, 382-12", raised mark. **$250-$350**

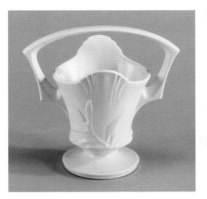

Ivory basket on a Velmoss blank, impressed mark, 9". **$75-$150**

Sunflower vase with flat shoulder, 492-10", unmarked, 10 1/4". **$1,500-$2,500**

Blue Windsor spherical vase, crisply decorated with ferns on both sides, unmarked, 7 1/2" x 7". **$600-$900**

Green Snowberry teapot, 1TP, sugar, 1S, and a creamer, 1C, all marked. **$250-$350**

Early Velmoss-type factory lamp base, paper label, 11" x 5 1/4". **$500-$700**

Tourmaline squat vessel with geometric embossed design around the rim, unmarked, 5" x 6 1/2". **$250-$350**

Brown Clemana flower frog, 23-4", impressed mark. **$100-$200**

Vista jardinière, unmarked, 10 1/2". **$400-$650**

Green Zephyr Lily cookie jar, 5-8", raised mark. **$200-$300**

Wincraft cylindrical vase with a climbing panther, 290-11", raised mark. **$350-$550**

Brown Pine Cone wall plate, unmarked, 8" d. **$400-$600**

Pair of green Peony bookends, #11, raised marks, 6" each. **$100-$200**

Brown Panel double bud vase with sunflowers, Rv ink mark, 5" x 7 1/2". **$150-$250**

Jonquil crocus pot, unmarked, 6 1/4" x 9 1/4". **$600-$800**

Weller Pottery

Weller Pottery was made from 1872 to 1945 at a pottery established originally by Samuel A. Weller at Fultonham, Ohio and moved in 1882 to Zanesville, Ohio.

Mr. Weller's famous pottery slugged it out with several other important Zanesville potteries for decades. Cross-town rivals such as Roseville, Owens, La Moro, and McCoy were all serious fish in a fairly small and well-stocked lake. While Mr. Weller occasionally landed some solid body punches with many of his better art lines, the prevailing thought was that his later production ware just wasn't up to snuff.

Samuel Weller was a notorious copier and, it is said, a bit of a scallywag. He paid designers such as William Long to bring their famous discoveries to Zanesville. He then attempted to steal their secrets, and, when successful, renamed them and made them his own.

After World War I, when the cost of materials became less expensive than the cost of labor, many companies, including the famous Rookwood Pottery, increased their output of

less expensive production ware. Weller Pottery followed along in the trend of production ware by introducing scores of interesting and unique lines, the likes of which have never been created anywhere else, before or since.

In addition to a number of noteworthy production lines, Weller continued in the creation of hand-painted ware long after Roseville abandoned them. Some of the more interesting Hudson pieces, for example, are post-World War I pieces. Even later lines, such as Bonito, were hand painted and often signed by important artists such as Hester Pillsbury. The closer you look at Weller's output after 1920, the more obvious the fact that it was the only Zanesville company still producing both quality art ware and quality production ware.

For more information on Weller pottery, see *Warman's Weller Pottery Identification and Price Guide* by Denise Rago and David Rago.

Ewer, Dickensware II, rare and unusual, shows a golfer and caddy along a deeply incised line of trees. Impressed mark, 11" x 5". **$3,000-$4,000**

Vase, Etna, corseted, decorated with stemmed pink flowers, impressed mark, 4 1/2" x 3 3/4". **$150-$250**

Vase, Dickensware II, ovoid, decorated by J. H. with a woman playing a mandolin on a crescent moon, impressed mark, 8 1/2". **$500-$700**

Vase, Dresden, tall cylindrical, painted by Levi Burgess with a panoramic Delft scene, signed LJB, stamped Weller Matt, 16" x 4 1/2". **$500-$750**

Ewer, Aurelian, painted with orange carnations, impressed Aurelian mark, 11 1/2". **$400-$600**

Double vase, Coppertone, formed by two jumping fish, impressed mark, 8 1/2". **$1,750-$2,750**

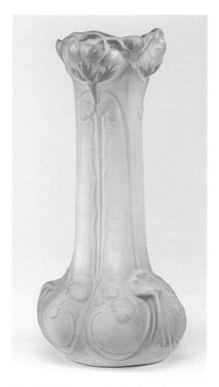

Vase, L'Art Nouveau, bottle-shaped, orange flowers and spade-shaped leaves, unmarked, 13" x 5". **$500-$700**

Vase, Floretta, large, bulbous, decorated with clusters of grapes, impressed Floretta mark, 12" x 8". **$200-$300**

Vase, Fru Russet, tapered, embossed with brown scarabs and red acanthus leaves on a blue and green ground, incised mark, 5" x 4 3/4". **$2,000-$3,000**

Vessel, Baldin, brown with a wide, squat body, 7" x 9". **$500-$700**

Vase, Auroro, undecorated other than the shaded blue background, incised mark, 6 1/2". **$500-$700**

Vase, Ardsley, partitioned, unmarked, 10 1/2" x 6". **$300-$400**

Vase, Dickensware I, four-sided, incised and painted with tulips and yellow scrolled design, impressed 672, 9 1/4" x 6". **$450-$650**

Umbrella stand, Forest, 22".
$1,000-$1,500

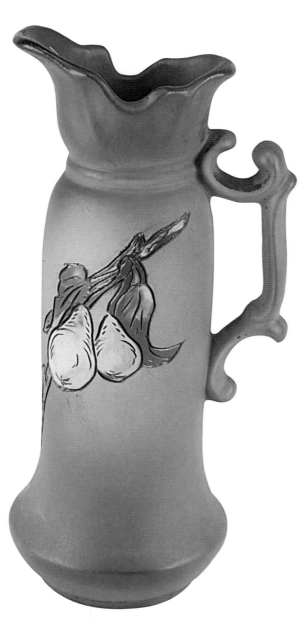

Ewer, Matt Floretta, incised with pears on a branch, incised mark, 10 1/2" x 4 1/2". **$250-$350**

Jardinière and pedestal set, Flemish, with birds and flowers on an ivory ground, unmarked, 30" overall, **$1,000-$2,000**

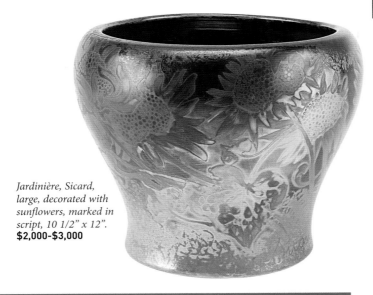

Jardinière, Sicard, large, decorated with sunflowers, marked in script, 10 1/2" x 12".
$2,000-$3,000

Vase, Matt Green, tall, with banded handles, 12".
$1,500-$2,000

Blank jardinière and pedestal set, Ivory on Baldin, both pieces with impressed marks, 37".
$600-$1,000

Figure of a woman holding her dress out to her sides, Hobart, impressed mark, 11" x 8". **$750-$1,250**

Vase, Cloudburst, ovoid, in brown, orange, and ivory, unmarked, 10 1/2" x 4". **$300-$400**

Vase, Jewell, embossed with men and women around the rim above a jeweled band, impressed mark, 10 3/4" x 5 1/2". **$1,500-$2,000**

Vase, Stellar, bulbous, blue, painted by Hester Pillsbury, incised mark and artist's initials, 6" x 6 1/2". **$700-$900**

Vase, Louwelsa, large, bulbous, painted by Frank Ferrell with a vine of grapes, impressed and artist's mark, 12" x 8". **$500-$700**

Vase, Eocean, ovoid, finely painted with flying birds, incised marks, 12". **$2,000-$3,000**

Jar, Selma, lidded, decorated with swans, impressed mark, 4 1/4". **$650-$950**

Vase, Glendale, bulbous, embossed with birds and their nest, stamped mark, 9 1/4" x 8 1/2". **$1,000-$1,500**

Vase, cylindrical, believed to be an example of a rare red Hudson, incised mark, 10" x 4 1/2". **$1,500-$2,000**

Umbrella stand, Marvo, green, ink stamp and paper label, 19 1/2" x 11". **$750-$1,000**

Vase, Xenia, ovoid, white circular flowers, 5 1/4".
$1,250-$1,500

Wall pocket, Warwick, stamped mark, foil Weller label, and Weller Warwick Ware paper label, 11".
$150-$250

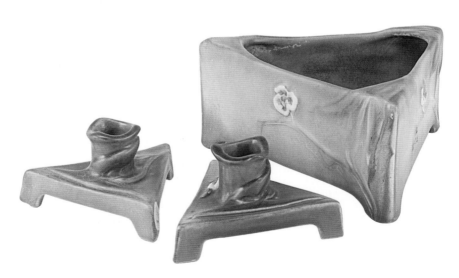

Console set, Tutone, green, comprised of a three-sided bowl and a pair of candlesticks, stamped mark, bowl 3 1/2" x 7". **$250-$350 set**

Pair of candlesticks, Rosemont, glossy black with banded red floral design, impressed mark, 8 3/4". **$200-$400 pair**

Vase, Silvertone, bulbous, with two twisted handles, covered in a brown and yellow trial glaze, unmarked, 7" x 6 1/2". **$700-$900**

Tankard, Woodcraft, embossed with foxes in their den, impressed mark, 13" x 7". **$800-$1,200**

Vase, LaSa, ovoid, painted with palm trees on a golden horizon, unmarked, 6 1/2" x 3 1/2". **$300-$500**

Hair receiver, Jap Birdimal, decorated with Viking ships, 2" x 4". **$400-$600**

Flower frog, Muskota, shaped as a frog perched on a rock, impressed mark, 3 3/4" x 5 1/4". **$400-$600**

Vase, Camelot, large and rare, unmarked, 12" x 5 1/2". **$2,000-$2,500**

European
Select English, European Makers

The **Amphora Porcelain Works** was one of several pottery companies located in the Teplitz-Turn region of Bohemia in the late 19th and early 20th centuries. It is best known for art pottery, especially Art Nouveau and Art Deco pieces. Several markings were used, including the name and location of the pottery and the Imperial mark, which included a crown. Prior to World War I, Bohemia was part of the Austro-Hungarian Empire, so the word "Austria" may appear as part of the mark. After World War I, the word "Czechoslovakia" may be part of the mark.

Belleek is thin-bodied, ivory-colored, almost-iridescent porcelain, first made in 1857 in County Fermanagh, Ireland. Production continued until World War I, was discontinued for a period of time, and then resumed. The Shamrock pattern is most familiar, but many patterns were made, including Limpet, Tridacna and Grasses.

Several American firms made a Belleek-type porcelain. The first was Ott and Brewer Company of Trenton, N.J., in 1884. Other firms producing this ware included The Ceramic Art Company (1889), American Art China Works (1892), Columbian Art Company (1893) and Lenox Inc. (1904). Irish Belleek bore specific marks during given time periods, which makes it relatively easy to date. Variations in mark color are important, as well as the symbols and words.

Capo-di-Monte: In 1743, King Charles of Naples established a soft-paste porcelain factory. The firm made figurines and dinnerware. In 1760, many of the workmen and most of the molds were moved to Buen Retiro, near Madrid, Spain. A new factory, which also made hard-paste porcelains, opened in Naples in 1771. In 1834, the Doccia factory in Florence purchased the molds and continued production in Italy.

Capo-di-Monte was copied well into the 20th century by makers in Hungary, Germany, France and Italy.

Capo-de-Monte

Figures (pair), Capo-di-Monte, classical females, one at desk with compass and scroll, other sculpting helmeted bust on stand, oval base, porcelain, Capo-di-Monte, 19th century, 6 1/2" high. **$510 pair**

Copeland   Spode

In 1749, **Josiah Spode** was apprenticed to Thomas Whieldon and in 1754 worked for William Banks in Stoke-on-Trent, Staffordshire, England. In the early 1760s, Spode started his own pottery, making cream-colored earthenware and blueprinted whiteware. In 1770, he returned to Banks' factory as master, purchasing it in 1776.

Spode pioneered the use of steam-powered, pottery-making machinery and mastered the art of transfer printing from copper plates. Spode opened a London shop in 1778 and sent William Copeland there in about 1784. A number of larger London locations followed. At the turn of the 18th century, Spode introduced bone china. In 1805, Josiah Spode II and William Copeland entered into a partnership for the London business. A series of partnerships between Josiah Spode II, Josiah Spode III and William Taylor Copeland resulted.

In 1833, Copeland acquired Spode's London operations and seven years later, the Stoke plants. William Taylor Copeland managed the business until his death in 1868. The firm remained in the hands of Copeland heirs. In 1923, the plant was electrified; other modernization followed.

In 1976, Spode merged with Worcester Royal Porcelain to become Royal Worcester Spode, Ltd.

Delftware is pottery with a soft, red-clay body and tin-enamel glaze. The white, dense, opaque color came from adding tin ash to lead glaze. The first examples had blue designs on a white ground. Polychrome examples followed.

The name originally applied to pottery made in the region around Delft, Holland, beginning in the 16th century and ending in the late 18th century. The tin used came from the Cornish mines in England. By the 17th and 18th centuries, English potters in London, Bristol and Liverpool were copying the glaze and designs. Some designs unique to English potters also developed.

Skinner Inc.

Plate, Delftware, England, 18th century, with polychrome decorated floral and bird designs, 11 3/4" diameter. **$444**

Augustus II, Elector of Saxony and King of Poland, founded the Royal Saxon Porcelain Manufactory in the Albrechtsburg, **Meissen**, in 1710. Johann Frederick Boettger, an alchemist, and Tschirnhaus, a nobleman, experimented with kaolin from the Dresden area to produce porcelain. By 1720, the factory produced a whiter, hard-paste porcelain than that from the Far East. The factory experienced its golden age from the 1730s to the 1750s under the leadership of Samuel Stolzel, kiln master, and Johann Gregor Herold, enameler.

The Meissen factory was destroyed and looted by forces of Frederick the Great during the Seven Years' War (1756-1763). It was reopened, but never achieved its former greatness.

In the 19th century, the factory reissued some of its earlier forms. These later wares are called "Dresden" to differentiate them from the earlier examples. There were several other porcelain factories in the Dresden region and their products also are grouped under the "Dresden" designation.

Many marks were used by the Meissen factory. The first was a pseudo-Oriental mark in a square. The famous crossed swords mark was adopted in 1724. A small dot between the hilts was used from 1763 to 1774, and a star between the hilts from 1774 to 1814. Two modern marks are swords with a hammer and sickle, and swords with a crown.

Gouda and the surrounding areas of Holland have been principal Dutch pottery centers for centuries. Originally, the potteries produced a simple utilitarian, tin-glazed Delft-type earthenware and the famous clay smoker's pipes.

When pipe making declined in the early 1900s, Gouda turned to art pottery. Influenced by the Art Nouveau and Art Deco movements, artists expressed themselves with freeform and stylized designs in bold colors.

In 1842, American china importer **David Haviland** moved to Limoges, France, where he began manufacturing and decorating china specifically for the U.S. market. Haviland is synonymous with fine, white, translucent porcelain, although early hand-painted patterns were generally larger and darker colored on heavier whiteware blanks than were later ones.

Haviland revolutionized French china factories by both manufacturing the whiteware blank and decorating it at the same site. In addition, Haviland and Company pioneered the use of decals in decorating china.

Haviland's sons, Charles Edward and Theodore, split the company in 1892. In 1936, Theodore opened an American division. In 1941, Theodore bought out Charles Edward's heirs and recombined both companies under the original name of H. and Company. The Haviland family sold the firm in 1981.

Charles Field Haviland, cousin of Charles Edward and Theodore, worked for and then, after his marriage in 1857, ran the Casseaux Works until 1882. Items continued to carry his name as decorator until 1941.

Thousands of Haviland patterns were made, but not consistently named until after 1926. The similarities in many of the patterns make identification difficult. Numbers assigned by Arlene Schleiger and illustrated in her books have become the identification standard.

Dresden/Meissen

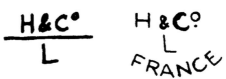

Gouda

Haviland

The **"KPM"** mark has been used separately and in conjunction with other symbols by many German porcelain manufacturers, among which are the Königliche Porzellan Manufactur in Meissen, 1720s; Königliche Porzellan Manufactur in Berlin, 1832-1847; and Krister Porzellan Manufactur in Waldenburg, mid-19th century.

Collectors now use the term KPM to refer to the high-quality porcelain produced in the Berlin area in the 18th and 19th centuries.

Creamware is a cream-colored earthenware created about 1750 by the potters of Staffordshire, England, which proved ideal for domestic ware. It was also known as "tortoiseshellware" or "Prattware" depending on the color of glaze used.

The most notable producer of creamware was Josiah Wedgwood. Around 1779, he was able to lighten the cream color to a bluish white and sold this product under the name "pearl ware." Wedgwood supplied his creamware to England's Queen Charlotte (1744-1818) and Russian Empress Catherine the Great (1729-1796), and used the trade name "Queen's ware."

The **Leeds Pottery** in Yorkshire, England, began production about 1758. Among its products was creamware that was competitive with that of Wedgwood. The original factory closed in 1820, but various subsequent owners continued until 1880. They made exceptional cream-colored ware, either plain, salt glazed or painted with colored enamels, and glazed and unglazed redware.

Leeds Pottery

Early wares are unmarked. Later pieces are marked "Leeds Pottery," sometimes followed by "Hartley-Green and Co." or the letters "LP."

Liverpool is the name given to products made at several potteries in Liverpool, England, between 1750 and 1840. Seth and James Pennington and Richard Chaffers were among the early potters who made tin-enameled earthenware.

By the 1780s, tin-glazed earthenware gave way to cream-colored wares decorated with cobalt blue, enameled colors and blue or black transfers.

Bubbles and frequent clouding under the foot rims characterize the Liverpool glaze. By 1800, about 80 potteries were working in the town producing not only creamware, but soft paste, soapstone and bone porcelain.

The reproduction pieces have a crackled glaze and often age cracks have been artificially produced. When compared to genuine pieces, reproductions are thicker and heavier and have weaker transfers, grayish color (not as crisp and black), ecru or gray body color instead of cream, and crazing that does not spiral upward.

Skinner Inc.

Coffeepot and cover, creamware, England, circa 1780, attributed to Liverpool, pear shape with black transfer "tea party" and "shepherd" prints, strap handle and ball knop, 10" high. **$355**

In 1793, **Thomas Minton** joined other entrepreneurs and formed a partnership to build a small pottery at Stoke-on-Trent, Staffordshire, England. Production began in 1798 with blueprinted earthenware, mostly in the Willow pattern. In 1798, cream-colored earthenware and bone china were introduced.

Minton

A wide range of styles and wares was produced. Minton introduced porcelain figures in 1826, Parian wares in 1846, encaustic tiles in the late 1840s, and majolica wares in 1850. In 1883, the modern company was formed and called Mintons Limited. The "s" was dropped in 1968.

Many early pieces are unmarked or have a Sevres-type marking. The "ermine" mark was used in the early 19th century. Date codes can be found on tableware and majolica. The mark used between 1873 and 1911 was a small globe with a crown on top and the word "Minton."

Mocha decoration usually is found on utilitarian creamware and stoneware pieces and was produced through a simple chemical action. A color pigment of brown, blue, green or black was made acidic by an infusion of tobacco or hops. When the acidic colorant was applied in blobs to an alkaline ground, it reacted by spreading in feathery designs resembling sea plants. This type of decoration usually was supplemented with bands of light-colored slip.

Types of decoration vary greatly, from those done in a combination of motifs, such as Cat's Eye and Earthworm, to a plain pink mug decorated with green ribbed bands. Most forms of mocha are hollow, e.g., mugs, jugs, bowls and shakers.

English potters made the vast majority of the pieces. Collectors group the wares into three chronological periods: 1780-1820, 1820-1840 and 1840-1880.

William Moorcroft was first employed as a potter by James Macintyre & Company Ltd. of Burslem, Staffordshire, England, in 1897. He established the Moorcroft pottery in 1913.

The majority of the art pottery wares were hand thrown, resulting in a great variation among similarly styled pieces. Colors and marks are keys to determining age.

Walter Moorcroft, William's son, continued the business upon his father's death and made wares in the same style.

The company initially used an impressed mark, "Moorcroft, Burslem;" a signature mark, "W. Moorcroft," followed. Modern pieces are marked simply "Moorcroft," with export pieces also marked "Made in England."

Sanford Alderfer Auction & Appraisal

Bowl, Moorcroft, china with fruit motif, grapevine and leaves in blue, purple and yellow on green ground, 8 3/4" diameter, 2 3/4" high. **$184**

Moorcroft

In 1794, the **Royal Bayreuth** factory was founded in Tettau, Bavaria. Royal Bayreuth introduced its figural patterns in 1885. Designs of animals, people, fruits and vegetables decorated a wide array of tableware and inexpensive souvenir items.

Tapestry wares, in rose and other patterns, were made in the late 19th century. The surface of the pieces feel and look like woven cloth.

The Royal Bayreuth crest used to mark the wares varied in design and color.

Royal Bayreuth

Derby Crown Porcelain Company, established in 1875 in Derby, England, had no connection with earlier Derby factories that operated in the late 18th and early 19th centuries. In 1890, the company was appointed "Manufacturers of Porcelain to Her Majesty" (Queen Victoria) and since that date has been known as "Royal Crown Derby."

Most of these porcelains, both tableware and figural, were hand decorated. A variety of printing processes were used for additional adornment.

Derby porcelains from 1878 to 1890 carry only the standard crown printed mark. After 1891, the mark includes the "Royal Crown Derby" wording. In the 20th century, "Made in England" and "English Bone China" were added to the mark.

Skinner Inc.

Royal Crown Derby bone china cockerel, England, circa 1952, polychrome enamel decorated, modeled standing on a tree stump, printed mark, 11 3/4". **$207**

Doulton pottery began in 1815 under the direction of John Doulton at the Doulton & Watts pottery in Lambeth, England. Early output was limited to salt-glazed industrial stoneware. After John Watts retired in 1854, the firm became Doulton and Company, and production was expanded to include hand-decorated stoneware such as figurines, vases, dinnerware and flasks.

ROYAL
DOULTON
FLAMBE

Royal Doulton

In 1878, Doulton's son, Sir Henry Doulton, purchased Pinder Bourne & Company in Burslem, Staffordshire. The companies became Doulton & Company, Ltd. in 1882. Decorated porcelain was added to Doulton's earthenware production in 1884.

Most Doulton figurines were produced at the Burslem plants, where they were made continuously from 1890 until 1978. After a short interruption, a new line of Doulton figurines was introduced in 1979.

Dickensware, in earthenware and porcelain, was introduced in 1908. The pieces were decorated with characters from Dickens' novels. Most of the line was withdrawn in the 1940s, except for plates, which continued to be made until 1974.

Character jugs, a 20th-century revival of early Toby models, were designed by Charles J. Noke for Doulton in the 1930s. Character jugs are limited to bust portraits, while Royal Doulton Toby jugs are full figured. The character jugs come in four sizes and feature fictional characters from Dickens, Shakespeare and other English and American novelists, as well as historical heroes. Marks on both character and Toby jugs must be carefully identified to determine dates and values.

Doulton's Rouge Flambé (Veined Sung) is a high-glazed, strong-colored ware.

Production of stoneware at Lambeth ceased in 1956.

Beginning in 1872, the "Royal Doulton" mark was used on all types of wares produced by the company.

Beginning in 1913, an "HN" number was assigned to each new Doulton figurine design. The "HN" numbers, which referred originally to Harry Nixon, a Doulton artist, were chronological until 1940, after which blocks of numbers were assigned to each modeler. From 1928 until 1954, a small number was placed to the right of the crown mark; this number, when added to 1927, gives the year of manufacture.

In 1751, the **Worcester Porcelain Company**, led by Dr. John Wall and William Davis, acquired the Bristol pottery of Benjamin Lund and moved it to Worcester. The first wares were painted blue under the glaze; soon thereafter decorating was accomplished by painting on the glaze in enamel colors. Among the most-famous 18th-century decorators were James Giles and Jeffery Hamet O'Neal. Transfer-print decoration was developed by the 1760s.

A series of partnerships took place after Davis' death in 1783: Flight (1783-1793); Flight & Barr (1793-1807); Barr, Flight & Barr (1807-1813); and Flight, Barr & Barr (1813-1840). In 1840, the factory was moved to Chamberlain & Company in Diglis, Worcester. Decorative wares were discontinued. In 1852, W.H. Kerr and R.W. Binns formed a new company and revived the production of ornamental wares.

In 1862, the firm became the Royal Worcester Porcelain Company. Among the key modelers of the late 19th century were James Hadley, his three sons, and George Owen, an expert with pierced clay pieces. Royal Worcester absorbed the Grainger factory in 1889 and the James Hadley factory in 1905. Modern designers include Dorothy Doughty and Doris Lindner.

The principal patron of the French porcelain industry in early 18th-century France was Jeanne Antoinette Poisson, Marquise de Pompadour. She supported the Vincennes factory of Gilles and Robert Dubois and their successors in their attempt to make soft-paste porcelain in the 1740s. In 1753, she moved the porcelain operations to Sevres, near her home, Chateau de Bellevue.

The **Sevres** soft-paste formula used sand from Fontainebleau, salt, saltpeter, soda of Alicante, powdered alabaster, clay and soap.

In 1769, kaolin was discovered in France, and a hard-paste formula was developed. The baroque designs gave way to rococo, a style favored by Jeanne du Barry, Louis XV's next mistress. Louis XVI took little interest in Sevres, and many factories began to turn out counterfeits. In 1876, the factory was moved to St. Cloud and was eventually nationalized.

Louis XV allowed the firm to use the "double L" in its marks.

Spatterware generally was made of common earthenware, although occasionally creamware was used. The earliest English examples were made about 1780. The peak period of production was from 1810 to 1840. Firms known to have made spatterware are Adams, Barlow, and Harvey and Cotton.

The amount of spatter decoration varies from piece to piece. Some objects simply have decorated borders. These often were decorated with a brush, requiring several hundred touches per square inch to achieve the spatter effect. Other pieces have the entire surface covered with spatter. Marked pieces are rare.

Collectors today focus on the patterns—Cannon, Castle, Fort, Peafowl, Rainbow, Rose, Thistle, Schoolhouse, etc. The decoration on flatware is in the center of the piece; on hollow ware, it occurs on both sides.

Aesthetics and the colors of spatter are key to determining value. Blue and red are the most common colors; green, purple, and brown are in a middle group; black and yellow are scarce.

In 1754, Josiah **Wedgwood** and Thomas Whieldon of Fenton Vivian, Staffordshire, England, became partners in a pottery enterprise. Their products included marbled, agate, tortoiseshell, green glaze and Egyptian black wares. In 1759, Wedgwood opened his own pottery at the Ivy House works, Burslem, Staffordshire. In 1764, he moved to the Brick House (Bell Works) at Burslem. The pottery concentrated on utilitarian pieces.

Wedgwood

Between 1766 and 1769, Wedgwood built the famous works at Etruria. Among the most-renowned products of this plant were the Empress Catherine of Russia dinner service (1774) and the Portland Vase (1790s). The firm also made caneware, unglazed earthenwares (drabwares), piecrust wares, variegated and marbled wares, black basalt (developed in 1768), Queen's or creamware, and Jasperware (perfected in 1774).

Skinner Inc.

Wedgwood solid black Jasper Dancing Hours bowl, England, 20th century, applied white classical relief with running laurel border above figures, impressed mark, 7" diameter. **$119**

Bone china was produced under the direction of Josiah Wedgwood II between 1812 and 1822 and revived in 1878. Moonlight Luster was made from 1805 to 1815. Fairyland Luster began in 1920. All luster production ended in 1932.

A museum was established at the Etruria pottery in 1906. When Wedgwood moved to its modern plant at Barlaston, North Staffordshire, the museum was expanded.

Vilmos Zsolnay (1828-1900) assumed control of his brother's factory in Pécs, Hungary, in the mid-19th century. In 1899, Miklos, Vilmos' son, became manager. The firm still produces ceramic ware.

Zsolnay Pottery

The early wares are highly ornamental, glazed and have a cream-colored ground. Eosin glaze, a deep, rich play of colors reminiscent of Tiffany's iridescent wares, received a gold medal at the 1900 Paris exhibition.

Originally, no trademark was used, but in 1878 the company began to use a blue mark depicting the five towers of the cathedral at Pécs. The initials "TJM" represent the names of Miklos' three children.

Clarice Cliff

Clarice Cliff was a designer for A.J. Wilinson, Ltd., Royal Staffordshire Pottery, Burslem, England, when it acquired the adjoining Newport Pottery Company, whose warehouses were filled with undecorated bowls and vases. In about 1925, Cliff's flair with the Art Deco style was incorporated into designs appropriately named "Bizarre" and "Fantasque," and the warehouse stockpile was decorated in vivid colors. These hand-painted earthenwares, all bearing the printed signature of designer Clarice Cliff, were produced until World War II and find enormous favor with collectors.

Note: Reproductions of the Clarice Cliff "Bizarre" marking appear on the market occasionally.

Skinner, Inc.

Bizarre ware vase, England, 20th century, Wilkinson Ltd., Rhodanthe pattern, baluster shape, backstamp, 10 5/8" high. **$593**

Skinner, Inc.

Bizarre ware charger, England, 20th century, Wilkinson Ltd., Rhodanthe pattern, backstamp, 18" diameter. **$652**

Skinner, Inc.

Bowl, England, 20th century, Wilkinson Ltd., Rhodanthe pattern, backstamp, 8 1/2" diameter. **$296**

Skinner, Inc.

Fantasque ware vase, England, 20th century, Wilkinson Ltd., Brown Lily pattern with polychrome banding, shape 269, backstamp, 5 7/8". **$415**

Skinner, Inc.

Wall pocket, England, 20th century, Newport Pottery Company, female nymph with flowers in her hair, with backstamp, 9" high. **$296**

Skinner, Inc.

Bizarre ware covered pot, England, 20th century, Newport Pottery Company, Delecia pattern with pansies, shape 335, wicker handle, backstamp, 6 1/4" diameter. **$385**

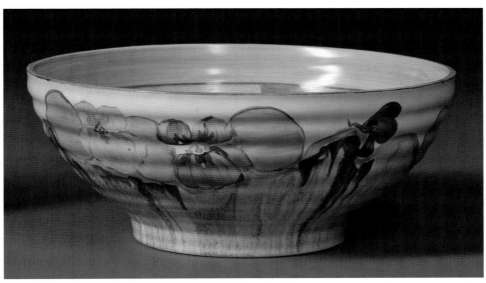

Skinner, Inc.

Bizarre ware bowl, England, 20th century, Newport Pottery Company, Delecia pattern with pansies and ribbed sides, backstamp, 9 1/4" diameter. **$296**

Skinner, Inc.

Two Bizarre ware jugs, England, 20th century, Wilkinson Ltd., each Aurea pattern to ribbed body, one Lotus form, 9 7/8" high, the other with spout, base with raised "563 GREEK," 9" high; each with backstamp. **$444**

Skinner, Inc.

Bizarre ware vase, England, 20th century, Newport Pottery Company, tulip-form, polychrome geometric pattern, shape 361, backstamp, 8 1/4" high. **$652**

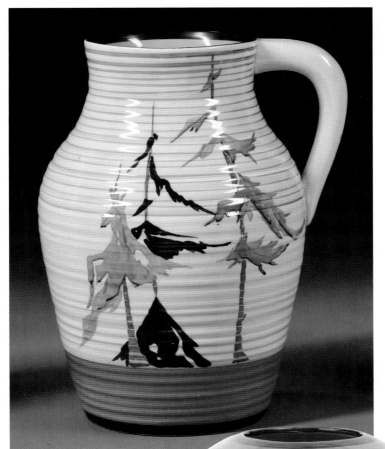

Skinner, Inc.

Bizarre ware Lotus Jug, England, 20th century, Wilkinson Ltd., ribbed body, Pine Grove pattern, backstamp and hand-painted blue "S," 11 3/8" high. **$1,126**

Bonhams

Moonlight vase, shape 370, printed factory marks, 6 1/2" high, 6 1/2" diameter. **$1,188**

Skinner, Inc.

Bizarre ware vase, England, 20th century, Newport Pottery Company, baluster-form with molded decoration and matte glaze in pastel colors, shape 390, backstamp, 8 1/2" high. **$326**

Bonhams

House and Bridge tea set, Stamford teapot, sugar bowl (restored) and creamer, two teacups and a saucer, printed marks, teapot 4 1/2" high x 5" wide x 3" deep. **$2,250**

Skinner, Inc.

Planter, England, 20th century, Wilkinson Ltd., Woodland pattern, three shaped feet, backstamp, 7 1/2" diameter. **$365**

Skinner, Inc.

Bizarre ware jug and coffeepot, England, 20th century, Wilkinson Ltd., each decorated with the Aurea pattern to a ribbed body, jug, 8 7/8" high, Lynton shape coffeepot, 7 1/2" high, each with backstamp, jug with raised "563 GREEK" to base. **$459**

Skinner, Inc.

Bowl and vase, England, 20th century, Newport and Wilkinson potteries, Bizarre ware bowl in Delecia pattern, shape 636, 8" diameter; flared vase, polychrome enameled with landscape, spreading foot, 9" high; each with backstamp. **$356**

Skinner, Inc.

Wall hanging, England, 20th century, female head adorned with flowers, designer's signature on reverse, 6 5/8". **$243**

Skinner, Inc.

Bizarre ware vase, England, 20th century, Newport Pottery Company, slightly tapered and ribbed body, Goldstone pattern with gilt and black spheres and fine gilt banding, shape 630 L/S, backstamp, 8" high. **$237**

Skinner, Inc.

Fantasque ware vase, England, 20th century, Wilkinson Ltd., frieze-decorated in Broth pattern with green, red, and black banding, shape 194, backstamp, 11" high. **$1,304**

Skinner, Inc.

Bizarre ware bowl, England, 20th century, Newport and Wilkinson potteries, green band to rim and interior with polychrome design of flowerheads and tree, three feet, backstamps for both firms, 7" diameter. **$326**

Skinner, Inc.

Bizarre ware vase, England, 20th century, Wilkinson Ltd., Aurea pattern, shape 362, backstamp, 8" high. **$474**

Skinner, Inc.

Bizarre ware bowl, England, 20th century, Wilkinson Ltd., ribbed body decorated with polychrome landscape dotted with cottages, shape 633, backstamp, 9 1/4" diameter. **$296**

Skinner, Inc.

Two figural condiment servers, England, 20th century, Newport Pottery Company, shaker on spreading foot, painted as a sailor, 3 3/8" high; jam pot with handle modeled as a human head and further decorated with polychrome banding, 4 3/8" high; each with backstamp. **$563**

Skinner, Inc.

Brangwyn Panels commemorative charger, England, 20th century, Wilkinson Ltd., depicting a scene with world peoples and animals in jungle setting, reverse with hand-painted inscription "The Brangwyn Panels Designed For the Royal Gallery of the House of Lords 1925 First Exhibited at Olympia 1933. Painted By Clarice Cliff From One of the Panels. A Wilkinson Ad. Royal Staffordshire. Pottery. Burslem Staffordshire," with Frank Brangwyn's monogram and signature, 17 1/4" diameter. **$2,963**

KPM

BY MELODY AMSEL-ARIELI

KPM plaques are highly glazed, enamel paintings on porcelain bases that were produced by Konigliche Porzellan Manufaktur (KPM), the King's Porcelain Factory, in Berlin, Germany, between 1880 and 1901.

Their secret, according to Afshine Emrani, dealer and appraiser at www.some-of-my-favorite-things.com, is KPM's highly superior, smooth, hard paste porcelain, which could be fired at very high temperatures.

"The magic of a KPM plaque is that it will look as crisp and beautiful 100 years from now as it does today," he said. Even when they were introduced, these plaques proved highly collectible, with art lovers, collectors, tourists, and the wealthy acquiring them for extravagant sums.

KPM rarely marketed painted porcelain plaques itself, however. Instead, it usually supplied white, undecorated ones to independent artists who specialized in this genre. Not all artists signed their KPM paintings, however.

While most KPM plaques were copies of famous paintings, some, commissioned by wealthy Americans and Europeans in the 1920s, bear images of actual people in contemporary clothing. These least collectible of KPM plaques command between $500 and $1,500 each, depending on the attractiveness of their subjects.

KPM marks

Gilded, hand-painted plaques featuring Middle Eastern or female Gypsy subjects and bearing round red "Made in Germany" stamps were produced just before and after World War I for export. They command between $500 and $2,000 each. Plaques portraying religious subjects, such as the Virgin Mary or the Flight into Egypt, command higher prices but are less popular.

Popular scenes of hunters, merrymakers, musicians, etc., generally fetch less than $10,000 apiece because they have been reproduced time and again. Rarer, more elaborate scenes, however, like "The Dance Lesson" and "Turkish Card Players," may be worth many times more.

Highly stylized portraits copied from famous paintings–especially those of attractive children or décolleté women–allowed art lovers to own their own "masterpieces." These are currently worth between $2,000 and $20,000 each. Romanticized portrayals of cupids and women in the nude, the most desirable KPMs subjects of all, currently sell for up to $40,000 each. Portraits of men, it must be noted, are not only less popular, but also less expensive.

Size also matters. A 4" x 6" inch plaque, whose subject has been repeatedly reproduced, may sell for a few thousand dollars. Larger ones that portray the same subject will fetch proportionately more. A "Sistine Madonna" plaque, fashioned after the original work by Rafael and measuring 10" x 7 1/2", might cost $4,200. One featuring the identical subject, but measuring 15" x 11", might cost $7,800. A larger plaque, measuring 22" x 16", might command twice that price.

The largest KPM plaques, measuring 22" x 26", for example, often burst during production.

MELODY AMSEI-ARIELI *is a freelance writer and frequent contributor to* Antique Trader. *She is the author of* Between Galicia and Hungary: The Jews of Stropkov, *as well as* Jewish Lives: Britain 1750-1950 *(Pen & Sword, 2013). She lives in Israel.*

Although no formula exists for determining prices of those that have survived, Afshine Emrani said that each may sell for as much as $250,000. Rare plaques like these are often found in museums.

The condition of a KPM plaque also affects its price. Most, since they were highly glazed and customarily hung instead of handled, have survived in perfect condition. Thus those that have sustained even minor damage, like scratches, cracks, or chips, fetch considerably lower prices. Those suffering major damage are worthless.

KPMs painted plaques arouse so much interest and command such high prices that, over the last couple of years, unscrupulous dealers have entered the market. According to dealer Balazs Benedek, KPM plaques are "the mother of all fakes. About 90 percent of KPM plaques are mid- to late-20th century reproductions. And about 70 percent are not hand painted."

Collectors should be aware that genuine KPM paintings always boast rich, shiny, glazes that preserve their colors, and though subject matter may vary, they typically feature nude scenes, indoor portraits of women, or group gatherings in lush settings. Anything wildly different should raise suspicion.

Genuine KPMs, on their backs or edges, feature small icons of scepters deeply set in the porcelain, over the letters KPM. These marks are sometimes accompanied by an "H" or some other letter, which may indicate their production date or size. Some are imprinted with the size of the plaque as well, which facilitated sorting or shipping. Shallow or crooked imprints may reveal a fake.

John Moran Auctioneers, Inc.

Porcelain vase with circular rim above scrolled handles entwined with serpents, elongated tapering body decorated with a frieze of mythological figures over a socle entwined with a serpent on a circular base raised on paw feet; underglaze blue scepter mark and overglaze blue beehive mark to underside; late 19th/early 20th century, 20 1/2" high x 5 3/4" diameter. **$3,000**

John Moran Auctioneers, Inc.

Porcelain plaque "Clementine" depicting an auburn-haired beauty adorned with sprigs of clementine leaves, after Conrad Kiesel (1846-1921, German); impressed KPM and scepter mark and incised "315-255" with a symbol, signed lower right "L. Schinzel"; late 19th century, 12 1/2" high x 10" wide, Italian Rococo-style carved gilt wood frame, overall 20 3/4" high x 15 3/4" wide x 3 3/4" deep. **$16,000**

John Moran Auctioneers, Inc.

Porcelain plaque depicting a female nude hovering over a moonlit lake holding a torch; unmarked, signed lower right "J. Sch./XR" with handwritten inscription verso, "Painted in the studio by J. Schumacher"; late 19th century, 11 3/4" high x 8 3/4" wide. Provenance: Collection of the estate of a resident of Artist Alley, Champion Place, Alhambra, California, prior to the 1960s. **$4,250**

John Moran Auctioneers, Inc.

Two plaques, each titled verso, the first "Medea" after N. Sichel (Nathaniel Sichel, 1843-1907, German), the second "L'esclave" (The Slave) after de Chatillon (Joseph de Chatillon, 1808-1881, American); unsigned, each with impressed "KPM" and scepter mark; late 19th/early 20th century, each 9 1/4" high x 6 1/2" wide, wooden frame with old trade label verso, each overall 14 1/2" high x 11 1/2" wide. **$4,250**

John Moran Auctioneers, Inc.

Plaque depicting a bearded man; impressed KPM and scepter mark, also incised "12. 9 3/4," signed "Horn" lower right; late 19th/ early 20th century, carved painted wooden frame, 12 1/2" high x 10 1/2" wide. **$1,600**

Skinner, Inc.

Porcelain plaque of Lorelei, painted after Willhelm Kray (1828-1889), the winged beauty in diaphanous drapery and seated on a ledge in a misty landscape; unsigned, impressed monogram and scepter mark; late 19th/early 20th century, framed, sight size 15 1/4" x 9 7/8". **$13,000**

Skinner, Inc.

Porcelain pate-sur-pate charger of a seated Venus scribing in a book supported by Cupid, on rose ground with cream border and gilt accents; signed "E. Dietrich" with blue scepter and red globus cruciger marks; third quarter 19th century, approximately 13 1/2" diameter, framed.
$10,000

Heritage Auctions, Inc.

Framed porcelain plaque by Franz Till, hand-painted decoration of a boy in a white gown; marks: (scepter) KPM, S, Fr. Till, Dresden; circa 1900, 6 1/2" high x 3 3/4" wide, frame 13" x 10 1/2".
$594

Heritage Auctions, Inc.

Framed rectangular porcelain plaque by Franz Till, hand-painted decoration of a young girl holding a "catch the ball" toy; marks: (scepter) KPM, S, Fr. Till, Dresden; circa 1900, 6 1/2" high x 3 3/4" wide, frame 13" x 10 1/2". **$813**

Courtesy of Bonhams

A KPM Berlin porcelain mantel clock, underglaze blue scepter mark, red factory mark and black iron cross stamp, 21 1/2" high, 31" wide, 9 1/2" deep. **$27,500.**

Skinner, Inc.

KPM Porcelain Portrait Plaque of a Woman, 19th century, the woman in a purple dress seated in a Victorian-style interior, impressed mark to base, 10 3/4" high, 8 7/8" wide. **$1,185**

Heritage Auctions, Inc.

Framed porcelain plaque depicting Ruth after Charles Landelle (French, 1821-1908); marks: impressed (scepter over KPM), S, 33, 20, original paper labels to reverse inscribed Kunst Institut Fur Porzellan-Malerai, Merkel-Heine, Wiesbaden, and 1119, Ruth by Landelle; circa 1900, 13" x 7 7/8", frame 22 1/4" x 20 1/4" wide. **$2,750**

Heritage Auctions, Inc.

Framed rectangular porcelain plaque by Ludwig Sturm, hand-painted decoration of nude female nymph with fish skin chased by a raven; signed L. Sturm, marks: (scepter) KPM, high, F; circa 1890, 14" x 8 7/8", frame 15 3/8" x 10 1/8". **$8,125**

Heritage Auctions, Inc.

Framed rectangular porcelain plaque with hand-painted decoration of young woman in Renaissance dress kneeling in prayer; marks: (scepter) KPM, C; circa 1890, 8 1/2" x 6", gilt wood and velvet frame 18 1/8" x 16 1/8". **$3,585**

Heritage Auctions, Inc.

Framed porcelain plaque depicting Bussende Magdalen after the painting by Correggio (Italian, 1489-1534); marks: lower right front: AH (conjoined), impressed marks to reverse: (scepter) KPM, high; circa 1890, 8 3/4" high x 10 7/8" wide, frame 11 1/8" x 13 1/4". **$2,625**

Heritage Auctions, Inc.

Framed porcelain plaque, "Grape and Melon Eaters" after Bartome Murillo; marks: (scepter) KPM, high; circa 1900, 11 1/2" x 9 1/2", frame 19 3/4" x 17 1/2". **$1,912**

Heritage Auctions, Inc.

Framed porcelain plaque, Ruth after Landelle; marks: (scepter) KPM, high, signed Kronller; circa 1900, 12 1/2" x 7 3/8", gilt wood frame 19 1/4" x 14 1/2". **$2,390**

Heritage Auctions, Inc.

Framed porcelain plaque of a man smoking a pipe; marks: (scepter) KPM, paper label reading 911 Rauchez; circa 1880-1900, 7 5/8" x 5 3/8", carved gilt frame 13" high x 10 3/4" wide. **$2,510**

Neal Auction Company of New Orleans

Oval porcelain plaque, impressed scepter and KPM marks; late 19th century, 16 3/4" high. **$2,750**

Skinner, Inc.

KPM Porcelain plaque of the Virgin Mother and Christ Child, Germany, 19th century, oval, depicting mother and child on a blue enamel and gilt-star background, with impressed factory mark to back, in velvet lining and gilt frame, 7" high (sight), 5" wide. Losses to gilt frame, plaque not examined outside of frame or velvet lining. **$365**

Heritage Auctions, Inc.

Framed plaque, "The Young Jesus"; late 19th century, 8 1/2" x 6 1/4", frame 15" high. **$2,987**

Heritage Auctions, Inc.

Rectangular porcelain plaque with hand-painted decoration of a self-portrait of artist Louise-Elisabeth Vigee Le Brun after the original painting; marks: KPM scepter; circa 1900, 7" by 5 1/8", gilt frame 11 1/2" by 9 1/2". **$3,500**

Heritage Auctions, Inc.

Framed rectangular plaque with hand-painted decoration of the Three Muses crossing a river into the forest; marks: (scepter) KPM, h, L, 275 223; circa 1890, 10 3/8" x 8 1/2", gilt wood frame 16 1/2" x 14 5/8". **$13,145**

Heritage Auctions, Inc.

*Framed rectangular
porcelain plaque
with hand-painted
decoration of a
young classically
dressed woman
feeding pigeons;
marks: (scepter)
KPM; circa 1890,
7 1/4" x 5", metal
and enamel frame
11" x 8 1/5".* **$4,481**

Heritage Auctions, Inc.

*Framed plaque,
"Othello Pleading
Before the Doge,"
depicts Othello
pleading before the
chief magistrate of
Venice or Genoa
and Brabantio,
Desdemona at his
side, member of the
Senate looking on;
signed "C. Hen" in
lower right, which is
unusual since most
KPM art was not
signed; circa 1900.*
$11,950

Heritage Auctions, Inc.

Porcelain plaque depicting three nymphs, one seated on a chariot pulled by winged cherubs, and another about to be shot by Cupid; marks: (scepter) K.P.M., J, J, 315, 255; late 19th century, 10 1/8" x 12 3/4". **$7,768**

Heritage Auctions, Inc.

Oval porcelain plaque with hand-painted decoration of a young shrouded woman looking upward; marks: (scepter) KPM, K; circa 1890, 8 7/8" x 6 1/2". **$2,330**

Majolica

In 1851, an English potter was hoping that his new interpretation of a centuries-old style of ceramics would be well received at the "Great Exhibition of the Industries of All Nations" set to open May 1 in London's Hyde Park.

Potter Herbert Minton had high hopes for his display. His father, Thomas Minton, founded a pottery works in the mid-1790s in Stoke-on-Trent, Staffordshire. Herbert Minton had designed a "new" line of pottery, and his chemist, Leon Arnoux, had developed a process that resulted in vibrant, colorful glazes that came to be called "majolica."

Trained as an engineer, Arnoux also studied the making of encaustic tiles, and had been appointed art director at Minton's works in 1848. His job was to introduce and promote new products. Victorian fascination with the natural world prompted Arnoux to reintroduce the work of Bernard Palissy, whose naturalistic, bright-colored "maiolica" wares had been created in the 16th century. But Arnoux used a thicker body to make pieces sturdier. This body was given a coating of opaque white glaze, which provided a surface for decoration.

Pieces were modeled in high relief, featuring butterflies and other insects, flowers and leaves, fruit, shells, animals and fish. Queen Victoria's endorsement of the new pottery prompted its acceptance by the general public.

When Minton introduced his wares at Philadelphia's 1876 Centennial Exhibition, American potters also began to produce majolica.

For more information on majolica, see *Warman's Majolica Identification and Price Guide* by Mark F. Moran.

Thirty-six-piece set of German turquoise bird and grape pieces including cake stand, platters, bowls, plates, cups, saucers. **$400+ all**

Other Majolica Makers

John Adams & Company, Hanley, Stoke-on-Trent, Staffordshire, England, operated the Victoria Works, producing earthenware, jasperware, Parian, majolica, 1864-1873. (Collector's tip: Jasperware is a fine white stoneware originally produced by Josiah Wedgwood, often colored by metallic oxides with raised classical designs remaining white.)

Another Staffordshire pottery, **Samuel Alcock & Company**, Cobridge, 1828-1853; Burslem, 1830-1859, produced earthenware, china and Parian.

The **W. & J.A. Bailey Alloa Pottery** was founded in Alloa, the principal town in Clackmannanshire, located near Edinburgh, Scotland.

The **Bevington** family of potters worked in Hanley, Staffordshire, England in the late 19th century.

W. Brownfield & Son operated in Burslem and Cobridge, Staffordshire, England from 1850-1891.

T.C. Brown-Westhead, Moore & Company produced earthenware and porcelain at Hanley, Stoke-on-Trent, Staffordshire, from about 1862 to 1904.

The **Choisy-le-Roi** faience factory of Choisy-le-Roi, France, produced majolica from 1860 until 1910. The firm's wares are not always marked. The common mark is usually a black ink stamp "Choisy-le-Roi" pictured to the right with a large "HBm," which stands for Hippolyte Boulenger, a director at the pottery.

William T. Copeland & Sons pottery of Stoke-on-Trent, Staffordshire, England, began producing porcelain and earthenware in 1847. (Josiah Spode established a pottery at Stoke-on-Trent in 1770. In 1833, the firm was purchased by William Copeland and Thomas Garrett. In 1847, Copeland became the sole owner. W.T. Copeland & Sons continued until a 1976 merger when it became Royal Worcester Spode. Copeland majolica pieces are sometimes marked with an impressed "COPELAND," but many are unmarked.)

Jose A. Cunha, Caldas da Rainha, southern Portugal, also worked in the style of Bernard Palissy, the great French Renaissance potter.

Julius Dressler, Bela Czech Republic, was founded 1888, producing faience, majolica and porcelain. In 1920, the name was changed to EPIAG. The firm closed about 1945.

Eureka Pottery was located in Trenton, N.J., circa 1883-1887.

Railway Pottery was established by S. Fielding & Company, Stoke, Stoke-on-Trent, Staffordshire, England, 1879.

There were two **Thomas Forester** potteries active in the late 19th century in Staffordshire, England. Some sources list the more famous of the two as Thomas Forester & Sons Ltd. at the Phoenix Works, Longton.

Established in the early 19th century, the **Gien** pottery works is located on the banks of France's Loire River near Orleans.

Joseph Holdcroft majolica ware was produced at Daisy Bank in Longton, Staffordshire, England, from 1870 to 1885. Items can be found marked with "J HOLDCROFT," but many pieces can only be attributed by the patterns and colors that are documented to have come from the Holdcroft potteries.

George Jones & Sons Ltd., Stoke, Staffordshire, started operation in about 1864 as George Jones and in 1873 became George Jones & Sons Ltd. The firm operated the Trent Potteries in Stoke-on-Trent (renamed "Crescent Potteries" in about 1907).

In about 1877, **Samuel Lear** erected a small china works in Hanley, Staffordshire. Lear produced domestic china and, in addition, decorated all kinds of earthenware made by other

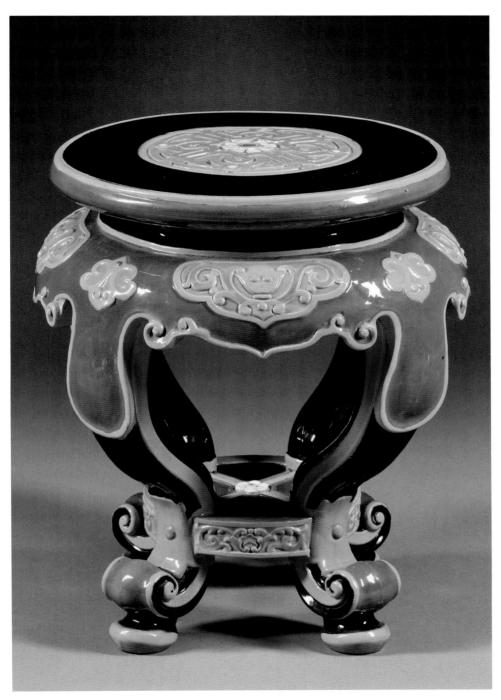

Skinner, Inc.

Minton garden seat, England, date cipher for 1867, circular seat with central medallion over shaped apron and four scrolled cabriole legs joined by circular stretcher, pad feet, impressed factory and cipher marks, 18 1/2" high. **$2,015**

manufacturers, including "spirit kegs." In 1882, the firm expanded to include production of majolica, ivory-body earthenware and Wedgwood-type jasperware. The business closed in 1886.

Robert Charbonnier founded the **Longchamp** tile works in 1847 to make red clay tiles, but the factory soon started to produce majolica. Longchamp is known for its "barbotine" pieces (a paste of clay used in decorating coarse pottery in relief) made with vivid colors, especially oyster plates.

Hugo Lonitz operated in Haldensleben, Germany, from 1868-1886, and later Hugo Lonitz & Company, 1886-1904, producing household and decorative porcelain, earthenware and metalwares. Look for a mark of two entwined fish.

The **Lunéville** pottery was founded about 1728 by Jacques Chambrette in the city that bears its name, in the Alsace-Lorraine region of northeastern France. The firm became famous for its blue monochromatic and floral patterns. Around 1750, ceramist Paul-Louis Cyfflé introduced a pattern with animals and historical figures. Lunéville products range from hand-painted faience and majolica to pieces influenced by the Art Deco movement.

The **Massier** family began producing ceramics in Vallauris, France, in the mid-18th century.

Skinner, Inc.

Pair of Minton cherubs on seahorses, England, date cipher for 1863, each modeled as a cherub holding a shell-form vase aloft while riding a seahorse, ovoid base, impressed marks to both, 17" high. **$11,850**

François Maurice, School of Paris, was active from 1875-1885 and also worked in the style of Bernard Palissy.

George Morley & Company was located in East Liverpool, Ohio, 1884-1891.

Morley & Company Pottery was founded in 1879, Wellsville, Ohio, making graniteware and majolica.

Orchies, a majolica manufacturer in northern France near Lille, is also known under the mark "Moulin des Loups & Hamage," 1920s.

Faïencerie de Pornic is located near Quimper, France.

Quimper pottery has a long history. Tin-glazed, hand-painted pottery has been made in Quimper, France, since the late 17th century. The earliest firm, founded in 1685 by Jean Baptiste Bousquet, was known as HB Quimper. Another firm, founded in 1772 by Francois Eloury, was known as Porquier. A third firm, founded by Guillaume Dumaine in 1778, was known as HR or Henriot Quimper. All three companies made similar pottery decorated with designs of Breton peasants, and sea and flower motifs.

The **Rörstrand** factory made the first faience (tin-glazed earthenware) produced in Sweden. It was established in 1725 by Johann Wolff, near Stockholm.

The earthenware factory of **Salins** was established in 1857 in Salins-les-Bains, near the French border with Switzerland. Salins was awarded with the gold medal at the International Exhibition of Decorative Arts in Paris in 1912.

Sarreguemines wares are named for the city in the Lorraine region of northeastern France. The pottery was founded in 1790 by Nicholas-Henri Jacobi. For more than 100 years, it flourished under the direction of the Utzschneider family.

Wilhelm Schiller and Sons, Bodenbach, Bohemia, was established 1885.

Thomas-Victor Sergent was one of the School of Paris ceramists of the late 19th century who was influenced by the works of Bernard Palissy.

St. Clement was founded by Jacques Chambrette in Saint-Clément, France, in 1758. Chambrette also established works in Lunéville.

The **St. Jean de Bretagne** pottery works are located near Quimper, France.

Vallauris is a pottery center in southeastern France, near Cannes. Companies in production there include Massier and Foucard-Jourdan.

Victoria Pottery Company was located in Hanley, Staffordshire, England from 1895-1927.

Wardle & Company was established 1871 at Hanley, Staffordshire, England.

Josiah Wedgwood was born in Burslem, Staffordshire, England, on July 12, 1730, into a family with a long pottery tradition. At the age of nine, after the death of his father, he joined the family business. In 1759, he set up his own pottery works in Burslem. There he produced cream-colored earthenware that found favor with Queen Charlotte. In 1762, she appointed him royal supplier of dinnerware. From the public sale of "Queen's Ware," as it came to be known, Wedgwood was able to build a production community in 1768, which he named Etruria, near Stoke-on-Trent, and a second factory equipped with tools and ovens of his own design. (Etruria is the ancient land of the Etruscans, in what is now northern Italy.)

Skinner, Inc.

Minton vase, England, circa 1875, squat urn-form with turquoise body and latticework to neck, oval foot, impressed factory mark and illegible date cipher, 4 1/2" high. **$306**

Skinner, Inc.

Wedgwood lobster dish and cover, England, circa 1871, oval form with molded lobster on cover, dish bordered with stiff leaves, impressed mark, 6 1/4". **$711**

Skinner, Inc.

Minton Nautilus shell centerpiece, England, date cipher for 1874, shell with seated mermaid to back and mermaid across front body with putti and seaweed garlands, shell supported by two mermen with tails scrolled together on oval base, impressed mark, 20 1/2" high. **$4,148**

Skinner, Inc.

Minton heron and fish ewer, England, date cipher for 1866, modeled and signed by Huges Protat, in the shape of heron with a pike in its beak, impressed mark, 21 1/2" high. **$4,148**

Skinner, Inc.

Minton centerbowl, England, date cipher for 1867, circular reticulated woven basket bordered by daisies with blue-glazed interior, tripod base with branches and three pigeons, impressed factory and cipher marks, bowl 12 1/4" diameter. **$1,778**

Skinner, Inc.

George Jones shell centerpiece, England, late 19th century, modeled as three stylized dolphins supporting a shell-form bowl with their tails the center between three shell-form dishes on three shell feet, pad mark, 9 3/4" high. **$889**

Pair of Brownfield ram's head ewers with ribbon and drapes of leaves and roses in high relief, professional handle, base and rim repairs, each 14" tall. **$200+ pair**

Skinner, Inc.

Continental mounted wall clock, circa 1870, black marble dial with gilded Roman numerals set within a cartouche with a lion's head flanked by putti, pendulum and winding key, unmarked, 17 1/2" high. **$711**

Skinner, Inc.

Pair of Wedgwood cornhusk vases, England, circa 1869, each with naturalistic modeling and enamels, impressed marks, 6 5/8" high. **$948**

Samuel Alcock butter dish, three pieces with shrimp handle atop bed of leaves, ferns and flowers, 6 1/2" diameter. **$900+**

Longchamp French asparagus set eight-piece, with four plates, sauce boat, platter, and platter with cradle. **$900+ set**

Hugo Lonitz figural Blackamoor center bowl, rim repair to bowl, 11" long, 8" tall. **$400+**

Skinner, Inc.

Wedgwood "Punch" teapot and cover, England, circa 1878, oval form with Toby finial, Punch handle, and Judy spout, impressed mark, 8 1/4". **$1,215**

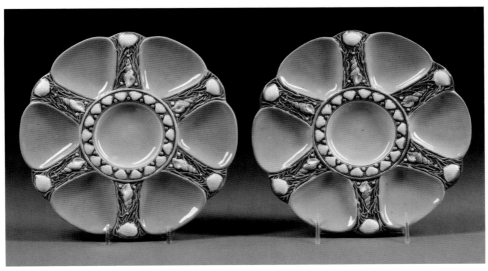

Skinner, Inc.

Pair of Minton oyster plates, England, 1874, 1876, each with molded shell-decorated compartments and shell border to central well, impressed marks, 9" diameter. **$972**

Skinner, Inc.

Wedgwood Rubens garden seat, England, circa 1867, raspberry-colored enameling to cream-colored ground, square tufted cushion set atop four scrolled legs adorned with fruiting festoons, impressed mark, 17 3/8" high. **$504**

Skinner, Inc.

Brownfield vase, England, circa 1871-1876, two kittens playing on an urn-form turquoise vase, carpet beneath, oval base, impressed "BROWNFIELD," registry, and other marks, 10 1/4" high. **$3,851**

Michaan's Auctions

Set of six Luneville artichoke plates, 9" diameter. **$275**

Skinner, Inc.

Minton dish and cover, England, late 19th century, gourd with bird on inside of dish and bird-shaped finial on cover, impressed marks, date cipher indistinct, 5 3/4" high. **$3,281**

Skinner, Inc.

Victoria Pottery Company strawberry dish, England, circa 1885, basket adorned with strawberries and blossoms, holders at base of handle for creamer and sugar bowl, impressed factory mark, 13" long. **$729**

Copeland floor jardinière with large vine handles and rim of grape clusters, cobalt ground with faces of mythological figures in high relief, professional repair to one handle, 29" wide, 17" tall. **$3,250+**

Skinner, Inc.

Palissy planter, France, late 19th century, modeled as tree base with central leaf and overhanging foliage to rim, front decorated with frogs, clams, nest of eggs to center, snake on bed of reeds and ferns, five organic-form feet, 11" high x 16 1/2" wide x 9 1/2" deep. **$790**

Skinner, Inc.

George Jones covered sardine dish and tray, England, late 19th century, cover with three fish, tray and dish with leaves, all on pink ground, blue pad mark to tray and pad mark to dish, total height 4 1/2", tray 8 1/4" long x 7 1/2" wide, box 5 3/4" long x 4 3/4" wide. **$3,185**

Skinner, Inc.

Mafra & Son Palissy wall plaque, Caldas, Portugal, 19th century, with coiled snake atop large frog, encrusted rim adorned with insects and lizard, impressed factory mark, 16 1/2" diameter. **$2,252**

Skinner, Inc.

Minton oyster server, England, date cipher for 1862, four graduated rows of oyster holders, finial modeled as two fish and snake, on stand, impressed mark, 10 1/2" high. **$7,350**

Skinner, Inc.

Victor Barbizet Palissy Barbotine wall plaque, Paris, France, second half 19th century, central pile of fish and eel surrounded by lizards, snakes, shellfish, leaves, individual turtle, frog, beetle, dragonfly on mottled blue ground, unmarked, 16" diameter. **$8,295**

Royal Worcester dragon-handled teapot with birds, flowers and vine in relief, minor professional spout repair, rare, 7 1/2" tall. **$3,000+**

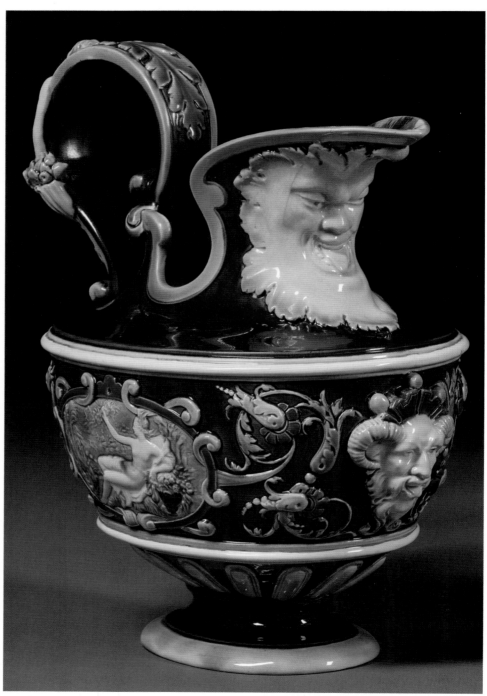

Skinner, Inc.

Minton majolica Palissy ewer, England, circa 1860, modeled by Hamlet Bourne after a Palissy design, head of a triton below spout, mermaid draped along handle and Renaissance-style cartouches and motifs across body, cobalt ground, 10 1/2" high. **$1,422**

Thomas Forester cobalt bird, water lily and cattail footed oval window jardinière, 17 1/2" long, 7 1/2" tall. **$1,000+**

Longchamp small basket-weave and shell three-well oyster plate, 8" diameter. **$325+**

Skinner, Inc.

George Jones cheese dish, England, late 19th century, cover molded with flowering cherry blossoms spreading from double-branch handle on light blue ground above a band of molded basketweave, repeated as border on rim of dish, impressed mark, 10 1/4" high, tray possibly married, dish diameter 11"; cover diameter 9". **$1,422**

Skinner, Inc.

Minton tulipiere, England, circa 1865-1875, five foliate stem vases on turquoise ground, rectangular foot, impressed factory mark and illegible date cipher, 8" high. **$1,094**

Shorter and Bolton bird and fan teapot, hairline crack to spout, 8 1/2" tall. **$250+**

Skinner, Inc.

Pair of Copeland Renaissance-style vases, England, late 19th century, six-panel design carved allover in low relief with six stylized portrait medallions, 11 3/8" high. **$1,304**

Holdcroft cobalt rustic floral strawberry basket with twig handles, professional rim repair, 12" long. **$400+**

Bevington cobalt swan topped figural pitcher, great color, 7 1/2" tall. **$700+**

French Maurice Palissy Ware lobster plaque, cobalt ground, professional repair to back rim and to lobster's head, 15 1/2" long. **$2,000**

Wilhelm Schiller and Sons (W.S. & S.) picket fence mottled sardine box with fish on cover, attached under plate. **$150+**

Three Delphin Massier floral place card holders, minor nicks to tips of flowers, each about 3 1/2" tall. **$1,300+ all**

Courtesy of Joan Sween

Wardle pitcher in gathered silk and grape leaves, 7 3/8" tall. **$275**

Samuel Lear water lily spooner, 5 1/4" tall. **$115+**

Brownfield pheasant and rabbit figural vase, great detail, professional rim repair to leaves of vase, Bacall Collection, 14" tall. **$5,000+**

Samuel Lear classical urn and sunflower tray with yellow rim, rim nick, 14" wide. **$250+**

Victoria Pottery Company boar's head covered tureen with floral, leaf and vine motif on base, professional repair to one handle, 15" wide. **$700+**

Clement Massier seven-piece tea set with teapot, creamer, sugar, and two cups and saucers with floral and dragonfly motif. **$300+ all**

Hugo Lonitz partridges with cattails under oak tree with oak leaves and acorns stand, professional repair to oak leaves and cattail leaves, 13 1/4" tall. **$4,200+**

Choisy-Le-Roi large wishing well, 27" tall, minor repair, atop Massier tree trunk pedestal, 26" tall. **$1,000+ pair**

Gerbing & Stefan cobalt vase with butterfly, putti, flowers and insects in relief, hairline crack, chips, 10" tall. **$400**

Sèvres

Some of the most desirable porcelain ever produced was made at the Sèvres factory, originally established at Vincennes, France, and transferred, through permission of Madame de Pompadour, to Sèvres as the Royal Manufactory about the middle of the 18th century. King Louis XV took sole responsibility for the works in 1759, when production of hard paste wares began. Between 1850 and 1900, many biscuit and soft-paste pieces were made again. Fine early pieces are scarce and high-priced. Many of those available today are late productions. The various Sèvres marks have been copied, and pieces in the "Sèvres Style" are similar to actual Sèvres wares but not necessarily from that factory.

Bonhams

Tureen and cover from the Imperial Compiegne Service produced for Napoleon III, mid-19th century, tureen of oval form with twin handles, integrated oval stand with scrolling handles, cover with pierced circular handle, body decorated in gilt with the initial N applied over interlaced foliate L's below a crown, white ground with gilt borders, 10" wide x 6" high, red printed S53 eagle mark. **$2,209**

Skinner, Inc.

Twelve pieces of Chateau des Tuileries pattern porcelain, France, 19th century, 11 plates each with celeste blue borders and gilt scrolls, painted with putti and gilt interlaced L's to center, 10" diameter; one compote with crowned "N" in center, 8 5/8" diameter; all marked on base with Chateau des Tuileries seal, Serves factory mark and serial numbers. **$2,726**

Susanin's Auctions

Pair of painted and gilt porcelain cache pots, 4 1/4" x 6". **$500**

Michaan's Auctions

Pair of gilt bronze-mounted flambe glazed covered urns, MP-Sevres in circle, each of baluster form with applied scroll handles, covers with berried knob finials, allover blue green mottled matte glaze, 19" high. **$900**

Michaan's Auctions

Pair of gilt cobalt glazed bottle vases, circa 1878, each in pear form with flaring rim above molded ring with repeating gilt stenciled leaf and floral scrollwork band, recessed foot, allover cobalt blue ground, each marked on base with S78 enclosed in a green circle symbol, Dore a Sevres circular mark 84, 13" high. **$3,250**

Skinner, Inc.

Eleven assorted cups and saucers, France, 19th century, five Chateau des Tuileries pattern, four with blue ground and the other with yellow; pair with portrait medallions on blue ground; and four of various motifs, all with gilt decoration and marked on base, height to 3 1/4", diameter to 5". **$1,580**

Elite Decorative Arts

Pair of 18th century French bronze-mounted chargers, 25 1/2" tall.
$3,000-$5,000

Skinner, Inc.

Pair of porcelain vases, France, late 19th century, elongated baluster-form with flared foot and rim, gilt base, gilt mounted handles, painted landscape to one side and couple and cupid to the other within gilt cartouches, signed "H. Poitevin," blue interlaced L's mark to covers and base, 26" high. **$2,844**

Pook & Pook, Inc.

Seven Chateau de St. Cloud dinner plates, 19th century, 9" diameter. **$119**

Bonhams

Late 19th century gilt metal and porcelain mounted clock garniture, neo-classical design, panels with birds, cherubs and flowers painted in reserves within a blue ground, cases with trailing floral swags and foliage, clock approximately 20" high. **$1,356**

Pook & Pook, Inc.

Set of 12 painted porcelain plates, circa 1900, 9 5/8" diameter. **$1,094**

Pook & Pook, Inc.

Porcelain oil lamp with courting scene, 19th century, 21" high. **$334**

Michaan's Auctions

Porcelain creamer, blue floral design and gold accents, repaired handle, 4 1/2" high. **$150**

Live Auctioneers

Set of eight 18th century plates, blue borders with gilt floral swags and floral medallions, centers decorated with birds in a tree, each plate carries the Sèvres mark but with various letters, 9 1/2" diameter. **$4,000**

Wedgwood

In 1754, Josiah Wedgwood and Thomas Whieldon of Fenton Vivian, Staffordshire, England, became partners in a pottery enterprise. Their products included marbled, agate, tortoiseshell, green glaze, and Egyptian black wares.

In 1759, Wedgwood opened his own pottery at the Ivy House works, Burslem. In 1764, he moved to the Brick House (Bell Works) at Burslem. The pottery concentrated on utilitarian pieces.

Between 1766 and 1769, Wedgwood built the famous works at Etruria. Among the most-renowned products of this plant were the Empress Catherina of Russia dinner service (1774) and the Portland Vase (1790s). The firm also made caneware, unglazed earthenwares (drabwares), piecrust wares, variegated and marbled wares, black basalt (developed in 1768), Queen's or creamware, and Jasperware (perfected in 1774).

Bone china was produced under the direction of Josiah Wedgwood II between 1812 and 1822 and was revived in 1878. Moonlight luster was made from 1805 to 1815. Fairyland luster began in 1920. All luster production ended in 1932.

A museum was established at the Etruria pottery in 1906. When Wedgwood moved to its modern plant at Barlaston, North Staffordshire, the museum was expanded.

Skinner, Inc.

Hand-painted bone china bowl, England, 1925, octagonal, with polychrome enamel decoration, exterior with foliate festoons, interior with fairies and acrobatic nymphs amongst foliate vines, inscribed date and printed mark, 2 5/8" diameter. **$2,252**

Skinner, Inc.

Fairyland luster bowl, England, circa 1920, Z4968, exterior with Woodland Bridge – Variation I to black sky, interior with Picnic by a River to day-lit sky, printed mark, 8" diameter. **$5,925**

Skinner, Inc.

Fairyland luster Melba centerbowl, England, circa 1920, Z4968 Garden of Paradise exterior to purple sky, interior with satin texture with Jumping Faun pattern, printed mark, 8" diameter. **$15,925**

Skinner, Inc.

Marsden's artware vase, England, circa 1885, buff ground rim and shoulder above dark brown body slip decorated with flowers, foliage, and scrolled vines, impressed mark, 8" high. **$237**

Skinner, Inc.

Pate-sur-pate plaque, England, circa 1875, oval, green ground and white slip depiction of young boy gazing through a telescope, impressed mark, 6" long, set in modern frame. **$2,133**

Skinner, Inc.

Wedgwood Queen's ware lobster bowl, England, 19th century, oval shell-form bowl with polychrome decorated brown transfer-printed sea vegetation, mounted atop a lobster's back set on raised oval base, silver plated trim ring, impressed mark, bowl 10 1/4" long. **$652**

Skinner, Inc.

Queen's ware mantel clock, England, circa 1873, vellum ground with gilded foliage to reddish-brown ground, polychrome floral panels to each corner, clock face inscribed J.W. Benson 25 Old Bond Street London, impressed mark, 12 1/4" high. **$889**

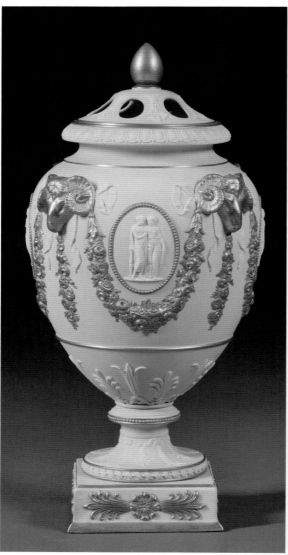

Skinner, Inc.

Gilded white stoneware potpourri vase and cover, England, 19th century, ram's heads supporting floral festoons surrounding classical medallions, pierced cover, impressed mark, 12 3/8" high. **$2,818**

Skinner, Inc.

Jasper-mounted cut-steel chatelaine, England, late 18th century, attributed to Matthew Boulton, faceted bead chain with octagonal three-color jasper medallion above five drops, three clips and two with blue jasper beads, seal, and pencil, overall 10 1/2" long, medallion 5/8" x 7/8". **$4,148**

Skinner, Inc.

Three Keith Murray design vases, England, circa 1940, green-glazed globular shape with incised concentric rings, 6" high; straw-glazed globular vase with concentric rings, 7 1/8" high; matte green cylindrical tumbler with fluted sides, 3 1/2" high; printed and impressed marks. **$593**

Skinner, Inc.

Pair of Queen's ware Design 63 canisters and covers, England, circa 1963, cylindrical, with printed geometric pattern in yellow and black, impressed and printed mark, 8 3/8" high. **$207**

Skinner, Inc.

Luster inkwell and cover, England, circa 1920, square tray with globular inkpot with Sybil finial, polychrome decorated and gilded with dragons and dogs, insert liner, printed mark, 4 1/8" high. **$1,126**

Skinner, Inc.

Butterfly luster Malfrey pot and cover, England, circa 1920, Z4832 with mother-of-pearl ground with gilded and enameled butterflies, printed mark, 9 3/8" high. **$1,541**

Skinner, Inc.

Powder blue bone china Malfrey pot and cover, England, circa 1915, body enamel decorated with hounds to blue ground, printed mark, 8 1/4" high. **$1,126**

Skinner, Inc.

Powder blue bone china fish vase, England, circa 1915, gilded fish to blue ground, printed mark, 9 1/2" high. **$711**

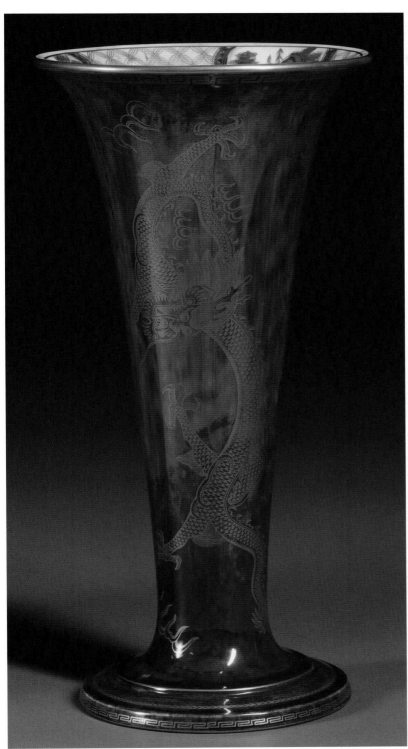

Skinner, Inc.

Dragon luster trumpet vase, England, circa 1920, purple exterior with gilded dragons, mother-of-pearl interior with paneled border of Chinese landscapes, printed mark, 11 3/8" high.
$1,422

Luster centerbowl, England, circa 1920, mother-of-pearl ground, exterior with paneled sides depicting wild cat in tented landscape, interior with floral bouquets surrounding central group with birds, bat, and flowers, printed mark, 11 1/4" diameter. **$8,295**

Skinner, Inc.

Fairyland luster argus pheasant vase, England, circa 1920, Z5486 decorated to mottled blue sky, printed mark, 8" high. **$5,206**

Skinner, Inc.

Modern Black Jasper dip vase and cover, England, mid-20th century, applied white Dancing Hours figures centering striped engine-turned borders, impressed mark, 9" high. **$444**

Skinner, Inc.

Flame Fairyland vase, England, circa 1920, Z5360 with Sycamore Tree with Feng Hwang, Bridge and Ship and Tree, printed mark, 8" high. **$13,035**

Skinner, Inc.

Black Jasper dip bowl, England, circa 1960, circular form with applied white Dancing Hours figures below a band of running laurel, impressed mark, 10 1/4" diameter. **$486**

Skinner, Inc.

Three-color Jasper clock, England, circa 1900, white jasper ground with applied lilac figures and green foliage, rectangular case mounted atop a raised rectangular base with running oak leaf border, impressed mark, 7 1/8" high. **$237**

Skinner, Inc.

Fairyland luster Picnic by a River plaque, England, circa 1920, rectangular, pattern Z5158 set to nighttime sky, printed mark, 4 3/4" x 10 3/4". **$13,035**

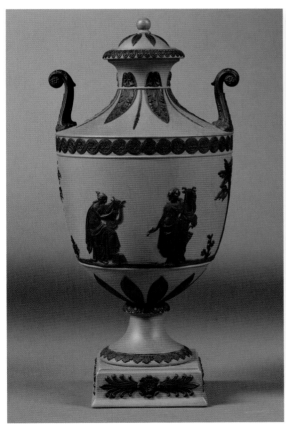

Skinner, Inc.

Modern solid lilac Jasper vase and cover, England, circa 1960, applied white relief with Bacchus head handles and Dancing Hours between foliate borders, impressed mark, 10 1/2" high. **$948**

Skinner, Inc.

Terracotta Jasper vase and cover, England, 1957, applied black jasper classical relief, impressed mark, 10 1/2" high. **$1,067**

Skinner, Inc.

Solid lilac Jasper vase and cover, England, 1960, applied white relief with snake handles terminating at Medusa masks, classical figures centering floral festoon and foliate borders, impressed mark, 12 3/4" high. **$770**

Skinner, Inc.

Modern solid blue Jasper "The Fall of Phaeton" plaque, England, 1977, rectangular, with applied white relief depiction, original modeled by George Stubbs, numbered 49 and impressed mark, approximately 11 1/2" x 19 3/4", giltwood frame, overall 17" x 25 1/4". **$1,304**

Skinner, Inc.

Nizami luster plate, England, circa 1920, W2191 with black and gilt trim to wide green ground border, printed mark, 10 3/4" diameter. **$6,518**

Skinner, Inc.

Fairyland luster Firbolgs bowl, England, circa 1920, Z5245 circular form with gilded deep purple firbolgs to red ground, mother-of-pearl interior with Thumbelina center, printed mark, 9 3/4" diameter. **$2,370**

Skinner, Inc.

Fairyland luster Lily tray, England, circa 1920, Fairy Gondola pattern to day-lit sky, exterior with flying geese to mottled purple/gray ground, printed mark, 13" diameter. **$20,825**

Skinner, Inc.

Fairyland luster poplar trees bowl, England, circa 1920, Z5360 with flame sky, interior with Woodland Elves V – Woodland Bridge and Mermaid center, signed MJ and printed mark, 11 1/4" diameter. **$6,518**

Skinner, Inc.

Fairyland luster Malfrey pot, England, circa 1920, Woodland Elves IV – Big Eyes to green sky, printed mark, 3" high. **$1,185**

Civil War Collectibles

The Civil War began April 12, 1861, at Fort Sumter, the Confederates surrendered at Appomattox Courthouse on April 9, 1865, and all official fighting ceased on May 26, 1865.

For some Civil War enthusiasts, collecting war relics is the best way to understand the heritage and role of the thousands who served.

It has become commonplace to have major sales of Civil War artifacts by a few major auction houses, in addition to the private trading, local auctions, and Internet sales of these items. These auction houses handle the majority of significant Civil War items coming to the marketplace.

The majority of these valuable items are in repositories of museums, universities, and colleges, but many items were also traded between private citizens. Items that are being released by museums and from private collections make up the base of items currently being traded and sold to collectors of Civil War material culture. In addition, many family collections amassed over the years have been recently coming to the marketplace as new generations have decided to liquidate some of them.

Civil War items are acquired by collectors in the same fashion as any material cultural item. Individuals interested in antiques and collectibles find items at farm auction sales, yard sales, estate sales, specialized auctions, private collectors trading or selling items, and the Internet and online auction sales.

Provenance is important in Civil War collectibles—maybe even more important than with most other collectibles. Also, many Civil War items have well-documented provenance as they come from family collections or their authenticity has been previously documented by auction houses, museums, or other experts in the field.

For more information on Civil War memorabilia, see *Warman's Civil War Collectibles Identification and Price Guide,* 3rd edition, by Russell L. Lewis.

Skinner, Inc.

Union presentation watch, English sterling silver presentation hunter case pocket watch with cabinet card, the watch hallmarked London, 1859, with engine-turned covers, inscription engraved to interior cover "Presented by the Members of Co. B 1st N.O. Vols. to 1st Lieut. D. N. Dunlop, as a mark of esteem," 2 1/4" diameter, together with a cabinet card photograph of Lieutenant Dunlap and his wife. **$705**

Cowan's Auctions, Inc.

Snare drum, one of the tension mounts stamped Horstmann's Phila., buff snares are in excellent condition and complete, batter head is in excellent condition, tension head has an 8" tear, 14" high x 16" wide. **$705**

Cowan's Auctions, Inc.

Images of General Abner Doubleday are popular, not only because his reputation as a Union officer, but because of the popular (but untrue) belief that he invented the game of baseball. **$250-$325**

Cowan's Auctions, Inc.

Officer's trunk inscribed on brass plate on leather lock cover, "Wm C. Couriey, Co. C, 60th Regt. N.Y.S. Vols." **$250-$400**

Quarter-plate tintype of an African-American Union soldier uniformed in standard nine-button frock coat and slouch hat. **$2,800-$3,300**

The Civil War Confederate Battle Flag of the 37th Mississippi Infantry, accompanied by a complete analysis package from noted flag authority Fonda Thomsen attesting to its authenticity; 43 1/4" on the hoist and 53 3/4" on the fly, constructed on a field of red wool English bunting, intersected by a 6 1/2"-7" blue wool bunting cross. The cross has 12 white cotton stars inserted into the fabric, three on each arm. The cross is trimmed with two layers of 1 1/4" off-white cotton fabric. The leading edge of the flag is turned to the reverse to form a 2" pole sleeve. Appliquéd on the obverse only, in two rows with 2" white cotton letters, "37th Reg: Miss./Infantry." In the other quadrants are the shadows of previously applied battle honors, Port Gibson (in an arc), Baker's Creek, and Vicksburg. **$50,787**

James D. Julia, Inc.

John Taylor Wood was Confederate Colonel of Cavalry and also served as a captain in the C.S. Navy. He saw much combat during the war, and a biography was written on him published by the University of Georgia. Before the war he taught at Annapolis, when this picture was probably taken. John Taylor Wood's name appears in back of case but not in contemporary ink. **$3,450**

Cowan's Auctions, Inc.

USN cartridge box, inside the cartridge is a large wood block, front of flap is embossed with USN, on the rear is a large belt loop. **$431**

Cowan's Auctions, Inc.

Shoulder straps worn by Brevet Colonel Samuel Goodman (1824-1914) CMOH, 28th PA.; mounted in a frame. Goodman entered service as 1st Lieutenant and Adjutant in October 1861 and was breveted four times during the war, including Gettysburg. Lt. Goodman won the Medal of Honor for saving the flag of the 107th OVI at Chancellorsville. The heroic officer was discharged in August 1864 as 1st lieutenant. **$920**

Skinner, Inc.

*Massachusetts 54th Regiment surgeon's kit,
Weiss, London, maker, mid-19th century,
in brass-bound mahogany case with
velvet-lined interior fitted with numerous
implements including bone saws, scalpels,
tourniquets, etc., case 14 5/8" x 7 1/4" x
2 5/8". Provenance: Descended directly in
the family of a member of the Massachusetts
54th regiment. The rounded-end bone
saw likely associated (differently patterned
handle not marked Weiss), brass tourniquet
handle not marked. Possibly lacking one
scalpel, and with one scalpel with some
damage to handle. Case with minor age
wear to case and interior, including small
age-typical shrinkage crack below brass at
one corner of lid.* **$3,081**

Skinner, Inc.

Heritage Auctions, Inc.

*Confederate cavalry officer's saber, exceptional untouched condition, Kraft, Goldschmidt & Kraft, Columbia,
S.C. Blade generally smooth and gray with light scattered surface rust, no pitting or nicks with three narrow
fullers on each side, extending to about 12" from the hilt. Blade retains original leather washer at the base,
iron scabbard utilizes a heavy brass throat affixed on one side with two small brass screws, and on the other
with a single larger brass screw, 1/2" wide brass ring mounts with incised line decoration on the edges, along
with brass rings. Saber is 44" overall with 38" straight blade with traces of engraved decoration.* **$28,680**

Heritage Auctions, Inc.

Early Civil War prototype/locally manufactured Confederate National/Battle Flag; one other similar documented example is known to exist. Accompanied by analysis from noted flag authority Fonda Thomsen; 33" on the hoist and 52" on the fly, constructed of one layer of red, white, and blue cotton fabric, with 13 five-pointed, white cotton stars appliquéd to each side of canton forming "X" pattern, center star slightly (1/8") larger than other stars. The 13 alternating red and white stripes are joined with plain seams, with seam selvages on the obverse, giving reverse side of flag the finished appearance. **$50,787**

Cowan's Auctions, Inc.

Albumen print of Meade's headquarters at Gettysburg from Alexander Gardner's 1865 series "Incidents of the War," 12" x 10". **$500-$750**

Heritage Auctions, Inc.

J. H. Dance & Bros., Columbia, Texas, .44 caliber percussion Confederate revolver, #220, with history of use by Horace G. Young, 5th Texas Cavalry. The gun overall has a deep dark patina with some scattered surface rust and some light pitting on areas of the cylinder. The gun is numbered on the frame, barrel housing, trigger guard, underside of grip strap, left side of loading lever, left lower side of hammer and cylinder. Missing the wedge and wedge screw. The letters H Y are deeply scratched in the underside of the grip strap. Retains the original brass blade front sight and has a good bore. **$56,762**

Skinner, Inc.

Small craft mahogany box binnacle made for the U.S. Navy, fold-down glass viewing door, bail handle, compass by Robert Merrill, New York, and unusual suspended overhead lighting device, printed paper label stating, in part, "Prestons Liquid Compass," 19 1/2" high. **$2,015**

Washington, May 25. 1862. 1 1/2 P.M.

Major Gen. McClellan

The enemy is moving North in sufficient force to drive Banks before him — precisely in what force we can not tell — He is also threatening Leesburg, and Geary on the Manassas Gap Railroad from both North and South — in precisely what force we can not tell — I think the movement is a general and a concerted one — such as could not be if he was acting upon the purpose of a very desperate defense of Richmond — I think the time is near when you must either attack Richmond, or give up the job and come to the defense of Washington — Let me hear from you instantly —

A. Lincoln

Abraham Lincoln telegram signed "A. Lincoln", one page, 9 7/8" x 7 1/2", "Washington, 25 May 1862, 1 1/2 P.M.," to Major General George B. McClellan. Lincoln's directive, "Send in cipher," is largely effaced from lower margin; some minor marginal tears and repairs, faint damp staining at left. Green morocco folding-case, russet morocco labels. **$482,500**

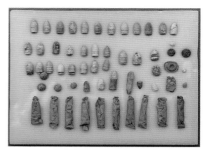

Cowan's Auctions, Inc.

Framed collection of cartridges, including round balls, mini balls and some paper cartridges. Some are battlefield pickups; some are in good condition. **$632**

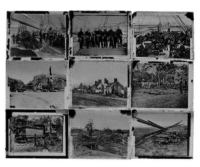

Cowan's Auctions, Inc.

Approximately 170 hand-colored lantern slides made from paper photographs and stereoviews originally produced by popular Civil War-era photographers including Mathew Brady, Alexander Gardner, Timothy O'Sullivan, A.J. Russell, and George Barnard. The majority of glass slides measure 3 1/4" x 4". Most lack a paper border and are not covered with a protective glass sleeve, and only a few have handwritten or paper labels. The collection is comprised of images of the leading military and political personalities of the war, post-battle shots capturing the dead in the field, broken earthworks, occupied forts, and bombed buildings, plus views of supply wagons, Union and Confederate camp scenes, hospitals, and prisons. **$5,287**

Sotheby's

Painted pine and tin Civil War toy soldier, American, early 20th century, the upright figure with kepee cap, nail head "buttons," and sword blade baffles; 21" high. **$7,500**

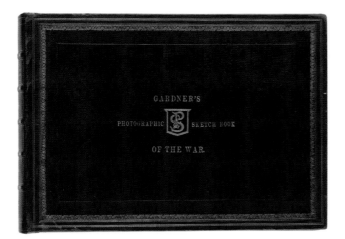

Sotheby's

Alexander Gardner's "Gardner's Photographic Sketch Book of the War," 1821-1882. Washington, D. C.: Philp & Solomons, 1866, two volumes containing 100 albumen photographs printed by Alexander Gardner from negatives by himself, James Gardner, Timothy O'Sullivan, David Knox, John Reekie, William R. Pywell, D.B. Woodbury, W. Morris Smith, Barnard & Gibson, and Wood & Gibson, each on a two-toned mount, the photographer's, printer's, and publisher's credits, and title, series title, date, and copyright in letterpress on the mount. Oblong folio, gilt-lettered morocco with gilt-decorative borders and publisher's gilt monogram, expertly re-backed, all edges gilt; in a modern custom-designed cloth box with gilt-lettered spine. Each plate 6 3/4" x 8 3/4" or the reverse. **$158,500**

Clocks

The clock is one of the oldest human inventions. The word clock (from the Latin word clocca, "bell"), suggests that it was the sound of bells that also characterized early timepieces.

The first mechanical clocks to be driven by weights and gears were invented by medieval Muslim engineers. The first geared mechanical clock was invented by an 11th century Arab engineer in Islamic Spain. The knowledge of weight-driven mechanical clocks produced by Muslim engineers was transmitted to other parts of Europe through Latin translations of Arabic and Spanish texts.

In the early 14th century, existing clock mechanisms that used water power were being adapted to take their driving power from falling weights. This power was controlled by some form of oscillating mechanism. This controlled release of power—the escapement—marks the beginning of the true mechanical clock.

James D. Julia, Inc.

Rare French two-faced swinging ceiling clock, mid-19th century, two-sided example of Sunburst Design intended to be suspended on a brass ceiling mount, clock mounted on a nine-rod compensating pendulum with alternating silver and brass elements: swings as one, enamel dials each with Roman numeral chapter ring, one dial with sweep seconds hand, approximately 54" long. **$6,000-$9,000**

Michaan's Auctions

Romilly a Paris carriage clock, 8 1/4" high. **$1,200**

Previous page:

James D. Julia, Inc.

French Vincenti Et Cie Empire-style crystal regulator, late 19th/early 20th century, retailed by Tiffany & Company and so marked on back plate of movement, back plate additionally stamped with Vincenti's Medaille d'Argent 1855 above the serial number 6373 69, stamped "Made in France," enameled dial with Roman numeral chapter ring and with time and strike apertures, fitted within a Classical rectangular brass case, top with step molding and inset corners, body sides each fitted with beveled glass panels, hinged door at front and back, on conforming plinth, accompanied by key and twin cylinder mercury pendulum, 14 1/2" high x 9 1/4" wide overall x 7" deep overall. **$1,000-$1,500**

French silvered and gilt brass great wheel skeleton timepiece with day, date and lunar calendar, early 19th century, form of colonnade with pierced and gilt columns each surmounted by biscuit putto, flanking a pierced frieze of inhabited foliate scrolls, pierced wire work urn, engraved oval base raised on gilt leaf and acorn feet, annular white enamel arabic chapter ring bordered by minute scales repeated at each hour interval, single pierced gilt scroll hand indicating both minutes and hours, in the center, four subsidiary rings, two of which revolve to indicate the day and its ruling deity, other two fixed, indicating date and age of moon by means of pierced scroll hands, movement with pierced arched brass frame united by four screwed pillars, wheelwork with "Y" crossings and wolf's teeth, anchor escapement with thread suspended pendulum, 16" high. **$35,000**

Meissen two-part mantel clock and Meissen plateau, third quarter 19th century to first quarter 20th century, German, porcelain case decorated overall with dense polychrome floral garlands, scrolling crest framed by songbirds, case with enameled dial with gilt bronze bezel centering a roman numeral chapter ring, eight-day brass movement mark "AS" with serial number "616279," case with scrolled feet on similarly decorated stand, each leg with scrolling leaf tips and floral garland raised on scrolled feet, all gilt decorated, plateau decorated with polychrome floral sprays, centering a cartouche with putti, clock with incised mark "B16," crossed swords in underglaze blue, small plateau with incised mark "B16," impressed mark "100," crossed swords in underglaze blue, large plateau impressed mark "23," crossed swords in underglaze blue, clock 13 3/4" high, small plateau 4 3/4" overall height x 9 3/4" overall length x 6 1/5" overall width, large plateau 4 1/3" overall height x 13 3/4" overall length x 9 3/4" overall width. **$8,000-$12,000**

Skinner, Inc.

Three-vial brass hour glass, France, circa 1763, three glass vials with spherical ampoules containing dark colored sand, centers joined by colored twine and lashed with gold thread, brass casing with chased scrolls, punch decorated frieze depicting stallions and marked 1763, twisted columns, lower door for access to vials and rotating mounting device on reverse, 11" high. **$2,489**

Skinner, Inc.

Hamilton Watch Company Model 21 two-day marine chronometer, Lancaster, Pennsylvania, No. 7641, circa 1940, 4" Arabic numeral silvered dial inscribed Hamilton Lancaster PA., U.S.A., 7641 and 1941, full plate nickel damascened movement marked Hamilton Watch Company, Lancaster, Penn., Model 21 14 Jewels, chain fusee, maintaining power, steel balance, helical hairspring, balance lock screw and spring detent escapement, all in weighted brass bowl and gimbal, walnut three-tiered brass-bound box with carrying handles, printed instructions under lid and "Break Circuit" attachment in base, overall dimensions, 10" high x 8 1/4" wide x 7 3/4" deep. **$1,659**

Bonhams

Rare American Federal inlaid mahogany dwarf clock with alarm, signed R. Tower, Kingston, case attributed to Henry Willard, circa 1821-1824, forward sliding hood with fretwork between three brass finials over arched cornice supported by plain columns, sides pierced with lozenge array of circular holes, trunk with crossbanded long door, crossbanded plinth with applied bead molding above French feet, finely painted white dial with foliage, urn and drapery in arch, gilt spandrels enclosing roman chapter ring, blued steel arrow hands, two barrel weight driven brass movement with rectangular plates joined by four pillars, anchor escapement, iron rod pendulum with brass bob, separately wound alarm train planted on side of movement, 50 1/2" high. **$91,500**

Skinner, Inc.

E. Howard No. 12 wall regulator, E. Howard & Company, Boston, circa 1875, black walnut case with turned molded bezel over 15" diameter painted zinc Roman numeral dial inscribed E. Howard & Company, Boston, lower door with black, gold and maroon painted tablet, eight-day damascened brass plate, time-only movement with dead-beat escapement, maintaining power and Geneva stop, iron weight and four jar etched glass mercury temperature compensating pendulum and looking glass behind, 62" high. **$26,070**

Skinner, Inc.

Arts & Crafts oak tall clock with Regina musical box, circa 1900, chamfered edge crown molding above glazed door opening to composite brass dial with Arabic numerals and cast brass spandrels, eight-day time and gong strike movement marked Seth Thomas, chain driven with two brass-cased weights, beveled glass waist door and side glass, all above Regina musical box playing six different tunes on single disc, with 14 bells, 90" high. **$7,110**

Skinner, Inc.

James Arthur Regulator with Remontoir, New York, 1901, maple case with molded top, glazed dial and waist doors and mirrored back, skeletonized movement stamped with maker's name and date with three front mounted dials, seconds at top, hours object lower right and minutes, lower left, dead-beat escapement with adjustable pallet faces, lever activated one minute remontoir rewound by large brass cased weight and internal "ball" pulley all regulated by steel grid iron pendulum and cylindrical bob, 81" high. **$15,405**

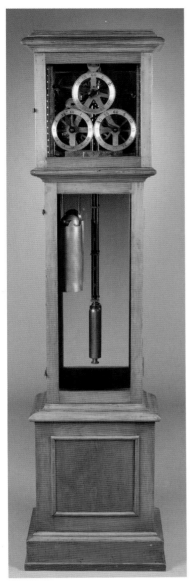

Skinner, Inc.

James Arthur drum-head tall clock, James Arthur, New York City, 1903, mahogany case with 14" brass Roman numeral dial stamped by maker, glazed waist door with eight-day time, wooden and brass wheeled skeletonized movement with dead-beat escapement, signed "James Arthur 1903" and "James Arthur Co. New York," transfer gearing to transmit power to hands, applied plaque stating "To Bessie Humphrey Arthur, From her Father James Arthur, October 24th, 1904," powered by two brass-cased weights and regulated by a brass bob, wooden rod pendulum, 87". **$4,444**

Benjamin Willard tall clock, Roxbury, Massachusetts, no. 207, circa 1780, silvered sheet brass dial engraved "Benja. Willard Roxbury, No. 207," and "Ab Hoc Momento Pendet Eternitas" with phoenix in arch, fret-top maple case with fan-carved waist door flanked by thumbnail corners, all on two-stage molded bracket foot base, eight-day time and strike movement with rack and snail strike regulated by wooden pendulum rod and brass-faced bob all powered by two period iron weights, 87 1/2" high. **$23,700**

Jan Gobels burl walnut marquetry tall clock, Amsterdam, circa 1760, case with blind sound fret in crest, flat fluted columns with Corinthian capitals flanking composite brass dial with silvered Roman numeral chapter ring engraved "Jan Gobels Amsterdam," engraved and matted center with calendar, cast brass four seasons spandrels, moon's age in arch with lunar and tidal calibrations, tombstone-shaped waist door with oval lentical and floral and scroll marquetry pattern inlays, bombe base with similar decoration all on hairy paw feet, eight-day time and Dutch striking movement with two bells, two iron cased weights and pendulum, 100 1/2" high. **$6,518**

Skinner, Inc.

Stephen Taber mahogany tall clock, New Bedford, Massachusetts, circa 1800, painted iron dial inscribed "S. Taber," Roman numerals, gilt corner spandrels and moon's age in arch, pierced fret top with brass stop-fluted free-standing columns flanking glazed hood door, fan inlaid rectangular waist, brass stop-fluted quarter columns and fan inlaid base on ogee feet, eight-day time and strike brass movement with pendulum and two iron weights, 89 1/2" high.
$18,960

Skinner, Inc.

Austrian 30-day skeleton clock, circa 1840, silvered case with two classical columns on oval base with engine-turned beading and acorn feet, 6 3/4" diameter dial with Roman numerals within engine-turned bezel, subsidiary dials indicating seconds at top, day-of-the-month object right and month-of-the-year object left, sweep minute hand and pierced hour hand, 30-day time-only movement with maintaining power, dead beat escapement and decorative star wheels to advance calendars all powered by silvered engine-turned weight and regulated by pendulum, 21 1/4" high. Provenance: Formerly in the collection of Norman Langmaid.
$14,220

Seth Thomas off-center pillar and scroll clock, Plymouth, Connecticut, circa 1818, painted wooden with Arabic numerals, inside minute track and gilt decoration, scroll top case with three brass finials, reverse-painted lower tablet depicting rural scene and off-center pendulum aperture, printed maker's label stating in part, "Patent Clocks Made and Sold by Seth Thomas, Plymouth, Conn.," 30-hour strap wooden movement with center mounted count-wheel all powered by two compound-hung weights and pendulum, 30" high. **$2,187**

Silas B. Terry mahogany balance wheel steeple clock, Terryville, Connecticut, circa 1845, painted wooden dial with Roman numerals, second's dial, cut outs for viewing escape and balance wheels, reverse painted tablet depicting mill scene, printed maker's label stating "Balance Clocks, Invented by Eli Terry, and Patented to him, August 9th, 1845, Manufactured by Silas B. Terry, Terryville, Conn.," 30-hour brass balance wheel escapement movement with count wheel strike and detached wooden fusees, 24 3/4" high. **$9,480**

French industrial cannon-form clock, circa 1890, cast brass and nickel cannon with time-only cylinder escapement timekeeper at end, 2 1/4" diameter silvered Roman numeral dial, anchor with mercury thermometer, brass swabbing basin with aneroid barometer and smaller one with compass, 11 long, 7" high. **$7,290**

Skinner, Inc.

Botsford's Improved Patent Lever Marine Timepiece, Jerome Manufacturing Company, New Haven, Connecticut, circa 1845-1855, with gilt, paint and mother-of-pearl decorated front, enameled dial with Roman numerals and inscribed "Mrs. Eliza Kelley" within a stylized banner, printed maker's label pasted on back with description as in title line and instructions, 30-hour patent lever escapement movement all mounted on gilt decorated pedestal with glass dome, 12 1/2" high. **$2,205**

Skinner, Inc.

Mahogany three-tune quarter-chiming table clock, attributed to Elliott, London, circa 1890, composite brass dial with raised Arabic numerals, cast brass spandrels, three subsidiary dials in arch for Chime-Silent, Fast-Slow and three-tune chime selection, all flanked by freestanding brass fluted columns and Corinthian capitals, caddy top with five acorn finials, all on scrolled foot base, eight-day time, strike and triple chime on eight bells and gongs fusee movement, 26" high. **$7,290**

Skinner, Inc.

Patinated bronze, gilt-bronze, and marble mantel clock, France, 19th century, polychrome enameled dial displaying hour, minute, and date in Arabic numerals, marked "Ridel a Paris," adorned with eagle above, male figure scribing and female figure reading, relief panel of figures making a burnt offering, on marble base frieze-decorated with sphinxes, on four raised feet, 21" high x 26" wide. **$17,775**

Bonhams

Rare gilt brass grande sonnerie quarter repeating center seconds carriage clock with calendar, moon phase and alarm, signed Breguet, No. 2443, last quarter 19th century, glazed gorge case with gilt mask enclosing white enamel dial with Roman chapters, gilt minute numerals and aperture for phase of moon, subsidiary dials for day, date and alarm, blued steel Breguet hands, twin barrel movement with fine nickel finished platform, straight line lever escapement with overcoiled spring, cut bimetallic balance with numerous gold screws, center seconds train planted on back plate, striking grande/petite sonnerie and quarter repeating on two gongs, strike/silent switch in base, accompanied by distressed leather covered carrying case, 7 3/4" high. **$23,750**

Bonhams

Ebony repeating bracket clock with alarm bearing the signature Joseph Knibb Londini fecit, caddy top with leaf tied handle and foliate scroll mounts, glazed side panels, gilt fret and scroll escutcheons to door, plinth base with later feet, 6 1/2" dial with winged cherub spandrels, silvered Roman chapter ring with fleur de lis half hour marks enclosing winding and date apertures in matted center, silvered alarm setting disc, twin fusee movement with five latched baluster pillars, renewed trains with knife edge verge escapement, restored hour repeating work activated by replaced brass bar, striking and repeating hour on single bell with alarm on second bell, back plate engraved with scrolls and flower heads, 14" high. **$46,250**

Bonhams

Rare patinated and gilt bronze mystery clock, Jean Eugene Robert-Houdin, Paris, mid-19th century, transparent glass dial within gilt bezel above vase-shaped patinated case, applied gilt putto supporting pair of chimerae concealing link to contrate wheels mounted within case and on back plate of two train circular movement, signed Robert-Houdin, Paris, anchor escapement striking hour and half hour on bell by means of count wheel, carved gilt wood base en suite, accompanied by glass dome, 13 1/2" high. **$18,750**

Coca-Cola Collectibles

BY ALLAN PETRETTI

Organized Coca-Cola collecting began in the early 1970s. The advertising art of The Coca-Cola Company, which used to be thought of as a simple area of collecting, has reached a whole new level of appreciation. Because of their artistic quality, these images deserve to be considered true Americana.

Coca-Cola art is more than bottles and trays, more than calendars and signage, more than trinkets, giveaways, and displays. It incorporates all the best that America has to offer. The Coca-Cola Company, since its conception in 1886, has taken advertising to a whole new level. So much so that it has been studied and dissected by scholars as to why it has proved to be so successful for more than 120 years.

Allan Petretti

Can soda pop advertising be considered true art? Without a doubt! The very best artists in America were an integral part of that honorary place in art history. Renowned artists like Rockwell, Sundbloom, Elvgren, and Wyeth helped take a quality product and advance it to the status of an American icon and all that exemplifies the very best about America.

This beautiful advertising directly reflects the history of our country: its styles and fashion, patriotism, family life, the best of times, and the worst of times. Everything this country has gone through since 1886 can be seen in these wonderful images.

For more information on Coca-Cola collectibles, see *Petretti's Coca-Cola Collectibles Price Guide*, 12th edition, by Allan Petretti.

ALLAN PETRETTI *is one of the world's top authorities on Coca-Cola memorabilia. He conducts seminars for Coca-Cola collector groups and has been interviewed by the* Wall Street Journal, *USA Today, the* London Times, *and the New York Times, and has appeared on many television shows, including "History Detectives."*

1927-1929 die-cut sign, 7 3/4" x 30".
$1,000
Other versions exist.

1898 calendar, 7 1/4" x 12 3/4". **$25,000**

1950s table lighter. **$185**

Late 1920s export bottle, paper labels. **$3,600**

1919 classic calendar, with bottle, near mint condition. **$7,000**

Early 1930s toy stove, 8 1/2" x 4 1/4" x 8 1/2". **$3,800** *Must be complete with original cord.*

Early 1900s silver glass holder for straight-sided glass. **$1,800**

1940s-1950s metal carrier. **$300** *Must be in near mint condition to warrant this value.*

Circa 1929 Glascock cooler, single case, junior size, all original choice condition. **$1,600**

Circa 1914-1916 counter display "Dutch Boy" and "Dutch Girl" set, each 5 1/4" x
7 3/4", die-cut, easel back, printed by the Sackett & Wilhelms Co. NY., rare when found as set.
Individual **$13,500**
Set of two **$36,000**

Circa 1896 30" x 40" cameo paper sign,
printed by J. Ottman Litho Company, New
York. **$35,000**
Pre-1900 paper signs are very rare.

1909 cardboard sign, 28 1/2" x 45". **$20,000**

1920s cardboard bottle cutout, 10" x 14", "Boy with Weiner." **$4,000**

*1910 cardboard cutout, 28 1/2" x 39 1/2",
"Man in the Grass" (with glass), printed by
American Lithography.* **$8,000**
This cutout also exists in a bottle version.

*1899 sign, 20" x 28", Hilda Clark, embossed tin,
rare.* **$30,000**

Circa 1912 watch fob, 1 1/2", celluloid. **$3,800**

Circa 1903 6" small hanging die-cut sign, rare, Chas. W. Shonk Company, Chicago. **$15,000**

Circa 1907 change receiver, 7", The Empire Ornamental Glass Company, New York. **$2,500**

1964 tin sign, 18" x 54". **$450**

1937 neon lightup counter clock. **$9,500**
Must be near mint or better working condition,
with no restoration, to warrant value shown.

1950s 7" x 12" x 9 1/2" cooler
music box (different versions).
$3,500

1930s 7' Kay Displays tin and wood festoon (rare when found complete as shown). **$4,500**

1930s 12" x 30" Kay Displays wood hanging sign, rare. **$3,000**

1907 8" x 10" celluloid "Satisfied" sign manufactured by Whitehead and Hoag Company, Newark, New Jersey. **$20,000**

This sign is very rare. The price range is for examples in high quality collector condition and complete with ornate corners as shown. Examples in lesser condition will be valued much lower.

1899 9 1/4" serving tray. **$24,000**

1935 cardboard sign, 13" x 21", two-sided. **$750**

1914 trolley sign. **$8,000**

1956 cardboard sign, 20" x 36". **$450**

1950s thermometer,
porcelain, 8" x 36".
$1,800

1933 cardboard cutout,
62", Clark Gable and
Joan Crawford, folds in
center. **$9,000**

1940s Santa Claus cutout, 32" x 42". **$850**

1934 4 1/2' Wallace Beery and Jackie Cooper foldout. **$4,800**

1957 serving tray. **$300**

1938 cardboard sign, 29" x 50", signed Sundblum, Niagara Litho, Buffalo, New York. **$3,000**

Coin-Operated Devices

Coin-operated devices fall into three main categories: amusement or arcade games, trade stimulators, and vending machines.

Electric baseball 1¢ arcade game, working, all original, nice labels on both sides, 17" tall. **$3,000**

Jennings Monte Carlo 5¢ prospector slot machine, working, rare and desirable machine in overall very fine, restored condition, 60 1/2" tall. **$3,600**

Mills 10¢ floor model, original wood finish and older paint restoration to castings, 59" tall. **$1,800**

Mills floor model golf ball vendor, working original 25-cent slot machine, motor for golf ball dispenser is intact and functional, restored castings, 59" tall. **$8,400**

10¢ American Coin Rol-A-Top machine, with castle board top, restored, 27" tall. **$3,300**

Miniature Baseball World Champion arcade game, working, original with nice labels on both sides of machine, includes a small sampling of tokens to be won, two small skulls and one Popeye charm, 16 1/2" tall. **$750-$1,250**

Mills 5¢ QT twin jackpot slot machine, working, brown spatter finish, 19" tall. **$3,000**

Mills 5¢ Hash Mark QT slot machine, working, all original, includes twin jackpot, 19" tall. **$1,560**

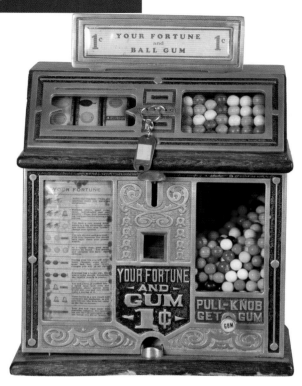

Superior Confection Company 1¢ trade stimulator, working, all original, includes gum vendor, 18" tall. **$1,320**

Two tabletop game vendors, both working, Booster machine and Select'em machine with dice and ball game, each 17" long. **$570**

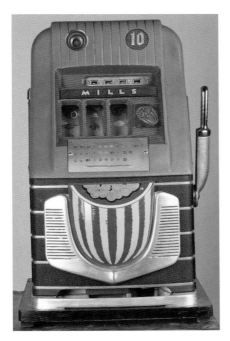

Mills 10¢ melon bell machine, all original, very fine condition, 26 1/2" tall. **$2,700**

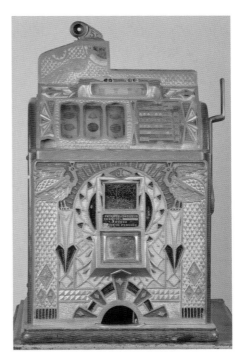

Jennings Peacock Escalator model, all original, as-found and untouched, 26" tall. **$2,280**

Nevada Club 25¢ four-reel Buckaroo machine, with red plastic light-ups and hand low jackpot, features the Lake Tahoe Reno figure on jackpot cover, castings have been replated, 27" tall. **$4,500**

Jennings $1 Nevada Club machine, open front model with green light up plastics, 27 1/2" tall. **$5,400**

Mills 10¢ floor model slot machine, bird's-eye maple cabinet, castings and cabinet have been restored, 59" tall. **$2,040**

Mills 25¢ floor model, brown paint, appears to be in as-found all original condition, 59" tall. **$3,900**

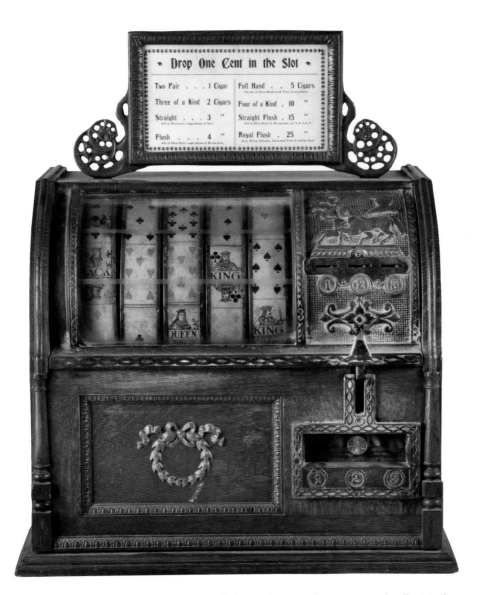

Drop One Cent in the Slot

Two Pair	. . . 1 Cigar	Full Hand	. . 5 Cigars
Three of a Kind	2 Cigars	Four of a Kind	. 10 "
Straight	. . 3 "	Straight Flush	. 15 "
Flush	. . . 4 "	Royal Flush	. 25 "

Mills jockey machine, turn-of-the-century, early fancy cabinet, machine appears to be all original except for cash drawer on right side, 21" tall. **$9,600**

Caille's Centaur upright slot machine, overall exceptional restoration to the quarter sewn oak cabinet with black oxidized finish, retains original oak back door, plays nickels, marquee is probably a replacement, 65" tall. **$24,000**

Superior Confection Company 5¢ trade stimulator, working, all original, includes gum vendor, 18" tall. **$1,920**

Jennings 10¢ Standard Chief machine, reel strips are original, machine has been restored with a hammered gold finish and refinishing to wood cabinet, 27" tall. **$1,440**

Comics

BY BRENT FRANKENHOFF

More sales records have been set for comics since the previous edition of *Warman's Antiques & Collectibles*, the biggest raising the bar to more than $2 million for the highest-price comic book sold.

On Nov. 30, 2011, online auction house ComicConnect.com sold a copy of *Action Comics* #1 (Jun 38, the first appearance of Superman) for $2.16 million. Previously part of actor Nicolas Cage's comics collection, the copy was graded 9.0 (very fine/near mint) on a 10-point grading scale by Certified Guaranty Company (CGC).

Brent Frankenhoff

Major media attention added to the excitement as the book broke the previous high of $1.5 million set by the sale of a lower-grade copy of *Action Comics* #1 (CGC-graded 8.5, very fine+), also sold by ComicConnect.com in 2010.

This record-setting copy of *Action* #1, which started comics' Golden Age, was stolen several years ago, but was recovered earlier in 2011 from a storage locker and later graded and consigned to ComicConnect.com. Going by specific marks on the book, ComicConnect.com co-founders Vincent Zurzolo and Stephen Fishler were able to identify it as coming from Cage's collection and as an issue they had sold to the actor a number of years earlier.

This marks the fourth comic book sold by the firm in the $1 million+ range. In addition to these two copies of *Action* #1, the firm first set a record earlier in 2010 with the $1 million sale of a CGC 8.0 (very fine) copy of *Action* #1. A year later, ComicConnect sold the first Silver Age comic book to exceed $1 million — a CGC-graded 9.6 (near mint+) copy of *Amazing Fantasy* #15 (Aug 62, the first appearance of Spider-Man) — for $1.1 million on March 7, 2011.

Heritage Comic Auctions set records in 2012 with a pair of sales. In February, the firm realized $8.79 million in a three-day event in New York City. Leading the charge was a consignment of more than 300 comics from an original-owner collection. Purchased between 1938 and 1941, the Billy Wright Collection was consigned to Heritage by Wright's great-nephew, Michael Rorrer, who acquired them after the death of his great-aunt. Billy Wright, an only child whose mother didn't throw away many of his possessions, had carefully kept the comics for nearly 60 years before his death in 1994.

Rorrer said that he took half the comics and gave the other half of the collection to his mother to give to his brother.

When Rorrer told a co-worker about a copy of *Captain America Comics* #2 (Apr 41) in the stack that he had, the co-worker said it would be great if a copy of *Action Comics* #1 was also in the collection. Rorrer checked — and found that he had one. Realizing that he was onto something, he called his mother and brother and compiled a list of all the comics in the collection.

Heritage Managing Director of Comics Lon Allen was contacted and came to Rorrer's mother's home to appraise the collection.

"This is just one of those collections that all the guys in the business think don't exist any more," Allen said, adding that the collection was jaw-dropping and that Wright appeared to have had an uncanny knack for picking up the key comics at the time.

While the $8.79 million sale was impressive, Heritage handily topped it in late July with another three-day sale, this time in Beverly Hills, California, as part of a multi-day pop-culture event with a series of auctions. The July 26-28 sale realized more than $10.47 million.

Original art was the big seller on this sale, as you'll read in the illustration art chapter, but comics did extremely well with a consignment dubbed the "Doug Schmeel/PedigreeComics.com Collection" realizing more than $3.94 million. Topping that group was Schmeel's copy of *X-Men* #1 (Sep 63), from the Pacific Coast Collection, which was CGC-graded 9.8 (near mint/mint) and sold for $492,938.

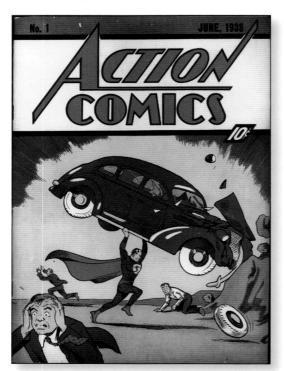

Record sales may have been the big news stories of comics in 2012, but there were also plenty of other trends to follow. The blockbuster success of *The Avengers* movie caused a surge of activity in sales of back issues including the team's first appearance in *Avengers* #1 (Sep 63). *The Dark Knight Rises*, the conclusion of director Christopher Nolan's Batman trilogy, had a lesser effect on the prices of back issues featuring the Caped Crusader. A similar minor bump was shown by the lackluster performance of *The Amazing Spider-Man*.

Over on the small screen, the continued success of AMC's "The Walking Dead," based on the Image Comics series by Robert Kirkman, has made back-issue prices for early issues continue to rise, despite their reprinting in various hardcover and softcover books. Speculation on later issues, which feature first appearances of characters that are expected to pop up in later seasons of the show, is also on the rise. A caution with such speculation is that this sort of interest can be short-lived and long-term investment is not a wise option. Do not hang on to back issues of currently "hot" series in the hopes of realizing a bigger gain later. Multiple reprintings and the rise of paperback and hardcover collections make such strategies a losing proposition for the most part.

BRENT FRANKENHOFF *is the editor of* Comics Buyer's Guide, *the longest-running U.S. magazine about comic books. A lifelong collector (he got his first comics when he was three and still has them), he's been following the comics market for more than 20 years.*

All prices and images courtesy of Heritage Comic Auctions.

Action Comics #1 (1938), CGC-graded 3.0 (good/ very good), from the Billy Wright Collection. **$298,750**

Adventure Comics #40 (1939), CGC-graded 8.0 (very fine), from the Billy Wright Collection. **$59,750**

All-American Comics #16 (1940), CGC-graded 8.0 (very fine), from the Billy Wright Collection. **$203,150**

All-Star Comics #8 (1942), CGC-graded 8.0 (very fine), from the Empire Comics Collection. **$56,763**

Amazing Fantasy #15 (1962), CGC-graded 7.5 (very fine-). **$49,294**

Avengers #1 (1963), CGC-graded 9.6 (near mint+), Pacific Coast pedigree copy from the Doug Schmeel Collection. **$274,850**

Batman #1 (1940), CGC-graded 8.5 (very fine+), from the Billy Wright Collection. **$274,850**

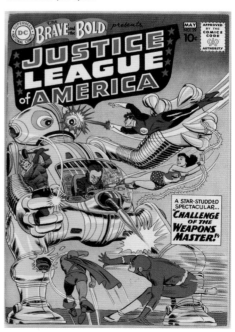

Brave and the Bold #29 (1960), CGC-graded 8.0 (very fine). **$5,975**

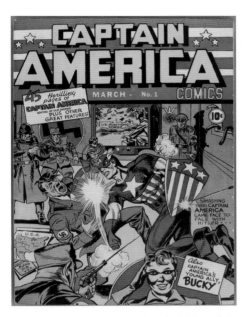

Captain America Comics #1 (1941), CGC-graded 7.0 (fine/very fine). **$89,625**

Captain America Comics #2 (1941), CGC-graded 9.4 (near mint), from the Billy Wright Collection. **$113,525**

Captain America Comics #3 (1941), CGC-graded 9.2 (near mint-), from the Billy Wright Collection. **$50,788**

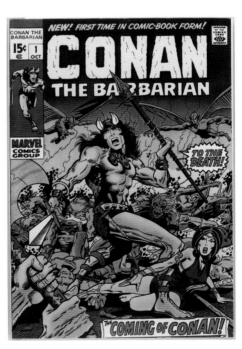

Conan the Barbarian #1 (1970), CGC-graded 9.8 (near mint/mint), from the Empire Comics Collection. **$3,884**

Detective Comics #27 (1939), CGC-graded 6.5 (fine+), from the Billy Wright Collection. **$522,813**

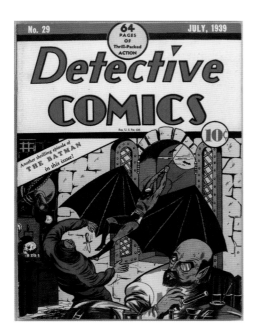

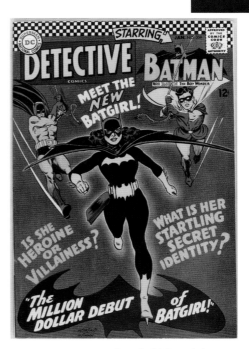

Detective Comics #29 (1939), CGC-graded 7.0 (fine/very fine), from the Billy Wright Collection. **$83,650**

Detective Comics #359 (1967), CGC-graded 9.2 (near mint-). **$1,613**

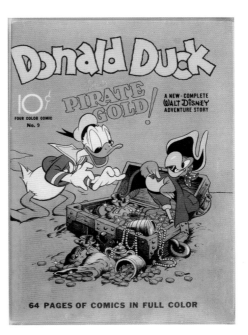

Fantastic Four #1 (1961), CGC-graded 9.2 (near mint-), White Mountain pedigree copy from the Doug Schmeel Collection. **$203,150**

Four Color #9 (1942), CGC-graded 8.5 (very fine+). **$7,768**

Four Color #386, aka Uncle Scrooge #1 (1952), CGC-graded 9.6 (near mint+). **$26,290**

Incredible Hulk #181 (1974), CGC-graded 9.8 (near mint/mint). **$9,560**

Journey into Mystery #83 (1962), CGC-graded 9.2 (near mint-). **$83, 650**

Marvel Comics #1 (1939), CGC-graded 7.5 (very fine-), from the Billy Wright Collection. **$113,525**

Showcase #22 (1959), CGC-graded 7.5
(very fine-). **$14,340**

Tales of Suspense #39 (1963), CGC-graded 9.6
(near mint+), Pacific Coast pedigree copy from
the Doug Schmeel Collection. **$262,900**

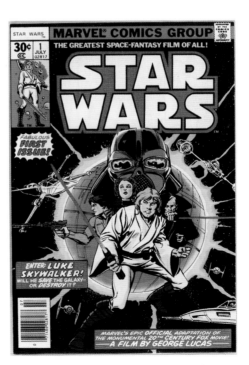

Star Wars #1 (1977), CGC-graded 9.2
(near mint-). **$508**

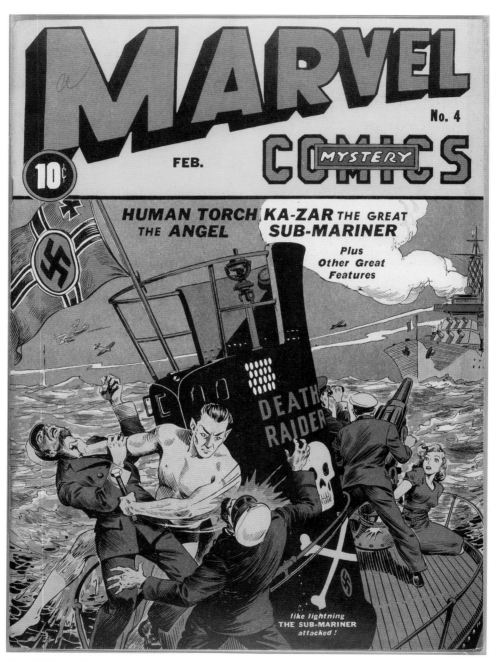

Marvel Mystery Comics #4 (1940), CGC-graded 9.2 (near mint-), from the Billy Wright Collection. **$50,788**

X-Men #1 (1963), CGC-graded 9.8 (near mint/mint), from the Doug Schmeel Collection. **$492,938**

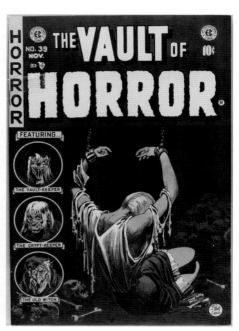

Teenage Mutant Ninja Turtles #1 (1984), CGC-graded 9.4 (near mint). **$5,378**

Vault of Horror #39 (1954), CGC-graded 9.8 (near mint/mint), Gaines File Copy #1. **$3,585**

Walking Dead #1 (2003), CGC-graded 9.8 (near mint/mint). **$1,434**

Whiz Comics #2 (1940), CGC-graded 1.0 (fair). **$9,560**

Cookie Jars

Cookie jars, colorful and often whimsical, are popular with collectors. They were made by almost every manufacturer in all types of materials. Figural character cookie jars are the most popular with collectors.

Cookie jars often were redesigned to reflect newer tastes. Hence, the same jar may be found in several different variations, and these variations can affect the price.

Many cookie-jar shapes were manufactured by more than one company and, as a result, can be found with different marks. This often happened because of mergers. Molds also were traded and sold among companies.

For more information on cookie jars, see *Warman's Cookie Jars Identification and Price Guide* by Mark F. Moran.

Pinocchio, two versions, by California Originals, both 12 1/4" tall, impressed marks on bottom, "Calif. Orig. G-131 USA." Also found unmarked or with only an impressed "USA." Unlike some other older jars, the color variations in these Pinocchios do not affect value. **$1,200+ each**

Little Old Lady by Abingdon, 9" tall, circa 1950, ink-stamped "Abingdon USA" and impressed "471." (Also found with other under-glaze decorations and in solid colors, similarly priced.) **$600+**

Plaid Dog by Brayton Laguna, 9" tall, 1950s, marked inside the lid with a hand-written "H" and stamped on the bottom, "Brayton California USA." **$500+**

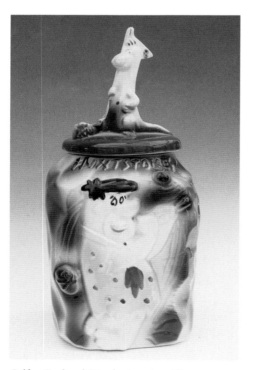

Golfing Fred and Dino by American Bisque, 14 1/4" tall, 1960s, impressed mark on back, "U.S.A." (Beware of smaller reproductions.) **$1,500+**

Queen by Hedi Schoop, 13 1/4" tall, 1950s, marked inside lid, "Hedi Schoop 2" and on bottom, "Hedi Schoop." **$700-$800**

Castle Turret, distributed by Cardinal, airbrush colors, 11 1/2" tall, 1950s, marked on reverse, "Cardinal Copyright (symbol) 310 USA." **$175-$200**

Gleep by Haeger, 11" tall, 1960s, ink-stamped on bottom, "Haeger USA Copyright (symbol)," foil label, "Glaze Tested United States Pottery Association." **$300**

Little Boy Blue marked "Hull-Ware Boy Blue U.S.A. 971-122" with cold paint. This jar was not produced, and there are only a few known to exist. **$5,000**

Dog with Basket by Brush, 12" tall, unmarked (sometimes found with paper label). **$800+**

Castle by Twin Winton, 10" tall, introduced in 1954, this example slightly later, soft impressed mark, "The Twin Wintons Copyright (symbol)." Found in other color combinations. **$250-$300**

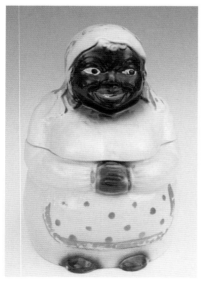

Mammy by National Silver, with cold-paint highlights on mouth, 9 1/2" tall, 1940s, marked on bottom, "USA NSCO." (Sometimes found with foil labels and the mark "NASCO.") **$500+**

Watermelon by Metlox, 10 1/8" tall, 1960s, impressed mark on bottom, "Made in Poppytrail Calif." with gold and brown foil label, "Metlox Manufacturing Co." **$1,000+**

Jocko by Robinson Ransbottom, with unusual glaze decoration, 12" tall, 1950s, impressed mark, "RRPCo. USA Roseville O." This example, **$750+**; in normal colors, **$350-$400**

Balloon Lady by Pottery Guild of America, 11 3/4" tall, 1940s, unmarked. **$175+**

Carousel by Red Wing, with distinct color and decorating styles, each 8" tall, 1950s, marked with two styles of ink stamp. **$800 each**

Clown by Regal China, 12" tall, 1950s, marked, "Translucent Vitrified China Copyright (symbol) C. Miller–54-439A." **$700+**

Humpty Dumpty by Purinton, 10 1/2" tall, 1950s, unmarked. **$225-$250+**

Water Lily blue cookie jar (1-8") by Roseville, raised mark, 9" x 10 1/4". **$400-$500**

Drum Major by Shawnee, 10" tall, late 1940s, impressed mark, "U.S.A.," also found marked "#10" and rarely in gold trim. **$700+**; *with gold trim,* **$1,200+**

ABC Bear by Sierra-Vista, 11 3/4" tall, late 1950s, with original foil label, "Genuine hand Painted Starnes California U.S.A.," otherwise unmarked. **$400+**

Queen Bee by Starnes, 10 3/4" tall, 1950s, unmarked. **$375+**

Rocking Horse by William Hirsch, 12" tall, raised mark on the bottom, "Copyright (symbol) 1950 Wm. Hirsch California." **$100**

Fawn at Stump by Ungemach, 9 1/4" tall, 1950s, impressed mark, "U.S.A." on the back. **$300+**

Leprechaun (in red) by McCoy, 12" tall, 1950s, unmarked, never put into wide production, but no one is certain just how many were made. (Widely reproduced slightly smaller.) In red, **$3,000+**

Folk Art

Folk art generally refers to items that originated among the common people of a region and usually reflect their traditional culture, especially regarding everyday or festive items. Unlike fine art, folk art is primarily utilitarian and decorative rather than purely aesthetic.

Exactly what constitutes the genre is a question that continues to be vigorously debated among collectors, dealers, museum curators, and scholars. Some want to confine folk art to non-academic, handmade objects. Others are willing to include manufactured material.

Folk art can range from crude drawings by children to academically trained artists' paintings of "common" people and scenery. It encompasses items made from a variety of materials, from wood and metal to cloth and paper.

The accepted timetable for folk art runs from is earliest origins up to the mid-20th century.

Bonhams

Pieced and appliqued "princess feather" cotton quilt, third quarter 19th century, borders embroidered with various initials, approximately 91 1/2" x 91 1/2". **$2,000**

Michaan's Auctions

Folk art wrought iron retailer's sign in shape of boot, 19th century, 33" high. **$500**

Pook and Pook, Inc.

Miniature tramp art dresser, circa 1900, 22" high x 12" wide. **$972**

Pook and Pook, Inc.

Joseph Lochbaum (Southeast Pennsylvania, active 1799-1806), ink and watercolor fraktur birth certificate, 12 3/4" x 14 3/4". **$711**

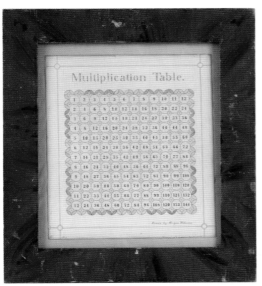

Pook and Pook, Inc.

Pen and ink schoolwork drawing of math table, inscribed drawn by Morgan Williams, JAN 28 1902, 12" x 10 1/2". **$948**

Pook & Pook, Inc.

Carved figure of eagle, circa 1900, 22" high. **$711**

Pook and Pook, Inc.

Pennsylvania floral hooked rug, 19th century, 36 1/2" x 36". **$243**

Pook and Pook, Inc.

Carved and painted figure of angel, 19th century, 14 3/4" high. **$273**

Pook & Pook, Inc.

Needlework of cat seated on pillow, early 19th century, 12" x 11 1/2". **$334**

Pook & Pook, Inc.

Oil on velvet theorem, 19th century, cornucopia of flowers and hummingbird, 17" x 23 1/2". **$334**

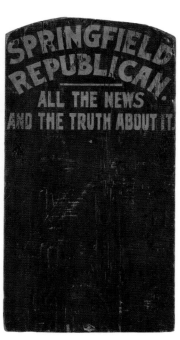

Pook & Pook, Inc.

Painted pine bulletin board, 19th century, titled Springfield Republican, 29 1/2" x 15 1/2". **$1,007**

Pook & Pook, Inc.

Tramp art box, 20th century, together with chipped carved wall box with mirror, taller item 7 1/4". **$148**

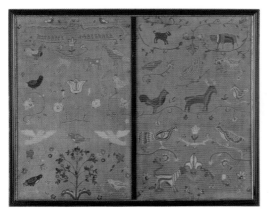

Pook & Pook, Inc.

Pair of crewelwork panels, dated 1734, wrought by Margaret Marshall, decorated with tulips, birds, stag, owl, etc., frame 28" x 34". **$2,844**

Pook and Pook, Inc.

Pennsylvania carved and painted cow, 19th century, 6" high x 7 1/2" long. **$91**

Pook & Pook, Inc.

Two hooked rugs, 20th century, one in shape of butterfly, the other inscribed East West Home's Best, larger rug 55" x 34 1/2". **$356**

Pook & Pook, Inc.

Patchwork and quilted table rug, 19th century, central floral decoration, 22" high. **$296**

Pook & Pook, Inc.

Tramp art doll's dresser, circa 1900, 23" high x 12 1/4" wide. **$243**

Pook & Pook, Inc.

Pine cutting board in shape of man, 19th century, 21" high. **$1,007**

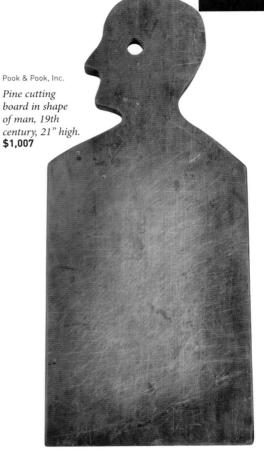

Pook & Pook, Inc.

Large American needlework and oil on silk banner, late 19th century, center panel depicting a naval battle, 42" x 25". **$415**

Pook & Pook, Inc.

Carved and painted wall plaque of fox, late 19th century, 8 1/4" high. **$486**

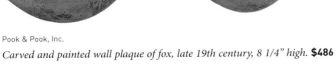

Pook & Pook, Inc.

Silk on linen sampler, 18th century, wrought by Elizabeth Brown 17__ Kingston, 17" x 12 3/4". **$122**

Pook and Pook, Inc.

Pennsylvania satinwood pincushion with drawer, early 19th century, initialed A.M.K, with tulip, 6" high x 6 1/2" wide. **$356**

Pook & Pook, Inc.

Tramp art clock hutch, dated 1919, horseshoe, heart and shield decoration, 15" high x 17 3/4" wide. **$356**

Pook & Pook, Inc.

Four tramp art trinket boxes, circa 1900, largest 8 1/4" high, together with two tramp art frames. **$356**

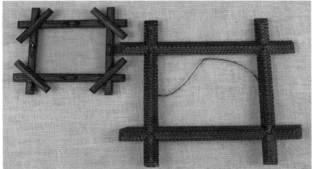

Pook & Pook, Inc.

Pair of tramp art frames, early 20th century, heart decoration, together with another tramp art frame, 22" x 19 1/2". **$356**

Pook and Pook, Inc.

Painted diorama of clipper ship, circa 1900, 36" high x 45 1/2" wide. **$830**

Pook & Pook, Inc.

Circular tramp art frame, mid-20th century, 25" diameter, together with three splint baskets. **$504**

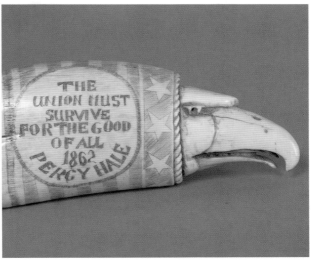

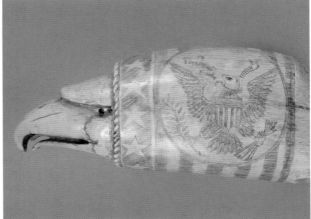

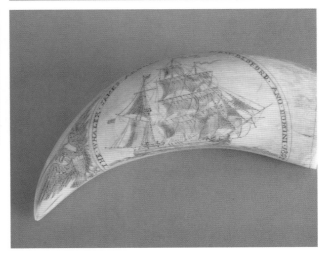

Pook & Pook, Inc.

Three scrimshaw whale teeth, 20th century, decorated with American eagle and the whaler James Arnold Out of New Bedford, 5" long, 7" long and 5 1/2" long. **$1,458**

Pook & Pook, Inc.

Carved folk art figure of seated cat, circa 1915, 11 3/4" high. **$1,067**

Pook and Pook, Inc.

Painted stick model of airplane, 43" high x 37 3/4" wide. **$395**

Pook & Pook, Inc.

Scrimshaw decorated tusk, 20th century, depicting the ship Mercury beneath eagle, 10" high. **$1,422**

Furniture

Furniture Styles

American

Style: Pilgrim Century
Dating: 1620-1700
Major Wood(s): Oak

General Characteristics:
Case pieces: rectilinear low-relief carved panels; blocky and bulbous turnings; splint-spindle trim
Seating pieces: shallow carved panels; spindle turnings

Style: William and Mary
Dating: 1685-1720
Major Wood(s): Maple and walnut

General Characteristics:
Case pieces: paint decorated chests on ball feet; chests on frames; chests with two-part construction; trumpet-turned legs; slant-front desks
Seating pieces: molded, carved crest rails; banister backs; cane, rush (leather) seats; baluster, ball and block turnings; ball and Spanish feet

Style: Queen Anne
Dating: 1720-50
Major Wood(s): Walnut

General Characteristics:
Case pieces: mathematical proportions of elements; use of the cyma or S-curve broken-arch pediments; arched panels, shell carving, star inlay; blocked fronts; cabriole legs and pad feet
Seating pieces: molded yoke-shaped crest rails; solid vase-shaped splats; rush or upholstered seats; cabriole legs; baluster, ring, ball and block-turned stretchers; pad and slipper feet

Style: Chippendale
Dating: 1750-85
Major Wood(s): Mahogany and walnut

General Characteristics:
Case pieces: relief-carved broken-arch pediments; foliate, scroll, shell, fretwork carving; straight, bow or serpentine fronts; carved cabriole legs; claw and ball, bracket or ogee feet
Seating pieces: carved, shaped crest rails with out-turned ears; pierced, shaped splats; ladder (ribbon) backs; upholstered seats; scrolled arms; carved cabriole legs or straight (Marlboro) legs; claw and ball feet

Style: Federal (Hepplewhite)
Dating: 1785-1800
Major Wood(s): Mahogany and light inlays

General Characteristics:
Case pieces: more delicate rectilinear forms; inlay with eagle and classical motifs; bow, serpentine or tambour fronts; reeded quarter columns at sides; flared bracket feet
Seating pieces: shield backs; upholstered seats; tapered square legs

---

Style: Federal (Sheraton)
Dating: 1800-1820
Major Wood(s): Mahogany and mahogany veneer and maple

General Characteristics:
Case pieces: architectural pediments; acanthus carving; outset (cookie or ovolu) corners and reeded columns; paneled sides; tapered, turned, reeded or spiral-turned legs; bow or tambour fronts, mirrors on dressing tables
Seating pieces: rectangular or square backs; slender carved banisters; tapered, turned or reeded legs

---

Style: Classical (American Empire)
Dating: 1815-1850
Major Wood(s): Mahogany and mahogany veneer and rosewood

General Characteristics:
Case pieces: increasingly heavy proportions; pillar and scroll construction; lyre, eagle, Greco-Roman and Egyptian motifs; marble tops; projecting top drawer; large ball feet, tapered fluted feet or hairy paw feet; brass, ormolu decoration
Seating pieces: high-relief carving; curved backs; out-scrolled arms; ring turnings; sabre legs, curule (scrolled-S) legs; brass-capped feet, casters

Style: Victorian – Early Victorian
Dating: 1840-1850
Major Wood(s): Mahogany veneer, black walnut and rosewood

General Characteristics:
Case pieces: Pieces tend to carry over the Classical style with the beginnings of the Rococo substyle, especially in seating pieces.

Style: Victorian – Gothic Revival
Dating: 1840-1890
Major Wood(s): Black walnut, mahogany and rosewood

General Characteristics:
Case pieces: architectural motifs; triangular arched pediments; arched panels; marble tops; paneled or molded drawer fronts; cluster columns; bracket feet, block feet or plinth bases
Seating pieces: tall backs; pierced arabesque backs with trefoils or quatrefoils; spool turning; drop pendants

Style: Victorian – Rococo (Louis XV)
Dating: 1845-1870
Major Wood(s): Black walnut, mahogany and rosewood

General Characteristics:
Case pieces: arched carved pediments; high-relief carving, S- and C-scrolls, floral, fruit motifs, busts and cartouches; mirror panels; carved slender cabriole legs; scroll feet; bedroom suites (bed, dresser, commode)
Seating pieces: high-relief carved crest rails; balloon-shaped backs; urn-shaped

splats; upholstery (tufting); demi-cabriole legs; laminated, pierced and carved construction (Belter and Meeks); parlor suites (sets of chairs, love seats, sofas)

Style: Victorian – Renaissance Revival
Dating: 1860-1885
Major Wood(s): Black walnut, burl veneer, painted and grained pine

General Characteristics:
Case pieces: rectilinear arched pediments; arched panels, burl veneer; applied moldings; bracket feet, block feet, plinth bases; medium and high-relief carving, floral and fruit, cartouches, masks and animal heads; cyma-curve brackets; Wooton patent desks
Seating pieces: oval or rectangular backs with floral or figural cresting; upholstery outlined with brass tacks; padded armrests; tapered turned front legs, flared square rear legs

Style: Victorian – Louis XVI
Dating: 1865-1875
Major Wood(s): Black walnut and ebonized maple

General Characteristics:
Case pieces: gilt decoration, marquetry, inlay; egg and dart carving; tapered turned legs, fluted
Seating pieces: molded, slightly arched crest rails; keystone-shaped backs; circular seats; fluted tapered legs

Style: Victorian – Eastlake
Dating: 1870-1895
Major Wood(s): Black walnut, burl veneer, cherry and oak

General Characteristics:
Case pieces: flat cornices; stile and rail construction; burl veneer panels; low-relief geometric and floral machine carving; incised horizontal lines
Seating pieces: rectilinear; spindles; tapered, turned legs, trumpet-shaped legs

Style: Victorian Jacobean and Turkish Revival
Dating: 1870-1890
Major Wood(s): Black walnut and maple

General Characteristics:
Case pieces: A revival of some heavy 17th century forms, most commonly in dining room pieces
Seating pieces:
Turkish Revival style features: oversized, low forms; overstuffed upholstery; padded arms; short baluster, vase-turned legs; ottomans, circular sofas
Jacobean Revival style features: heavy bold carving spool and spiral turnings

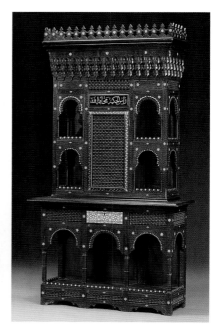

Style: Victorian – Aesthetic Movement
Dating: 1880-1900
Major Wood(s): Painted hardwoods, black walnut, ebonized finishes

General Characteristics:
Case pieces: rectilinear forms; bamboo turnings, spaced ball turnings; incised stylized geometric and floral designs, sometimes highlighted with gilt
Seating pieces: bamboo turning; rectangular backs; patented folding chairs

Style: Art Nouveau
Dating: 1895-1918
Major Wood(s): Ebonized hardwoods, fruitwoods

General Characteristics:
Case pieces: curvilinear shapes; floral marquetry; whiplash curves
Seating pieces: elongated forms; relief-carved floral decoration; spindle backs, pierced floral backs; cabriole legs

Style: Turn-of-the-Century (Early 20th Century)
Dating: 1895-1910
Major Wood(s): Golden (quarter-sawn) oak, mahogany hardwood stained to resemble mahogany

General Characteristics:
Case pieces: rectilinear and bulky forms; applied scroll carving or machine-pressed designs; some Colonial and Classical Revival detailing
Seating pieces: heavy framing or high spindle-trimmed backs; applied carved or machine-pressed back designs; heavy scrolled or slender turned legs; often feature some Colonial Revival or Classical Revival detailing such as claw and ball feet

Style: Mission (Arts and Crafts movement)
Dating: 1900-1915
Major Wood(s): Oak

General Characteristics:
Case pieces: rectilinear through-tenon construction; copper decoration, hand-hammered hardware; square legs
Seating pieces: rectangular splats; medial and side stretchers; exposed pegs; corbel supports

---

Style: Colonial Revival
Dating: 1890-1930
Major Wood(s): Oak, walnut and walnut veneer, mahogany veneer

General Characteristics:
Case pieces: forms generally following designs of the 17th, 18th and early 19th centuries; details for the styles such as William and Mary, Federal, Queen Anne, Chippendale or early Classical were used but often in a simplified or stylized form; mass-production

in the early 20th century flooded the market with pieces which often mixed and matched design details and used a great deal of thin veneering to dress up designs; dining room and bedroom suites were especially popular
Seating pieces: designs again generally followed early period designs with some mixing of design elements.

Style: Art Deco
Dating: 1925-1940
Major Wood(s): Bleached woods, exotic woods, steel and chrome

General Characteristics:
Case pieces: heavy geometric forms
Seating pieces: streamlined, attenuated geometric forms; overstuffed upholstery

Style: Modernist or Mid-Century
Dating: 1945-1970
Major Wood(s): Plywood, hardwood or metal frames

General Characteristics: Modernistic designers such as the Eames, Vladimir Kagan, George Nelson and Isamu Noguchi lead the way in post-War design. Carrying on the tradition of Modernist designers of the 1920s and 1930s, they focused on designs for the machine age, which could be mass-produced for the popular market. By the late 1950s many of their pieces were used in commercial office spaces and schools as well as in private homes.

Case pieces: streamlined or curvilinear abstract designs with simple detailing; plain round or flattened legs and arms commonly used; mixed materials including wood, plywood, metal, glass and molded plastics
Seating pieces: streamlined and abstract curvilinear designs generally using newer materials such as plywood or simple hardwood framing; Fabric and synthetics such as vinyl were widely used for upholstery with finer fabrics and real leather featured on more expensive pieces; seating made of molded plastic shells on metal frames and legs used on many mass-produced designs

Style: Danish Modern
Dating: 1950-1970
Major Wood(s): Teak

General Characteristics:
Case and Seating pieces: This variation of Modernistic post-war design originated in Scandinavia, hence the name; designs were simple and restrained with case pieces often having simple boxy forms with short rounded tapering legs; seating pieces have a simple teak framework with lines coordinating with case pieces; vinyl or natural fabric were most often used for upholstery; in the United States dining room suites were the most popular use for this style although some bedroom suites and general seating pieces were available

English

Style: Jacobean
Dating: Mid-17th century
Major Wood(s): Oak, walnut

General Characteristics:
Case pieces: low-relief carving, geometrics and florals; panel, rail and stile construction; applied split balusters
Seating pieces: rectangular backs; carved and pierced crests; spiral turnings ball feet

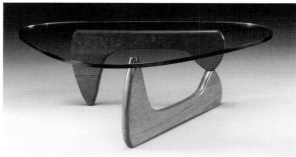

Style: William and Mary
Dating: 1689-1702
Major Wood(s): Walnut, burl walnut veneer
General Characteristics:
Case pieces: marquetry, veneering; shaped aprons; 6-8 trumpet-form legs; curved flat stretchers
Seating pieces: carved, pierced crests; tall caned backs and seats; trumpet-form legs; Spanish feet

Style: Queen Anne
Dating: 1702-1714
Major Wood(s): Walnut, mahogany, veneers
General Characteristics:
Case pieces: cyma curves; broken arch pediments and finials; bracket feet
Seating pieces: carved crest rails; high, rounded backs; solid vase-shaped splats; cabriole legs; pad feet

Style: George I
Dating: 1714-1727
Major Wood(s): Walnut, mahogany, veneer and yew wood

General Characteristics:
Case pieces: broken arch pediments; gilt decoration, japanning; bracket feet
Seating pieces: curvilinear forms; yoke-shaped crests; shaped solid splats; shell carving; upholstered seats; carved cabriole legs; claw and ball feet, pad feet

Style: George II
Dating: 1727-1760
Major Wood(s): Mahogany

General Characteristics:
Case pieces: broken arch pediments; relief-carved foliate, scroll and shell carving; carved cabriole legs; claw and ball feet, bracket feet, ogee bracket feet
Seating pieces: carved, shaped crest rails, out-turned ears; pierced shaped splats; ladder (ribbon) backs; upholstered seats; scrolled arms; carved cabriole legs or straight (Marlboro) legs; claw and ball feet

Style: George III
Dating: 1760-1820
Major Wood(s): Mahogany, veneer, satinwood

General Characteristics:
Case pieces: rectilinear forms; parcel gilt decoration; inlaid ovals, circles, banding or marquetry; carved columns, urns; tambour fronts or bow fronts; plinth bases

Seating pieces: shield backs; upholstered seats; tapered square legs, square legs

Style: Regency
Dating: 1811-1820
Major Wood(s): Mahogany, mahogany veneer, satinwood and rosewood
General Characteristics:
Case pieces: Greco-Roman and Egyptian motifs; inlay, ormolu mounts; marble tops; round columns, pilasters; mirrored backs; scroll feet

Seating pieces: straight backs, latticework; caned seats; sabre legs, tapered turned legs, flared turned legs; parcel gilt, ebonizing

Style: George IV
Dating: 1820-1830
Major Wood(s): Mahogany, mahogany veneer and rosewood

General Characteristics: Continuation of Regency designs

Style: William IV
Dating: 1830-1837
Major Wood(s): Mahogany, mahogany veneer

General Characteristics:
Case pieces: rectilinear; brass mounts, grillwork; carved moldings; plinth bases
Seating pieces: rectangular backs; carved straight crest rails; acanthus, animal carving; carved cabriole legs; paw feet

Style: Victorian
Dating: 1837-1901
Major Wood(s): Black walnut, mahogany, veneers & rosewood

General Characteristics:
Case pieces: applied floral carving; surmounting mirrors, drawers, candle shelves; marble tops
Seating pieces: high-relief carved crest rails; floral & fruit carving; balloon backs, oval backs; upholstered seats, backs; spool, spiral turnings; cabriole legs, fluted tapered legs; scrolled feet

Style: Edwardian
Dating: 1901-1910
Major Wood(s): Mahogany, mahogany veneer & satinwood

General Characteristics: Neo-Classical motifs & revivals of earlier 18th century & early 19th century styles.

Antique Furniture

Skinner, Inc.

Classical carved mahogany and mahogany veneer gilt stencil-decorated sofa, circa 1825, embellished with gilt cornucopias, rosettes, and compotes of flowers, original decoration is well-preserved, 36 1/2" high x 91" wide x 24" deep. **$4,266**

Skinner, Inc.

Painted pine chest over two drawers, New England, early 18th century, the hinged top on a single arch-molded case of two false drawers and two working drawers below, with applied molding at base, on turned feet, with three original brass escutcheons, old surface, 39" high, case 37 1/2" wide, top 19" deep. **$2,844**

Skinner, Inc.

Federal mahogany slant-lid desk, probably Massachusetts, circa 1790-1800, the molded lid opens to an interior of three central drawers inlaid with an arch of stringing centering a diamond escutcheon, with flanking long drawer, short drawers, and valanced compartments, on a case of four scratch-beaded graduated drawers and dovetailed bracket base, old brasses, refinished, 44 1/4" high x 41" wide x 20 1/2" deep. **$1,185**

Skinner, Inc.

Federal inlaid mahogany demilune card table, possibly Charlestown, Massachusetts, circa 1800, old refinish, 29" high x 34 1/2" wide x 17" deep. **$2,133**

Skinner, Inc.

Federal maple carved and inlaid one-drawer stand, possibly Vermont, circa 1825, with contrasting inlay in drawer front, and vase- and ring-turned spiral-carved legs, pulls appear to be original, refinished, 29 3/4" high x 18" wide x 17 3/4" deep. **$889**

Skinner, Inc.

Federal cherry and bird's-eye maple and mahogany veneer half sideboard, made in the shop of Hastings Warren (1779-1845), Middlebury, Vermont, 1814, the cockbeaded inlaid drawers with opalescent Sandwich glass pulls, added in 1833, (old refinish), 39 1/2" high, case 40 1/2" wide x 19" deep. Note: An inscription on the underside of the top right hand drawer traces the history of the piece. It reads in part "Huldah Chipman's daughter of Maj'r Gen. Timothy F. Chipman. Purchased of Brig. Gen. Hastings Warren of Middlebury, Vt./Shoreham, Vt./Nov'm. 1814." **$5,629**

Skinner, Inc.

Cherry one-drawer stand, possibly New England, early 19th century, the square scratch-beaded top above a drawer and ring-turned tapering legs, old refinish, 25 1/2" high x 15 3/4" wide x 16" deep. **$444**

Skinner, Inc.

Glazed cherry corner cupboard, possibly Ohio, circa 1830, the doors opening to three shelves with plate grooves, 86" high, 53 1/2" wide. **$770**

Skinner, Inc.

Windsor braced bow-back side chair, partial brand of I. ALWAYS, New York, late 18th century, with swelled spindles and bulbous vase and ring-turnings, refinished, 37" high, seat 17" high. **$429**

Skinner, Inc.

Federal mahogany card table, possibly southern New England, circa 1800, the rectangular folding top with molded edge above a cockbeaded drawer and straight beaded skirt joining square tapering legs inlaid with diamonds at the cuff, brasses appear to be original, old refinish, 29 1/2" high, 35 3/4" wide, 16 1/2" deep. **$652**

Skinner, Inc.

Federal tiger maple and cherry inlaid chest of drawers, Asa Loomis, Shaftsbury, Vermont, 1816, the case of cockbeaded drawers and flanking bird's-eye maple panels, refinished, replaced brass pulls, inscribed on the underside of the top by the cabinetmaker "Made by Asa Loomis in the year 1816," 45 1/4" high, case 42 1/2" wide x 20 3/4" deep. Provenance: Sold at Skinner, American Furniture and Decorative Arts, Bolton, Massachusetts, March 23, 1997, lot 80. **$6,518**

Skinner, Inc.

Rare and important Federal tiger maple and mahogany, flame birch and bird's-eye maple veneer inlaid bureau, Rutland, Vermont, 1805-1815, replaced brasses, refinished, 41 1/2" high, case 42" wide, top 20 1/4" deep. Provenance: Nathan Liverant and Son; Israel Sack, Inc.; Christie's New York, Important American Furniture, Silver, Folk Art and Decorative Arts, June 23, 1993, lot 204, pp. 132-33. **$65,175**

Skinner, Inc.

Queen Anne carved maple and cherry slant-lid desk, Massachusetts or New Hampshire, late 18th century, fitted with an elaborate interior of blocked and shaped drawers, on bandy legs ending in pad feet, replaced brasses, old refinish, 44 1/2" high, case 37 1/2" wide, 18 1/2" deep. **$5,036**

Skinner, Inc.

Red-painted sack-back Windsor chair, Newport, Rhode Island, area, late 18th century, with curved arm supports and carved seat, old red-painted surface over earlier green, 36 1/2" high, seat 16 1/4" high. Provenance: Consigned by a descendant of John Goddard, the 18th century Newport, Rhode Island, cabinetmaker. **$7,703**

Skinner, Inc.

Chippendale carved mahogany oxbow slant-lid desk, Massachusetts, circa 1770-1780, old replaced brasses, refinished, 44" high, 42 1/2" wide, 22" deep. There is a full-length strip of mahogany at the back of the top, about 1 1/2" wide. **$1,422**

Pook & Pook, Inc.

Victorian wire three-tier plant stand, 19th century, 48 1/2" high, 31" wide. **$119**

Skinner, Inc.

Small brown-painted pine lift-top desk on frame, New England, early 19th century, shaped gallery with beaded hinged lid opening to compartments, drawer below, on square tapering legs, brass pulls probably replaced, old surface, 39 3/4" high, 25" wide, 18" deep. **$563**

Pook & Pook, Inc.

New England Chippendale figured maple chest on chest, circa 1770, 75" high, 39" wide. **$7,703**

Pook & Pook, Inc.

Pennsylvania writing arm Windsor chair, circa 1810, retaining an old black surface. **$972**

Pook & Pook, Inc.

Regency Chinoiserie decorated sewing stand, circa 1830, 28 1/2" high, 17" wide. **$237**

Pook & Pook, Inc.

Pennsylvania painted child's rope bed, early 19th century, retaining a vibrant blue surface, 29 1/2" high, 72" wide, 38" deep. **$652**

Skinner, Inc.

Federal carved cherry and mahogany veneer inlaid swell-front chest of drawers, probably southeastern New England, circa 1810, the top with reeded edge on four cockbeaded drawers and base of flaring French feet with inlaid crossbanding, old oval brasses, refinished, 37" high, case 40" wide, 21 1/2" deep. **$1,185**

Skinner, Inc.

Federal mahogany inlaid card table, Rhode Island, circa 1795, the hinged top with string-inlaid edge, on a straight conformingly shaped base joining four square tapering legs with bookend-inlaid dies continuing to icicles and string inlay, old surface, 29" high, 34 1/2" wide, 17" deep. **$533**

Skinner, Inc.

Grain-painted six-board chest, New England, late 18th century, with cutout ends and applied base molding, original surface of faux mahogany graining, 23 1/2" high, case 39" wide, 18" deep. **$276**

Skinner, Inc.

Federal mahogany and wavy birch inlaid desk bookcase, probably Massachusetts, circa 1800-1810, the top section with three hinged doors opening to compartments and drawers, with lower section having a fold-out writing surface above four graduated drawers on cutout bracket base, original brasses, refinished, 57 1/4" high, 38 1/4" wide, 21 1/4" deep. **$2,607**

Skinner, Inc.

Mustard yellow-painted maple glazed two-part step-back cupboard, Pennsylvania, circa 1830-1840, upper section with hinged doors open to a three-shelf interior with plate grooves, above projecting lower section with two shelves, 81" high, 49" wide, 20" deep. **$2,252**

Skinner, Inc.

Federal mahogany inlaid piano forte, Benjamin Crehore and Alpheus Babcock, Milton, Massachusetts, circa 1805, the case attributed to John and Thomas Seymour, Boston, with floral polychrome decoration on the nameboard attributed to the shop of John Ritto Penniman, 32 1/2" high, 63 1/4" deep. **$18,960**

Pook & Pook, Inc.

Pine wall cupboard with two raised panel doors, circa 1790, 67 1/2" high, 33" wide. **$563**

Pook & Pook, Inc.

Miniature Baltimore painted fancy chair, mid-19th century, 16 1/2" high. **$1,541**

Pook & Pook, Inc.

Unusual painted pine bench with four drawers and boot jack ends, 18" high, 71" long, 13" deep. **$3,081**

Pook & Pook, Inc.

Pennsylvania painted pine spice chest, 19th century, retaining a smoke decoration on a red ground, 16 1/2" high, 17" wide. **$1,778**

Pook & Pook, Inc.

Pennsylvania painted pine bucket bench, circa 1840, retaining its original red painted surface, 40 3/4" high, 33" wide. **$1,422**

Pook & Pook, Inc.

Painted pine hanging shelf with scalloped sides, circa 1830, 32 3/4" high, 21 3/4" wide. **$563**

Pook & Pook, Inc.

Pennsylvania painted pine plant stand, 19th century, with two curving tiers, 28" high, 46 1/2" wide.
$326

Pook & Pook, Inc.

American classical mahogany work table, attributed to Isaac Vose, Boston, circa 1830, 30 1/4" high, 24" wide. **$889**

Pook & Pook, Inc.

New England pine sawbuck table, 19th century, retaining an old stained surface, 28 1/4" high, 80" wide, 28" deep. **$668**

Pook & Pook, Inc.

Pennsylvania two-piece walnut Dutch cupboard, circa1820, the upper section with glazed doors and candle drawers, 89" high, 59 1/2" wide. **$1,778**

Pook & Pook, Inc.

Mid Atlantic classical mahogany card table, circa 1815, 28 3/4" high, 37 1/2" wide. **$2,133**

Pook & Pook, Inc.

New England Federal mahogany lyre pedestal card table, circa 1810, 30" high, 36" wide. **$516**

James D. Julia, Inc.

Mid-Atlantic Sheraton carved mahogany crib, first half 19th century, probably Baltimore, each ring-turned swelled cylindrical post headed by an acorn finial joined to the four spindled sides, 53 1/2" high x 32" wide overall x 52" long overall. Provenance: By descent through the family of the original owners. **$253**

Pook & Pook, Inc.

Pennsylvania Federal cherry two-part secretary, circa 1805, with unusual chamfered corners with single flute, 87" high, 39 1/2" wide. **$3,555**

Pook & Pook, Inc.

Pennsylvania walnut candlestand, circa 1790, with a tilting dish top and tripod base, 29" high, 24 1/2" diameter. Provenance: Muhlenberg family. **$830**

Modern Furniture

Pair of armchairs, Charles and Ray Eames design, 1950, manufactured by Zenith Plastics Company for Herman Miller, molded fiberglass with wire rod base and red Naugahyde pad, Model No. LAR-6, each 24" x 24 3/4" x 24". **$4,063**

Wire mesh (Eiffel Tower) chair, Charles and Ray Eames design, 1951-1953, manufactured by Herman Miller, Model No. DKR, 32" x 18 1/2" x 17". **$1,250**

"Home Office" desk, George Nelson design, 1946, manufactured by Herman Miller, Model Nos. 4658 & 601. This example contains the original Pendaflex file basket, which was a special order, 40 1/2" x 54 1/2" x 28". **$6,875**

Grasshopper chair, Eero Saarinen design, 1945, manufactured by Knoll, Model No. 61U, 35 1/2" x 26 1/2" x 33". **$1,800-$2,500**

Non Stop Sofa, Ueli Berger design, 1972, manufactured by de Sede, Ueli Berger, Eleonore Peduzzi-Riva and Heinz Ulrich, Model No. DS-600, approximately 30" x 174" x 39 1/2". **$8,750**

Oval drop-leaf dining table, Edward Wormley design, circa1950, manufactured by Dunbar, from the "Career Group," Model No. 4913, Dunbar Berne Indiana label, closed: 29" x 72" x 18 1/4"; open: 29" x 72" x 72". **$3,125**

Dressers (2), Edward Wormley design, circa 1955, manufactured by Dunbar, retains Dunbar label in one drawer, each 38" x 41 1/2" x 18". **$2,500**

Bookcase, Wilhelm Lutjens design, 1953, manufactured by Den Boer, Netherlands, bent plywood with beech veneer, 52" x 58 1/2" x 11 1/2". **$3,125**

Side table, Carl Aubock design, circa 1950, manufactured by Aubock, 16 1/2" x 29" x 21 1/2". **$2,000-$3,000**

Sleeper sofa, Marco Zanuso design, 1954, manufactured by Arflex, 32" high x 74" long x 35" deep. **$1,750**

Group of three sofas and two coffee tables, George Nelson design, 1956, manufactured by Herman Miller, pair of coffee tables (not illustrated), from the Contract Bench System, retains Herman Miller medallion, each sofa: 26 3/4" x 90" x 30"; each coffee table: 15" x 32" x 32". **$4,750**

Glass

American Brilliant Cut Glass

Cut glass is made by grinding decorations into glass by means of abrasive-carrying metal or stone wheels. An ancient craft, it was revived in 1600 by Bohemians and spread through Europe to Great Britain and America.

American cut glass came of age at the Centennial Exposition in 1876 and the World Columbian Exposition in 1893. America's most significant output of high-quality glass occurred from 1880 to 1917, a period now known as the Brilliant Period. Glass from this period is the most eagerly sought by collectors.

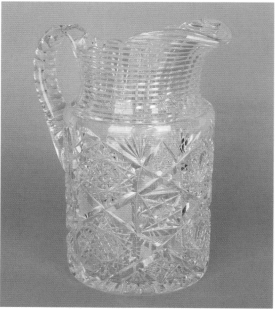

Pook & Pook, Inc.

Hoare signed pitcher, circa 1900, 10 1/2" high. **$415**

Michaan's Auctions

Pitcher, 13 1/2" high. **$80**

Pook & Pook, Inc.

Five pieces of glass, tallest 12". **$415**

DuMouchelles
Libbey dish, circa 1900,
acid stamp at the well,
11 3/4" diameter. **$200**

Pook & Pook, Inc.

Large squat vase, 9 1/2" high, together with a large centerpiece bowl, 6 3/4" high x 16" wide x 8 1/4" long.
Provenance: Collection of Charlene Sussel, Garrett Park, Maryland. **$889**

Burchard Galleries, Inc.
Pair of decanters, deeply cut glass with some clouding, 11 3/4" high x 6" diameter. **$1,400**

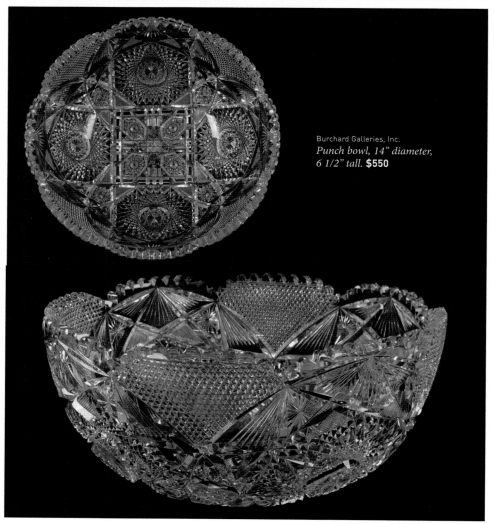

Burchard Galleries, Inc.
Punch bowl, 14" diameter, 6 1/2" tall. **$550**

Mark Mussio, Humler & Nolan

Handled basket, silver cut with four poinsettias balanced about rim accompanied by smaller flowers and feathery foliage, 24-point hobstar cut in the base, double notched handle with cuttings at tips, cut rim, 12" high, 7 1/2" x 11 3/4" rim.
$1,200-$1,500

Mark Mussio, Humler & Nolan

Bowling pin vase with a large hobstar gracing each side flanked by double diamond fields in cane and connected by strawberry diamonds and fans, concave polished neck, cut ray in basee, 14" high.
$2,200

Mark Mussio, Humler & Nolan

Basket showing two cathedral panels with decorative buttons alternating with wheel cut poinsettia flowerheads and feathered foliage bordered by interlocking ribbons, scallop cut edge, step cut sides and star in base, 14 1/2" high, body 4 1/2" x 10".
$200-$300

Mark Mussio, Humler & Nolan

Tazza pedestal vase, open flower inside, vessica petals cut in buttons flanked by cane, wreath of hobstars at curve, Harvard pattern encircles sawtooth scalloped rim, step cut stem, decorative base repeats Harvard pattern and frames a hobstar. 10 1/2" high. **$1,200**

Mark Mussio, Humler & Nolan

Handled basket showing gathered notched prism "drape" at either end held by flashed stars; hobstars and large optical bull's-eye on sides; flaring base has strawberry diamond fields and a surround of vertical notched prism, double notched and X cut handle and sawtooth rim. 21" high, body 13 1/2" long x 6 1/4" wide. **$3,000-$5,000**

Mark Mussio, Humler & Nolan

Slender pedestal vase cut with vertical bars of hobstars that alternate with decorative hobstar buttons and fans bordering, neck band cut with step cutting and topped with scalloped edge, 32-point hobstar cut into base, 18" high. **$3,500**

Mark Mussio, Humler & Nolan

Tazza created at Blackmer Cut Glass Company, New Bedford, Massachusetts, cut with Sultana pattern consisting of hobstars and fans, stem has St. Lewis diamond cutting and base has 24-point hobstar and scalloped edge. 14" high. **$2,500-$3,500**

Mark Mussio, Humler & Nolan

Handled vase wheel cut with a trio of sunflowers on either side surrounded by 32 hobstars on lower section of body plus six more hobstars poised at flaring rim, triple notched handles, ray cut on bottom. 15 1/2" high. **$2,500**

Banana compote attributed to Libbey, 7" body cut with hobstars flanked by fields of cane and decorative fans, scalloped rim, triple cut hobstar base, decorative fluting to stem and bowl measuring 12 3/4" x 6 3/4", possible trim to base. **$1,800-$2,400**

Mark Mussio, Humler & Nolan

Art Glass

Art glass is artistic novelty glassware created for decorative purposes. Types of art glass include leaded glass, molded glass, blown glass, and sandblasted glass. Tiffany, Lalique, and Steuben are some of the best-known types of art glass. Daum Nancy, Baccarat, Galle, Moser, Mount Washington, Fenton, and Quezal are a few others.

Rockwell glass vase with silver overlay etched in flying goose design, Rockwell Silver Company, Meriden, Connecticut, circa 1930, marks: (shield) ROCKWELL, 12 5/8" high. **$1,187**

Durand & Company

Durand & Company blue iridescent glass vase with everted rim, Newark, New Jersey, circa 1900, marks: DURAND, 1713, 7" high. **$437**

Loetz pink glass vase with pinched sides and ruffled rim, Formosa pattern, Glasfabrik Johann Loetz Witwe, Klostermuhle, Austria, circa 1900, 5 1/2" high. **$812**

Lalique vase, clear and opalescent glass with orchid decoration to each side, Wingen-sur-Moder, France, post-1945, marks: Lalique, France, 6 1/8" high. **$2,375**

Czechoslovakian glass vase, light amber glass with applied blue handles and enameled bird and foliate decoration, attributed to Ludwig Moser, Karlovy Vary, Czechoslovakia, circa 1900, unmarked, 12 1/4" high. **$1,187**

Victorian pink glass cabinet vase with applied gilt and floral enamel decoration, circa 1900, 3 1/2" high. **$191**

Frank Lloyd Wright (American, 1867-1959) leaded glass window with stylized geometric trees executed in colored glass in transparent green, amber and white, and opaque opalescent, gold and iridized gold glass, each piece set at slightly different angle, in brass canes; from the Darwin D. Martin House, Buffalo, New York, produced by Linden Glass Company, Chicago, circa 1904, unmarked, 25 3/8" x 16 1/2". This is the upper portion of a Tree of Life window from the Martin House (1904-1905), one of more than 60 windows and doors in this pattern created for the house. The window, which originally extended to stylized trunk and roots, was removed from the home, which was abandoned from 1938 to 1954 and remodeled in the 1960s. At the time of the remodeling, many irreplaceable parts of the house were sold or scrapped. This window was salvaged from a Buffalo dump, with damage beyond repair to the bottom segment. Other examples of this window are represented in the collections of the Corning Museum of Glass, Art Institute of Chicago, and National Gallery of Australia. **$21,250**

James D. Julia

Pair of Peking glass vases, 18th century, China, deep pink cased bottle form examples with high foot rim, 9" high. **$3,335**

Pair of Tiffany Studios Favrile glass candlesticks with ribbed base, circa 1910, marks: LCT, FAVRILE, 1825, 12" high. **$3,750**

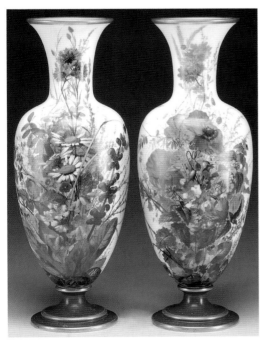

James D. Julia

Pair of Bristol type opaque glass vases, late 19th century, artist signed with monogram "NV," each baluster form vase decorated with floral garden montage, polychrome painted on opaque ivory ground with gilt borders continuing to stepped mauve bases, 23 1/2" h. **$6,900**

Frederick Carder Steuben jade green amphora form glass vase with alabaster handles, later pressed glass base, Corning, New York, circa 1920, 10 1/2" high (vase). **$1,625**

James D. Julia

Peking glass vase, Ch'ien Lung mark and possibly of the period (1735-1796), cobalt blue eight-panel faceted bottle-shaped example, 7 1/4" high. **$7,475**

Mount Washington Royal Flemish glass vase, rose to blue with gilt geometric design with dragon and trefoil lip, Mount Washington Glass Company, New Bedford, Massachusetts, circa 1900, unmarked, 14 1/2" high. **$1,187**

Baccarat gilt and patinated bronze and glass bull's head designed by Chaumet, titled Feria, gilt and patinated bronze horns, eyes, ears and nose, original fitted case, letter of authentication included; House of Chaumet for Baccarat, Baccarat, France, circa 1950, marks: BACCARAT, FERIA, PIECE UNIQUE, CHAUMET, 10 1/2" x 11" x 14". **$7,500**

Carnival Glass

BY ELLEN T. SCHROY

Carnival glass is what is fondly called mass-produced iridescent glassware. The term "carnival glass" has evolved through the years as glass collectors have responded to the idea that much of this beautiful glassware was made as giveaway glass at local carnivals and fairs. However, more of it was made and sold through the same channels as pattern glass and Depression glass. Some patterns were indeed giveaways, and others were used as advertising premiums, souvenirs, etc. Whatever the origin, the term "carnival glass" today encompasses glassware that is usually pattern molded and treated with metallic salts, creating that unique coloration that is so desirable to collectors.

Ellen Schroy

Early names for iridescent glassware, which early 20th century consumers believed to have all come from foreign manufacturers, include Pompeiian Iridescent, Venetian Art, and Mexican Aurora. Another popular early name was "Nancy Glass," as some patterns were believed to have come from the Daum, Nancy, glassmaking area in France. This was at a time when the artistic cameo glass was enjoying great success. While the iridescent glassware being made by such European glassmakers as Loetz influenced the American market place, it was Louis Tiffany's Favrile glass that really caught the eye of glass consumers of the early 1900s. It seems an easy leap to transform Tiffany's shimmering glassware to something that could be mass produced, allowing what we call carnival glass today to become "poor man's Tiffany."

Carnival glass is iridized glassware that is created by pressing hot molten glass into molds, just as pattern glass had evolved. Some forms are hand finished, while others are completely formed by molds. To achieve the marvelous iridescent colors, a process was developed where a liquid solution of metallic salts was put onto the still hot glass form after it was unmolded. As the liquid evaporated, a fine metallic surface was left, which refracts light into wonderful colors. The name given to the iridescent spray by early glassmakers was "dope."

Many of the forms created by carnival glass manufacturers were accessories to the china American housewives so loved. By the early 1900s, consumers could find carnival glassware at such popular stores as F. W. Woolworth and McCrory's. To capitalize on the popular fancy for these colored wares, some other industries bought large quantities of carnival glass and turned them into "packers." This term reflects the practice where baking powder, mustard, or other household products were packed into a special piece of glass that could take on another life after the original product was used. Lee Manufacturing Company used iridized carnival glass as premiums for its baking powder and other products, causing some early carnival glass to be known by the generic term "Baking Powder Glass."

Classic carnival glass production began in the early 1900s and continued about 20 years, but no one really documented or researched production until the first collecting wave struck in 1960. It is important to remember that carnival glasswares were sold in department stores as well as mass merchants, rather than through the general store often associated with a young America. Glassware by this time was mass-produced and sold in large quantities by such enterprising companies as Butler Brothers. When the economics of the country soured in the 1920s, those interested in purchasing iridized glassware were not spared. Many of the leftover inventories of glasshouses found their way to wholesalers who, in turn, sold the wares to those who offered the glittering glass as prizes at carnivals, fairs, circuses, etc. Possibly because this was the last venue people associated the iridized glassware with, it became known as "carnival glass."

ELLEN T. SCHROY, *one of the leading experts in her field, is the author of* Warman's Carnival Glass Identification and Price Guide *and other books on collectible glassware. Her books are the definitive references for glass collectors.*

Blackberry Spray ruffled hat, red opalescent, made by Fenton. **$650**

Acorn Burrs punch bowl and base with four cups (not shown), green, incredible iridescence, made by Northwood. **$1,800 for all**

Acorn Burrs punch bowl, base and six cups, ice green, made by Northwood, very few known. **$23,000**

Northwood Grape and Cable bonbon, stippled, aqua opalescent. **$4,000**

Cherry Chain bonbon, large size, red, made by Fenton. **$5,000**

Blueberry ruffled-top tankard, blue, made by Fenton, 10" high. **$1,000-$1,400**
Outstanding example **$4,500**

Embroidered Mums ruffled bowl, ice blue with beautiful pastel iridescence, made by Northwood. **$950**

Northwood Daisy and Plume rose bowl, aqua opalescent, footed, one of three known, possibly only butterscotch. **$7,000**

Fenton Grape and Cable bowl, ice-cream shape, red slag, 6". **$225**

Dandelion ice blue tankard and tumbler by Northwood.
Tankard **$4,500-$6,000**
Tumbler **$150-$350**

Daisy and Drape vase, turned in, ice green, made by Northwood. **$4,000**

Dragon and Lotus eight-ruffled bowl, red, made by Fenton, 9" diameter.
$1,500-$2,500
Outstanding example **$5,000**

Feather and Heart water pitcher and six tumblers, dark marigold, made by Millersburg. **$875**

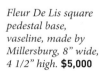

Frolicking Bears water pitcher and one tumbler, green, one of three known, made by U.S. Glass. **$42,000**

Fleur De Lis square pedestal base, vaseline, made by Millersburg, 8" wide, 4 1/2" high. **$5,000**

Curved Star epergne, marigold, 18" high, 12" wide, possibly made by U.S. Glass. **$750-$1,000 (rare)**

Heavy Iris water pitcher, tankard, peach opalescent, made by Dugan. **$2,000**

Fashion compote, smoke, made by Imperial. **$900**

Good Luck bowl, enameled, only one known, blue, made by Northwood. **$800**

Rare Broken Arches ruffled punch bowl and base, purple, 13" diameter, made by Imperial. **$2,500-$3,000**

Gay Nineties water pitcher and one tumbler, green, made by Millersburg. Only one perfect known, second known pitcher, second known tumbler. **$24,000**

Strawberry stippled bowl, ruffled edge, aqua opalescent, one of two known, made by Northwood. **$15,000**

Holly ruffled bowl, red, made by Fenton, 9" diameter. **$1,200**

Scales plate, deep and round, marigold over milk glass, made by Westmoreland. **$250**

Inverted Feather water pitcher, marigold, made by Cambridge. **$8,100**

Imperial Grape plate, purple, 9". **$1,000-$1,400** *Outstanding example* **$2,200**

Northwood Grape and Cable standard size punch set, electric purple. **$4,500**

Hearts and Flowers compote, powder blue opalescent, made by Northwood, 6". **$2,200-$3,100 (rare)**

Ripple vase, purple, 8" high, 2-1/2" base. **$125-$175**

Multi-Fruits and Flowers water pitcher, green, made by Millersburg. **$15,000**

Northwood Peacock and Urn master bowl, blue stippled, ice cream shape, 10" diameter. **$1,500-$2,500**
Outstanding example **$4,200**

Grape and Cable cracker jar in aqua opalescent. **$45,000**
This is the only known perfect example.

Grape Arbor water pitcher and one tumbler, ice green, one of three known, made by Northwood. **$10,000**

Three Fruits bowl, sapphire, made by Northwood. **$2,200**

Peacock at the Fountain master berry bowl, ice blue, straight up. **$650**

Peacocks on the Fence ruffled bowl, electric green, made by Northwood, 8 1/2" diameter. **$1,350**

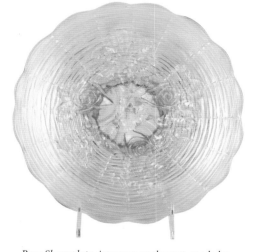

Rose Show plate, ice green opalescent, made by Northwood. **$10,000**

Northwood Poppy Show plate, marigold, 9" diameter. **$900-$1,600**

Strawberry spittoon by Millersburg, marigold, rare, 4" wide x 1 1/2" base. **$5,000-$6,000**

Little Stars ice cream shaped bowl, marigold, made by Millersburg, 9" diameter, rare size. **$850**

*Imperial Poppy Show vase, purple, rare,
12" high.* **$3,000-$5,500**
Outstanding example **$12,000**

*Palm Beach vase, whimsy, marigold, made
by U.S. Glass, 6 1/2" high,
3 1/2" base.* **$800**

Raspberry water pitcher and five tumblers (four shown), ice blue, made by Northwood. **$1,400**

Daum Nancy

Daum Nancy fine glass, much of it cameo, was made by Auguste and Antonin Daum, who founded a factory in 1875 in Nancy, France. Most of their cameo and enameled glass was made from the 1890s into the early 20th century.

Cameo glass is made by carving into multiple layers of colored glass to create a design in relief. It is at least as old as the Romans.

James D. Julia, Inc.

French cameo large bulbous vase of medium blue decorated with a design of allover Oriental poppies and stars in transparent glass with gold and black highlighting, all on an acid-etched ground, gilding at top and bottom, signed on underside "Daum Nancy" with Cross of Lorraine, 5 1/2" tall x 7 1/2" across. **$3,750-$4,750**

James D. Julia, Inc.

French cameo and enamel powder jar, allover multi-shaded green foliage pattern with berries in shades of orange, background glass is mottled in greens and other earthen hues, signed on the side of the jar in cameo "Daum Nancy" with Cross of Lorraine, 3 1/4" tall x 5 1/4" diameter. **$3,000-$4,000**

James D. Julia, Inc.

French cameo and enameled ewer, yellow and orange mottled ground decorated with poppy pattern in oranges with gold highlighting foliage, finished at foot with a gold and clear floral motif, signed "Daum Nancy" with Cross of Lorraine to underside of foot, 9 1/2" tall. **$7,500-$8,500**

James D. Julia, Inc.

French cameo and enamel vase with rouge-hued flower petals and green foliage set against a yellow to purple mottled ground, baluster shape flows to a flared rim, signed on side in cameo "Daum Nancy" with Cross of Lorraine, 8" tall. **$3,500-$4,500**

James D. Julia, Inc.

French cameo handled bowl, diminutive size with two applied glass handles, mottled green and purple with a forest scene around entire bowl, signed on underside "Daum Nancy" with Cross of Lorraine, 4" x 1 1/4". **$2,000-$3,000**

James D. Julia, Inc.

French cameo miniature egg-shaped vase with irregular top, features a Dutch winter windmill scene in cameo and enameling, signed on underside "Daum Nancy D," 1 3/4" tall. **$2,012**

James D. Julia, Inc.

French cameo miniature tumbler-shaped vase decorated with a winter scene featuring deciduous trees and snow on the ground, all on a mottled yellow and orange ground, signed on underside "Daum Nancy" with Cross of Lorraine and "M.L.," 2" tall. **$1,750-$2,250**

James D. Julia, Inc.

French cameo fuchsia tumbler-shaped vase decorated with fuchsia pattern in mauve, purple, green and brown on purple and frosted mottled ground, signed in cameo on side of vase "Daum Nancy" with Cross of Lorraine, 5" tall. **$1,600-$1,800**

James D. Julia, Inc.

French cameo farm scene vase, rare scenic vase, shows farm and house with rapeseed in full bloom, decorated with pastures and trees enameled in bright green with deeper earthen hues, all set on a sky blue mottled ground; square shape with four pulled corners, signed on the side in enamel "Daum Nancy" with the Cross of Lorraine and artist initials "L.S.," 6 1/2" tall. **$9,200**

James D. Julia, Inc.

French cameo and enameled bulbous-form vase with flared rim with mottled yellow background, floral pattern in burgundy with green foliage and brown stems, circular foot, signed on the side in cameo "Daum Nancy France" with Cross of Lorraine, 11 3/4" tall. **$3,500-$4,500**

James D. Julia, Inc.

French cameo miniature vase, enameled in cameo, spring scene is set against a mottled white, purple and green ground, signed on underside "Daum Nancy" with Cross of Lorraine, 1 1/2" tall. **$1,600-$2,000**

James D. Julia, Inc.

French cameo vitrified ashtray, blue-purple grapes with green leaves set against a multi-shaded yellow, pink and purple background glass, signed in center of ashtray in cameo "Daum Nancy" with Cross of Lorraine, 5". **$1,250-$1,500**

James D. Julia, Inc.

Cameo vase with marine scene, acid etched with multiple ships in full sail decorating the entire circumference, dark brown sailing vessels are on mottled green, yellow and dark orange background, overall surface of background decorated with open bubbles, signed in cameo on the side "Daum Nancy" with the cross of Lorraine,14" tall. **$2,750-$3,750**

James D. Julia, Inc.

French cameo pillow vase, cameo and enamel summer scene of trees with green and yellow foliage against an internally decorated mottled yellow background, signed on underside in black enamel "Daum Nancy" with cross of Lorraine, 3" tall. **$1,495**

James D. Julia, Inc.

Cameo and silver vase, thistle design against peach-colored acid textured background, thistles highlighted with gold gilding, vase finished with a silver foot decorated with thistle design and plain silver lip, vase signed in gold with upside down "Daum Nancy" signature partially obscured by the silver foot mounting, 5" tall. **$402**

James D. Julia, Inc.

Cameo and enameled bowl, winter scene of deciduous trees with shrubbery in background, ground is enameled in white to represent snow, quadrefoil shape, signed on underside in enamel "Daum Nancy" with cross of Lorraine, 2 1/2" x 5". **$1,380**

James D. Julia, Inc.

French cameo rare boat-shaped winter scene vase with orange and yellow mottled ground and deciduous snow-tipped trees above a snow-covered landscape, signed "Daum Nancy" with Cross of Lorraine, 1 3/4" x 7". **$3,500-$4,500**

James D. Julia, Inc.

Cameo and enameled spring scenic vase, cameo decoration of trees along a river, trees are enameled in yellows, rust and green with distant shore enameled in background with an internal blue band against a mottled purple and blue background, signed on underside in black enamel "Daum Nancy" with Cross of Lorraine and "1588," 9" tall. **$5,865**

James D. Julia, Inc.

French cameo and enamel creamer, extremely rare, thumbprint design and applied glass handle, depicts two children holding an umbrella in the rain with trees surrounding them, reverse shows two plants in bloom in mauve and purple with gold highlighting, all set on frosted opalescent ground, signed on underside "Daum Nancy" with Cross of Lorraine, 3" tall. **$3,162**

Depression Glass

BY ELLEN T. SCHROY

Depression glass is the name of colorful glassware collectors generally associated with mass-produced glassware found in pink, yellow, crystal, or green in the years surrounding the Great Depression in America.

Ellen T. Schroy

The housewives of the Depression-era were able to enjoy the wonderful colors offered in this new inexpensive glass dinnerware because they received pieces of their favorite patterns packed in boxes of soap, or as premiums given at "dish night" at the local movie theater. Merchandisers, such as Sears & Roebuck and F. W. Woolworth, enticed young brides with the colorful wares that they could afford even when economic times were harsh.

Because of advancements in glassware technology, Depression-era patterns were mass-produced and could be purchased for a fraction of what cut glass or lead crystal cost. As one manufacturer found a pattern that was pleasing to the buying public, other companies soon followed with their adaptation of a similar design. Patterns included several design motifs, such as florals, geometrics, and even patterns that looked back to Early American patterns like Sandwich glass.

As America emerged from the Great Depression and life became more leisure-oriented again, new glassware patterns were created to reflect the new tastes of this generation. More elegant shapes and forms were designed, leading to what is sometimes called "Elegant Glass." Today's collectors often include these more elegant patterns when they talk about Depression-era glassware.

Depression-era glassware is one of the best-researched collecting areas available to the American marketplace. This is due in large part to the careful research of several people, including Hazel Marie Weatherman, Gene Florence, Barbara Mauzy, Carl F. Luckey, and Kent Washburn. Their books are held in high regard by researchers and collectors today.

Regarding values for Depression glass, rarity does not always equate to a high dollar amount. Some more readily found items command lofty prices because of high demand or other factors, not because they are necessarily rare. As collectors' tastes range from the simple patterns to the more elaborate patterns, so does the ability of their budget to invest in inexpensive patterns to multi-hundreds of dollars per form patterns.

The Depression-era glassware researchers have many accurate sources, including company records, catalogs, magazine advertisements, oral and written histories from sales staff, factory workers, etc.

For more information on Depression glass, see *Warman's Depression Glass Identification and Price Guide*, 5th Edition, or *Warman's Depression Glass Field Guide*, 5th Edition, both by Ellen T. Schroy.

ELLEN T. SCHROY, *one of the leading experts in her field, is the author of* Warman's Depression Glass Identification and Price Guide *and* Warman's Depression Glass Field Guide. *Her books are the definitive references for Depression glass collectors.*

Bubble, royal ruby 3" old fashioned glass. **$12**

American, crystal 10" bowl. **$48**

Cube, green covered powder jar. **$30**

Aunt Polly, blue sherbet. **$16**

Cameo, yellow 3 1/4" creamer. **$25**

Colonial, crystal wine. **$15**
Cocktail. **$18**

Jubilee, yellow goblet. **$150**

Adam, green ashtray. **$28**
Pink pitcher. **$65**

Iris, iridescent 9" vase. **$25**

Fire King Charm, Azur-ite cup and saucer. **$12**

Daisy, amber creamer. **$10**

Old Café, royal ruby bowl with handles and original label. **$15**

Coin, red candy dish with cover. **$120**

Florentine No. 1, pink 8 1/2" berry bowl. **$28**

Cloverleaf, green sherbet. **$15**

Holiday, pink 4" tumbler. **$28**
Cup. **$12**

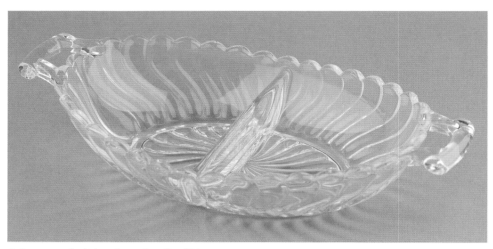

Colony, crystal relish with two handles. **$20**

Early American Prescut, crystal cake plate. **$25**

Cherry Blossom, pink cup. **$28**

Diamond Quilted, green one-handled bowl. **$15**

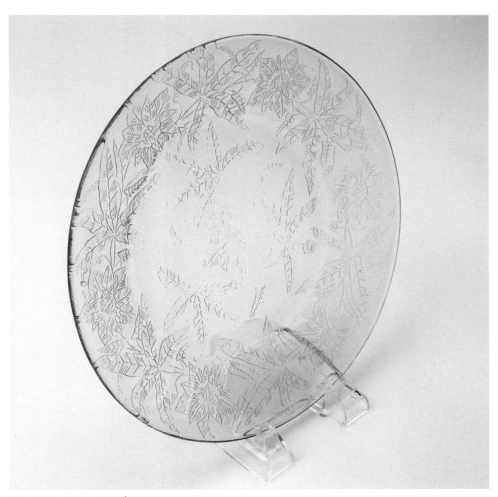

Floral, pink dinner plate. **$22.50**

Fairfax, green nut cup. **$20**
Rare topaz two-part chilled juice tumbler. **$12**
Ice bowl with liner. **$36.50**

Georgian, green sherbet. **$16**

Swirl, ultramarine sugar. **$15**

Creamer. **$12**

Twisted Optic, pink 6" diameter sherbet plate. **$3**

Florentine No. 2, green dinner plate. **$12**

Mayfair Open Rose, green fruit bowl. **$50**

New Century, green salt and pepper shakers. **$45**

Princess, green octagonal salad bowl. **$40** *Cookie jar.* **$65**

Strawberry, pink 5-3/4" footed comport. **$60**

Miss America, pink 10" oval vegetable bowl. **$55**

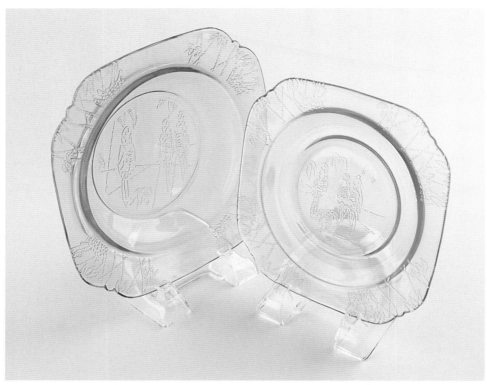

Parrot, amber jam dish. **$35**

Green sherbet plate. **$35**

Seville, amber 9 1/2" diameter dinner plate. **$12.50**

Royal Ruby, 5 1/2" tilted ball pitcher. **$45**

Queen Mary, pink oval open sugar. **$12**   *Oval creamer.* **$14**

Patrician, amber pitcher, molded handle, 8" high, 75 oz. **$110**

Fenton Art Glass

The Fenton Art Glass Company was founded in 1905 by Frank L. Fenton and his brother, John W., in Martins Ferry, Ohio. They initially sold hand-painted glass made by other manufacturers, but it wasn't long before they decided to produce their own glass. The new Fenton factory in Williamstown, West Virginia, opened on Jan. 2, 1907. From that point on, the company expanded by developing unusual colors and continued to decorate glassware in innovative ways.

Two more brothers, James and Robert, joined the firm. But despite the company's initial success, John W. left to establish the Millersburg Glass Company of Millersburg, Ohio, in 1909. The first months of the new operation were devoted to the production of crystal glass only. Later iridized glass was called "Radium Glass." After only two years, Millersburg filed for bankruptcy.

Fenton's iridescent glass had a metallic luster over a colored, pressed pattern, and was sold in dime stores. It was only after the sales of this glass decreased and it was sold in bulk as carnival prizes that it came to be known as carnival glass.

Fenton became the top producer of carnival glass, with more than 150 patterns. The quality of the glass, and its popularity with the public, enabled the new company to be profitable

Chocolate glass footed bowl in Vintage, circa 1908, 6" diameter. **$125+**

Green Opalescent plate in Northern Star, circa 1910, 10 1/2" diameter. **$50+**

through the late 1920s. As interest in carnival subsided, Fenton moved on to stretch glass and opalescent patterns. A line of colorful blown glass (called "off-hand" by Fenton) was also produced in the mid-1920s.

During the Great Depression, Fenton survived by producing functional colored glass tableware and other household items, including water sets, table sets, bowls, mugs, plates, perfume bottles and vases.

Restrictions on European imports during World War II ushered in the arrival of Fenton's opaque colored glass, and the lines of "Crest" pieces soon followed.

In the 1950s, production continued to diversify with a focus on milk glass, particularly in Hobnail patterns.

In the third quarter of Fenton's history, the company returned to themes that had proved popular to preceding generations, and began adding special lines, such as the Bicentennial series.

Innovations included the line of Colonial colors that debuted in 1963, including amber, blue, green, orange and ruby. Based on a special order for an Ohio museum, Fenton in 1969 revisited its early success with "Original Formula Carnival Glass." Fenton also started marking its glass in the molds for the first time.

The star of the 1970s was the yellow and blushing pink creation known as Burmese, which remains popular today. This was followed closely by a menagerie of animals, birds, and children.

In 1975, Robert Barber was hired by Fenton to begin an artist-in-residence program, producing a limited line of art-glass vases in a return to the off-hand, blown-glass creations of the mid-1920s.

Shopping at home via television was a recent phenomenon in the late 1980s when the "Birthstone Bears" became the first Fenton product to appear on QVC (established in 1986 by Joseph Segel, founder of The Franklin Mint).

In the latter part of the century, Fenton established a website—www.fentonartglass.com—as a user-friendly online experience where collectors could learn about catalog and gift shop sales, upcoming events and the history of the company.

In August 2007, Fenton discontinued all but a few of its more popular lines, and in 2011 ceased production entirely.

For more information on Fenton Art Glass, see *Warman's Fenton Glass Identification and Price Guide, 2nd edition*, by Mark F. Moran.

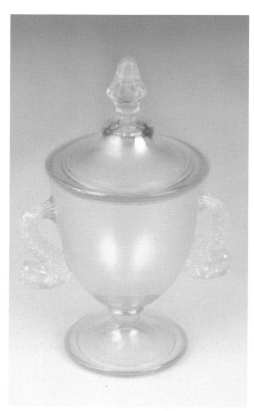

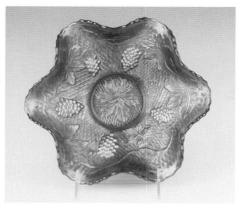

Green deep bowl with ruffled edge in Lattice and Grape, with paneled back, 9" diameter. **$400+**

Topaz stretch-glass covered candy jar with dolphin handles, early 1920s, 8" high. **$110+**

Green Opalescent tumblers in Rib Optic, with cobalt handles, 1920s, 4 1/2" high. **$65+ each**

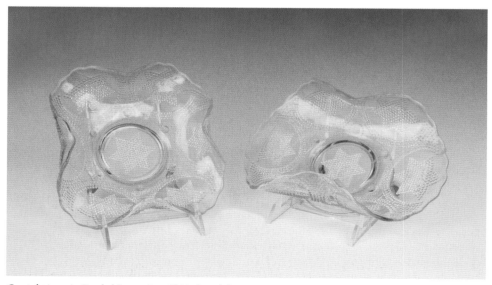

Crystal pieces in Beaded Stars, circa 1910, from left: square crimp bonbon and banana boat, each 8 1/2" wide. **$45+ each**

Mulberry crimped bowl in Diamond Optic, 1942, 10" diameter. **$125+**

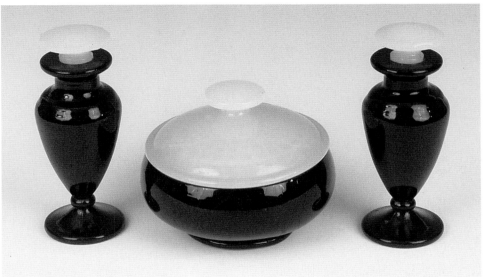

Moonstone and Ebony vanity set (found in other colors), two perfumes, powder box and rectangular tray (not pictured), early 1930s; perfumes, each 5" high; box, 4 1/4" diameter. **$600+ set**

Celeste Blue stretch-glass candleholders and footed console bowl (also called an "orange bowl"), circa 1920; candleholders, 8 1/2" high. **$80+ pair; Bowl, 11" diameter.** **$275+**

Peacock Periwinkle Blue flared vase, mid-1930s, 7 1/2" high. **$150+**

*Green Overlay basket in Coin Dot, early 1940s,
7 1/2" high x 7" wide.* **$500+**

*Black (Ebony) Empress vase, 1935,
7 1/2" high.* **$110+**

*Dancing Ladies Topaz Opalescent footed bowl,
mid-1930s, 8 1/2" wide.* **$750+**

Santoy Etched decanter, 1936, 9" high. **$150+**

Mosaic off-hand handled vase, mid-1920s, 7" high.
$1,800+

*Sapphire bowl in Basket Weave
with open edge,
6 1/4" diameter.* **$250+**

*Peach Crest single-horn epergne, made for L.G. Wright,
1940s, 16 1/2" high, 12 1/2" diameter.* **$350+**

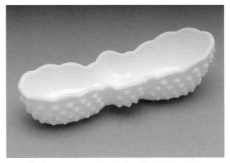

Milk-glass spooner in Hobnail, 1950s, 7" long.
$100+

Amethyst water pitcher and six tumblers in Butterfly and Fern. **$1,050**

Ruby Silver Crest ribbed cornucopia candleholders with smooth tulip crimp, 1940s, each 6" high. **$180-$200+ pair**

Cranberry Polka Dot footed ivy bowl, 1955, 8 1/2" high. **$225**

Silver Crest melon-form perfume bottle with Charleton decoration by Abels, Wasserberg of New York, mid-1940s, 7" high. **$85**

Amethyst Snow Crest four-horn epergne in Threaded Optic, 1940s, made for L.G. Wright, 17" high. **$800+**

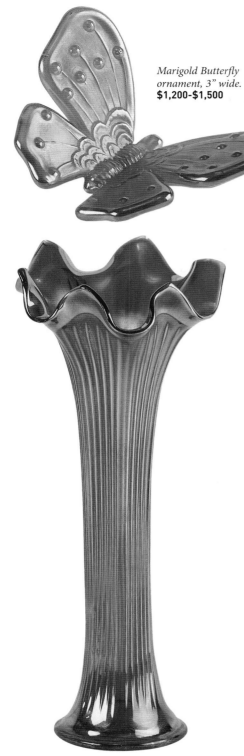

Marigold Butterfly ornament, 3" wide. **$1,200-$1,500**

Two Blue Snow Crest vases in Spiral Optic, 1950-1951, 9" high. **$180+**
11" high. **$250+**

Red vase in Fine Rib, 10" high. **$300-$500**

Cranberry apothecary jar in Dot Optic, made for L.G. Wright, 1960s, 10" high. **$275+**

Rose Overlay crimped vase in Wild Rose and Bowknot, early 1960s, 7 1/2" high. **$50+**

Experimental melon vase, multi-colored cased Milk-glass tri-crimp, with Crystal Overlay and multi-colored "frit," sample made 10/13/64, 7 1/2" high. **$100+** *(Frit is composed of partly fused materials of which glass is made.)*

Marigold jardinière in Diamond and Rib, 6 1/2" high. **$1,500-$1,800**

Green Transparent basket in Big Cookies, with rattan handle, 1930s, 11" wide. **$125+**

Ruby Satin Cardinal hood ornament or car mascot, circa 1970, made for Crawford Auto Museum, Cleveland, Ohio, 6" high. **$200**

Green table set in Butterfly and Berry, including creamer, covered sugar, covered butter dish and spooner; butter, 6" high; creamer, 5" high; spooner, 4 1/4" high; sugar, 6 1/2" high. **$2,500+/set**
Also found in marigold and cobalt blue, and rarely in amethyst.

Black amethyst vase in April Showers, 12" high. **$80-$150**

Purple stretch-glass four-horn epergne, 1970s, made for Levay Company, 13" high. **$375+**

Aqua opalescent ruffled bowl in Peacock and Grape, 8 3/4" diameter. **$5,000+**

Green flat plate in Holly, 9 1/2" diameter. **$700-$900**

Blue whimsy vase in Paneled Dandelion, no handle, made from a water pitcher. **$16,000**

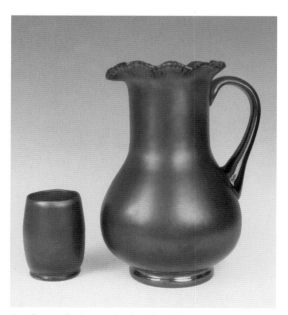

Purple stretch-glass tankard and tumbler, part of a water set that would have included six tumblers, 1980s; tankard, 10 1/2" high; tumbler, 4" high. **$500+ for complete set**

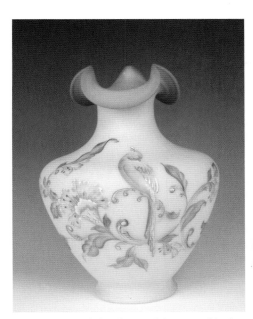

Burmese vase with hand-painted flowers and birds by Martha Reynolds, 1990s, 12" high. **$350+**

Honey Amber Overlay tri-crimp vase in Hobnail, mid-1960s, 11" high. **$110+**

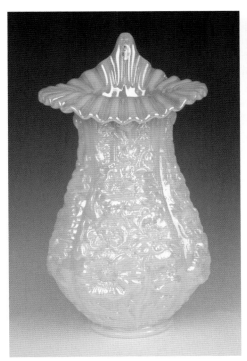

Iridescent Burmese Poppy Show Vase using an old Imperial mold, 2003, custom-made for Singleton Bailey, 13 3/4" high. **$185+**

Cranberry cameo glass platter with sand-carved floral decoration by Martha Reynolds, 1994, one of 500, 14 1/2" diameter. **$275+**

Lalique

René Jules Lalique was born on April 6,1860, in the village of Ay, in the Champagne region of France. In 1862, his family moved to the suburbs of Paris.

In 1872, Lalique began attending College Turgot where he began studying drawing with Justin-Marie Lequien. After the death of his father in 1876, Lalique began working as an apprentice to Louis Aucoc, who was a prominent jeweler and goldsmith in Paris.

Lalique moved to London in 1878 to continue his studies. He spent two years attending Sydenham College, developing his graphic design skills. He returned to Paris in 1880 and worked as an illustrator of jewelry, creating designs for Cartier, among others. In 1884, Lalique's drawings were displayed at the National Exhibition of Industrial Arts, organized at the Louvre.

At the end of 1885, Lalique took over Jules Destapes' jewelry workshop. Lalique's design began to incorporate translucent enamels, semiprecious stones, ivory, and hard stones. In 1889, at the Universal Exhibition in Paris, the jewelry firms of Vever and Boucheron included collaborative works by Lalique in their displays.

In the early 1890s, Lalique began to incorporate glass into his jewelry, and in 1893 he took part in a competition organized by the Union Centrale des Arts Decoratifs to design a drinking vessel. He won second prize.

Lalique opened his first Paris retail shop in 1905, near the perfume business of François Coty. Coty commissioned Lalique to design his perfume labels in 1907, and he also created his first perfume bottles for Coty.

In the first decade of the 20th century, Lalique continued to experiment with glass manufacturing techniques, and mounted his first show devoted entirely to glass in 1911.

During World War I, Lalique's first factory was forced to close, but the construction of a new factory was soon begun in Wingen-sur-Moder, in the Alsace region. It was completed in 1921, and still produces Lalique crystal today.

In 1925, Lalique designed the first "car mascot" (hood ornament) for Citroën, the French automobile company. For the next six years, Lalique would design 29 models for companies such as Bentley, Bugatti, Delage, Hispano-Suiza, Rolls Royce, and Voisin.

Lalique's second boutique opened in 1931, and this location continues to serve as the main Lalique showroom today.

René Lalique died on May 5, 1945, at the age of 85. His son, Marc, took over the business at that time, and when Marc died in 1977, his daughter, Marie-Claude Lalique Dedouvre, assumed control of the company. She sold her interest in the firm and retired in 1994.

For more information on Lalique, see *Warman's Lalique Identification and Price Guide* by Mark F. Moran.

(In the descriptions of some of the Lalique pieces that follow, you will find notations like this: "M p. 478, No. 1100." This refers to the page and serial numbers found in René Lalique, Maître-Verrier, 1860-1945: Analyse de L'oeuvre et Catalogue Raisonné *by Félix Marcilhac, published in 1989 and revised in 1994. Printed entirely in French, this book of more than 1,000 pages is the definitive guide to Lalique's work, and listings from auction catalogs typically cite the Marcilhac guide as a reference. A used copy can cost more than $500. Copies in any condition are extremely difficult to find, but collectors consider Marcilhac's guide to be the bible for Lalique.)*

"Deux Sirenes" box in amber glass, circa 1921, 10" diameter. (M p. 230, No. 43) **$3,000+**

"Louise" ashtray in satin glass, circa 1929, 3" diameter. (M p. 275, No. 301) **$600+**

"Flora-Bella" coupe (shallow bowl with broad rim), circa 1930, in clear and opalescent glass, stenciled "R. Lalique France," 15 1/2" diameter. (M p. 299, No. 407) **$2,700-$3,000**

"Perche" hood ornament/car mascot designed in 1929, this example circa 1950, in clear and frosted glass with blue patina, molded "R. Lalique," 6" long. (M p. 503, No. 1158) **$1,200-$1,400**

"Coq De Jungle," a decorative sculpture, circa 1936, in clear and frosted glass, stenciled "R. Lalique France," signature obscured by polishing, 16" tall. (M p. 493, No. 1124) **$1,500-$1,800**

"Serpents" inkwell in amber glass, circa 1920, 6" diameter. (M p. 317, No. 432) **$4,000+**

"Ronces" red vase, formed branches encircling vase, signed on underside with etched signature "R. Lalique France," 9" high. **$12,000-$15,000**

"Blidah" cold drinks service, circa 1931, in amber glass, with jug and six tumblers, together with a complimentary tray in the "Setubal" pattern, all stenciled "R. Lalique France," jug 8" tall. (M p. 797, No. 3681, and p. 799, No. 3684) **$2,000-$2,500/set**

"Ronces" vase circa 1921, in cased yellow glass, molded "R. Lalique," engraved "Lalique," 9 1/2" tall. (M p. 427, No. 946) **$4,800-$5,400**

James D. Julia, Inc.

"Moineaux" ATO clock, case features impressed design of love birds, clock finished with rare glass face with sunburst center and impressed ATO, clock case carries remnants of brown patination; unsigned, 8 1/2" wide x 6 1/4" high. **$3,500-$4,500**

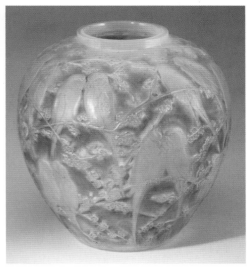

"Perruches" vase, circa 1919, in cased opalescent glass with blue patina, molded "R. Lalique," 10" tall. (M p. 410, No. 876) **$6,000-$7,000**

"Fleur" bowl, circa 1912, in clear and frosted glass with sepia patina and black enamel, molded "R. Lalique," 4 1/2" diameter. (M p. 727, No. 3100) **$650-$750**

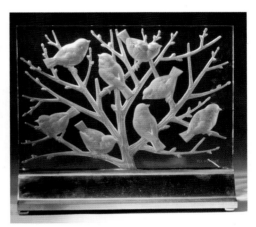

"Fauvettes A" illuminating surtout de table, circa 1930, in clear and frosted glass with original nickel-plated metal illuminating base, wheel-cut "R. Lalique," 13 1/2" tall. (M p. 486, No. 1171) **$11,000-$13,000**

"Lunaria" perfume bottle in clear and frosted glass with sepia patina, circa 1912, 3 1/8" tall. (M p. 326, No. 482) **$1,500+**

James D. Julia, Inc.

"Tournesols" vase, tournesols or sunflowers decorate entire body, which is finished with a small collar and flared lip, signed on underside "R. Lalique France No 1007," 4 3/4" tall. **$1,840**

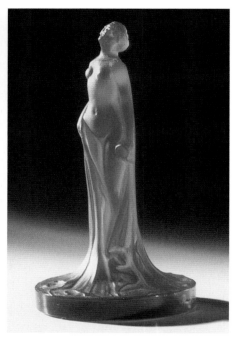

"Statuette Drapee" letter seal in blue glass with white patina, circa 1912, 2 1/2" tall. (M p. 249, No. 181) **$5,500+**

"Quatre Cigales" perfume bottle in clear and frosted glass with sepia patina, circa 1910, 5 1/8" tall. (M p. 325, No. 475) **$2,000+**

"Pan" vase circa 1937, in clear and frosted glass with gray patina, stenciled "R. Lalique France," 12 1/2" long. (M p. 465, No. 10-904) **$5,500-$6,000**

Quezal

The Quezal Art Glass Decorating Company, named for the quetzal—a bird with brilliantly colored feathers found in tropical regions of the Americas—was organized in 1901 in Brooklyn, New York, by Martin Bach and Thomas Johnson, two disgruntled Tiffany workers. They soon hired Percy Britton and William Wiedebine, two more former Tiffany employees.

The first products, unmarked, were exact Tiffany imitations. Quezal pieces differ from Tiffany pieces in that they are more defined and the decorations are more visible and brighter. No new techniques were developed by Quezal.

Johnson left in 1905. T. Conrad Vahlsing, Bach's son-in-law, joined the firm in 1918, but left with Paul Frank in 1920 to form Lustre Art Glass Company, which in turn copied Quezal pieces. Martin Bach died in 1924, and by 1925, Quezal had ceased operations.

The "Quezal" trademark was first used in 1902 and placed on the base of vases and bowls and the rims of shades. The acid-etched or engraved letters vary in size and may be found in amber, black or gold. A printed label that includes an illustration of a quetzal was used briefly in 1907.

James D. Julia, Inc.

Quezal decorated bulbous vase with flared rim and saucer foot, decorated with allover random design in gold against an ivory ground, outstanding iridescent finish with strong pink and blue highlights, signed on underside "Quezal," 6 1/4" tall.
$2,000-$3,000

James D. Julia, Inc.

Three Quezal art glass shades with large openings, decorated with a green and gold heart and vine pattern and then overlaid with applied glass threading, each shade signed "Quezal," 2 1/4" fitter x 6" tall. **$287**

James D. Julia, Inc.

Quezal dome-shaped art glass shade, green pulled feather design with gold trim on a white ground with gold interior, signed "Quezal," 3 3/4" opening; 10 1/4" diameter. **$1,295**

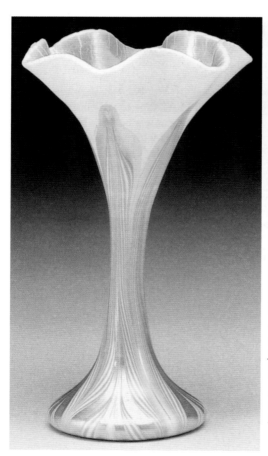

James D. Julia, Inc.

Quezal decorated flowerform vase with deep gold stretched glass mouth, exterior has pulled green feather design with gold complements, all on ivory ground, signed on underside "Quezal," 6 1/2" tall. **$1,495**

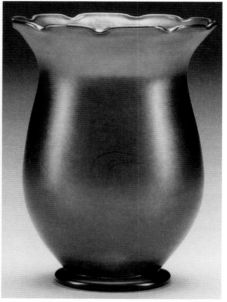

James D. Julia, Inc.

Quezal blue shade vase with platinum iridescent finish to interior and exterior, inverted tulip shape with scalloped border, signed on underside "Quezal," 5 1/2" tall. Provenance: Gift from Martin Bach to Cecelia Stolz in 1913, thence by descent to her daughter, Therese Kershow, to the present consignor. **$517**

James D. Julia, Inc.

Quezal innovation vase with brown, yellow and beige swirling colors surrounding the baluster body with slightly flaring rim, signed on underside "Quezal," 4 1/2" tall. Provenance: Gift from Martin Bach to Cecelia Stolz in 1913, thence by descent to her daughter, Therese Kershow, to the present consignor. **$1,150**

James D. Julia, Inc.

Quezal decorated blue open salt, rare, trefoil-shaped rim resting atop a bulbous base having a single thumbprint design and decorated with a platinum King Tut design overall, signed on underside "Quezal," 2". **$690**

James D. Julia, Inc.

Quezal art glass vase, gold cauldron shape with flared rim and vertical ribbing, iridescent finish with pink and purple highlights, signed on underside "Quezal," 2 1/4" tall. **$143**

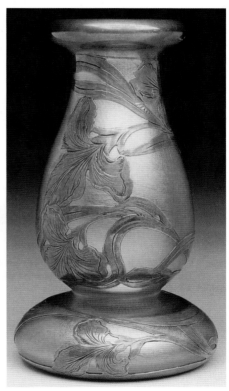

James D. Julia, Inc.

Quezal silver overlay vase with light blue iridescent finish and strong pink highlights near base, decorated with sterling silver overlay in the form of Art Nouveau leaves and stems. Silver is marked with the Alvin hallmark as well as "999/1000 Patented 15," vase is marked in the polished pontil "Quezal," 5 1/4" tall. **$1,840**

Tiffany Glass

Tiffany & Company was founded by Charles Lewis Tiffany (1812-1902) and Teddy Young in New York City in 1837 as a "stationery and fancy goods emporium." The store initially sold a wide variety of stationery items, and operated as Tiffany, Young and Ellis in lower Manhattan. The name was shortened to Tiffany & Company in 1853, and the firm's emphasis on jewelry was established.

The first Tiffany catalog, known as the "Blue Book," was published in 1845. It is still being published today.

In 1862 Tiffany & Company supplied the Union Army with swords, flags and surgical implements.

Charles' son, Louis Comfort Tiffany (1848-1933) was an American artist and designer who worked in the decorative arts and is best known for his work in stained glass. Louis established Tiffany Glass Company in 1885, and in 1902 it became known as the Tiffany Studios. America's outstanding glass designer of the Art Nouveau period produced glass from the last quarter of the 19th century until the early 1930s. Tiffany revived early techniques and devised many new ones.

More information on Tiffany is located in the "Lamps & Lighting" section.

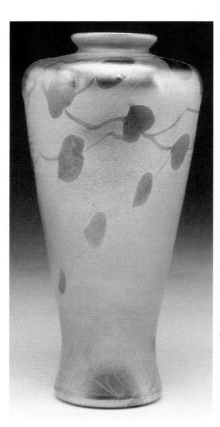

James D. Julia, Inc.

Tiffany Studios decorated vase, gold Favrile baluster form with wide shoulders and flared lip, overall design of hearts and vines in deep green with platinum iridescent finish, signed on underside "2283H L.C. Tiffany F Favrile," 9" tall.
$4,000-$5,000

James D. Julia, Inc.

Tiffany Studios black decorated Egyptian form bulbous vase with elongated neck, background has blue and platinum peacock feather decoration to main body of vase, signed on underside "L.C.T. D740," 12" tall. **$25,300**

James D. Julia, Inc.

Tiffany Studios decorated vase, squat form with King Tut pattern in platinum and blue with highlights of purple and gold iridescence, signed on underside "L.C. Tiffany Q 9938 Favrile," 4" tall x 4 3/4" across. **$4,025**

James D. Julia, Inc.

Tiffany Studios millifiori vase in green glass with dark purple iridescent finish, gold iridescent heart and vine decoration with interspersed millefiori flowers, signed on underside "L.C.T. U7158," 5 1/4" tall. **$6,900**

James D. Julia, Inc.

Tiffany Studios pastel decorated compote, lemon yellow glass decorated with white feather decoration, clear twisted glass stem receding into milky white inverted saucer foot, signed on underside "1840 L.C.T. Favrile," 7 1/2" tall x 8" across. **$805**

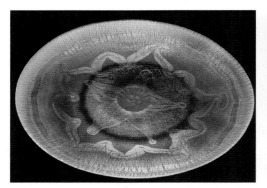

James D. Julia, Inc.

Tiffany Studios Favrile rondel, gently curved edge stretched with platinum Art Nouveau decoration and star pattern in center, middle of star has intaglio cut design, Favrile glass has pink, blue, green, platinum and purple iridescent finish, signed on reverse edge "48E L.C. Tiffany Favrile," 8" diameter. **$2,530**

James D. Julia, Inc.

Tiffany Studios intaglio cut and decorated vase, organic form slightly ribbed, greenish-brown base color, decorated with platinum pulled feather design from neck to shoulder with four intaglio carved insects in flight, signed on underside "L.C.T.," 4 1/2" tall x 5 3/4" across. **$4,500-$5,500**

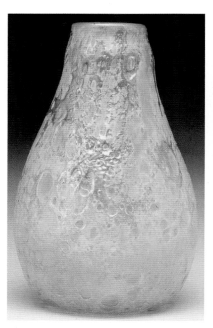

James D. Julia, Inc.

Tiffany Studios Cypriote cabinet-sized organic vase made of rare Cypriote glass that Tiffany Studios created to replicate early Roman glass; iridized background with heavy iridescence to Cypriote decoration, signed on underside in button pontil "L.C.T. Favrile V271," 5 3/4" tall. **$7,000-$9,000**

James D. Julia, Inc.

Tiffany Studios large decorated Favrile glass vase with pulled feather decoration to top and bottom, circular platform with cat's paw feet and row of bronze beading with green-brown patina finish. Bronze is signed "Tiffany Studios New York 09775" with Tiffany Glass & Decorating logo, vase marked with matching number "09775," 15 1/2" x 10" across at bottom. **$15,000-$25,000**

James D. Julia, Inc.

Early Tiffany Studios Favrile bulbous Egyptian form vase, shouldered, flares to small neck, gold Favrile glass has a phantom luster and is decorated with ivory hooked design at shoulder as well as a pulled feather pattern below, signed on underside "L.C.T.," 8" tall. **$2,500-$3,500**

James D. Julia, Inc.

Tiffany Studios scarab desk lamp with deep gold iridescence and flashes of red and blue. Shade supported by a two-arm base with vertically ribbed foot and shell-shaped arm ends where shade connects to base. Base has center switch at bottom of arms with beaded bronze border around bottom of shade. Base has brown patina with green and red highlights. Signed on underside of base "Tiffany Studios New York S1343" as well as the Tiffany Glass & Decorating Company logo; 8 1/2" tall. **$9,200**

James D. Julia, Inc.

Rare Tiffany Studios miniature red vase, classical Egyptian-form with red glass exterior and yellow interior, slight iridescent finish, signed on underside "1296J L.C. Tiffany Favrile," 2 3/4" tall. **$4,600**

James D. Julia, Inc.

Tiffany Studios Heraldic pattern inkwell in hammered silver, green painted ground, complete with large glass insert, signed on underside "Tiffany Studios New York 2045," 3" tall x 4" across. **$700-$900**

James D. Julia, Inc.

Tiffany Studios linenfold desk lamp, gold dore harp base with ribbed foot that supports a six-panel linenfold shade with linenfold trim pieces at the bottom. Shade marked "Tiffany Studios New York 1942 Pat. Apl'd For." Base is marked "Tiffany Studios New York 614"; 13 1/2" tall. **$4,720**

James D. Julia, Inc.

Tiffany Studios flower form vase, gold Favrile glass flower form with large cup and deeply scalloped rim, stretched glass rim, supported by a translucent bulbed stem on inverted saucer foot, iridescent finish in purples, pinks and greens, signed on underside "L.C.T. 4492A" with a "Favrile Glass Tiffany Registered Trademark" label in pontil, 16" tall. **$4,500-$5,500**

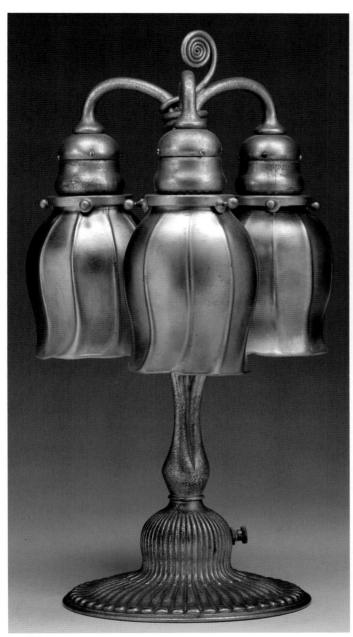

James D. Julia, Inc.

Tiffany Studios candlestick, bronze gold dore with four cat's paw feet on pedestal base finished with small Favrile glass shade with iridescent clambroth finish and gold hooked feather design, top of shade finished with scalloped border. Candlestick signed "Tiffany Studios New York 1201," shade signed "S7733," 14" tall overall. **$1,610**

James D. Julia, Inc.

Tiffany three-light tulip lamp, Art Nouveau designed base with vertically ribbed foot and three organic-looking stems intertwining and curving outward to support sockets and shade holders, fourth twining stem extending up the middle, wrapping around support arms and curling to form a finial. Lamp finished with three vertically ribbed tulip shades with gold iridescence showing strong purple, blue, and green highlights. Base is finished in gold dore. Each shade signed "LCT Favrile." Base is signed on underside "Tiffany Studios New York 339"; 16" tall. **$10,925**

James D. Julia, Inc.

Tiffany Studios nasturtium table lamp, red, yellow, and cream-colored flowers set against a background of large green, white, and yellow nasturtium leaves. Background between leaves is blue with bright green striations. Border glass is rippled cream and tan. Shade signed with 1" tag "Tiffany Studios New York." Shade rests atop trumpet base with three-socket cluster and rich brown patina with green highlights. Base is signed on underside "Tiffany Studios New York 573"; shade 20 1/2" diameter, lamp 26" tall overall. **$57,500**

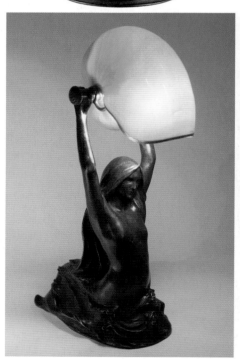

Stefek's Auctioneers & Appraisers

Tiffany Studios bronze Nautilus desk lamp, American, early 20th century. Impressed under foot "Tiffany Studios New York" and numbered "28635." Modeled by Louis Gudebrod. Bronze base impressed "Gudebrod." With a mermaid rising from the sea and supporting a Nautilus shell shade with silver rim; 15 1/2" tall. **$20,000-$30,000**

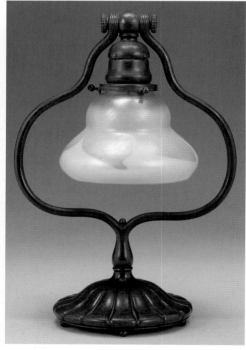

James D. Julia, Inc.

Tiffany Studios harp desk lamp with vertically ribbed inverted saucer foot and five ball feet. Base is finished with rich brown patina with green highlights and houses a Tiffany bell-shaped shade with gold pulled feather design against a creamy pearlescent background. Shade signed "LCT." Base is signed on underside "Tiffany Studios New York 419" and has swivel ring for hanging the lamp on a wall to create a sconce; shade 5 1/2" diameter; lamp 13 1/2" tall. **$3,500-4,500**

Halloween Collectibles

BY MARK B. LEDENBACH

Mark B. Ledenbach

As a collector of vintage Halloween memorabilia for nearly 25 years, I find the evolution of the imagery for this fun hobby endlessly fascinating.

Halloween became quite the event in the first decade of the last century, mainly through the exchange of festive postcards. Those cards, with the art drawn by such luminaries as Winsch and Clapsaddle, typically accented the agricultural roots of Halloween, then branched out into the more whimsical realm of witches, black cats, blazing JOLs, bats, cavorting devils and the like.

As Halloween became an event to be celebrated with parties – primarily given by and for adults through the 1920s – the imagery began to change. From about 1909 through 1913, manufacturers of party supplies like Dennison of Framingham, Massachusetts, simply offered an array of seasonally decorated crepe papers from which the host would fashion decorations and party favors. The imagery from this period tends to be more subdued and somewhat pedestrian. However, as the manufacturers became more entranced by the business possibilities of offering finished goods for sale, the lines of available products exploded into a dazzling array of seals, silhouettes, tally cards, place cards, invitations, diecuts, aprons, and costumes. To keep up with the seemingly endless kinds of products to be sold to adults, the imagery became more complex, scary and perhaps sometimes chilling.

The most innovative purveyor of such complex Halloween imagery was the Beistle Company of Shippensburg, Pennsylvania. They provided nut cups, diecuts, lanterns, games, table decorations, and other small paper decorations that are especially coveted by collectors today. The firm's design sensibilities are easily recognized today for their ingenuity in extending Halloween imagery beyond what was offered previously by other manufacturers. Examples of this would be Beistle's 1930-1931 identical dual-sided lantern and 1923 fairy clock.

Imagery through about 1940 tends to be more adult-focused. However, as trick-or-treating become more of an entrenched feature of Halloween celebrations, the target market segment for parties ceased to be adults and moved inexorably toward juveniles. The impact on Halloween imagery was profound. Out were the more complex and scary images of devils, witches and black cats, to be replaced by less threatening, less interesting and less memorable imagery of apple-cheeked witches, grinning, plump devils and friendly black cats. The air of implied menace, so evocative of early Halloween imagery, had been replaced by a sugar-high-inducing cuteness that any retailer could carry without censure.

Through the present day, cuteness has been dethroned by goriness. One can shop at any mass retailer and find diecuts of skulls with worms wriggling through eye sockets, costumes complete with wretch-inducing masks trumpeting various deformities or tortures, and other horrors meant to shock and perhaps dismay. The sense of subtlety and artistry so apparent in

Lithographed-paper hatbox candy container, Germany, 1920s, approximately 4" high. **$850**

Celluloid witch on jack-o'-lantern, 1920s, United States, 4" high. **$650**

Composition jack-o'-lantern-headed woman nodder with pink sunbonnet, Germany, 1920s, approximately 7" high. **$800**

the majority of decorations made prior to 1940 is nowhere in evidence today.

As with many hobbies, certain sub-categories have done better than others. Hotter categories are embossed German diecuts; U.S. diecuts, especially those made by Dennison and Gibson; Beistle paper products; boxed seals, silhouettes and cut-outs from Dennison; tin tambourines; and German candy containers and figurals as well as Halloween-themed games. Colder categories include tin noisemakers, U.S. pulp and hard plastic.

Collecting vintage Halloween memorabilia became a red-hot hobby complete with sky-rocketing prices and always scarce supply in the early 1990s. Even with all of the economic cycles since and the rise of more efficient supply channels like ebay, prices continue to climb for nearly all genres of near-mint or better items. For example, embossed German diecuts sold then for between $30-$75. Today many examples bring $100-$400, with the rarest items like a winged bat devil and a large fireplace screen topping $2,250. Even ephemera like a 1932 Beistle grandfather clock mechanical invitation bring astronomical prices. One recently sold for over $1,700.

As referenced above, not all categories have benefited. The garish hard plastic made in such huge quantities during the 1950s used to command head-scratching prices of $40-$1,000. Today prices have decreased to about half of the market's height given more collector awareness of the ubiquity of these items.

Unlike Christmas items, Halloween decorations were purchased with the intention of using them once, then tossing them out after the event with no sentiment. This is the primary supply driver behind the rapid escalation of prices today. The primary demand driver is the large number of new collectors entering this fun field as each Halloween season comes around.

As with all hobbies wherein the values have risen tremendously, reproductions and fantasy pieces are a problem. Consult other collectors and buy the right references before plunking down cash. Get in the habit of asking a lot of questions. Don't be shy!

MARK B. LEDENBACH *is the author of* Vintage Halloween Collectibles: An Identification and Price Guide, *2nd Edition published in 2007 by Krause Publications. His website is www.HalloweenCollector.com.*

Celluloid witch in pram; 1920s, United States, 4" long. **$500**

Witch face transparency, 1940s, Beistle, United States, 8" high. **$90**

Witch steering a flying saucer, 1960s, Beistle, United States, 11 1/4" high x 14 1/2" wide. **$45**

Composition candy container, German, 1920s, approximately 6" high. **$650**

Cardboard slot-and-tab jack-o'-lantern, mid-1950s, Alberts Display & Novelty Company, United States, 6" high. **$50**

Composition candy container on cardboard tube, German, 1920s, approximately 4 1/2" high. **$325**

Devil face horn with rolled tongue, 1910s, Germany, 4 1/4" high x 8 3/4" long. **$325**

Germany, mid-1930s, approximately 14 3/4" high. **$1,000**

Black cat face diecut, late 1920s, Dennison, United States, 11" high x 10" wide. **$45**

Composition candy container, 1930s, German, approximately 9 1/2" high. **$750**

Cat-in-the-Box, 1910s, Germany, 3 1/4" high (lid closed). **$650**

Porcelain sugar shaker, 1913, German, approximately 4 1/4" high. **$1,750**

Lithographed-paper pipe noisemaker, Germany, 1920s, approximately 4" high. **$130**

Jewelry

Hearts on Fire legendary necklace, 6.28-6.52 carat diamonds set in 18k white gold. **$28,000**

Jewelry Styles

Jewelry has been a part of every culture throughout time. It is often reflective of the times, as well as social and aesthetic movements, with each piece telling its own story through hidden clues that, when interpreted, will help solve the mysteries surrounding them. Jewelry is generally divided into periods and styles. Each period may have several styles, with some of the same styles and types of jewelry being made in both precious and non-precious materials. Additionally, there are recurring style revivals, which are interpretations of an earlier period. For example, the Egyptian Revival that took place in the early and late 1800s, and then again in the 1920s.

For more information on jewelry, see *Warman's Jewelry,* 4th Edition by Kathy Flood.

Georgian, 1760-1837. Fine jewelry from this period is quite desirable, but few good-quality pieces have found their way to auction in recent years. Sadly, much jewelry from this period has been lost.

Victorian, 1837-1901. Queen Victoria of England ascended the throne in 1837 and remained queen until her death in 1901. The Victorian period is a long and prolific one; abundant with many styles of jewelry. It warrants being divided into three sub-periods: Early or Romantic period dating from 1837-1860; Mid or Grand period dating from 1860-1880; and Late or Aesthetic period dating from 1880-1901.

Sentiment and romance were significant factors in Victorian jewelry. Often, jewelry and clothing represented love and affection, with symbolic motifs such as hearts, crosses, hands, flowers, anchors, doves, crowns, knots, stars, thistles, wheat, garlands, horseshoes and moons. The materials of the time were also abundant and varied. They included silver, gold, diamonds, onyx, glass, cameo, paste, carnelian, agate, coral, amber, garnet, emeralds, opals, pearls, peridot (a green gemstone), rubies, sapphires, marcasites, cut steel, enameling, tortoise shell, topaz, turquoise, bog oak, ivory, jet, hair, gutta percha and vulcanite.

Sentiments of love were often expressed in miniatures. Sometimes they were representative of deceased loved ones, but often the miniatures were of the living. Occasionally, the miniatures depicted landscapes, cherubs or religious themes.

Hair jewelry was a popular expression of love and sentiment. The hair of a loved one was placed in a special compartment in a brooch or a locket, or used to form a picture under a glass compartment. Later in the mid-19th century, pieces of jewelry were

Pearl Society; Matthew Arden photo

Oriental pearls necklace sewn with white horsehair to mother-of-pearl plates, given to Miss Constance Wharton by her mother with a note (in her hand) indicating it had been made circa 1820 for her great-grandmother. Note small neck size, under 13", 3/4" wide. Members of this family included writer Edith Wharton and founders of the Wharton School of Economics. **$2,150**

Bonhams

Enamel and diamond flexible bangle bracelet, circa 1860, composed of rose-cut diamonds, gross weight approximately 52.3 g., mounted in 18 carat gold, 2 3/8" diameter. **$4,375**

made completely of woven hair. Individual strands of hair would be woven together to create necklaces, watch chains, brooches, earrings and rings.

In 1861, Queen Victoria's husband, Prince Albert, died. The queen went into mourning for the rest of her life, and Victoria required that the royal court wear black. This atmosphere spread to the populace and created a demand for mourning jewelry.

Mourning jewelry is typically black. When it first came into fashion, it was made from jet, fossilized wood. By 1850, there were dozens of English workshops making jet brooches, lockets, bracelets and necklaces. As the supply of jet dwindled, other materials were used such as vulcanite, gutta percha, bog oak and French jet.

By the 1880s, the somber mourning jewelry was losing popularity. Fashions had changed and the clothing was simpler and had an air of delicacy. The Industrial Revolution, which had begun in the early part of the century, was now in full swing and machine-manufactured jewelry was affordable to the working class.

Edwardian, 1890-1920. The Edwardian period takes its name from England's King Edward VII. Though he ascended the throne in 1901, he and his wife, Alexandria of Denmark, exerted influence over the period before and after his ascension. The 1890s were known as La Belle Epoque. This was a time known for ostentation and extravagance. As the years passed, jewelry became simpler and smaller. Instead of wearing one large brooch, women were often found wearing several small lapel pins.

In the early 1900s, platinum, diamonds and pearls were prevalent in the jewelry of the wealthy, while paste was being used by the masses to imitate the real thing. The styles were reminiscent of the neo-classical and rococo motifs. The jewelry was lacy and ornate, feminine and delicate.

Arts & Crafts, 1890-1920. The Arts & Crafts movement was focused on artisans and craftsmanship. There was a simplification of form where the material was secondary to the design. Guilds of artisans banded together. Some jewelry was mass-produced, but the most highly prized examples of this period are handmade and signed by their makers. The pieces were simple and at times abstract. They could be hammered, patinated and acid etched. Common materials were brass, bronze, copper, silver, blister pearls, freshwater pearls, turquoise, agate, opals, moonstones, coral, horn, ivory, base metals, amber, cabachon-cut garnets and amethysts.

Steve Fishbach Collection jewelry; Linda Lombardo photo

14k white gold pendant, blue and white enamel, diamonds, from a Newark, New Jersey jeweler, circa 1910, 19" chain with 1 1/2" drop. **$3,500**

Pin, diamond, enamel and 18k gold, Art Nouveau style, designed as a pair of large scrolled leaves enameled in bluish green and framed by looping leaves and arching blossoms and buds bead-set with single-cut diamond, suspending a freshwater pearl drop, early 20th century. **$2,250**

Doyle New York

Diamond ring, platinum and vertically set European-cut diamonds, approximately 4.25 carats, elongated pierced openwork mount set throughout with numerous single-cut diamonds, circa 1915, approximately 4 dwt, 1 3/16" long. **$12,000**

Art Nouveau, 1895-1910. In 1895, Samuel Bing opened a shop called "Maison de lArt Nouveau" at 22 Rue de Provence in Paris. Art Nouveau designs in the jewelry were characterized by a sensuality that took on the forms of the female figure, butterflies, dragonflies, peacocks, snakes, wasps, swans, bats, orchids, irises and other exotic flowers. The lines used whiplash curves to create a feeling of lushness and opulence.

1920s-1930s. Costume jewelry began its steady ascent to popularity in the 1920s. Since it was relatively inexpensive to produce, there was mass production. The sizes and designs of the jewelry varied. Often, it was worn a few times, disposed of and then replaced with a new piece. It was thought of as expendable, a cheap throwaway to dress up an outfit. Costume jewelry became so popular that it was sold in both the upscale stores and the "five and dime."

During the 1920s, fashions were often accompanied by jewelry that drew on the Art Deco movement, which got its beginning in Paris at the "Exposition Internationale des Arts Décoratifs et Industriels Modernes"

Bonhams

*Pair of retro ruby and 18k gold earclips, Cartier, circa 1945, signed
Cartier, no. 1597/2332, accompanied by signed box, estimated total
oval-shaped ruby cabochon weight 1.75 carats, 9/16" diameter (14k
gold findings).* **$1,625**

Bonhams

*Art Deco diamond and synthetic
emerald brooch/pendant, circa
1925, estimated total diamond
weight 2.20 carats, mounted in
platinum, 2 3/8" long.* **$3,500**

held in 1925. The idea behind this movement was that form follows function. The style was
characterized by simple, straight, clean lines, stylized motifs and geometric shapes. Favored
materials included chrome, rhodium, pot metal, glass, rhinestones, Bakelite and celluloid.

One designer who played an important role was Coco Chanel. Though previously reserved
for evening wear, Chanel wore it during the day, making it fashionable for millions of other
women to do so, too.

With the 1930s came the Depression and the advent of World War II. Perhaps in response
to the gloom, designers began using enameling and brightly colored rhinestones to create
whimsical birds, flowers, circus animals, bows, dogs and just about every other figural form
imaginable.

Retro Modern, 1939-1950. Other jewelry designs of the 1940s were big and bold. Retro
Modern had a more substantial feel to it and designers began using larger stones to enhance
the dramatic pieces. The jewelry was stylized and exaggerated. Common motifs included
flowing scrolls, bows, ribbons, birds, animals, snakes, flowers and knots.

Sterling silver now became the metal of choice, often dipped in a gold wash known as
vermeil.

Designers often incorporated patriotic themes of American flags, the V-sign, Uncle Sam's
hat, airplanes, anchors and eagles.

Post-War Modern, 1945-1965. This was a movement that emphasized the artistic approach
to jewelry making. It is also referred to as Mid-Century Modern. This approach was occurring
at a time when the Beat Generation was prevalent. These avant-garde designers created jewelry
that was handcrafted to illustrate the artist's own concepts and ideas. The materials often used
were sterling, gold, copper, brass, enamel, cabochons, wood, quartz and amber.

Jelly shell brooch, Lucite and sterling silver, uncommon, unsigned, 2 3/8", 1944-1946. **$250-$350**

1950s-1960s. The 1950s saw the rise of jewelry that was made purely of rhinestones: necklaces, bracelets, earrings and pins.

The focus of the early 1960s was on clean lines: pillbox hats and A-line dresses with short jackets were a mainstay for the conservative woman. The large, bold rhinestone pieces were no longer the must-have accessory. They were now replaced with smaller, more delicate gold-tone metal and faux pearls with only a hint of rhinestones.

At the other end of the spectrum was psychedelic-colored clothing, Nehru jackets, thigh-high miniskirts and go-go boots. These clothes were accessorized with beads, large metal pendants and occasionally big, bold rhinestones. By the late 1960s, there was a movement back to mother nature and the "hippie" look was born. Ethnic clothing, tie dye, long skirts, fringe and jeans were the prevalent style and the rhinestone had, for the most part, been left behind.

DeLizza & Elster coral gold stippled cabochon set in peach from the early 1960s. Necklace, pin, bracelet and earrings; price depends on color. **$1,500-$2,500+ set**

*Penny Preville cuff
in 18k yellow gold
with 0.68 carat
diamonds in flower
and scroll accents.*
$15,380

Hamilton Jewelers of Natural Color Diamond Association

Hamilton Heritage diamond bracelet with radiant-cut fancy yellow and colorless diamonds. **$79,000**

Doyle New York

David Webb ear clips, platinum, 18k gold, hoops set with 198 round diamonds approximately 11.00 carats, flared bombe platinum ribbons lined with slender, polished gold bands, signed Webb for David Webb, approximately 19.7 dwt., 1 5/8". **$16,000**

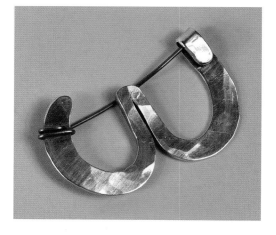

HeavenlyTreasures.com jewelry

Heart drop earrings, 18k white gold, .90 carat-weight black diamonds, .54 carat-weight white diamonds, pierced, 1 1/2". **$1,450**

Woodbury Auction

Alexander Calder sterling silver brooch. **$22,140**

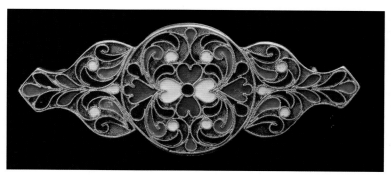

Michaan's Auctions

Russian enamel and silver brooch, cloisonné enamel in silver mounting measuring approximately 52 mm x 21 mm, pin stem and catch. **$250**

Michaan's Auctions

22k yellow gold jewelry suite, including one 22k yellow gold linked bracelet and matching earrings, 11.8 dwts. **$1,000**

Michaan's Auctions

Suite of Bohemian garnet and gilt metal jewelry, cluster motif necklace, brooch and earrings, prong and bezel set in gilt metal. **$750**

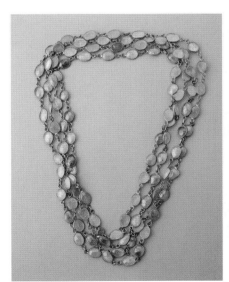

Michaan's Auctions

Sapphire and silver necklace composed of numerous rose-cut multicolored sapphires, each bezel set in blackened silver link chain, 68" long. **$325**

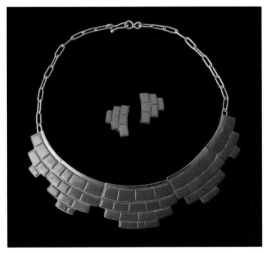

Michaan's Auctions

Suite of coral and sterling silver jewelry, including brick motif sterling silver necklace and matching ear clips, both signed CAE. **$475**

Bonhams

Pair of retro citrine earclips, French, circa 1940, French assay mark, mounted in 18k gold, 1" long. **$15,000**

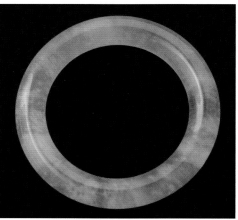

Michaan's Auctions

Carved jadeite bangle, approximately 12 mm wide and 53 mm internal diameter. **$1,100**

Bonhams

Eighteen karat gold fish necklace weighing approximately 186.2 g., 16" long. **$9,750**

Michaan's Auctions

Jade necklace with beads in various shapes and sizes, 35" long. **$425**

Bonhams

Diamond solitaire ring together with insert ring, central diamond approximately 3.20 carats, remaining diamonds approximately 1.40 carats, mounted in platinum and 14 karat white gold, respectively, sizes 5 1/4. **$15,000**

Bonhams

Diamond, synthetic gem, enamel, and 14k bicolor gold bangle charm bracelet depicting stages of courtship, gross weight approximately 65.0 g., 2 1/4" diameter. **$13,750**

Bonhams

Gold coin, diamond and 18k gold pendant, South African Krugerrand 1983 gold coin, gross weight approximately 67.7g., 3 1/8" long. **$4,375**

Bonhams

Art Deco diamond and emerald ring, circa 1925, centering a modified square-cut diamond weighing approximately 1.10 carats, mounted in platinum, size 4 1/4. **$8,125**

Bonhams

Eighteen karat gold astrological pendant, Van Cleef & Arpels, French, depicting sign of Cancer, signed VCA, no. 71/115405, French assay mark, approximately 60.7 g., 3 3/8" long. **$4,750**

Mother-of-pearl, diamond, ruby and sapphire beetle brooch, Russian, partial Russian assay mark, mounted in 14k gold, 2" long. **$1,375**

Bonhams

Agate cameo brooch, Russian, depicting Cupid and Psyche, Russian assay mark, mounted in 14k gold, 2 9/16" x 2 1/4". **$3,125**

Bonhams

Eighteen karat gold geometric ring, David Webb, signed Webb for David Webb, size 2 3/4, with inner sizing spring. **$1,375**

Bonhams

Tortoiseshell and ruby Blackamoor clip brooch, Nardi, signed Nardi, 1 11/16" long. **$2,125**

Bonhams

Enamel and diamond pansy brooch, Cartier, signed Cartier, no. 17745, accompanied by signed box, mounted in 14k gold, 1 1/4" diameter. **$2,000**

Bonhams

Emerald, diamond, white sapphire, and enamel tassel pendant/necklace, endless chain, estimated total emerald weight 58 carats, estimated total white sapphire weight 5.70 carats, estimated total diamond weight 2.35 carats, mounted in 18k white and blackened gold, 24" long. **$16,250**

Bonhams

Ruby, sapphire and diamond brooch, Oscar Heyman & Brothers, waving American flag composed of fancy-cut sapphires, calibré-cut rubies, round brilliant, baguette and pear-shaped diamonds, maker's mark for Oscar Heyman & Brothers, no. 75239, estimated total diamond weight 3.30 carats, mounted in platinum, 2" long. **$31,250**

Bonhams

Shell cameo brooch mounted in 14k gold, 3 1/2" long. **$1,250**

Bonhams

Emerald, ruby and diamond pendant/brooch, central oval-shaped emerald cabochon weighing approximately 30 carats, estimated total diamond weight 7.30 carats, gross weight approximately 51.6 g., mounted in 18k gold and platinum; 2 1/4" long. **$23,750**

Bonhams

Antique citrine and seed pearl fringe choker necklace, circa 1900, graduated pear-shaped citrines measuring approximately 12.7 mm x 8.9 mm x 6.0 mm to 5.9 mm x 4.2 mm x 3.1 mm, mounted in 14k and 18k gold, 13 1/4" long. **$3,125**

Bonhams

Antique turquoise and diamond locket pendant, circa 1880, gross weight approximately 34.4 g., mounted in 18k gold, 2 1/4" long. **$1,500**

Bonhams

Pair of diamond earrings, Chopard, signed Chopard, no. 82/3043/9134057, estimated total diamond weight 8.70 carats, mounted in platinum, 2 3/4" long. **$15,000**

Bonhams

Art Deco black onyx, coral and diamond bracelet, circa 1925, mounted in platinum, 7" long. **$1,875**

Bonhams

Art Deco star sapphire and diamond ring, circa 1935, oval-shaped star sapphire cabochon weighing approximately 18 carats, mounted in platinum, size 5 3/4. **$4,750**

Bonhams

Art Deco black onyx and diamond dress-set, circa 1920, pair of cufflinks and four vest buttons, mounted in 18k gold. **$1,750**

Bonhams

Pair of Art Deco diamond brooches, circa 1930, accompanied by 14k white gold brooch frame, estimated total diamond weight 4.70 carats, mounted in platinum, 1 1/8" long. **$6,875**

Bonhams

Art Deco diamond hatpin, circa 1930, estimated total diamond weight 4 carats, mounted in 14k white gold, 2 3/8" long. **$2,125**

Bonhams

Two jadeite jade bangle bracelets, hinged, mounted in 14k gold, 2 1/4" and 2" diameter. **$1,500**

Bonhams

Art Deco diamond and green stone ring, circa 1925, central old European-cut diamond weighing approximately 0.75 carats, mounted in 18k white gold, size 7 1/4. **$1,875**

Bonhams

Peridot and diamond ring, oval-shaped peridot measuring approximately 15.8 mm x 12.3 mm x 8.6mm, estimated total diamond weight 1.50 carats, mounted in 18k gold, size 7 1/4. **$2,000**

Bonhams

Carved hardstone, gem-set and diamond bracelet, Santagostino, "Caribbean reef" collection, including opal, coral, turquoise and cultured pearl, signed Santiagostin, accompanied by extra link, mounted in 18k gold, 7 1/4" long. **$10,000**

Bonhams

American sterling silver brooch, George W. Shiebler & Company, New York, NY, circa 1890, "Homeric," #723, weight approximately 0.5 oz troy, 1 3/4" high. **$313**

Bonhams

Jadeite jade and ruby dragon motif ring, oval-shaped jadeite jade cabochon measuring 12.9 mm x 18.1 mm x 5.7 mm, mounted in 14k gold, size 7 1/4. **$6,000**

Bonhams

Pink sapphire and black diamond spider brooch, articulated legs, estimated total diamond weight 3.50 carats, mounted in blackened 18k gold, 2" long. **$1,875**

Bonhams

Diamond sheaf of wheat clip brooch, estimated total diamond weight 4.30 carats, mounted in platinum, 3 1/8" long. **$4,375**

Bonhams

Diamond and gem-set floral motif double-clip brooch composed of buff-topped rubies, sapphires, emeralds, amethysts, and black onyx with round brilliant-cut diamond borders, estimated total diamond weight 2.10 carats, mounted in platinum-topped 18k gold, 2 1/2" wide. **$6,250**

Bonhams

Jadeite jade and diamond clip brooch mounted in 14k and 18k white gold, 1 7/8" long. **$3,750**

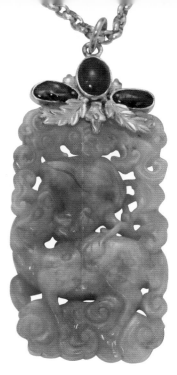

Bonhams

Collection of three diamond and gem-set flower brooches, including peridot, pink sapphire and garnet, estimated total diamond weight 1.45 carats, mounted in 18k white and blackened gold, 2" and 1 7/8" long. **$4,750**

Bonhams

Carved jade, sapphire, spinel and 24k gold pendant with 24k gold chain, jadeite jade depicting deer and peach approximately 66.8 mm x 38.9 mm x 10.5mm, chain only weighing approximately 35.7 g., pendant 3 3/4" long, chain 21 7/8" long. **$2,250**

Bonhams

Antique diamond necklace, circa 1890, estimated total old mine-cut diamond weight 2 carats, mounted in 14k gold, 15 1/4" long. **$1,875**

Bonhams

Multicolor tourmaline bead double strand necklace, drop-shaped tourmaline beads measuring approximately 21.3 mm x 14 mm to 7.9 mm x 4.7 mm, mounted in 18k gold, 18 3/4" long. **$3,500**

Bonhams

Ruby and diamond ring, oval-shaped ruby weighing approximately 2.50 carats, estimated total diamond weight 1.30 carats, mounted in platinum, size 5 1/2. **$6,250**

Bonhams

Lava cameo, cultured pearl, emerald and diamond brooch, cultured pearls measuring approximately 12.9 mm to 10.7 mm, mounted in 18k gold, 2 15/16" long. **$1,625**

Bonhams

Ruby, sapphire and diamond bouquet brooch, French, featuring carved rubies and oval-shaped sapphire cabochons, French assay mark and maker's mark, mounted in 18k gold and platinum, 2 7/8" long. **$6,250**

Lamps & Lighting

BY MARTIN WILLIS

A fine lamp provides both illumination as well as a decorative focal point for a room. This dual-purpose trend had its origins in the mid-to-late 1800s with American lighting. As with most game-changing style movements, timing was key in this evolution.

Arguably, the vanguard name of decorative lighting was Louis Comfort Tiffany (1848-1933) of New York City. Urban homes became electrified on a wide scale near the end of the 19th century; it was then that Tiffany was becoming recognized as a designer as well as a commercial success.

Martin Willis

Tiffany's first stained glass shade for an electric lamp was designed by Clara Driscoll around 1895. Since their introduction over a century ago, Tiffany's shades have always had a unique, glowing quality to them due to their masterful designs and chemically compounded stained glass colors. Today, Tiffany Studios lamps remain collector's favorites. Rare and unusual designs – including the Hanging Head Dragonfly, Peony, Apple Blossom, and Wisteria patterns – generate the most interest and dollars; outstanding examples have commanded up to $2 million. More common items such as Acorn, Tulip, or Favrile art glass shade lamps have experienced falling prices relative to a decade ago.

Tiffany's commercial success catalyzed the creation of many new stained glass lamp companies. Contemporaries included Duffner & Kimberly, Suess, Chicago Mosaic, and Wilkinson. See Mosaic Shades II by Paul Crist, for more information.

There were several other companies in the United States making fine glass lamps at the turn of last century. These included Handel, from Meriden, Connecticut, and Pairpoint, from New Bedford, Massachusetts. Handel was known primarily for its reverse painted shades. Fine examples of the company's landscape, Aquarium, and other unusual motifs have garnered prices up to $85,000. Pairpoint opened in 1880 and soon merged with Mt. Washington Glass of Boston. They created reverse painted shades as well, the most popular being their "Puffy" shade. Prices for Pairpoint lamps start around $1,000 and peak about $25,000 for top examples.

Perhaps the most notable European glass lamp manufacturer from the late 19th century was Daum, founded by Jean Daum in France in 1878. The company is still in business today, manufacturing crystal art glass. Daum's lamps were made of cameo glass, produced through a proprietary technique of using acid to cut through layers of fused glass. This creates dramatic

---

MARTIN WILLIS *is the Director of the Decorative Arts at James D. Julia, Inc., one of the nation's premier auction galleries. Formerly of New Hampshire, Willis comes from a family of auctioneers: His father, Morgan Willis, developed and ran the Seaboard Auction Gallery in Eliot, Maine, which Martin eventually took over. He has 40 years of experience in the antique auction business from companies in Maine, New Hampshire, Massachusetts, Colorado and California. He spent six years with Clars Auction Gallery of Oakland, California, as senior appraiser, cataloger and auctioneer, handling the estate of TV mogul Merv Griffin as well as talk show host Tom Snyder. In 2009, Martin launched Antique Auction Forum, a biweekly podcast on the art and antiques trade with followers across North America and throughout the world.*

color reliefs. During the heyday, 1895-1914, Daum produced beautiful cameo glass lamp bases and shades. Today, early examples can be purchased starting at $1,000. Exceptional pieces may garner up to $80,000.

It is important to note that when it comes to vintage lamps, reproductions and fakes dominate the secondary market. If a price seems too good to be true, it probably is. It is imperative to buy from a reputable dealer or an auction house that will stand behind an item's authenticity. If a piece has the word "style" as part of its description, i.e., a "Tiffany style" lamp, this indicates that it is either a reproduction or that the seller is uncertain of its origins. Always ask plenty of questions before investing in a fine art lamp.

As always, anything is worth whatever someone will pay, and there are often good buys available – even from top manufacturers. With the exception of the very rarest examples, enthusiasts should be able to find and afford a nice authentic vintage lamp to admire and enjoy.

James D. Julia, Inc.

Pairpoint Ravenna Puffy shade table lamp, two large floral garland wreaths reverse painted in mauves, oranges, pinks and whites, reminiscent of Art Nouveau wallpaper in hues of greens, yellows, rose and white.
$12,500

James D. Julia, Inc.

Tiffany Studios table lamp in Greek Key pattern, mottled glass in green and yellow. **$37,950**

James D. Julia, Inc.

Tiffany Studios Acorn table lamp, leaded geometric background of yellow lemon glass decorated with a single band of acorns in green striated glass. **$6,000**

James D. Julia, Inc.

Rare Handel Peacock floor lamp, domical glass shade decorated and acid etched on exterior with two peacocks being the central focus, surrounded by a floral and foliage pattern. **$23,575**

James D. Julia, Inc.

Tiffany Studios Poinsettia table lamp with fully leaded shade, intense dichroic geometric background shows yellow and green when unlit, turns orange and red when illuminated. **$48,875**

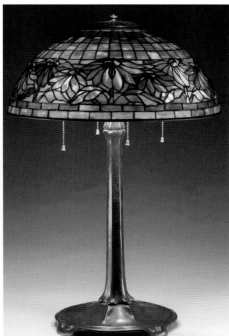

James D. Julia, Inc.

Daum Nancy boudoir lamp with wooded landscape scene, unusual white, pink, and green enameled and cameo scene on mottled amethyst and green background, signed "Daum Nancy." **$13,800**

James D. Julia, Inc.

Handel Aquatic table lamp, reverse painted shade depicts aquatic life with fish, coral and other underwater vegetation in deep green, bright yellow and brown. **$14,000**

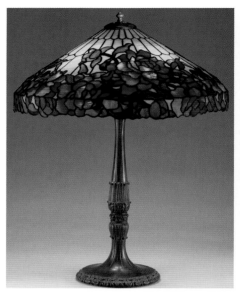

James D. Julia, Inc.

Duffner & Kimberly table lamp in Peony pattern, shaded red glass and green leaves against a striated green and brown background. **$35,000**

James D. Julia, Inc.

Tiffany Studios turtleback table lamp, row of green turtlebacks with blue iridescence surrounding the shade, set against a background of geometric heavily mottled emerald green panels. **$60,000**

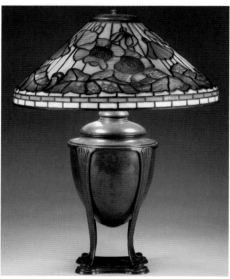

James D. Julia, Inc.

Tiffany Studios Poppy table lamp, leaded shade with orange poppies against a butterscotch background. Poppies have acid etched bronze overlay on exterior for stamens while interior has acid etched overlay to show veining on leaves, bottom of shade is encircled by green leaves, shade rests on four-legged urn base with three-light cluster. **$35,000**

James D. Julia, Inc.

Tiffany Studios Moorish double student lamp with twisted wire Moorish decoration on bronze base that supports two bronze overlay shades with blown out green glass inserts. **$12,000**

James D. Julia, Inc.

Rare Pairpoint Puffy owl lamp with exaggerated, blown out, molded Pairpoint shade resting atop owl-shaped metal base. The shade, painted in brown, green, white and yellow, features two large oyster-shaped eye areas painted white with highlights and centered with yellow irises and black pupils; beak painted in shades of white and maize. **$86,250**

James D. Julia, Inc.

Tiffany Studios Peony table lamp with peony shade, red and pink peonies against a mottled yellow background, flower petals executed with red and pink glass swirled with white. **$82,500**

James D. Julia, Inc.

Handel Wisteria table lamp with massive leaded shade, recurring design of 12 wisteria flowers in purple, lavender, amethyst, and blue with yellow centers, set against foliage in green hues, hanging wisteria vines in earthen hues, accentuated irregular border gives the shade a three-dimensional affect. **$17,500**

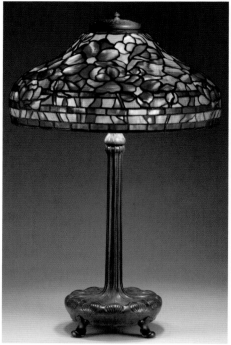

James D. Julia, Inc.

Tiffany Studios Peony table lamp with allover peony design, red mottled peony petals and yellow amber stamens set against a background of mottled and shaded green. **$80,000**

James D. Julia, Inc.

Exceptional Pairpoint Puffy three-color azalea table lamp, closed top shade with pink, red and white azaleas against a green leafy background. **$14,000**

James D. Julia, Inc.

Handle Treasure Island table lamp with dome shaped shade, reverse painted with a decoration of palm trees, ocean and sailing ships against a moonlit bay, predominantly blues, greens and earthen tones. **$14,400**

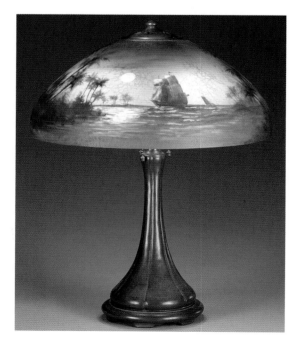

James D. Julia, Inc.

Daum Nancy ribbed table lamp with purple-blue raised vertical ribs against a shaded green to raspberry ground on shade and maize-yellow to powdered blue mottled on base. **$13,800**

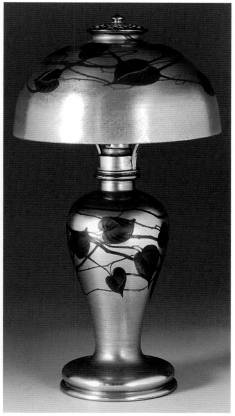

James D. Julia, Inc.

Tiffany Studios Dragonfly table lamp with shade surrounded by seven dragonflies with olive green bodies and multicolored wings with yellow, pink and amber all set against a green background of heavily mottled glass. **$69,000**

James D. Julia, Inc.

Tiffany Studios intaglio cut table lamp with gold Favrile glass shade heavily carved with intaglio cut green leaves and vines. Shade supported by gold Favrile glass base with matching green intaglio cut leaves and vines. **$13,800**

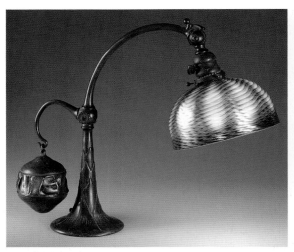

James D. Julia, Inc.

Rare Tiffany Studios counterbalance lamp with pendulous turtleback tile counterweight, artichoke design stand, and blue decorated damascene shade. **$32,775**

James D. Julia, Inc.

Handel Cattail lamp with heavily overlaid shade depicting cattails and reeds, colors predominantly amber and green on a caramel ground. **$11,500**

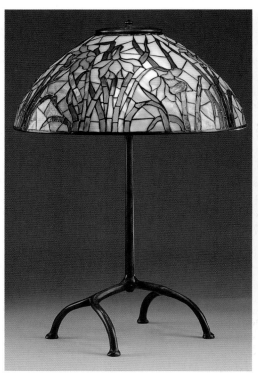

James D. Julia, Inc.

Tiffany Studios Daffodil table lamp with yellow daffodils, centers created with heavily ribbed glass with dark green stems and leaves against a light green background shading to creamy white. **$39,100**

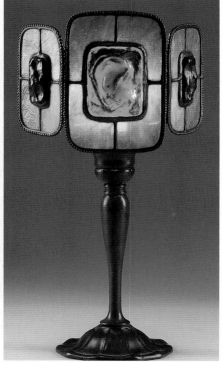

James D. Julia, Inc.

Unusual Tiffany Studios turtleback lamp with bronze base, ribbed inverted saucer foot, and simple turned stem. **$12,075**

James D. Julia, Inc.

Tiffany Studios Fireball lamp with leaded orb shade with flame design in mottled red and orange glass against a textured green and brown swirled background. **$48,875**

James D. Julia, Inc.

Handel crane lamp, reverse painted with a single crane on three sides. **$10,350**

James D. Julia, Inc.

Handel bird lamp with domical shaped shade, sand finished exterior, painted on interior with three colorful parrots perched on branches with complementary foliage painted in shades of rose and yellow with green foliage. **$15,813**

James D. Julia, Inc.

Handel floral and butterfly table lamp with reverse painted shade with floral pattern in lavender, amethyst, aquamarine, blue, and green that encompasses two-thirds of shade. **$11,500**

James D. Julia, Inc.

Massive Handel overlay table lamp with textured butterscotch glass, obverse painted emerald green within peacock feather metal overlay design. **$10,350**

James D. Julia, Inc.

Pairpoint Puffy apple tree lamp with background of green leaves with bluish highlights and pink apple blossoms surrounding green and red apples, pair of bumblebees on one side and two butterflies on opposing side. **$23,575**

James D. Julia, Inc.

Handel bird lamp with domical shade, reverse painted with two pairs of exotic birds and a floral and foliate pattern, birds painted in yellows, oranges, and blues with mauve peonies and five-petal yellow flowers. **$13,800**

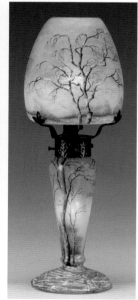

James D. Julia, Inc.

Daum Nancy winter scenic lamp with detail including snow on branches against a shaded and mottled orange to yellow background. **$16,800**

Maps & Globes

Throughout the ages, pictorial maps have been used to show the industries of a city, the attractions of a tourist town, the history of a region or its holy shrines. Ancient artifacts suggest that pictorial mapping has been around since recorded history began. "Here be dragons" is a mapping phrase used to denote dangerous or unexplored territories, in imitation of the medieval practice of putting sea serpents and other mythological creatures in blank areas of maps.

Skinner, Inc.

Cary's 14" terrestrial table globe on stand, London, 1826, circle cartouche reads, "Cary's New Terrestrial Globe, Drawn from the most recent Geographical Works, shewing the whole of the New Discoveries with the Tracks of the Principle Navigators and every improvement in Geography to the present Time." London, published by G & J Cary, St. James's, Jan. 4, 1826, the 12 engraved paper gores with countries and territories shaded in various colors, the coasts outlined, Alaska labeled "Russian America," the American southwest labeled "Mexico," South Africa shown as "Unknown Parts," the oceans marked with tracks of various explorers, brass meridian ring with degrees and polar hour ring, paper on wood red-rimmed horizon ring with decorative border and Gregorian and Zodiacal calendars, string-inlaid frame, on three turned mahogany legs joined by stretchers, 22 3/4" high. **$3,851**

Michaan's Auctions

Weber Costello Co. terrestrial 16" floor globe on stand, 38" high. **$225**

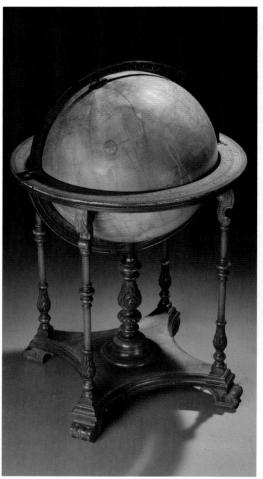

Skinner, Inc.

W. & A. K. Johnston, Ltd. 18" terrestrial library globe, Edinburgh, Scotland, circa 1900, printed gores with states and countries highlighted in different colors, maker's cartouche in Pacific stating 18 Inch Terrestrial Globe, Terrestrial Globe, A.J. Nystrom & Co., Chicago, Ill., Analemma or Table of Equation of Time chart, brass hour circle at the pole and calibrated meridian ring, paper on wood horizon ring with signs of zodiac and calendar, all on turned and carved walnut base with central carved shaft support and four supporting legs, 40" high. **$2,252**

Heritage Auctions, Inc.

Illuminated electric globe, maker unknown, French, circa 1930, on stepped chromed metal base, labeled in French, 9 3/8" high. **$300**

Framed 1856 map of California with inset of San Francisco, frame 27" x 23". **$120**

Colonial map of Virginia, Maryland, Carolina, and New England. **$325**

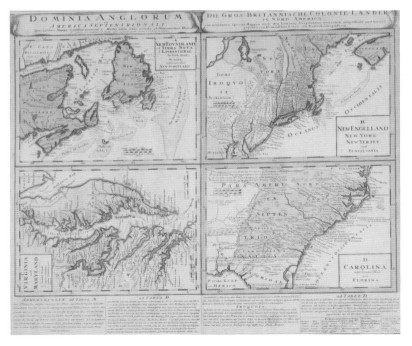

Bonhams

American cast iron terrestrial floor globe, Gilman Joslin, Boston, third quarter 19th century, 15" globe raised on a painted foliate and scroll cast iron standard, 42" high, 21 1/2" diameter. **$6,875**

Heritage Auctions, Inc.

"A New Map of the United States of America, from the Latest Authorities," London, John Cary, 1806. First edition taken from Cary's New Universal Atlas from 1808. Contemporary hand-coloring, 20 1/4" x 26 1/4". Cary (1754-1835) was one of the finest and most prolific English cartographers of the 19th century. He also became the foremost globe maker of his day. **$1,375**

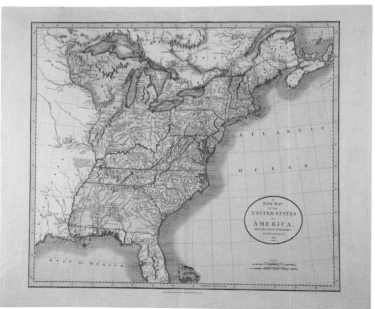

Pook & Pook, Inc.

Silk embroidered map of England and Wales, dated 1804, wrought by Mary Walker, York, 19" x 15 1/2". **$711**

Heritage Auctions, Inc.

Atlas, New York and vicinity, New York, F. W. Beers, A. D. Ellis & G. G. Soule, 1867. First edition of Beers' atlas, this copy complete. Folio. 17 1/2" x 14 1/4". Twelve lithographic maps printed on onionskin paper inserted throughout, 61 hand-colored lithographic maps and uncolored lithographic views, publisher's quarter brown morocco over cloth boards, boards paneled in blind, front cover lettered in gilt, embossed stamp of Kettner & Walker, Bookbinders on lower corner of front free endpaper. **$625**

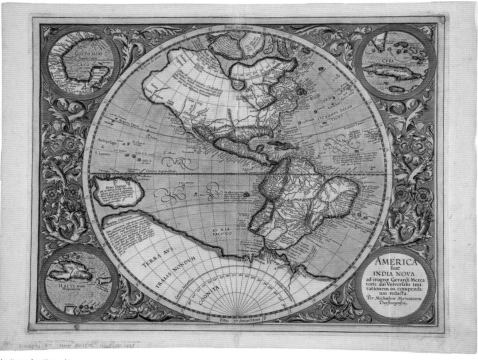

Heritage Auctions, Inc.

Michael Mercator, "America sive India Nova, ad magnae Gerardi Mercatoris avi Universalis imitationem in compendium redacta." Amsterdam, Hondius, 1595 [actually 1613-1630]. Taken from either the 1613, 1623, or 1630 editions of Hondius, identical to scarce 1595 first appearance, Latin text on verso, hand-colored map, initial "Q" on verso also hand-colored. 15 1/4" x 20 1/4". Details include possible first appearance of Great Lakes ("Mare Dulcium Aquarum") and three insets depicting Cuba and southern tip of Florida, Gulf of Mexico and Yucatan Peninsula, Haiti and West Indies. **$2,000**

Heritage Auctions, Inc.

Hand-colored atlas, "Descriptio Orbis Antiqui," Jo. Davide Koelero [Johann David Koehler]. Nuremberg, Homann family, [n.d., ca. 1760]. Later reprint of original 1720 edition published by Christoph Weigel. Folio. 15 1/2" x 10". Engraved title page, engraved index, and 44 double-page hand-colored maps and views (complete), all leaves and plates mounted on stubs, most maps have engraved vignettes or examples of coinage from the countries depicted, bound in near contemporary half-mottled calf over patterned paper boards, spine ruled and tooled in gilt, burgundy gilt morocco lettering label on front board. **$1,750**

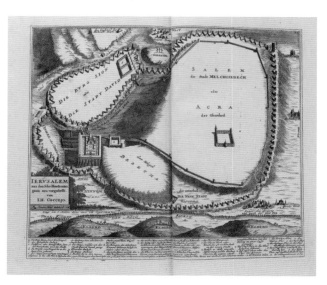

Pook & Pook, Inc.

*Pen and ink hand-
drawn map of the
United States, mid-
19th century, 8 3/4"
x 10 1/2".* **$830**

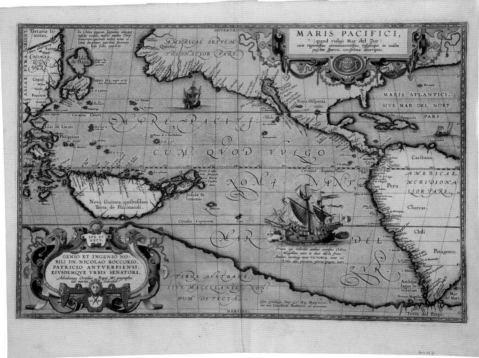

Heritage Auctions, Inc.

*First printed map devoted to Pacific Ocean, Abraham Ortelius, "Maris Pacifici, (quod volgò Mar del Zur)
cum regionibus circumiacentibus, insulisque in eodem passim sparsis, novissima descriptio." Antwerp,
Plantin Press, 1589 [actually 1590 or 1592]. First edition of copperplate map, first state, first issue, presumed
second printing from 1592, hand-colored, 16" x 20 1/4". First map devoted to the Pacific; one of the earliest
maps to differentiate North and South America by name; first map to show Japan and New Guinea as being
closer to Asia than to America; one of the earliest maps to show California as a peninsula; depicts the west
coast of North America more accurately than any maps before it. Near the center is a depiction of Magellan's
surviving ship, the Victoria.* **$6,875**

Neal Auction Co.

*Weber Costello Company 12"
terrestrial globe, early 20th
century, cartouche reads, "Made
by Weber Costello Co., Chicago
Heights, Illinois," on a turned
wooden pedestal, 20" high.* **$700**

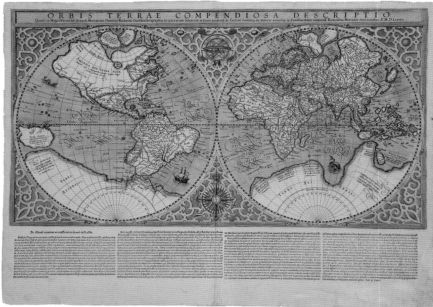

Heritage Auctions, Inc.

*World hemispherical projection map, Rumoldus Mercator, "Orbis Terrae Compendiosa
Descriptio," 1587 [actually 1595]. First atlas edition of this important map, excised from Gerardus
Mercator's "Atlas sive cosmographicae meditationes de fabrica mundi et fabricati figura," published
in 1595. Contemporary hand coloring, one of the earliest maps to show New Guinea. 15 1/2" x
21". Gerardus Mercator (1512-1594) was the most important and influential cartographer of the
16th century. He is famous for producing the most accurate maps of his day and for the invention
of the Mercator Projection, in which the world is pictured in a cylindrical-like fashion, showing
the entire globe in a single map. The above map is by his youngest son, Rumoldus (1545-1599),
who based it on his father's designs of the original map of 1567, after Gerardus died in 1594. The
Mercators are considered the most important cartographers after Ptolemy.* **$4,750**

Pook & Pook, Inc.

"A Map of the Country round Philadelphia including part of New Jersey, New York, Staten Island & Long Island," hand engraved, 7" x 8 3/4". **$385**

Pook & Pook, Inc.

Hand-colored lithograph map titled "Magnae Britannia" by Henrici Hondij, dated 1631, 17" x 21 1/2". **$334**

Movie Posters

BY NOAH FLEISHER

There is magic in old movie posters; the best directly channel the era from which they came. The totality of movie poster art, the oldest and rarest going back more than a century, taken as a whole, is no less than a complete graphic survey of the evolution of graphic design and taste in Western culture.

The broad appeal of movie posters stems from that nostalgia and from the fact that so many pieces can be had at very fair prices. This makes it an attractive place for younger collectors, many of whom don't even realize they are starting on the incredible journey that collecting can be. Most are simply looking to fill space on a wall or give a gift, and they fill it with art from a movie they loved when they were kids, or one that meant something to them at a specific point in their lives.

Noah Fleisher

"There's a natural evolution with many of them," said Grey Smith, director of movie posters at Heritage Auctions, Inc.. "As they progress in their lives they tend to progress as collectors, trading up as they go. When it's all said and done, you see accomplished, broad-based collections."

Movie posters can rightly be called a gateway collectible for that very reason. Very few true collectors just collect one thing and, for more than a few, the first taste comes in the form of movie posters.

So where, exactly, is the top of the market and how has it fared in the last few years?

"As always, Universal horror is the top of the market," said Smith. "Top examples of any great film – the older the better – will always bring respectable prices. As a whole, though, the market is off from five and 10 years ago when top posters were bringing $250,000 and $350,000, but it's been steady at the bottom of the high end and in the middle."

What does this mean to today's collectors? It means that a cooled market constitutes incredible opportunity to the trained eye. The untrained eye can benefit by association with reputable dealers and auction houses, by keeping a steady eye on prices in various auctions and on eBay, and by learning what they like, where to get it and when to buy.

Any dealer or auction house worth its salt is going to spend some time with you – if you want – at whatever level you are collecting, to help you figure out what you can get within your budget. From $100 to $1,000 and up into five and six figures, there are relative bargains to be had right now and, to go back to the top of this discussion, the artwork just can't be beat.

"Ultimately, I would tell anyone looking to buy a movie poster to buy it because they like it," said Smith, echoing the first rule of the business across all categories. "It's all about individual taste. Never get into something for the money because you'll be disappointed."

Besides buying online or from auction houses – at least a few of which, like Heritage, have weekly offerings online to complement its larger thrice yearly events – good posters can be found, for the intrepid explorer, in country auctions, flea markets and antiques shows across the country.

The movies are universal and every town had a movie house. The result is that posters were distributed everywhere and, while not meant for display purposes in the long-term, many found second lives as insulation in walls or as a single layer in a thick, glued board of movie posters, as theater owners would wallpaper the posters over each other from week to week.

Heritage Auctions, Inc.

"Dracula" (Universal, 1931), one sheet (27" x 41"), Style F: Early Universal Studios horror posters are the most desirable posters in the hobby and few, if any, more so than Dracula. From the Berwick Discovery. **$143,400**

The erudite eye can pick out the corners of one of these constructs, or can recognize the quality of paper and the neat folds of a quietly stashed one-sheet. The result can often be a treasure, financially and artistically.

Two aspects of movie poster collecting that get much attention and much misinformation are restorations versus forgeries and fakes.

Every collector should be wary of fakes and forgeries: If it seems too good to be true, ask questions and consult reputable sources. There are always unscrupulous people looking to take advantage of the unsuspecting. A pro will know, based on a variety of factors, whether you have a once-in-a-lifetime find or if you're looking at a clever reprint.

This should never be confused, however, with respectable restoration. Older posters often come with the damage of age – they were not printed on the highest quality paper, as they were not meant to be lasting mementos. Movies played for a few weeks and were replaced, as were the posters. If a poster is linen-backed or framed, there has likely been restoration work on it, and a good dealer or auctioneer will be very up front about this.

"Oftentimes a poster would not have been saved had it not been for quality restoration," said Smith. "Good restoration work is respectful of the original and will enhance the value of a piece, not hurt it. A fake is a fake, no matter what, and should never be portrayed as an original. Educate yourself, check your sources and you should do just fine."

NOAH FLEISHER *received his Bachelor of Fine Arts degree from New York University and brings more than a decade of newspaper, magazine, book, antiques and art experience to his position as Public Relations Director of Heritage Auctions, one of the country's foremost auction houses. He is the former editor of* Antique Trader, New England Antiques Journal *and* Northeast Antiques Journal, *is the author of* Warman's Modern Furniture, *and has been a longtime contributor to* Warman's Antiques & Collectibles.

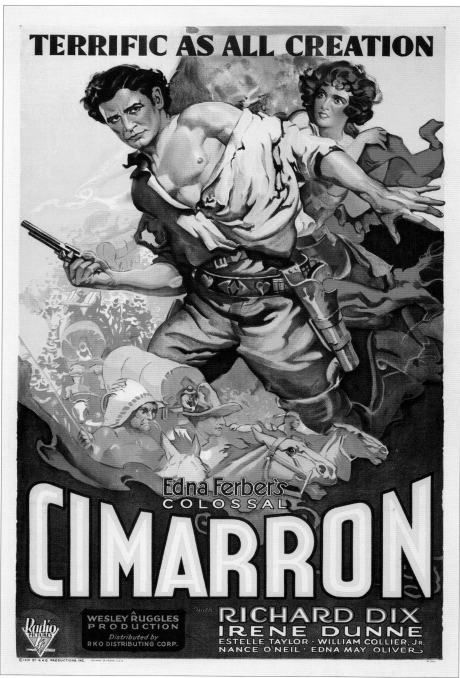

Heritage Auctions, Inc.

"Cimarron" (RKO, 1931), one sheet (27" x 41"): "Cimarron," starring Richard Dix and Irene Dunne, emerged as a big-budget prestige picture from RKO and went on to claim Best Picture Oscar for 1931. Expert professional restoration. From the Berwick Discovery. **$101,575**

Heritage Auctions, Inc.

"The Public Enemy" (Warner Brothers, 1931), one sheet (27" x 41"), Style B: Paper from this classic film is rare. Expert professional restoration. From the Berwick Discovery. **$59,750**

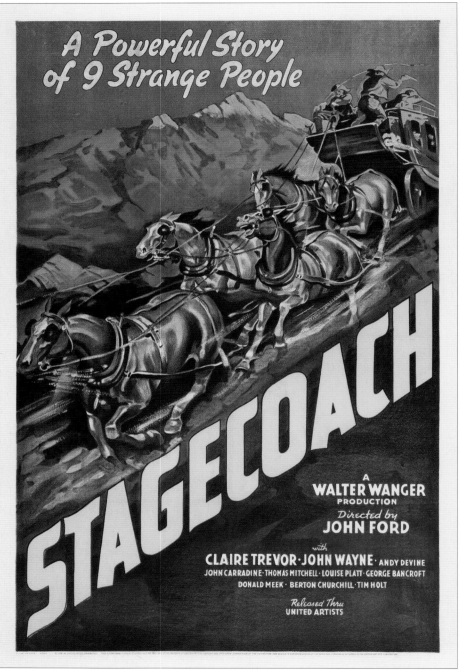

Heritage Auctions, Inc.

"Stagecoach" (United Artists, 1939), one sheet (27" x 41"): This is one of the greats and one of the rarest of the movie poster hobby for the film that made John Wayne a superstar. John Ford directs Wayne in his classic Western drama. Expert professional restoration. **$56,763**

Heritage Auctions, Inc.

"Little Caesar" (Warner Brothers – First National, 1931), one sheet (27" x 41"), Style B: One of only two copies known to exist. Expert professional restoration. From the Berwick Discovery. **$41,825**

Heritage Auctions, Inc.

"Casablanca" (Warner Brothers, 1942), one sheet (27" x 41"): A simple layout of six key scenes from the film swirls around Ingrid Bergman and Humphrey Bogart. **$28,680.**

Heritage Auctions, Inc.

"My Man Godfrey" (Universal, 1936), one sheet (27" x 41"), Style C: Rare one sheet poster for one of the 1930s' classiest screwball comedies featuring William Powell and Carole Lombard. **$28,680**

Heritage Auctions, Inc.

"Tarzan and His Mate" (MGM, 1934), lobby streamer (161 1/2" x 43 1/2"): Lithographed on hard cardboard, one side only, with several perforations drilled in each piece as was manufactured; this is a rarity and few streamers have survived from any film. The center piece pictures Johnny Weissmuller as Tarzan and Maureen O'Sullivan as Jane, both astride an elephant. **$26,290**

Heritage Auctions, Inc.

"The Little Giant" (First National, 1933), one sheet (27" x 41"): Master portrait artist Irving Sinclair displays his talent on this rarely sold one sheet, with Edward G. Robinson flanked by Mary Astor and Helen Vinson as the "saint and sinner" of the film. **$21,510**

Heritage Auctions, Inc.

Mickey Mouse stock poster (United Artists, 1932), one sheet (27" x 41"): United Artists picked up the Disney franchise when Columbia dropped it in 1932, and this rare stock sheet was probably the first to be distributed by the studio's new distributor. **$20,315**

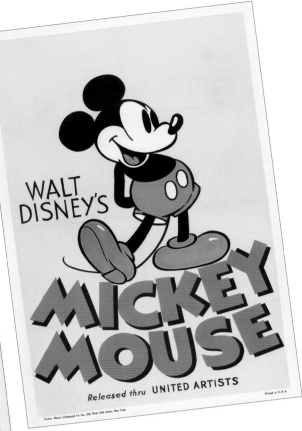

Heritage Auctions, Inc.

"Society Dog Show" (RKO, 1939), one sheet (27" x 41"): Mickey Mouse enters Pluto in a ritzy dog show in this animated short, the last before Mickey's redesign. His next appearance would depict him with pupils in his eyes. **$21,510**

"The Maltese Falcon" (Warner Brothers, 1941), window card (14" x 22"): An unrestored, magnificent condition window card to perhaps the greatest film noir classic of all time. **$16,730**

"Ten Cents a Dance" (Columbia, 1931), one sheet (27" x 41"), Style A: An early "pre-Code" starring vehicle for Barbara Stanwyck based on a popular song by Richard Rogers and Lorenz Hart. Professional restoration. **$16,730**

Heritage Auctions, Inc.

"A Dog's Life" (First National, 1918), three sheet (41" x 81"): Charlie Chaplin's initial film for First National Pictures, a 40-minute comedy and also his first three-reeler. Scraps the dog co-starred along with regular co-star Edna Purviance. **$14,340**

Heritage Auctions, Inc.

"Cat People" (RKO, 1942), one sheet (27" x 41"): Val Lewton produced this film on a modest budget and turned it into one of the most frightening films of the 1940s. Simone Simon stars as a woman who turns into a panther when emotionally charged. **$13,145**

Heritage Auctions, Inc.

"Only Angels Have Wings" (Columbia, 1939), one sheet (27" x 41"), Style A: Cary Grant and Jean Arthur have plenty of chemistry in Howard Hawks' film about a small mail delivery service in South America that flies a dangerous route. **$13,145**

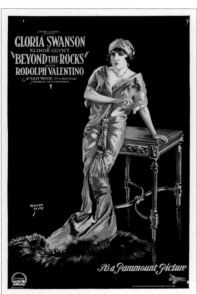

Heritage Auctions, Inc.

"Beyond the Rocks" (Paramount, 1922), one sheet (27" x 41"): Artist Henry Clive (1881-1960) renders Gloria Swanson in jewel tones against an onyx background. **$11,950**

Heritage Auctions, Inc.

"Baby Face" (Warner Brothers, 1933), one sheet (27" x 41"): One of the most controversial of the 1930s "pre-Code" films starring Barbara Stanwyck. Rich, vibrant colors. **$10,755**

Heritage Auctions, Inc.

"The Black Room" (Columbia, 1935), title lobby card (11" x 14"): From one of Boris Karloff's best films, a macabre gothic tale about an ancient family curse. One of only three or four copies known. **$11,950**

Heritage Auctions, Inc.

"Flying Tigers" (Republic, 1942), one sheet (27" x 41"), Style A: This poster depicts one of the Flying Tigers engaged in combat. The 1942 film starring John Wayne was met with critical and commercial success, as it was released shortly after America entered the war. **$7,768**

Heritage Auctions, Inc.

"2001: A Space Odyssey" (MGM, 1968), Cinerama one sheet (27" x 41"), Style C: The style C was only used in theaters presenting the film in Cinerama, and since not many theatres were set up for it, these posters were distributed in small quantities. From one of the most monumental science fiction films ever made. **$4,780**

Heritage Auctions, Inc.

"Snow White and the Seven Dwarfs" (RKO, 1937), one sheet (27" x 41"), Style B: With its saturated colors, this is one of the best copies of this style B one sheet ever seen. The artwork by Gustaf Tenggren on this style poster is superior to the other style released for the film. **$10,158**

Heritage Auctions, Inc.

"Blonde Crazy" (Warner Brothers, 1931), insert (14" x 36"): A rare insert for this racy "pre-Code" title with Joan Blondell and James Cagney. **$10,158**

Heritage Auctions, Inc.

"Creature From the Black Lagoon" (Universal International, 1954), one sheet (27" x 41"): Richard Carlson and Julia Adams star in this timeless Universal horror tale of an expedition to the dark waters of the Amazon that uncovers the existence of a half-human, half-amphibian Gill Man, one of the most popular monsters of all time. **$9,740**

Heritage Auctions, Inc.

"Follow the Fleet" (RKO, 1936), one sheet (27" x 41"): Ginger Rogers and Fred Astaire star in another RKO musical in which they perform one of their greatest dance numbers, Irving Berlin's "Let's Face the Music and Dance." **$8,963**

Heritage Auctions, Inc.

"Superman" (Columbia, 1948), three sheet (41" x 81"): A stellar large format poster featuring the ultimate superhero in action. **$8,963**

Heritage Auctions, Inc.

"Sunset Boulevard" (Paramount, 1957), Polish one sheet (22 1/2" x 33 1/4"): The Polish version of this poster, Billy Wilder's "Sunset Boulevard" features standout performances by William Holden and Gloria Swanson. The film was nominated for 11 Academy Awards, and ranks high in the top 100 American films list by AFI. **$7,768**

Heritage Auctions, Inc.

"How to Fish" (RKO, 1942), one sheet (27" x 41"): Produced during the first year of Disney's How To series, Goofy shows every man how not to go about the task of the angler. **$8,963**

Heritage Auctions, Inc.

"Greed" (MGM, 1924), window card (14" x 22"): The original cut of Greed by director Erich Von Stroheim was 42 reels with a running time of over nine hours. Producer Irving Thalberg condensed it to just more than two hours, resulting in a film with continuity gaps. One of the few known to exist. **$8,365**

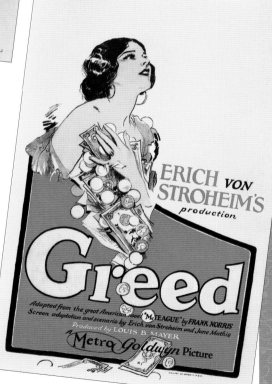

Heritage Auctions, Inc.

"Dracula" (Universal, 1931), uncut pressbook (13 1/2" x 19 1/2", eight pages): Rarely seen complete pressbook for the classic Universal Horror film "Dracula." **$8,365**

Heritage Auctions, Inc.

"The Virginian" (Paramount, 1929), one sheet (27" x 41"), Style B, silent version: A stone litho one sheet depicting the juxtaposition of romance and gunplay for this classic Western starring Gary Cooper, Walter Huston and Mary Brian. **$7,469**

Heritage Auctions, Inc.

"Spartacus" (Universal International, 1960), road show autographed one sheet (27" x 41"): The rare Saul Bass-designed poster was used only for the short road show distribution prior to the Academy Awards and pictures the cast of Kirk Douglas, Laurence Olivier, Jean Simmons and Charles Laughton. This copy is autographed by Tony Curtis, Woody Strode, Joanna Barnes, producer Edward Lewis, editor Robert Lawrence and the artist, all acquired in 1991. **$6,573**

Heritage Auctions, Inc.

"Breakfast at Tiffany's" (Paramount, 1961), one sheet (27" x 41"): Paperback artist Robert McGinnis delivered this splendid and now indelible image of Audrey Hepburn as Holly Golightly posing in her iconic Givenchy gown. **$5,378**

Heritage Auctions, Inc.

"Forbidden Planet" (MGM, 1956), one sheet (27" x 41"): This one sheet continues to be one of the most coveted science fiction posters in the hobby. This example has superb color and few flaws. **$6,573**

Music Memorabilia

BY SUSAN SLIWICKI

Despite the slow economy, the state of the hobby for those who collect music and related memorabilia is healthy, according to Jacques van Gool of Backstage Auctions.

Based in Houston, the boutique online auction house specializes in authentic rock memorabilia consigned directly by legendary musicians and entertainment professionals.

Jacques van Gool

"I have not seen a massive exodus or departure from collecting music memorabilia as a hobby," van Gool said. "I think the number of collectors and buyers is just as high as it was three or five years ago. But there is definitely a bigger interest for lower- to mid-range items."

Before the economy went south, multiple buyers might be in the market for a pricey item, such as a fully signed photo of The Beatles. The resulting bidding battle could drive that lot's price up to $10,000. These days, fewer people are looking for that type of lot to begin with, and those who are interested likely would pay less for it, too. Instead, buyers are gravitating toward low- to mid-price lots that previously might not have been considered for auction, van Gool said. And, the acts that buyers are interested in aren't necessarily your parents' favorites.

"There is definitely a new generation of collectors, which is people that currently age-wise are between 35 and 55, who didn't grow up listening to '60s music," van Gool said.

Artists from the late 1970s and 1980s, especially hard rock, heavy metal and pop acts, are poised to be the next generation of headlining acts for collectors, van Gool said. He listed Guns N' Roses, Motley Crüe, Bon Jovi, U2, Prince and Madonna as prime examples.

And just as the desired artists are changing, so, too, are some of the items that are being collected.

"Obviously, concert posters are becoming more and more extinct, because there hardly is a need to do concert posters anymore," van Gool said. "Back in the '60s, it was almost the only way to communicate that hey, there's a concert coming, and you would see these posters staple-gunned to phone poles. These days, you announce concerts via e-mail and websites and text messages and Facebook and Twitter and all of that."

Also on the endangered species list: ticket stubs, printed magazines, handbills and promotional materials. The sharp decline of many record companies and the rise of CD and digital formats have combined to reduce the production of promotional items, van Gool said.

T-shirts, on the other hand, have come into their own.

"T-shirts really didn't start taking off as either a promotion or concert merchandise item until the mid-'70s or beyond," van Gool said. "The whole T-shirt collection is more of a next-generation kind of thing. Of course, there are exceptions; there are old concert shirts for Led Zeppelin and the Stones. But in terms of sheer volume and numbers, that's not anything like the next decade."

And those reports you've heard about the pending demise of vinyl records in the wake of digital formats? Don't believe 'em.

"Vinyl is far from dead. Vinyl is alive and kicking," van Gool said. "Of '60s artists, vinyl is a prime collectible. But the same holds true for collectors of '80s bands or artists. They are just as intrigued and as interested in vinyl as the previous generation."

Whatever your interest in music and memorabilia, van Gool offers one key piece of advice.

"I have never looked at collecting music memorabilia as an investment," he said. Instead, he recommends building a collection around your passion, be it punk music, concert posters or all things Neil Diamond.

"If you just collect for the sheer and simple fact of pleasure and passion, then the money part, the investment part, becomes, at best, secondary," van Gool said. "In a way, collecting represents pieces of history. Whether it's an old handbill or a ticket stub or a T-shirt, every picture tells a story. When you buy that 1978 Blue Öyster Cult Wichita, Kansas, T-shirt, you've bought a piece of history."

Collecting Tips

There are a few things you should consider as you invest in your hobby, according to van Gool.

1. Condition, condition, condition. Strive to acquire items that are in the best condition possible, and keep them that way.

"One universal truth will always be condition," van Gool said. "Obviously, the more mint an item, the more it'll hold its value. That was true back then, it's true today, and it'll be true 40 years from now."

From poster frames to ticket albums to record storage sleeves, bags and boxes, there are ways to preserve basically every collectible you might seek.

Rolling Stones 1978 "Some Girls" tour T-shirt with printing on front and back, size large, 18" armpit to armpit, 28" top to bottom. **$202**

"It's money well spent to make sure you preserve your items well," van Gool said.

2. Put a priority on provenance. Some collectors feel that personal items, like an artist's jewelry, stage-worn clothing or even a car, have more value than other pieces. But the personal nature of a piece doesn't matter if you can't prove its pedigree.

"Personal items are considered valuable, but you'd better have the provenance to back it up, and provenance is harder to come by than the actual item," van Gool said.

Working with reputable auctioneers and dealers is a great way to boost the likelihood that an item is everything you want. But even if you acquire a personal item with an impeccable provenance, keep in mind that doesn't necessarily make it more valuable than something of a less personal nature.

"What I've seen is that a fully signed Beatles item may be worth $10,000. But there's an enormous amount of nonpersonal items that are worth more. We've seen certain concert posters sell for $20,000, $50,000, even $100,000," van Gool said.

3. Weigh quantity and rarity. "You always want to collect those types of items that there are the fewest of — promotional items or items that are local, for instance," van Gool said. "Anything that is made in smaller quantities or made for promotional purposes or a local purpose, like a concert, eventually will be more collectible."

4. Take advantage of opportunities geared toward collectors. "Record Store Day is once a year, and I really think that it pays off to go to your local record store and buy the releases that will be unique for Record Store Day only," van Gool said. "The vinyl that is going to be offered is typically limited to 1,000 or 3,000 or 5,000 copies, and those limited editions will always become more valuable as time goes by."

Today, some bands release limited-edition vinyl LPs or singles in addition to CDs and MP3s. Van Gool recommends music lovers buy one format to enjoy (be it CD, vinyl or MP3) and buy a copy of the vinyl record to keep — still sealed, of course — in your collection.

"Because there are fewer records pressed, if you keep yours sealed, 20, 30 years from now, there's a good chance that you'll be happy you did that," he said.

5. Refine the focus of your collection. The hottest acts tend to have the most collectors and, by extension, the most items you can collect, van Gool said. If you try to collect everything that is available, you'll need a lot of time to chase pieces down and a lot of money to acquire them.

"Figure out what really excites you as a collector," van Gool said. "If you do that, you make the hobby a lot more fun for yourself. You set some parameters so you protect yourself from spending an enormous amount of money."

6. Think before you toss. Good-condition, once-common items that date back before World War II — like advertising posters, Coca-Cola bottles, 78 RPM records and hand tools — today are cherished by collectors.

"Nothing saddens me more than people going through their basements, garages, storage facilities, attics, etc., with big plastic bags and just putting it out for the trash," van Gool said. "Eventually, true historic treasures are just being thrown away. Why keep that concert poster? Well, you can pitch it, but that might be the only piece of evidence for that particular venue, and now it's gone."

SUSAN SLIWICKI'S *favorite childhood memories are of hours spent hanging out with her oldest brother, who let her listen to his collection of albums, including Pink Floyd's "Dark Side of the Moon" and Deep Purple's "Machine Head," in exchange for her silence as long as the record was still spinning on the turntable. A journalist by trade, Sliwicki brought her two greatest passions — words and music — together when she joined Goldmine magazine in 2007 and became its editor in 2011.*

Rare promotional T-shirt for Slayer's 1988 "South of Heaven" promotional T-shirt, known as "Mandatory Suicide" T-shirt, it was banned due to its suggestive graphics. Size large, 19" armpit to armpit, 25" top to bottom. **$545**

Rare Ozzy Osbourne L.A. Sports Arena concert T-shirt and press release signed by Osbourne and guitarist Randy Rhoads. One-page press release regarding 1981's "Diary Of A Madman" album was signed by Osbourne and Rhoads at an after party following a New Year's Eve concert performance at the L.A. Sports Arena. Size small T-shirt from same show. **$3,376**

Signed Aerosmith concert set list from Dec. 31, 1998 concert at Fleet Center in Boston, signed by all five original band members: Steven Tyler, Joe Perry, Joey Kramer, Tom Hamilton and Brad Whitford. **$325**

Sex Pistols black and white glossy photograph signed in blue felt-tip pen by punk rock legends Johnny Rotten, Steve Jones, Glen Matlock and Paul Cook, 14" x 11". **$596**

"We Are the World" sheet music signed in black felt-tip pen by song co-authors Michael Jackson and Lionel Richie, inscribed with "We Are the World" by Richie above his signature. Three pages, each 8 1/2" x 11". **$10,630**

Custom-made leather outfit owned and worn by Keith Moon, drummer of The Who, with certificate of authenticity. **$12,543**

Mick Jagger's stage-worn jacket used during The Rolling Stones' 1994-95 "Voodoo Lounge" tour. **$7,594**

Elvis Presley's personal sheet music for songs from the album "From Elvis Presley Boulevard, Memphis, Tennessee." Released in May 1976, this album was recorded at a studio set up in Elvis' Graceland home. Following overdub sessions in March 1976, producer Felton Jarvis gave Elvis seven charts (six different songs; two included for "Solitaire"). **$937**

Original front cover album art by Robert Crumb for "The Cheap Suit Serenaders Party Record" (Red Goose, 1978). Crumb, a collector of 78 RPM records and an artist of the Underground Comix movement, created this illustration for one of his 10-inch records. Ink and gouache on bristol board., image area 10" x 10", matted to 12-3/4" x 13". **$11,950**

Mick Jagger's owned and stage-worn, custom-made military jacket from The Rolling Stones' "Steel Wheels" tour. Western Costume Co. tag sewn inside. **$11,402**

James Brown's stage-worn bow tie, accompanied by copy of a letter from curator James Camisar. **$446**

Elvis Presley's custom-made, 14-karat white gold and diamond Longines wristwatch, a gift from his manager, Col. Tom Parker. Features 14 full-cut diamonds along sides of case, plus seven more set in ornate letter "P" on clasp. Initials EAP engraved on back of watch. **$16,250**

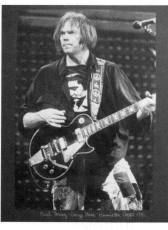

Neil Young's stage-used guitar strap from his 1991 tour with Crazy Horse, accompanied by black and white photograph showing Young wearing the guitar strap at a 1991 show at Hamilton, Ontario, Canada. **$10,630**

Grateful Dead-signed original cover artwork for the band's "House of Cards" album. Signatures include: Jerry Garcia, Bob Weir, Phil Lesh, Mickey Hart, Bill Kreutzmann and Vince Welnick. **$4,000**

Bruce Springsteen's stage-worn black vest used during a performance on his "Darkness on the Edge of Town" tour, accompanied by a letter from consignor, who worked with Springsteen for more than 10 years, and photograph of Springsteen wearing vest on stage. **$5,191**

Queen lead singer Freddie Mercury's black-and-white harlequin stage costume inspired by costumes from the ballet "Carnaval." Mercury wore this and similar costumes onstage in the 1970s; this particular costume was featured in the 2011 "Queen Forever" exhibit in Japan. **$35,271**

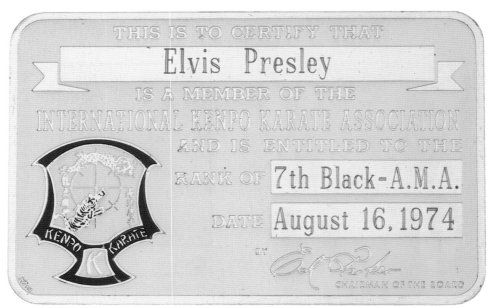

Elvis Presley's International Kenpo Karate Association membership card, dated Aug. 16, 1974, made of gold-colored metal, 2 1/4" x 3 1/2". **$4,375**

Ted Nugent's stage-worn, Indian-style boots, worn on countless stages, album covers and posters evidenced by hundreds of photos from the late 1970s to 1980s. Includes original certificate of authenticity signed by Nugent from his personal auction in 2005; signed original black and white photo; and signed board-mounted poster of Nugent wearing the boots. **$3,080**

Custom-made costume for dance sequence scene in Elvis Presley's movie "Jailhouse Rock." Jacket features 6240, the number Elvis' costume bore. MGM labels inside jacket collar and pants waist, MGM stamps on inside of back of jacket and pants. With photo of Presley from "Jailhouse Rock" dance sequence and letter of provenance from Bill Tuttle, head of makeup department at MGM who did all of Elvis' makeup for "Jailhouse Rock." **$32,211**

Ballet shoes worn by Queen lead singer Freddie Mercury during the band's performance at a free concert in Hyde Park, London, that drew more than 150,000 spectators on Sept. 18, 1976. **$6,270**

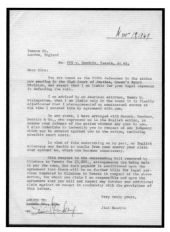

Jimi Hendrix-signed document regarding PPX v. Hendrex, Yameta, et al. Early in his career, Hendrix had signed contracts both with PPX and Yameta, and the two signings resulted in a lawsuit. Signed by Hendrix in black ink in the lower left-hand corner of the page, dated Nov. 19, 1969. **$15,700**

David Lee Roth's concert-worn T-shirt from Van Halen's Sept. 10, 1982, show at the L.A. Forum in Inglewood, California. Roth frequently wore official Van Halen tour merchandise during the group's concerts. **$903**

Psychedelic-themed poster featuring artwork by Frank Carson to promote Cat Stevens' "Tea For the Tillerman" album, 1971. Rolled, unrestored poster, 12 1/2" x 39 1/2". **$203**

Junior Walker and The All Stars original boxing-style poster for shows held July 1-4 at Penthouse Nightclub in Washington, D.C. Cardboard, 22" x 28". **$541**

Six guitar picks for James Hetfield (rhythm guitarist) and Kirk Hammett (lead guitarist) of the band Metallica. **$82**

RIAA Platinum Record Award for Van Halen's self-titled debut album, presented to Warner Bros. Records in recognition of one million albums sold. Sales of "Van Halen" eventually surpassed 10 million units in the U.S. alone, making it one of the most successful debuts in history. 17" x 21". **$1,195**

Collection of vintage Foreigner promotional necklaces for band's 1978 "Double Vision" LP. **$84**

Pink Floyd promotional display and assorted swag from the 1970s-2000. Includes "Us And Them" promotional card; pig mobile; Pink Floyd banner display; matching set of two promotional flats from 1979; die-cut banner display and cassette counter display for 1983's "The Final Cut"; head band from 1988 World Tour; five-piece "Shine On" mobile display from 1992; two-sided promotional flat for "Beyond the Dark Side of the Moon" from 2000; and floor display, counter display and sticker from the 20th anniversary of The Wall in 2000. **$373**

Monkees vintage dolls, lunchbox and thermos (1967), complete set of all four 5-inch dolls by Hasbro, plus Monkees-themed vinyl lunchbox with original thermos bottle. **$375**

1964 Topps Beatles "A Hard Day's Night" high-grade collection, including six cards (Nos. 11, 14, 17, 19, 31 and 46) graded PSA Mint 9 and five cards (Nos. 27, 39, 43, 46 and 51) graded PSA Near Mint-Mint 8. **$1,434**

Paul McCartney designed, painted and signed surfboard created for Surfers Against Sewage. **$19,489**

The Whisky

Neon marquee from famed Whisky A Go Go club used in 1980s and 1990s when it was commonly known as The Whisky. Located on Los Angeles' Sunset Strip, the club launched careers of The Doors, Frank Zappa, Buffalo Springfield, Van Halen and Guns N' Roses. Replaced in 2004 with new marquee that returned "A Go Go" to the club's moniker. With certificate of authenticity. 13' long x 3 1/2' tall x 10" wide. **$34,529**

Beatles harmonica with original box, mounted on original packaging card, manufactured by Hohner in 1964, card opens to reveal songbook featuring two Beatles tunes. Packaging blister separated from card at top left corner. Harmonica is 5". **$1,500**

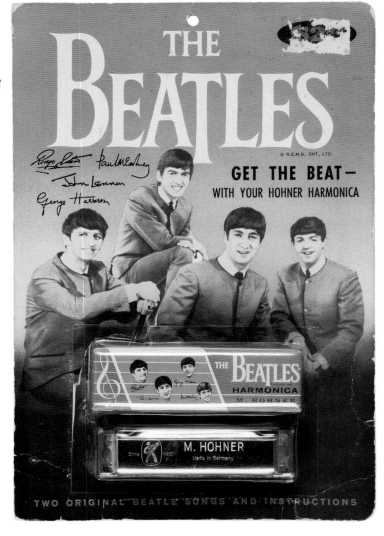

Unused Maple Leaf Gardens full ticket for The Beatles' 4 p.m. concert on Aug. 17, 1965. The band played two shows at this venue that day. Accompanied by original envelope. **$1,135**

Led Zeppelin promotional blow-up blimp with Atlantic Records logo. **$300**

Alice Cooper poster with original production artwork for Aug. 21, 1971, show at The Park in Baltimore, created and signed by artist Gary Grimshaw, poster features mixed media on board with separate celluloid overlay, both pieces framed to 21" x 26". **$656**

Original program for 1968 Newport Pop Festival featuring acts including Jefferson Airplane, The Byrds, The Grateful Dead, and Blue Cheer, 8 1/2" x 11". **$200**

Musical Instruments

Musical instruments—devices designed to make musical sounds—fall into four basic categories: string, wind, brass, and percussion. Their visual beauty, history, technology, acoustic ability, and investment potential appeal to many people.

Collectors of musical instruments may focus on an individual instrument or family of instruments, on instruments from a particular geographic region, or on a specific manufacturer.

Antique instruments that pre-date the 20th century can be valuable because of their craftsmanship and historical significance. The violin, also called the fiddle, is one of the most popular antique instruments. It is the smallest, highest-pitched member of the violin family, which includes the viola, cello and double bass. Antique violins are often viewed as investments because of their likelihood to increase in value.

Instruments owned or played by famous musicians, such as Johnny Cash, Elvis Presley, and Jimi Hendrix, or played at well-known concerts such as Woodstock, are also highly desirable. In this segment of the hobby the most popular instrument is the guitar, which has ancient roots and is used in a wide variety of musical styles. It typically has six strings, but four-, seven-, eight-, 10-, 11-, 12-, 13- and 18-string guitars also exist. The size and shape of the neck and the base also vary. There are two main types of guitars: electric and acoustic.

For more information on other music-related collectibles, please see the "Music Memorabilia" and "Records" sections.

Backstage Auctions

Scott Ian-used and signed 2005 Washburn Ian Pro SI75 guitar with "Matrix" movie-themed finish, mahogany body, ebony fretboard and Scott Ian "Anthagram" inlays. Ian, guitarist for the band Anthrax and fan of "The Matrix" movie series, had two guitars custom built that featured this hologram finish. One remains in his collection; this one was used on several tours in the mid-2000s. Ian signed top in silver marker; included leather strap and Anthrax set list. **$3,500**

Backstage Auctions

KISS tour-used, grill-covered Marshall speaker cabinet, used during its 1977-1978 Love Gun/Alive II tours; stage setup included illuminated stairs and fire-breathing dragons. **$5,094**

Heritage Auctions, Inc.

All-original, complete 1950s-era Gibson Electraharp pedal steel guitar, clean, very good condition, working order, includes original hard case. **$687**

Bonhams

Roger Waters' Fender Precision bass guitar, Sunburst-finish body, serial no. 274352, "F" series neckplate with serial, two-piece pickup, bolt-on maple neck and rosewood fingerboard with dot markers, includes plush-lined, hard Fender case and copy of program for Pink Floyd's "Dark Side of the Moon" 1974 U.K. tour. **$17,636**

Heritage Auctions, Inc.

1956 Gibson CF-100 Sunburst acoustic guitar, serial no. V-6305, all-original finish, heavily weather checked, pick guard shrinkage crack under E-string, two visible top cracks at bass lower bout area, original, full-thickness bridge needs to be reglued, original tuners, light wear to original frets, straight neck, soft case included. **$3,500**

Heritage Auctions, Inc.

Circa 1923 Gibson A-2 walnut mandolin, serial No. 72751, moderate play wear, back binding loose toward neck on both sides, neck heel appears to have been reglued at some point, back of neck and area of sides where neck joins have been refinished, frets show light wear, hard case included. **$1,434**

Heritage Auctions, Inc.

1949 Bigsby bird's-eye maple, solid-body electric guitar with original hard case; based on serial number (No. 51649), this guitar was likely completed May 16, 1949. One of the rarest, early guitars of Bigsby, it influenced most of the solid-body electric models that would follow. According to the Bigsby company, this is one of only six standard guitars still in existence. Only example seen of bridge posts mounted directly into top, like Gibson eventually did on Les Paul guitars starting with 1954 Les Paul Custom. **$266,500**

Heritage Auctions, Inc.

Circa late 1970s Ibanez walnut double-neck, solid-body electric guitar with hard case, moderate play wear, 12-string pickups appear to be replaced and have output, six-string does not, electronics function intermittently. **$897**

Heritage Auctions, Inc.

Johnny Cash's personally owned and stage-played acoustic guitar, custom built by Danny Ferrington; original handwritten label inside guitar indicates this guitar (No. 9) was built June 30, 1978, in Nashville, Tennessee. Cash used this black-finish guitar on his 1978 TV Christmas special, on his next spring TV special and on various recordings including his 25th anniversary album. Dreadnought-style instrument with bound body, neck (with mother-of-pearl inlays), and peghead (with Schaller tuners). Abalone purfling on top and soundhole. Includes narrow leather strap, capo, and worn, vintage case. **$30,000**

Heritage Auctions, Inc.

Elvis Presley-owned and used 1973 Giannini Craviola acoustic guitar with original case, serial number AWKN 6. Elvis gave this guitar to Gary Pepper, Tankers Fan Club president, in the mid-1970s after giving Pepper several lessons on it. Includes certificate of authenticity from Joe Esposito. **$18,125**

Heritage Auctions, Inc.

1935 Martin D-18 natural acoustic guitar, serial No. 59325, top shows signs of light overspray, back and sides oversprayed and buffed, crack-free, inside is clean with exception of deep gouging in No. 1 and 2 back braces, original bridge and bridge plate in good condition, frets not original but properly installed, soft case included. **$17,500**

Heritage Auctions, Inc.

1960 Gibson Les Paul Standard Sunburst, left-handed, solid-body electric guitar, original hard case, serial no. 0 1475, professionally repaired headstock break, otherwise all-original, one odd route in bridge position because of left-handed construction, moderate weather checking and fret wear, frets may have been dressed. Guitar consigned by The United States Marshals Service, profits to benefit victims of Aspen Energy Oil and Gas Investment Scheme. **$134,500**

Skinner Auctioneers & Appraisers

1923 Gibson mandolin, Gibson Mandolin-Guitar Company, Kalamazoo, with original rectangular case, labeled "THE GIBSON MASTER MODEL. STYLE F5 NUMBER 73673. APPROVED JUNE 13, 1923," signed LLOYD LOAR; slight running of ink on signature. All original parts, missing mounting screws for pick guard. **$120,000**

Heritage Auctions, Inc.

1959 Gibson Les Paul Standard Sunburst left-handed, solid-body electric guitar with original hard case, serial no. 9 0136, neck pickup ring appears to be a later replacement, jackplate replaced, original broken piece in case, electronics original but cover removed from bridge pickup, finish checking around tuners and on back of headstock, tuners replaced with older Kluson single wind tuners with no writing on back, finish is original, neck refretted. Consigned by The United States Marshals Service, profits to benefit victims of Aspen Energy Oil and Gas Investment Scheme. **$194,500**

Skinner Auctioneers & Appraisers

1914 Italian violin, Romeo Antoniazzi, Cremona, maker's label, surface scratches and abrasions to top varnish, repaired treble side saddle fracture, fracture under chinrest and top fracture on treble side of neck joint, varnish wear to soldier contact area of back, upper treble rib, includes certificate from William Moennig & Son, Inc., Philadelphia, June 21, 1976, with case, length of back 355 mm. **$63,600**

Skinner Auctioneers & Appraisers

Viennese violoncello, Johann Christoph Leidolff, Vienna, circa 1750, maker's label and repair label ANTON FISCHER, REPARAVIT 1840, repaired hairline saddle fractures, wing cracks, fractures at neck joint of top and fractures from lower edge, repair to upper button of back, repaired hairline crack upper edge of bass side, neck recently reset, with case. **$26,400**

Skinner Auctioneers & Appraisers

American flute, Harry Bettoney, Boston, circa 1905, head and foot joints stamped H BETTONEY, BOSTON, EDH WURLITZER, body stamped H BETTONEY, BOSTON MASS, 725, Grenadilla body, nickel silver keys, with case. **$270**

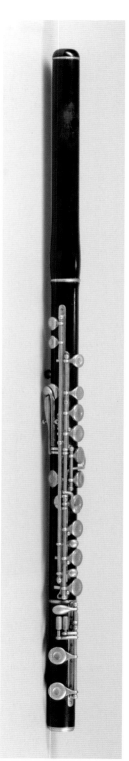

Skinner Auctioneers & Appraisers

German violin, circa 1830, labeled JOANES BAPTISTA FILIUS LORENTUS, button repair, maple crown on button, various repaired top fractures, soundpost fracture, wear to top edges, varnish loss, with case and three bows. **$5,100**

North American Indian Artifacts

BY RUSSELL E. LEWIS

This section covers collectible items commonly referred to as American Indian artifacts. Our interest in Native American material cultural artifacts has been long-lived, as was the Indian's interest in many of our material cultural items from an early period.

During recent years, it has become commonplace to have major sales of these artifacts by at least four major auction houses, in addition to the private trading, local auctions, and Internet sales of these items.

Anthropologists have written millions of words on American Indian cultures and societies and have standardized various regions of the country when discussing these cultures. Those standard regional definitions are continued here.

We have been fascinated with the material culture of Native Americans from the beginning of our contact with their societies. The majority of these valuable items are in repositories of museums, universities, and colleges, but many items that were traded to private citizens are now being sold to collectors of Native American material culture.

Native American artifacts are now acquired by collectors in the same fashion as any material cultural item. Individuals interested in antiques and collectibles find items at farm auction sales (an especially good place for farm family collections to be dispersed), yard sales, estate sales, specialized auctions, and from private collectors trading or selling items.

Native American artifacts are much more difficult to locate for a variety of reasons including the following: scarcity of items; legal protection of items being traded; more vigorous collecting of artifacts by numerous international, national, state, regional, and local museums and historical societies; frailties of the items themselves, as most were made of organic materials; and a more limited distribution network through legitimate secondary sales.

However, it is still possible to find some types of Native American items through the traditional sources of online auctions, auction houses in local communities, antique stores and malls, flea markets, trading meetings, estate sales, and similar venues. The most likely items to find in the above ways would be items made of stone, chert, flint, obsidian, and copper. Most organic materials will not have survived the rigors of a marketplace unless they were recently released from some estate or collection and their value was unknown to the previous owner.

For more information on Native American collectibles, see *Warman's North American Indian Artifacts Identification and Price Guide* by Russell E. Lewis.

RUSSELL E. LEWIS *is a university professor, anthropologist, collector and author of several books, including* Warman's North American Indian Artifacts Identification and Price Guide.

Coeur d'Alene Art Auction

Chief Joseph's war shirt, circa 1877. Joseph was the name given by a missionary in the 1830s to Tuekakas (1840-1904), chief of a Nez Perce band living in the Wallowa Valley of northeastern Oregon. **$865,000**

Coeur d'Alene Art Auction

Chief Black Bird, an Ogalalla Sioux, bronze statue (No. 1 casting) by Adolph Weinman (1870-1952), inscribed in base: "A.A. Weinman | No. 1 | Roman Bronze Works N-Y-," 18 1/4" high. **$304,200**

Oil portrait of Sioux Chief Sitting Bull, painted by H. H. Cross in 1882 and signed by Sitting Bull, 14 1/2" x 18 1/2", 18" x 22" framed. Cross was one of the best-known Western painters of the day and is believed to have produced some 1,000 works, half of which were Western subject matter. **$83,650**

Crow painted parfleche envelope, 26" x 13". **$948**

Plains beaded hide knife sheath, circa late 19th century, 10". **$674**

Sotheby's

Wood and metal pipe tomahawk composed of light ash-wood haft of tapering cylindrical section, surmounted by steel spontoon-style head, tooled with bat-wing cutout, stamped on one side: "Owned by Red Cloud, A Sioux Cheaf [sic] 1876," 25 1/2" long. **$50,000**

Heritage Auctions, Inc.

Pipe tomahawk by J. Wilson, circa 1850, hand-forged iron blade decorated on one side with brass inlaid foliate motif and cold stamped five-point stars at corners, opposing side rocker engraved with similar foliate design and same cold stamped stars, blade fitted to ash-wood handle with carved scallop pattern near top, hot file branding overall, deep brown patina, 23" overall length, blade 8 1/2" long. **$8,962**

Heritage Auctions, Inc.

Three Native American rugs, 1960s, all made of wool; first in black, brown, and tan, woven with square-shaped patterns and lines resembling a "W"; second in brown, beige, and red, woven with diamond-shaped patterns; third in brown, tan, and beige, woven with zigzag-shaped patterns; together with an Alpaca wool blanket made in Peru, in beige, brown, gray, and white, featuring an image of two lamas in center, never used as original tag is still attached. **$8,962**

Heritage Auctions, Inc.

Cheyenne pictographic dance shield depicting warriors on horseback, circa 1890, thin rawhide base and native tanned hide cover painted with two mounted warriors, each wearing eagle feather bonnets with trailers, set against a yellow background; below central black horizon band is image of buffalo painted in black against blue-green background; red and navy blue wool cloth banner is tied to rim in classic Plains fashion; 16" diameter. **$8,365**

Heritage Auctions, Inc.

Native American adaptation of mid-19th century percussion rifle, barrel cut down, presumably to make weapon easier to use on horseback, original rawhide wraps, old bone inlay, 29" long. **$3,585**

Heritage Auctions, Inc.

Portrait of Native American, circa 1850, tintype, unidentified Prairie Indian posed wearing military coat, silver peace medal, and holding pipe stem, photographer unknown; 2 1/2" x 2 1/4". **$2,125**

Skinner, Inc.

Two Acoma polychrome pottery jars, smaller jar circa 1910, larger jar circa 1930s, larger jar approximately 9" high and 6" wide; smaller jar approximately 8" high and 4 1/8" wide. **$1,580**

"Young Buck of the Tesuque Pueblo," oil on canvas painted in 1916 by Robert Henri, 1865-1929, signed Robert Henri and inscribed, *"To my Friend Capt. Dan Stevens, l.l.";* also inscribed *"Robert Henri and Young Buck of the Tesuque Pueblo"* on the reverse, 24" x 20". **$842,500**

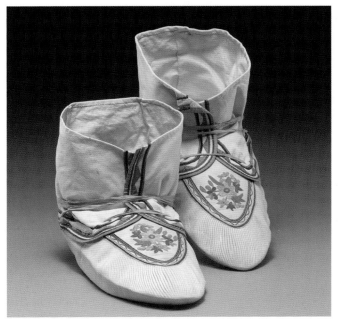

Pair of Cree or Metis embroidered hide moccasins composed of tanned hide, silk and cotton thread, 10" long. **$13,750**

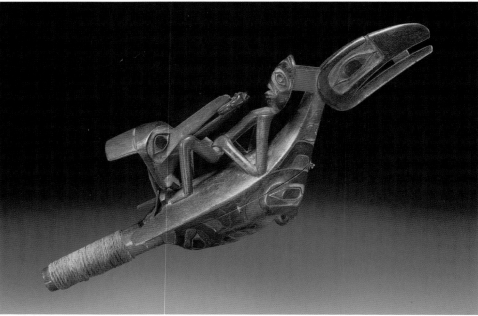

Sotheby's

Northwest Coast polychrome wood ceremonial rattle, probably Tlingit, classic form in two sections with twine on cylindrical grip, birdlike face with hooked beak and form line details on underbelly, body in form of flying raven holding disk, probably a representation of the sun, in beak, flattened backswept wings supporting reclining shaman with angular body and limbs, hands resting on abdomen, mask-like face, confronting another bird with short backswept feather crest holding a frog in its beak, 12 7/8" long. **$116,500**

Sotheby's

Early Cheyenne beaded hide tobacco bag, finely tanned hide, sinew sewn on each side in blue and white pony beads with pattern of alternating stripes, centermost enclosing box designs, similar beaded decoration on long sides, trimmed with tin cone pendants along lower edge, 15 1/2". **$36,000**

Skinner Inc.

Two Plains beaded items, commercial clasp bag and pouch with loom beaded American flag design, flag pouch 6 1/2" x 4 1/2" (excluding fringe); clasp bag is sinew sewn; flag bag is thread sewn. **$415**

Skinner, Inc.

Apache pictorial basketry olla, circa early 20th century, flared rim and decorated with meandering vertical devices framing row of human figures and two rows of animals, 13 1/2" high. **$1,126**

Skinner Inc.

Lakota beaded and quilled pipe bag, large, 39" long, including fringe. **$711**

Sotheby's

Skinner Inc.

History of the Indian Tribes of North America by Thomas L. McKenney and James Hall, Philadelphia: D. Rice & A. N. Hart, 1855 (Vol. 1); Rice, Rutter & Co., 1870 (Vols. 2-3), three volumes, 8vo (10 1/4" x 6 1/2"); 119 (of 120) fine hand-colored lithographs heightened with gum Arabic. Publisher's brown morocco block-stamped with arabesque panel, spines in six compartments lettered gilt, marbled endpapers, gilt edges. **$7,500**

Heavy Navajo silver and turquoise bracelet with three irregularly cut stones, 4". **$563**

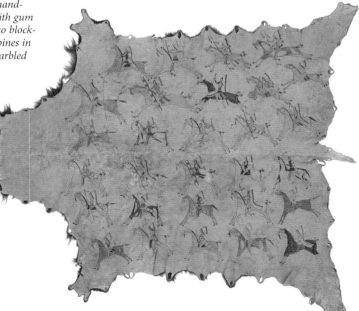

Sothby's

Sioux painted pictorial buffalo hide with series of equestrian figures in various postures, some wearing feather or split-horn bonnets or carrying shields, feathered lances, rifles, or coup sticks, inscribed with Heye Foundation number 14/5680, and 9311; 105 3/4" long. **$110,500**

Perfume Bottles

BY KYLE HUSFLOEN

Although the human sense of smell isn't nearly as acute as that of many other mammals, we have long been affected by the odors in the world around us. Science has shown that scents or smells can directly affect our mood or behavior.

No one knows for certain when humans first rubbed themselves with some plant or herb to improve their appeal to other humans, usually of the opposite sex. However, it is clear that the use of unguents and scented materials was widely practiced as far back as Ancient Egypt.

Some of the first objects made of glass, in fact, were small cast vials used for storing such mixtures. By the age of the Roman Empire, scented waters and other mixtures were even more important and were widely available in small glass flasks or bottles. Since that time glass has been the material of choice for storing scented concoctions, and during the past 200 years some of the most exquisite glass objects produced were designed for that purpose.

Kyle Husfloen

It wasn't until around the middle of the 19th century that specialized bottles and vials were produced to hold commercially manufactured scents. Some aromatic mixtures were worn on special occasions, while many others were splashed on to help mask body odor. For centuries it had been common practice for "sophisticated" people to carry on their person a scented pouch or similar accoutrement, since daily bathing was unheard of and laundering methods were primitive.

Commercially produced and brand name perfumes and colognes have really only been common since the late 19th and early 20th centuries. The French started the ball rolling during the first half of the 19th century when D'Orsay and Guerlain began producing special scents. The first American entrepreneur to step into this field was Richard Hudnut, whose firm was established in 1880. During the second half of the 19th century most scents carried simple labels and were sold in simple, fairly generic glass bottles. Only in the early 20th century did parfumeurs introduce specially designed labels and bottles to hold their most popular perfumes. Coty, founded in 1904, was one of the first to do this, and they turned to Rene Lalique for a special bottle design around 1908. Other French firms, such as Bourjois (1903), Caron (1903), and D'Orsay (1904) were soon following this trend.

People collect two kinds of perfume bottles—decorative and commercial. Decorative bottles include any bottles sold empty and meant to be filled with your choice of scent. Commercial bottles are any that were sold filled with scent and usually have the label of the perfume company.

The rules of value for perfume bottles are the same as for any other kind of glass—rarity, condition, age, and quality of glass.

The record price for perfume bottle at auction is something over $200,000, and those little sample bottles of scent that we used to get for free at perfume counters in the 1960s can now bring as much as $300 or $400.

For more information on perfume bottles, see *Antique Trader Perfume Bottles Price Guide* by Kyle Husfloen.

KYLE HUSFLOEN, *Southern California representative for Kaminski Auctions, is a well-respected expert on antiques and collectibles. He was an editor with Antique Trader publications for more than 30 years.*

Scent bottle with cap, cameo glass, bulbous creamy white ground overlaid in orange, cameo-carved with large flowers and leafy vines, silver band on small neck with hinged cap opening to original glass stopper, raised on silver foot band, silver marked "C and M" and rearing lion and "G" in shield, signed in cameo on side, Gallé, French, 5 1/2" high. **$1,438**

Scent holder, Bessamin box or spice tower, silver, domed foot and slender stem support bulbous tower-form container set with colored stones below pierced neck, conical cover, middle European, 19th century, 6" high. **$1,200-$1,500**

Perfume bottle and stopper, wide low pyramidal black glass bottle with block-molded panels decorated with gilt metal filigree bands trimmed with large green triangular stone and faux pearls with small jewel-set bands around the base and neck, tall flat clear rectangular stopper with beveled corners etched with a scene of Leda and the swan, signed, Czechoslovakian, circa 1930s, 6 1/4" high. **$800-$900**

Scent bottle and stopper, cameo glass, wide ovoid amethyst body with small cylindrical neck, cameo-carved with floral blossoms and leaves trimmed in gold, frosted clear ball stopper, signed on bottom by Daum Nancy, French, late 19th/early 20th century, 6" high. **$1,035**

Skinner, Inc.

Wedgwood solid blue Jasper perfume bottle, England, late 18th/early 19th century, octagonal shape with applied white classical figures within foliate frames, silver rim and cover, one side heavy with hairlines, 2 3/4". **$533**

Scent bottle with cap, cameo glass, cylindrical form in white cut to blue with flower and leaf design, silver cap and base band, English, late 19th century, 2 3/4" high. **$690**

Heritage Auctions, Inc.

Two perfume bottles with silver tops by Thomas Webb and Sons, circa 1890, larger with roundel, both with English silver hallmarks, no interior stoppers, taller one 6". **$5,078**

Heritage Auctions, Inc.

Rare R. Lalique perfume bottle for "Raquel Meller" fragrance by Roditi & Sons, enameled on each face in orange and black, circa 1925, molded signature, 2 7/8".
$20,315

Heritage Auctions, Inc.

R. Lalique Le Baiser Du Faune perfume bottle for Molinard, original presentation box, circa 1928, molded: R. Lalique, Molinard, France; bottle remains over three-quarters full of perfume, 7 1/2" high.
$15,535

International Perfume Bottle Association

Baccarat-designed perfume bottle for Patanwalla, containing the perfume Bhagwan, figural bottle of Indian male deity with enameled detail and housed in original luxury box. This bottle had only been known to exist through the drawings in the Baccarat archives before it sold at the International Perfume Bottle Association's 24th annual convention in May 2012. **$63,600**

Heritage Auctions, Inc.

Gallé cameo glass perfume bottle and stopper, cameo overlay bleeding heart decoration, Nancy, France, circa 1900, Gallé (cameo) mark, 4 1/2" high. **$2,250**

Heritage Auctions, Inc.

Two Lubin perfume bottles with salamander decoration, circa 1925, both molded LUBIN to base, smaller with fragrance name "Au Soleil" in gilt, both with original stoppers, taller one 8 1/2". **$2,270**

Heritage Auctions, Inc.

American spherical green glass perfume bottle and stopper with silver overlay etched and engraved in lily design, attributed to Alvin Corp., Providence, Rhode Island, circa 1900, STERLING mark, 6" high. **$468**

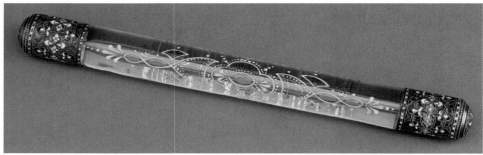

Heritage Auctions, Inc.

Viennese silver gilt cloisonné enamel and glass perfume bottle, maker unknown, Vienna, Austria, circa 1900, Arabic script decoration, cloisonné enamel and silver caps to top and bottom, marks: 3 dogs head A), A, Ottoman import marks, 8 1/4" long. **$1,875**

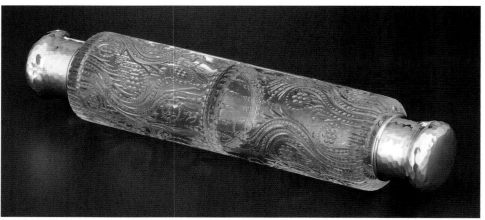

Heritage Auctions, Inc.

American glass and silver double perfume bottle, divided cut glass with design of dotted scrolls, silver cap to either end with hand hammered finish, Tiffany & Company, New York, New York, circa 1883, marks: TIFFANY & CO., STERLING, M, 7510, 3 (4 to opposite cap), 8074, 8 1/2" long. **$776**

Scent bottles and stoppers, cut glass, spherical clear bodies cut with band of strawberry diamond and hobstars above panel-cut bottom and shoulder with flaring neck, fitted with pointed sterling-capped stopper, silver marked by Tiffany and Company, American, circa 1900, 5 1/4" high. **$1,150**

Skinner, Inc.

Reticulated sterling and colorless glass four-part perfume bottle set, early 20th century, William W. Hayden Company makers, round frame pierced with entwined heart design, fitted with four three-sided colorless glass bottles with scroll-engraved sterling spherical lids, 4 3/4" high. **$385**

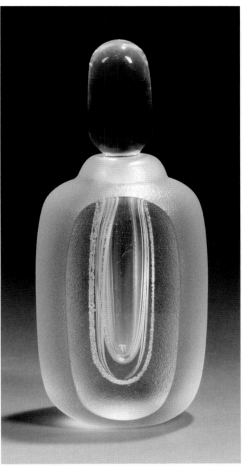

Skinner, Inc.

Göran Wärff for Kosta perfume bottle, art glass, Sweden, ovoid body in frosted glass with one faceted side exposing narrow hollowed interior, clear glass stopper, incised on base "Kosta Ateljé G. Wärff 82-821," 7 3/4" high. **$148**

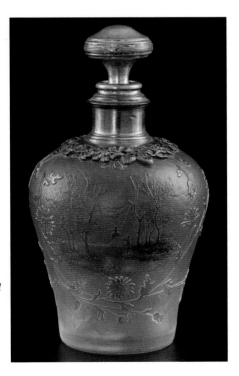

Heritage Auctions, Inc.

Daum Freres perfume bottle and stopper with silver gilt mounts and scene featuring two children and swing, circa 1890, stopper possibly not original, marks: painted signature in gilt, 6 1/2". **$1,434**

Sotheby's

Edwardian silver-mounted Nephrite perfume bottle, Frank Hyams, Ltd., London, 1905, applied with naturalistic salamanders, bee, snakes, and foliate sprays, topped by a frog, marked on body and cover, 5 1/2" high. **$5,625**

Heritage Auctions, Inc.

Gallé green glass perfume bottle and stopper with violet cameo overlay in water lily motif, circa 1900, Gallé (cameo) mark, original stopper, 4 1/2" high. **$2,629**

Scent bottle with caps, double-ended style, short oblong facet-cut cobalt blue bottle with gadrooned silver caps at each end, unmarked, probably English, circa 1880s, 3 1/2" long. **$250-$300**

Heritage Auctions, Inc.

Czech Art Deco perfume bottle, base molded with figures, arrowhead stopper (married), circa 1930, 6 1/4". **$1,015**

Heritage Auctions, Inc.

Retro diamond and gold perfume bottle by designer John Rubel, features single-cut diamonds weighing approximately 0.90 carat, set in hand-engraved 14k gold, stopper twists off revealing gold wand, marked John Rubel & Co., 2 1/8" x 1". **$1,792**

Heritage Auctions, Inc.

Thomas Webb and Sons ivory glass perfume bottle with gilt metal mounts and screw cap, original sepia patina, circa 1885, etched mark on base, no interior stopper, 3 1/2". **$507**

Heritage Auctions, Inc.

Daum Freres perfume bottle with silver mount and cover, painted signature in gilt, silver with French poinçon, maker and retailer marks, original interior stopper, circa 1895, 7". **$7,170**

Heritage Auctions, Inc.

14k gold perfume bottle with sunburst pattern front and back connected by ribbed side, scalloped cup form finial to screw-in wand, maker unknown but probably American, circa 1900, 14K mark, 1 1/8" high. **$567**

Heritage Auctions, Inc.

R. Lalique clear glass De Vigny D'ou Vient-Il perfume bottle, circa 1922, molded: LALIQUE, 3 3/4" high. **$8,962**

Heritage Auctions, Inc.

Gallé yellow glass perfume bottle and stopper with orange cameo overlay in floral motif, original stopper, circa 1900, Gallé (cameo) marks, 6 1/2" high. **$1,314**

Petroliana

Petroliana covers a broad range of gas station collectibles from containers and globes to signs and pumps and everything in between.

The items featured in this section are organized by type and have been selected at the high end of the market. The focus is on the top price items, not to skew the values, but to emphasize the brands and types that are the most desirable. Some less valuable items have been included to help keep values in perspective.

As with all advertising items, factors such as brand name, intricacy of design, color, age, condition, and rarity drastically affect value.

Beware of reproduction and fantasy pieces. For collectors of vintage gas and oil items, the only way to avoid reproductions is experience: making mistakes and learning from them; talking with other collectors and dealers; finding reputable resources (including books and websites), and learning to invest wisely, buying the best examples one can afford.

Marks can be deceiving, paper labels and tags are often missing, and those that remain may be spurious. Adding to the confusion are "fantasy" pieces, globes that have no vintage counterpart, and that are often made more for visual impact than deception.

How does one know whether a given piece is authentic? Does it look old, and to what degree can

Standard's Supreme (with Ethyl) Gasoline globe, 15" lenses in a high-profile metal body. **$2,300+**

age be simulated? What is the difference between high-quality vintage advertising and modern mass-produced examples? Even experts are fooled when trying to assess qualities that have subtle distinctions.

There is another important factor to consider. A contemporary maker may create a "reproduction" sign or gas globe in tribute of the original, and sell it for what it is: a legitimate copy. Many of these are dated and signed by the artist or manufacturer, and these legitimate copies are highly collectible today. Such items are not intended to be frauds.

But a contemporary piece may pass through many hands between the time it leaves the maker and wind up in a collection. When profit is the only motive of a reseller, details about origin, ownership, and age can become a slippery slope of guesses, attribution, and—unfortunately—fabrication.

As the collector's eye sharpens, and the approach to inspecting and assessing petroliana improves, it will become easier to buy with confidence. And a knowledgeable collecting public should be the goal of all sellers, if for no other reason than the willingness to invest in quality.

For more information about petroliana, consult *Warman's Gas Station Collectibles Identification and Price Guide* by Mark Moran.

Photo acknowledgments to Aumann Auctions, Rich Gannon, George Simpson, and John Hudson.

Globes

Blue Crown one-piece, possibly original paint, 17" tall, metal collar. (The blue Crown is the rarest color, followed by gold and red.) **$800+**

Co-op Gasoline globe single lens in a narrow glass body. **$2,000+**

Conoco globe with Ethyl
logo, 13 1/2" lenses, green
plastic body. **$900+**

Calso's Supreme
Gasoline globe with
Ethyl logo, 15" single
lens in a high-profile
metal body. **$1,600+**

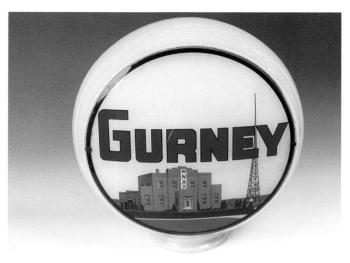

Gurney Seed globe 13 1/2" lenses, showing radio station, Yankton, S.D., in a wide white glass body. **$1,500+**

Koolmotor jewel-body globe, 15" lenses, 19 1/2" tall overall, circa 1930s. **$5,000+**

Mobiloil Gargoyle large oval globe, one-piece body, probably new old stock. **$2,900+**

Ride with Rose Regular Gasoline globe, 13 1/2" single lens in Capco body. **$2,750+**

Texaco leaded stained-glass metal body globe, slight fading, smaller size.
$4,500+

Sinclair Oils one-piece globe, etched, 15" tall.
$2,000+

Signs

Bulko Gasoline porcelain pump plate, small chip at right mounting hole, 11" x 12 1/2". **$3,500+**

Chevron Supreme Gasoline single-sided tin sign, minor paint loss on bottom edge, 24" diameter. **$2,600+**

Mobil-gloss single-sided tin die-cut sign, 48" x 24". **$1,400+**

(The) Crystal-Flash Line single-sided porcelain sign, edge chips, 47" x 99". **$2,250+**

Shell Premium Gasoline porcelain pump plate, dime-size chip around bottom hole, 12" x 12". **$1,700+**

Phillips 66

Go With the Gasoline that Won The West single-sided tin sign, some field wear, 16" x 15 1/2". **$325+**

Sinclair truck single-sided porcelain sign, 9" x 12". **$500+**

Standard Oil Products "cloud" double-sided porcelain sign, neon added, three chips in field, 30" x 60". **$2,600+**

Wil-Flo Motor Oil double-sided tin oval sign, 17" x 23", display side restored, reverse total loss. **$3,100+**

United Motors Service (with arrow, rare) double-sided porcelain sign, new old stock, 42" x 18". **$6,000+**

Union 76 single-sided porcelain die-cut truck door sign, minor edge chip, 7" x 7". **$2,900+**

Texaco (black T) "keyhole" single-sided porcelain truck sign. **$475+**

Malco porcelain pump plate, few light scratches, 12" diameter. **$1,300+**

Photography

BY ERIC BRADLEY

Modern photographic images date back to the 1820s with the development of chemical photography. The first permanent photograph was an image produced in 1826 by the French inventor Nicéphore Niépce. However, the picture took eight hours to expose, so he went about trying to find a new process. Working in conjunction with Louis Daguerre, they experimented with silver compounds based on a Johann Heinrich Schultz discovery in 1724 that a silver and chalk mixture darkens when exposed to light. Niépce died in 1833, but Daguerre continued the work, eventually culminating with the development of the daguerreotype in 1837.

Eric Bradley

Many advances in photographic glass plates and printing were made all through the 19th century. In 1884, American George Eastman developed the technology to replace photographic plates, leading to the technology used by film cameras today.

Eastman patented a photographic medium that used a photo-emulsion coated on paper rolls. The invention of roll film greatly sped up the process of recording multiple images.

American collectors are becoming more mature in their appreciation of fine (and even not so fine) photography for display and investment. Tens of thousands of photographs are sold at auction each year, and in 2012 one online auction seller recorded most lots of photographs sold for between $100 and $500. Many of the pieces in that price range include silver prints by American modernist Man Ray or Bert Stern's prints from Marilyn Monroe's "Last Sitting" or even a couple hundred vintage motion picture press photographs.

The top end of the market continues to be dominated by modernism's use of photography as an art form. Artists such as Alfred Stieglitz, Philippe Halsman and Edward Weston have seen works flirt with the six figure mark and surpass it.

Vernacular photography is quickly becoming one of the hottest collecting genres in its own right. In late 2011, a book filled with mug shots of early 20th century California prison inmates sold for $2,150 at a small Oregon auction company. The 40-page folio of 710 silver prints was once owned by the San Francisco Police Department, an early proponent in using photography in identifying criminals. Four months after it was sold and featured, the collection was offered at a February 2012, auction – this time through Swann Auction Galleries in New York with a $4,000-$6,000 estimate. It sold for $31,200 (including buyer's premium) to a collector, setting a record auction price for an album of vernacular photography.

ERIC BRADLEY is public relations associate at Heritage Auctions, the world's third largest auction house. He is former editor of Antique Trader magazine and is the author of Antique Trader 2013 Antiques and Collectibles Price Guide, America's no. 1-selling guide to the antiques and collectibles market. An award-winning investigative journalist with a degree in economics, Bradley has written hundreds of articles about antiques and collectibles and has made several media appearances as an expert on the antiques market at MoneyShow San Francisco, on MSN Money, Nasdaq.com and on AdvisorOne.com. His work has received press from The New York Times and The Philadelphia Inquirer.

Nest Egg Auctions

Alfred Cheney Johnston (American, 1885-1971), Katherine Moylan, Ziegfeld, circa 1920-1929, vintage gelatin silver, recto: artist's stamp, signed in pencil on mount, verso: titled in ink, 13 1/4" x 10". **$2,000**

Edward Weston, "Portrait of
a Woman," 1916, large format
gelatin silver print, signed
"Weston" and dated in ink
on recto, 15 7/8" x 11 7/8".
$110,000

Nest Egg Auctions

Philippe Halsman, "Refugee
Girl," Paris, 1938, gelatin silver
print, copyright credit stamp
on the verso, 11 3/4" x 9 3/8".
$9,500

Original Alfred Cheney Johnston (American, 1885-1971) photographs,
Dorothy Graves Ziegeld Girl, three photographs, identified en verso, each
approximately 10" x 13". **$1,900**

Alfred Stieglitz (American, 1864-1946), Studio
291, "291-Picasso-Braque Exhibition," 1915,
similar to National Gallery of Art Key Set: 393,
appearance consistent with platinum print,
hinged to mat, image 7 5/8" x 9 5/8". Research
indicates that the photograph, although titled
"Picasso-Braque Exhibition," represents a
temporary installation of two Picasso drawings
paired with an African reliquary mask and
a wasp's nest, staged to challenge viewers to
consider the relationship between emerging
modern art, "primitive art," and nature.
$170,000

*Edward Curtis hand-signed original silver gelatin print photograph, "Three Chiefs –
Piegan," taken in the summer of 1900, 11" x 14" (18" x 21" framed).* **$2,500**

Nest Egg Auctions

*Original Alfred
Cheney Johnston
(American,
1885-1971)
photograph,
Marie Stevens,
high gloss print,
identified en
verso, with
ACJ stamp,
approximately
10" x 13".* **$600**

A. Aubrey Bodine (American, 1906-1970), "Harbor at Night," circa 1940, color photograph, signed in ink in lower right margin: A. Aubrey Bodine, 12 3/4" x 17 1/2". Provenance: NYNEX Government Affairs, Washington, D.C. (label verso). **$937**

Chromogenic color print of Marilyn Monroe by Bert Stern, hand-signed and numbered, Stern signature in ink, from Stern's famous 1962 "The Last Sitting" session. In this session Stern photographed Monroe, just weeks before her death, over a three-day period in June 1962, 20" x 24". **$700**

Swann Auction Galleries

San Francisco Police Department inmate mug shots, 40-page folio, 710 silver prints. **$31,200**

William Klein, Rome, 1957, photographer's "William Klein / VIVA" stamp on reverse, annotated in unidentified hand in pencil on the reverse, 9.4" x 11.7". **$2,200**

1920s Chinese and Japanese album of photographs, over 300 photographs depicting the Forbidden City, boats, pagodas, agriculture, parades, landscapes, shrines, etc., 3 1/2" x 5 3/4". **$2,000**

Richard Margolis (American, 20th century), Brooklyn Bridge, circa 1985, silverprint, three images, 20" x 16". Provenance: NYNEX Corp., White Plains, New York (label verso). **$275**

Political Items

BY ERIC BRADLEY

Initially, American political campaign souvenirs were created to celebrate victories. There is a wide variety of campaign items—buttons, bandannas, tokens, pins, etc. The only limiting factor has been the promoter's imagination. The advent of television campaigning has reduced the quantity of individual items, and modern campaigns do not seem to have the variety of materials that were issued earlier.

Expert Enoch Nappen wrote in his bible of memorabilia that the quality and quantity of political memorabilia hit a sharp decline in 1968. Perhaps it was because the advent of television as the preferred medium of reaching the masses or that the election itself marked the end of the New Deal coalition, a highly organized and effective push that put millions of dollars behind Democratic candidates for more than 35 years.

Eric Bradley

At around that time, the variety, diversity and downright quirky buttons, ribbons, novelties and advertisements collectors seek became obsolete. Values now depend on design and novelty. Jugates, depicting two portraits side by side, remain popular and in high demand. Items decorated with real photo depictions of candidates or popular historic figures remain the most valuable of all political memorabilia collectibles. Ephemera and other paper items in excellent condition can be solid investments as well. Items from obscure or extinct political parties are desired, especially if the item features popular issues of the day, such as Prohibition, slavery, suffrage or civil rights.

Heritage Auctions, Inc.

Abraham Lincoln, 1864 campaign medal, Sullivan-DeWitt AL-1864-10, silvered brass, obverse inscription: "Abraham Lincoln For President 1864," retains 90-95% of original silvering, 31 mm. **$262**

However, the interest in collecting political memorabilia is increasing. The top lot of a June 2012 sale at Kaminski Auctions in Beverly, Mass., was a collection of over 200 political buttons, from Teddy Roosevelt through Richard Nixon. Highlights of the lot included hat and rider and old pin backs. Drawing attention in the weeks leading up to the sale, the lot generated interest from enthusiastic collectors all over the country. And after a round of fast-paced bidding, the valuable collection sold for an impressive $16,440, more than 20 times its original estimate.

For more information on political collectibles, consult *Warman's Political Collectibles* by Dr. Enoch L. Nappen.

ERIC BRADLEY *is public relations associate at Heritage Auctions, the world's third largest auction house. He is former editor of* Antique Trader *magazine and is the author of* Antique Trader 2013 Antiques and Collectibles Price Guide, *America's no. 1-selling guide to the antiques and collectibles market. An award-winning investigative journalist with a degree in economics, Bradley has written hundreds of articles about antiques and collectibles and has made several media appearances as an expert on the antiques market at MoneyShow San Francisco, on MSN Money, Nasdaq.com and on AdvisorOne.com. His work has received press from* The New York Times *and* The Philadelphia Inquirer.

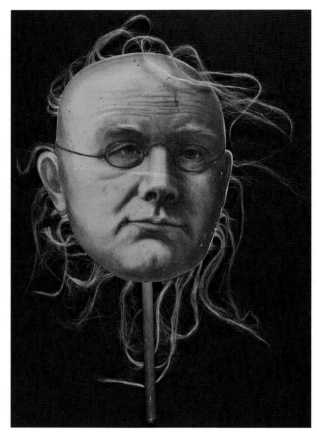

Heritage Auctions, Inc.

Satirical campaign hand fan, Horace Greeley, Liberal Republican and Democratic candidate for president in 1872, front lampoons Greeley's wispy white hair and chin whiskers through attachment of actual hair clippings, back shows vignettes and cartoons ridiculing Greeley's career, accomplishments, and political aspirations, wooden dowel handle, 7 1/2" x 9 1/2".
$1,195

Heritage Auctions, Inc.

Zachary Taylor, folksy campaign bandanna, "Gen. Taylor Rough and Ready" in central medallion, surrounded by stars, rays, and floral border, four corners list victorious battles: Matamoras, Palo Alto, Monterey, and Buena Vista; printed in two shades of brown, likely only example extant, 26" x 23".
$10,157

Hakes

One-of-a-kind resin Franklin D. Roosevelt figure in wood and wire wheelchair, fully painted, wire frame glasses, cigarette in trademark holder, teeth showing, precise detailing of eyes, facial wrinkles and graying hair, figure 9 1/2" tall, 9 1/2" diameter wooden base, 12 1/4" tall glass dome for display. Provenance: Made for FDR enthusiast Mark Furr's collection, circa 2002, by an artist in Annapolis, Maryland. **$442**

Heritage Auctions, Inc.

McKinley and Hobart 1896 campaign whiskey flask, molded clear glass, portraits of McKinley and Hobart on either side, inscribed "Genuine Distilled Protection For Sound Money Only," name of candidate beneath each portrait, cap and contents no longer present, 4 3/4" high. **$215**

Heritage Auctions, Inc.

Horatio Seymour, "Reluctant Candidate," rare greenback portrait flag, 1868, shows him in place of Salmon Chase on greenback, spread diagonally across stripes, surrounded by "Horatio Seymour for President"; bill has various campaign slogans, central one advocates payment of bonds issued to finance the Civil War in greenbacks rather than gold, as advocated by the Republicans; demands "Equal Taxation One Currency for the Government, the People, and the Laborer, and the Office Holder, The Producer and the Bondholder"; 37 stars, 12" x 18". **$7,767**

Kaminski

More than 200 political buttons, Teddy Roosevelt through Richard Nixon and other candidates, including hat and rider and assorted antique and vintage pin backs. **$16,440**

Hakes

Rare "Keep Rosy with Roosevelt" license plate, aluminum and steel in three layers, front layer consists of mounting holes and high relief name "Roosevelt" in cast aluminum, middle layer is aluminum with unpainted letters and painted pair of 1/4" thick red and green roses with stems, leaves and flowers, backed by a rectangle of steel plus final layer of three riveted steel strips that rise above body of design, each with 1/8" thick five-point gold star, 5" x 9 3/4". Provenance: From the FDR Collection of Mark Furr. **$1,581**

Hakes

Rare King Bee Cigarettes complete set of presidents in cellophane with easel backs, 1 1/8" thin tin rim with full color cellophane insert of Presidents Washington through McKinley, reverse has fold-out wire easel and covered tin back reading "King Bee Tobacco And Cigarettes" at center with rim text "City Button Works New York Patented February 23, 1897," only full set known. Only the 1897 set by Whitehead & Hoag was issued as early as this. **$1,391**

Hakes

Patriotic order Sons of America, five ornate ribbon badges, all include celluloid accents. First specifies "Credential Committee" for event at Williamsport, Pennsylvania in 1902; second features large celluloid shield picturing Washington for early 1900s group in Bonnair, Pennsylvania; third is dated 1907 for "Carnival of Nations/Committee"; fourth is for 1917 event in Havre de Grace, Maryland; fifth is for 1920 event in Sudlersville, Maryland, featuring Washington celluloid in shield; last two are both "Delegate" badges; largest 10 3/4". **$86**

Hakes

Grant/Colfax uniface ferrotype jugate pin, brass frame with beveled edge, embossed eagle with cut-out center windows holding ferrotypes with candidate's full names above their images, shield below includes word "For" and ribbons have tiny words "President" and "V. Pres.," reverse has tin back with vertical stickpin, 1 1/16". **$1,175**

Hakes

Autographed Barack Obama 2008 limited edition national campaign fundraiser poster, high quality stiff paper poster with "Yes We Can" slogan, pencil inscribed "1509/5,000," signed "Barack Obama" in person for a friend and member of his legal team and longtime Democratic Party activist, 25" x 39". **$316**

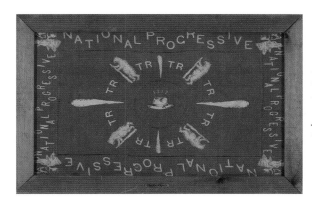

Heritage Auctions, Inc.

National Progressive Party cloth campaign bandanna for Theodore Roosevelt's National Progressive Party, better known as the Bull Moose Party, for presidential election, 1912, 50 1/8" x 77". Provenance: Elton Hyder III Collection, formerly at University of Texas School of Law. **$750**

Hakes

Extremely rare Parker/Roosevelt opposing candidates jugate button, 1904, Baltimore Badge paper, U.S. capitol with scales by Fairbanks company showing Parker outweighing Theodore Roosevelt; includes "Parker and Davis" above with rooster below next to cartoon balloon reading "Judge! We're 'It.' " Button curl reads "Copyright - Sept-6-1904." Button surface is flat as made, 1 3/4". Provenance: This button has been in the family of a Baltimore Badge employee who decided to save one for himself 107 years ago. (The name "Fairbanks" references the measuring device company founded in 1830, but is also a play on the name of Roosevelt's running mate.) **$6,122**

Hakes

Framed 1880 single-day event poster, Oct. 23, 1880, Pottstown, Pennsylvania event celebrating Republican victories in Ohio and Indiana, "A Tidal Wave! Rolling Eastward! A Grand Demonstration and Torchlight Parade in Honor of the Republican Victories in Ohio and Indiana Will Be Held at Pottstown on Saturday, Oct. 23, 1880. The Parade Will Move at 8.00 p.m. Garfield and Arthur Campaign Clubs From Philadelphia, Norristown, Phoenixville, Bridgeport, Reading and Other Places Will Take Part." Poster printed by Ledger Steam Power Job-Printing House as marked below main text, fold lines, 39 1/2" x 71 3/4" frame with glass. **$5,094**

Hakes

Rare "Van Buren & Democracy" sulfide brooch, beveled glass in brass frame with vertical pin and clasp, frame has curved lines in alternating directions with tiny diamond accent shape at each corner, 1 x 1 1/8". Provenance: From the Philip G. Straus Collection. **$9,323**

Quilts

Each generation made quilts, comforters and coverlets, all intended to be used. Many were used into oblivion and rest in quilt heaven, but for myriad reasons, some have survived. Many of them remain because they were not used but stored, often forgotten, in trunks and linen cabinets.

A quilt is made up of three layers: the top, which can be a solid piece of fabric, appliquéd, pieced, or a combination; the back, which can be another solid piece of fabric or pieced; and the batting, which is the center layer, which can be cotton, wool, polyester, a blend of poly and cotton, or even silk. Many vintage quilts are batted with an old blanket or even another old, worn quilt.

The fabrics are usually cotton or wool, or fine fancy fabrics like silk, velvet, satin, and taffeta. The layers of a true quilt are held together by the stitching, or quilting, that goes through all three layers and is usually worked in a design or pattern that enhances the piece overall. The term "quilt" has become synonymous with bedcover to many people, and we include tied quilts, comforters and quilt tops, none of which are true quilts in the technical description.

Quilts made from a seemingly single solid piece of fabric are known as wholecloth quilts, or if they are white, as whitework quilts. Usually such quilts are constructed from two or more pieces of the same fabric joined to make up the necessary width. They are often quilted quite elaborately, and the seams virtually disappear within the decorative stitching. Most wholecloth quilts are solid-colored, but prints were also used. Whitework quilts were often made as bridal quilts and many were kept for "best," which means that they have survived in reasonable numbers.

Wholecloth quilts were among the earliest type of quilted bedcovers made in Britain, and the colonists brought examples with them according to inventory lists that exist from colonial times. American quiltmakers used the patterns early in the nation's history, and some were carried with settlers moving west across the Appalachians.

Appliqué quilts are made from shapes cut from fabric and applied, or appliquéd, to a background, usually solid-colored on vintage quilts, to make a design. Early appliqué quilts dating back to the 18th century were often worked in a technique called broderie perse, or Persian embroidery, in which printed motifs were cut from a piece of fabric, such as costly chintz, and applied to a plain, less expensive background cloth.

Appliqué was popular in the 1800s, and there are thousands of examples, from exquisite, brightly colored Baltimore Album quilts made in and around Baltimore between circa 1840 and 1860, to elegant four-block quilts made later in the century. Many appliqué quilts are pictorial—with floral designs the predominant motif. In the 20th century, appliqué again enjoyed an upswing, especially during the Colonial Revival period, and thousands were made from patterns or appliqué kits that were marketed and sold from 1900 through the 1950s.

Pieced or patchwork quilts are made by cutting fabric into shapes and sewing them together to make a larger piece of cloth. The patterns are usually geometric, and their effectiveness depends heavily on the contrast of not just the colors themselves, but of color value as well. Patchwork became popular in the United States in the early 1800s.

Colonial clothing was almost always made using cloth cut into squares or rectangles, but after the Revolutionary War, when fabric became more widely available, shaped garments

Double Irish Chain, circa 1825 (top), maker unknown. Stamped on front: J.D.W. Randall. Probably United States. Purchased as top, quilted by Eileen Russell, Galena, Ohio, in 1999. Multicolored cotton prints and solids, cream background, new narrow cotton print border, new muslin back, new gray binding, new hand quilting. **$2,000-$3,000**

were made, and these garments left scraps. Frugal housewives, especially among the westward-bound pioneers, began to use these cutoffs to put together blocks that could then be made into quilts. Patchwork quilts are by far the most numerous of all vintage-quilt categories, and the diversity of style, construction and effect that can be found is a study all its own.

Dating a quilt is a tricky business unless the maker included the date on the finished item, and unfortunately for historians and collectors, few did. The value of a particular example is affected by its age, of course, and educating yourself about dating methods is invaluable. There are several aspects that can offer guidelines for establishing a date. These include fabrics; patterns; technique; borders; binding; batting; backing; quilting method; and colors and dyes.

The quilts shown here were made in the United States, with a few from England, almost all pre-1950s.

For more information on quilts, see *Warman's Vintage Quilts Identification and Price Guide* by Maggi McCormick Gordon.

Dove in the Window, circa 1930 (top), maker unknown. Quilted by Jo Ann Peterson, circa 2000. United States. Multicolored cotton print and solid scraps, white cotton backgrounds, blue cotton sashing with yellow cotton corners, new narrow yellow inner border, new blue-on-blue stripe cotton outer border, new blue floral back, blue striped cotton binding, hand-quilted outline in blocks, cable in sashing, double crosshatch in blue border. **$750-$1,000**

Grandmother's Flower Garden, circa 1930, maker unknown. United States. Multicolored cotton prints and solids, hexagons arranged in lozenge shapes, pink cotton double "path," cream cotton back, cream binding. **$400-$600**

Jacob's Ladder on Point, circa 1900, maker unknown. Iowa. Blue cotton prints, pale cotton microdot spacers, set on point, muslin back, red and white microdot binding, hand-quilted grid. **$400-$600**

Lone Star, circa 1900, maker unknown. Minnesota. Pink, blue, green, and mauve cotton solids on rose pink cotton background, rose pink and blue border of alternating pieced diamonds, pink back, knife-edge quilting, hand-quilted grid, crosshatch, and outline. **$250-$400**

New York Floral, 1860, maker unknown. Probably New York. Red and green (fading to blue) cotton solids hand appliquéd on white background, nine blocks with cherry vines between main motifs and on border, cherries are stuffed, muslin back, green (blue) binding piped with red, hand-quilted clamshell and outline. **$1,500-$2,000**

Red and white Shoofly, circa
1935, maker unknown.
United States. Red and white
cotton prints and solids,
hand-pieced blocks, white
cotton inner border, red
cotton outer border, machine
assembly, white cotton
back, white binding, hand-
quilted hanging diamonds
and parallel diagonal lines.
$400-$600

Straight Furrow Log
Cabin, circa 1870,
maker unknown.
United States. Cotton
prints and solids,
red cotton centers,
gray and tan cotton
stripe back, back-to-
front self-binding, no
quilting. **$600-$750**

Touching Six-Point Stars, circa 1910, maker unknown. United States. Multicolored cotton prints including many indigo colors set to make six-point stars, white cotton spacer hexagons, pink with white polka dot cotton back, pink binding, hand quilted outline. **$750-$1,000**

Turkey Tracks, circa 1930, maker unknown. United States. Yellow and green cotton solids on white cotton background, green cotton border, muslin back, knife-edge binding, hand-quilted floral motifs in spaces, cables in border, pattern was once called Wandering Foot. **$750-$1,000**

Tree of Life, circa 1875 (top), maker unknown. Quilted by Jo Peterson, 2004. United States. Green and red cotton broadcloth tree trunks and leaves, white cotton backgrounds and spacers, triple border in blue-green, white, and blue-green cotton, new back, new red binding, hand quilted crosshatch grid, star motifs in spacers. **$1,000-$1,500**

Whirligig Pinwheel, circa 1870, maker unknown. Missouri. Gray and white cotton prints and stripes, double pink spacers, brown and red print inner border, double pink outer border, dark-brown print back, matching binding, hand-quilted crosshatch, unwashed and unused. **$750-$1,000**

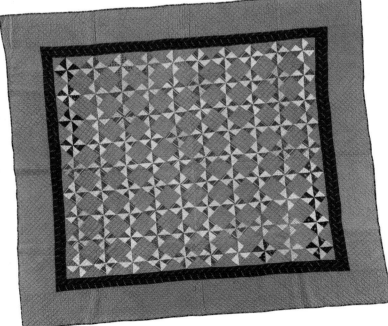

Records

BY SUSAN SLIWICKI

Values for records — much like those for other collectibles — are dependent on a mix of factors, including condition, rarity, overall demand, market trends, and past sales results. Here are some key points to remember as you buy, sell, and value your records.

Discern the record's quality, which is not the same thing as condition. Quality relates to the materials that were used in the first place. When 78 RPM blues records were pressed in the 1920s to 1930s, manufacturers used either stock shellac or laminated discs. Stock shellac discs had a lower-quality playing surface, which made them prone to more noise at playback, while laminated discs (which were used by labels including Columbia and OKeh) featured a higher quality playing surface.

Likewise, quality can vary for vinyl records. For 12" records, the low end of the scale is 120 gram vinyl (4.23 ounces), with 150 grams (5.29 ounces) considered a "heavy" weight, and anything pressed on 180 grams (6.35 grams) or more deemed audiophile grade. The higher the weight, the higher the quality and durability.

Be ruthless when you assess condition. *Goldmine* magazine established (and continues to follow) the Goldmine Grading Standard, which determines how well a record, cover, or sleeve has survived since its creation. These are high standards, and they are not on a sliding scale. A record or sleeve from the 1950s must meet the same standards as one pressed today.

Rarity does not guarantee value. You thought you bought a copy of Lynyrd Skynyrd's "Street Survivors" album; the cover and labels were correct, after all. But when you put it on the turntable, you discovered the A-side was actually Steely Dan's "Aja." Or maybe the labels were wrong, but the music was what you thought you bought. Or perhaps you bought a still-sealed record that advertised one group on the cover and contained a completely different artist's album inside. These types of scenarios happened more often than you might think at a record pressing plant. While these records are snowflakes, they don't possess the types of errors that draw big bucks from collectors; if anything, they negatively impact value. Depending on the music fan, these errors may only be a source of frustration, because the listener was anticipating "What's Your Name" and got "Black Cow" instead.

A record can be old without being valuable, and vice versa. Head to a garage sale, a thrift store or a relative's attic, and chances are good you'll find some old records. We're not saying you'll never find a beauty or two in the mix, but you're far more likely to find copies of Frankie Yankovic's "40 Hits I Almost Missed," Tom Jones' "Live In Las Vegas," and Glenn Miller's "The Carnegie Hall Concert" (worth $5 or less apiece) than a rare 78 RPM of Charley Patton's "High Water Everywhere" Parts 1 and 2 on the Paramount label, which sold for $5,000 in March 2012. Condition, quality, demand and rarity are far more important than age when determining value.

The laws of supply and demand rule. Meat Loaf's claim that "Two Out of Three Ain't Bad" doesn't count if the missing No. 3 is demand. No demand means no value; it doesn't matter how fine or rare the record is unless others want to buy it and own it. Supply figures in, too. A quality record in great condition that also is in great supply means buyers deem what the market is worth.

SUSAN SLIWICKI'S *favorite childhood memories are of hours spent hanging out with her oldest brother, who let her listen to his collection of albums, including Pink Floyd's "Dark Side of the Moon" and Deep Purple's "Machine Head," in exchange for her silence as long as the record was still spinning on the turntable. A journalist by trade, Sliwicki brought her two greatest passions — words and music — together when she joined* Goldmine *magazine in 2007 and became its editor in 2011.*

Backstage Auctions

KISS vintage vinyl collection, 1974-1987: "Kiss" (1974, LP, second pressing); "Dressed to Kill" (1975, LP, first pressing, light blue label); "Dressed to Kill" (1975, LP, first pressing, dark blue label); "Dressed to Kill" (1975, LP, third pressing, desert scene label); "Alive!" (1975, two LPs, first pressing with booklet); "Alive!" (1975, two LPs, second pressing, without booklet); "Alive!" (1975, two LPs, third pressing, without booklet); "The Originals" (1976, three LPs, second pressing with booklet, sticker and cards); "Rock and Roll Over" (1976, LP, first pressing); "Rock and Roll Over" (1976, LP, second pressing); "Alive II" (1978, two LPs, no inserts); "Double Platinum" (1978, two LPs, no inserts); "Paul Stanley" (1978, LP, no inserts); "Gene Simmons" (1978, LP, no inserts); "Ace Frehley" (1978, LP, no inserts); Peter Criss (1978, LP, no inserts); "Dynasty" (1979, LP, with poster); "Unmasked" (1980, LP, with poster); "The Elder" (1981); "Creatures of the Night" (1982); "Lick It Up" (1983); "Asylum" (1985); "Crazy Nights" (1987); "Beth" (1976, 7" promotional single in Casablanca sleeve); "Sure Know Something" (1979, 7" single, Casablanca); "All Hell's Breakin' Loose" (1984, 7" single, Japanese pressing). **$253**

Trying to sell a record but not getting the price you seek? Get a second, third or more opinion on the record in question. Has your record gotten a better grade than it deserves? Is it a first pressing? Or is it a reissue or a counterfeit? Are similar-condition copies selling for wildly different amounts on the Internet or with other dealers? This will give you a better picture of what you have, what it's worth, and how in-demand it really is.

If you feel a dealer is offering an unfair price, make a counter offer. If the dealer shows no interest in negotiating, ask why he or she arrived at the price offered. Keep in mind that reputable dealers offer what they feel are fair prices, based on the costs and risks they assume for the items they acquire.

Collect what you love and what you can afford. Don't raid your 401(k) account to buy a too-good-to-be-true rarity under the guise that it is an investment. Enjoy the thrill of the chase within your budget, buy the best that you can afford, and always take time to appreciate what you have, from super-cool sleeves and covers to great-sounding music.

Gotta Have Rock and Roll

Pretenders debut album signed in various inks; includes Chrissie Hynde's signature. **$656**

PROMOTIONAL RECORDS: These records were never meant for retail sale; they typically were sent to radio stations, music reviewers and other industry professionals. Promos typically bear a white label (or a label that somehow differs from the company's usual design or color scheme) and may include the words or phrases "Demonstration — Not For Sale," "Audition Record," "For Radio-TV Use Only" or "Promotional Copy."

While promo records have definitely been drawing fans on eBay sales, many promos sell for roughly the same amount as stock copies of the same catalog number.

Goldmine's Record Grading Guide

Record grading uses both objective and subjective factors. Our advice: Look at everything about a record — its playing surface, the label, the record's edges, the cover and/or sleeve — under a strong light. If you're in doubt, assign the record a lower grade. Many dealers grade records, sleeves, or covers and sometimes even labels separately. The grades listed below are common to vinyl records, including EPs, 45s, LPs and 12" singles.

MINT (M): Perfect in every way. Often rumored, but rarely seen. Never played, and often still factory sealed. Never use Mint as a grade unless more than one person agrees that a record or sleeve truly is in this condition. Mint price is best negotiated between buyer and seller.

NEAR MINT (NM OR M-): Nearly perfect. Looks and sounds like it just came from a retail store and was opened for the first time. Jackets and sleeves are free of creases, folds, markings, or seam splits. Records are glossy and free of imperfections. Many dealers won't use a grade higher than NM, implying that no record or sleeve is ever truly perfect.

VERY GOOD PLUS (VG+) or EXCELLENT (E): Except for a few minor things, slight warps, scuffs, or scratches that don't affect playback, ring wear on the labels, a turned up corner, cut-out hole, or seam split on the sleeve or cover, this record would be NM. Most collectors, especially those who want to play their records, are happy with a VG+ record, especially if it's toward the high end of the grade (VG++ or E+). Worth 50 percent of NM value.

VERY GOOD (VG): Many of the imperfections found on a VG+ record are more obvious on a VG record. Surface noise, groove wear, and light scratches can be found on VG records.

You may find stickers, tape or writing on labels, sleeves, and covers, but no more than two of those three problems. VG records are among the biggest bargains in record collecting. Worth 25 percent of a NM record.

GOOD (G), GOOD PLUS (G+), or VERY GOOD MINUS (VG-): Expect a lot of surface noise, visible groove wear and scratches on the vinyl, as well as more defects and repairs to labels, sleeves, and covers. Unless the record is unusually rare, G/G+ or VG- records are worth 10 to 15 percent of the NM value.

POOR (P) and FAIR (F): Records are cracked, impossibly warped, or skip and/or repeat when an attempt is made to play them. Covers and sleeves are heavily damaged, if they even exist. Unless they are incredibly rare, P and F records sell for 0 to 5 percent of the NM value (if they sell at all).

Backstage Auctions

Rare Led Zeppelin vinyl records of live performances between 1973 and 1975: "Fractured Ribs: Live in Dallas May 18, 1973" (two LPs, U.K. pressing, The Amazing Kornyfone record label); "Persistence — Live at Kezar Stadium San Francisco June 2, 1973" (two LPs, Roon Dog Records); "Trouble at the Front — England/Scotland January 1973 (two LPs, Tropo Records); and "Legerdomain — Montreal 1975" (two LPs, U.K. pressing, The Amazing Kornyfone record label). Album sleeves show common signs of storage, use and wear. **$388**

Bonhams

"Aladdin Sane" album autographed by David Bowie, front cover signed and inscribed in black felt-tip pen, "To Chris with thanks Bowie 82." **$547**

Gotta Have Rock and Roll

The Police "Zenyatta Mondatta" album cover signed in black and blue felt-tip ink by band members Sting, Stewart Copeland and Andy Summers. **$255**

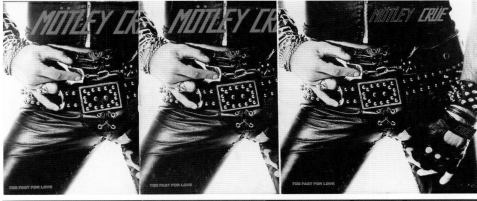

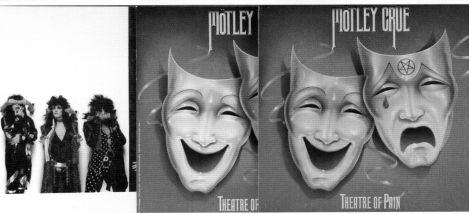

Backstage Auctions

Mötley Crüe vintage vinyl collection,1981-1985. Rare LPs, promos, including: "Too Fast For Love," 1981, Leathür Records, second pressing, insert; "Too Fast For Love," 1982, Elektra Records, insert; "Too Fast For Love," 1982, Elektra Records, white label promotional pressing; "Shout at the Devil," 1983, promotional pressing; "Shout at the Devil," 1983, white-label promotional pressing, merchandise sheet; "Theatre of Pain," 1985, merchandise sheet. **$222**

Gotta Have Rock and Roll

"Greetings From Asbury Park" album signed in black felt-tip pen by Bruce Springsteen and E Street Band members Clarence Clemons, Garry Tallent, and Vini Lopez. **$1,465**

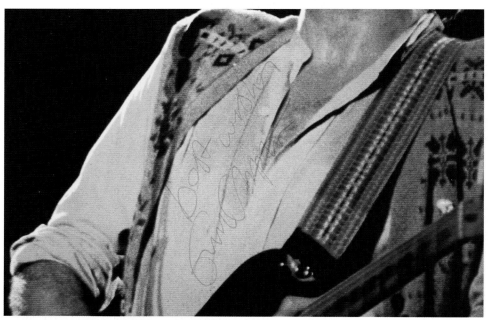

Backstage Auctions

Multi-artist autographed "Just One Night" album cover by Eric Clapton (1980), who used a ballpoint pen to inscribe album's gatefold with "Best Wishes Eric Clapton." He also wrote his home address and phone number on a separate slip of paper that is included. On back side of album cover are signatures (also in ballpoint pen) of five musicians who played on the album: Albert Lee, Nils Lofgren, Dave Markee, Chris Stainton, and Henry Spinetti. **$588**

Backstage Auctions

Collection of 1980-1985 vintage Iron Maiden vinyl records, including promotional records, foreign pressings and 12" EPs: "Iron Maiden" (1980, LP); "Sanctuary" (1980, four-song, 12" EP, Dutch pressing); "Maiden Japan" (1981, five-song, 12" EP); "Maiden Japan" (1981, five-song, 12" EP, German pressing); "Run to the Hills" (1982, 12" EP, German pressing); "The Number of the Beast" (1982, LP); "Cross-Eyed Mary" (1983, promotional release, 12" EP); "Piece of Mind" (1983, promotional LP, two merchandise sheets); "Powerslave" (1984, promotional LP). Also two related LPs that feature members of Iron Maiden: "Shock Tactics" by Samson (1981, U.K. pressing, features singer Bruce Dickinson, insert); and "Hot Tonight" by Lionheart (1984, features guitarist Dennis Stratton). **$174**

Heritage Auctions, Inc.

Guns N' Roses band-signed "Appetite For Destruction" LP, 1987. U.K. pressing (WX 125) signed by all five members: frontman Axl Rose, lead guitarist Slash, bassist Duff McKagan, guitarist Izzy Stradlin, and drummer Steven Adler. Rarer robo/ rape cover version, record is red vinyl pressing. **$812**

Backstage Auctions

Autographed promotional copy of Van Halen's 1978 "Van Halen" album, signed with silver marker by all four original members: guitarist Eddie Van Halen, drummer Alex Van Halen, bass player Michael Anthony, and singer David Lee Roth. **$633**

Heritage Auctions, Inc.

Led Zeppelin promotional pressing of 1969 "Led Zeppelin" LP (Atlantic SD 8216). Stereo, white-label promo of legendary group's first LP. **$286**

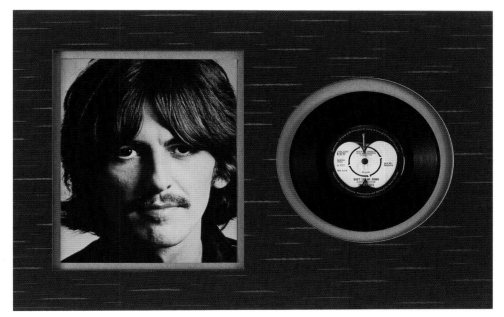

Heritage Auctions, Inc.

George Harrison-autographed 45 RPM record (UK - Apple 5777, 1969). The Beatles' lead guitarist signed B-side label of U.K.-released pressing of "Get Back"/"Don't Let Me Down." Mounted with color 8" x 10" photo of Harrison; includes letter of authenticity from Perry Cox; overall 22" x 14 1/2". **$1,000**

Heritage Auctions, Inc.

Rare Decca pressing of Tony Sheridan and The Beat Brothers (better known as The Beatles), "My Bonnie"/"The Saints" 45 RPM record (Decca 31382, 1962). Rarest of U.S. Beatles singles, including pink label promotional version of record. "My Bonnie" attracted few takers in the United States when it originally was released, and most copies pressed were trashed, explaining why promotional copies outnumber the stock commercial version. Once Beatlemania hit the United States in 1964, the record was re-released on the MGM label, where it reached No. 26 on the Billboard Hot 100 charts. Collecting experts estimate only 25 stock copies of Decca 31382 are still in existence. **$16,875**

Heritage Auctions, Inc.

Group of R&B 45 RPM records from 1955-1965. EP records: Smokey Robinson and the Miracles "Going to a Go-Go" (Tamla Jukebox, EP 60267); The 5 Satins, "The 5 Satins Sing Vol. 2" (Ember 101), black label; Lee Allen and His Band, "Walkin' With Mr. Lee" (Ember 103). Picture sleeves and 45 RPM singles: Louis Armstrong and His All-Stars, "The Beat Generation"/"Some Day You'll Be Sorry" (MGM 12809); Fats Domino, "Be My Guest"/"I've Been Around" (Imperial 5629); The Drifters, "The Christmas Song"/"I Remember Christmas" (Atlantic 2261); Sarah Vaughan, "Sole, Sole, Sole"/"How's the World Treating You" (Mercury 72300). Also included: color slick/proof of The Five Keys' EP, the group's first (Capitol 572). **$312**

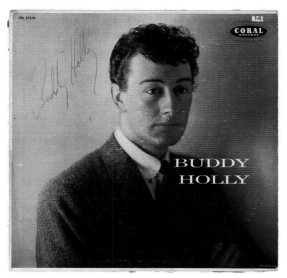

Heritage Auctions, Inc.

Buddy Holly-signed eponomous LP (Coral 57210). First pressing, maroon-label LP released in 1958 his first "solo" LP. **$3,000**

Gotta Have Rock and Roll

Noel Redding's personal 45 RPM Emidisc acetate of Jimi Hendrix Experience "Hey Joe"/"Stone Free" from 1966. Original sleeve has acetate's information handwritten in blue ballpoint pen. Redding played bass with the Jimi Hendrix Experience. **$888**

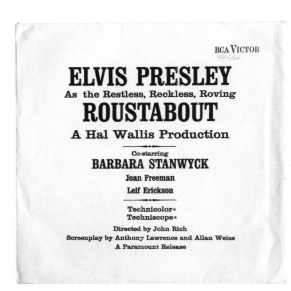

Heritage Auctions, Inc.

Elvis Presley "Roustabout" promotional sleeve (RCA, 1964), one of the rarest Presley picture sleeves because it was only produced for promotional purposes. Because RCA record number isn't indicated, sleeve was likely produced before associated disc was pressed. The date "10/26/64" is written on front and back of this copy, with three stamps on back for "RECEIVED Dec 23 1964 ALL STAR SHOWS." **$1,875**

Bonhams

Autographed copy of The Beatles' "Day Tripper"/"We Can Work It Out," (1965, Parlophone R-3589), inscribed "Best Wishes The Beatles" and signed in purple felt-tip pen by John Lennon, Paul McCartney, George Harrison, and Ringo Starr. Includes reel-to-reel tape of four-minute interview with group conducted for BBC radio at Capitol Cinema in Cardiff, Wales; 5" Zonatape spool in original box and dated 12/12/65; cassette copy of interview also included. **$21,554**

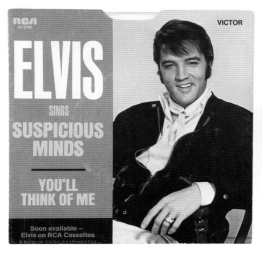

Heritage Auctions, Inc.

Elvis Presley's personally owned, yellow label promotional copy of "Suspicious Minds" (RCA 9764) 45 RPM record, 1969. Certificate of authenticity provided by Joe Esposito, member of Elvis' inner circle. **$625**

Heritage Auctions, Inc.

Group of 46 pop and rock 45 RPM records, including promotional pressings, from 1950s-1960s: The Four Lovers with Frankie Valli, "Honey Love" (RCA 6519); five records by The Skyliners, including "Since I Don't Have You" (Calico 103); Miller Sisters, "There's No Right Way to Do Me" (Sun 230); Donnie and the Dreamers, "Count Every Star" (Whale 101); Hot-Toddys, "Rockin' Crickets" (Shan-Todd 28987); Rochell and The Candles, "So Far Away" (Swingin' 634); The Who, "Substitute" (Polydor 1200) picture sleeve, Holland pressing; and The Tokens, "Tonight I Fell in Love" (Warwick 615). Other artists included: The Angels, Browns, Cascades, Chordettes, Crests, Crew-Cuts, James Darren (promo), Diamonds, Duprees, Echoes, Fireflies, Four Voices, Hollywood Argyles, Kingsmen, Lovin' Spoonful, Mystics, Newbeats, Playmates, Raiders, Regents, Ron-dels, Royal Teens, Royaltones, Shadows of Knight, Swinging Blue Jeans, Tokens and Westbrooks. **$250**

Heritage Auctions, Inc.

RCA's Elvis Presley Model 7HF-45 record player, 1956. Cherry wood, still in working order, accompanied by framed copy of ad for Elvis and other RCA artists and a copy of RCA EP "Perfect For Parties" issued with Elvis-dominated paper sleeve only offered as promotional mail-order item. **$1,553**

Heritage Auctions, Inc.

Thirteenth Floor Elevators pair of white-label promotional 45 RPM records for "You're Gonna Miss Me"/ "Tried to Hide" (International Artists IA-107), 1966. **$112**

Heritage Auctions, Inc.

Group of Beatles 45 RPM records/sleeves dating between 1964 and 1966: "Cry For a Shadow"/"Why" (MGM 13227); "Ain't She Sweet"/"Nobody's Child" (Atco 6308); "Please Please Me"/"From Me to You" (Vee-Jay 581), special Christmas sleeve; "Twist and Shout"/"There's a Place" (Tollie 9001), green print with logo in box; "A Hard Day's Night"/"I Should Have Known Better" (Capitol 5222); "Eight Days a Week"/"I Don't Want to Spoil the Party" (Capitol 5371); and "Nowhere Man"/"What Goes On" (Capitol 5587). **$836**

Science & Technology

BY ERIC BRADLEY

Grouping science and technology in a collecting genre is a relatively new theme, although these unique objects have been highly sought after for decades. Scientific models, diagrams and lab equipment are now hot collectibles, thanks to a boost in the Steampunk design movement and the rise of "geek chic."

It's cool to be smart and it's a cool collector who has at least a few fascinating objects devoted to mankind's pursuit to knowing more about the world we live in. From books to microscopes to calculators and even quack medical devices, this collecting category spans several object classes.

Eric Bradley

Increasingly, auction houses are pursuing this trend with specialty-themed sales. Bonhams, Heritage, Skinner, and even Sotheby's have all offered major technological auctions, many with strong results. However, the undisputed leader in this category is based in Germany. Auctin Team Breker, located in Cologne, offers several sales each year on office antiques, photographica and film. The sales are just one more example of how auction houses are seeking to cater not only to what collectors collect, but how collectors collect.

Trends in this area are likely to be centered on the dawn of personal computing. The first personal computer sold to the public was Simon, a hulk of wire and cabinetry holding a simple mechanical brain. It debuted in 1950 for $600 ($5,723 in today's dollars) and was able to perform addition, negation, greater than, and selection. It's rare for these early computers to come to market, however, when they do collectors and investors take notice.

A rare 1976 Apple I computer brought $374,500 at a June 2012 auction. Similar models don't sell for nearly as much money, with provenance, condition and exposure key to an object's auction value.

Rare examples aside, collecting scientific and technology collectibles is a very affordable hobby and one that stands an excellent chance to grow as today's tech-savvy youth become the nostalgic collectors of the future.

ERIC BRADLEY *is public relations associate at Heritage Auctions, the world's third largest auction house. He is former editor of Antique Trader magazine and is the author of* Antique Trader 2013 Antiques and Collectibles Price Guide, *America's no. 1-selling guide to the antiques and collectibles market. An award-winning investigative journalist with a degree in economics, Bradley has written hundreds of articles about antiques and collectibles and has made several media appearances as an expert on the antiques market at MoneyShow San Francisco, on MSN Money, Nasdaq.com and on AdvisorOne.com. His work has received press from* The New York Times *and* The Philadelphia Inquirer.

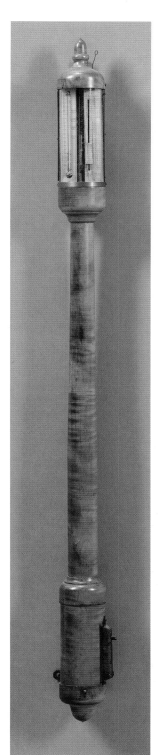

Pook & Pook, Inc

Table-mounted candleholder, 19th century, with iron extending arm. **$1,580**

English mahogany book press, 18th/19th century, 15" high x 13 3/4" wide. **$474**

Skinner, Inc.

Turned maple patent stick barometer, Charles Wilder, Peterboro, New Hampshire, circa 1860, with acorn finial over silvered metal thermometer and barometer with curved glass cover, thermometer with stamped marks "Woodruff's Pat. June 5 1860/C. Wilder Peterboro N.H.," 39" high. **$652**

James D. Julia, Inc.

Rare 17th century German engraved brass and silver table clock, "Gottfried Kruger" engraved on bottom plate of movement, hexagonal case with stepped molded edge inset with silver dial engraved with Roman numeral chapter ring within Arabic chapter ring, each side-mounted with glass panel beneath a row of colonnettes, case raised on turned suppressed ball feet. Rare example striking the hours and quarters on two bells situated within the gallery, mock pendulum and fusee chain movement with verge escapement. Piece accompanied by custom-made hexagonal display case. 4" high x 6 1/4" diameter overall. **$8,050**

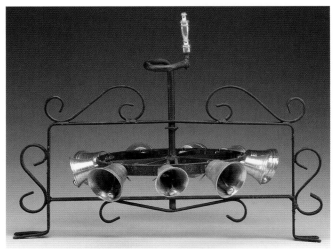

James D. Julia, Inc.

Rare architectural wrought iron and brass doorbell, late 19th/early 20th century, wrought iron rectangular frame of S-scrolls centering reel mounted with 10 brass bells joined to wrought iron crank terminating in turned brass handle, 16" long overall x 12 1/2" deep x 11" wide of wheel. **$805**

Pook & Pook, Inc.

English mahogany banjo form barometer, 19th century, signed D. Fagoli, London, 39" high. **$326**

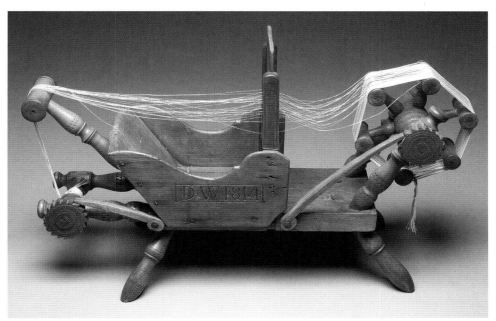

Jeffrey S. Evans & Associates

Pennsylvania turned and carved wood tape loom, bed mounted with box with cut-out sides and rosehead-nail construction, inscribed "DW 1814" on one side, reel and bobbin each with ratchet locks, whole raised on four splayed feet mortised through bed. Possibly Berks Co., first quarter 19th century, 18 1/2" height overall, 30" length overall. Provenance: Property of Museum of Early Southern Decorative Arts (MESDA). Deaccessioned and sold to benefit the Acquisition Fund. **$4,888**

Jeffrey S. Evans & Associates

American painted softwood and tin candle mold, frame fitted with 36 tubes and raised on cut-out feet, frame with original dry painted surface, probably Pennsylvania, mid-19th century, 12" high, 10 1/2" x 11". **$1,150**

Pook & Pook, Inc.

Lace making apparatus in leather case. **$178**

Pook & Pook, Inc.

Jupiter cast iron pencil pointer by Guhl & Harbeck, Hamburg, 5" x 13". Provenance: Pennsylvania educational institution. **$296**

Jeffrey S. Evans & Associates

Victorian rosewood tabletop stereoptical viewer, hinged and adjustable with fold-up extra magnifying lens, small group of common cards, second half 19th century, 9 1/4" x 16" base. **$316**

Auction Team Breker

*Musical gold snuff box, circa 1810, probably Geneva/
Switzerland, solid gold, 18K, total weight 91g, double-
tooth sectional-comb movements in engine-turned gold
case with sunburst motif on lid, geometric borders and
corner sways, key, 2 1/5" x 1 2/5" x 3/4".* **$18,222**

Pook & Pook, Inc.

*Watling How Much Do
You Weigh coin scale,
dated 1928, 72 1/2" high
x 24 1/4" wide.* **$830**

Skinner, Inc.

*Brass goniometer with
turned wood platform,
Secretan, Paris, 19th
century.* **$3,308**

Skinner, Inc.

Cased brass naturalist's microscope, W&S Jones, 30 Holborn, London, England, early 19th century, 4 1/4". **$4,444**

Skinner, Inc.

Holtzapffel & Deyerlein ornamental turning lathe and accessories, No. 1378, London, circa 1827, mahogany bench with foot treadle, flywheel and six drawers below iron bed with traversing mandrel headstock marked Holtzapffel & Deyerlein London and 1378, 50" high x 44" wide x 30" deep, accessory cabinet 73" high x 38" wide x 18 1/2" deep. **$65,175**

Skinner, Inc.

Three varied forms of simple microscopes, 19th century, cased Withering-type with tools having circular stage supported by brass posts, another small microscope with turned wood handle, brass and glass eyeloop, height to 2 1/4", length to 2 3/4". **$4,740**

Skinner, Inc.

Brass armillary sphere, probably England, 19th century, hour circle at pole, calibrated and adjustable equatorial and meridian rings, large equatorial ring inscribed with signs of zodiac, turned wooden stand, 20" high. **$3,555**

Skinner, Inc.

Culpeper-type compound monocular microscope, attributed to Mathew Loft, circa 1750, turned lignum vitae body with leather wrapped single draw tube, brass eyepiece and sliding cover, outer card body covered in ray skin, 16" high. **$14,220**

Auction Team Breker

"The Keaton Music Typewriter," 1947, rare American musical note typewriter in extraordinary design, original case. **$5,206**

Skinner, Inc.

Three Bakelite crystal models, American, mid-20th century, colored spheres mounted on metal rods demonstrate each crystal's molecular structure, 7" high. **$858**

Skinner, Inc.

Large Bakelite model of a crystal, American, 1957, colored spheres mounted on metal rods demonstrate the crystal's molecular structure, on wooden base, 17" high. **$504**

Auction Team Breker

Desk telephone "coffee grinder" by L. M. Ericsson, 1895, rare, Swedish, crank inductor, rolled lithographed tin case, wooden base, "Ericsson" handset, export model. **$22,127**

Auction Team Breker

"The Burns No. 1," 1894, rare American upstroke typewriter with full keyboard by Frank Burns, made by The Burns Typewriter Company, Buffalo, New York, serial no. 3. **$9,110**

Skinner, Inc.

Black-painted brass spectroscope, Fasse, Berlin, late 19th century, three legs with thumbscrew-adjusted feet for leveling, 11" high overall, 14 3/4" long overall. **$3,308**

Skinner, Inc.

One-inch five-draw brass spyglass, Paris, marked on eyepiece tube, "Levasseur, Optien, quai de l'horolge, No.53, Paris," decorated with mother-of-pearl and faux rubies at objective, length extended 3 1/2". **$415**

Auction Team Breker

Collection of glass eyes, circa 1925, 50 various artificial eyes in cardboard box, handmade by ocularist using white and colored glass. **$650**

Auction Team Breker

Floor telephone Kongliga Telegrafverkets Apparater, 1894, exclusive model for Royal Swedish castles, wooden case, metal front with coat of arms, double bell, four magnets inductor, original headset with speaking horn, adjustable cast iron base with inscription "Kongliga Telegraf-Verkets," few examples known worldwide. **$39,048**

Silver

Silver has been known since ancient times and has long been valued as a precious metal, used to make ornaments, jewelry, tableware and utensils, and coins.

Pure silver is too soft to be fashioned into strong, durable, and serviceable utensils. Therefore, a way was found to give silver the required degree of hardness by adding alloys of copper and nickel. Silversmithing in America goes back to the early 17th century in Boston and New York and the early 18th century in Philadelphia. Boston artisans were influenced by the English styles; New Yorkers by the Dutch.

Silver-plated items are made from a base metal coated with a thin layer of silver.

For more information on sterling silverware, see *Warman's Sterling Silver Flatware*, 2nd edition, by Phil Dreis.

Bonhams

Victorian sterling silver presentation shield by Charles Frederick Hancock, London, 1883, circular, representing a scene and characters from Sir Walter Scott's Ivanhoe, 1820, center with high relief plaque depicting Wilfred of Ivanhoe as "Desdichado" defeating Templar knight Brian de Bois-Guilbert in the tournament at Ashby, within a Celtic knot band surrounded by five portrait medallions of King Richard I, Rebecca, Rowena, Cedric of Rotherwood, and Wilfred of Ivanhoe, within a further band, lower edge molding engraved "Hancocks' & Co 39 Bruton Street London," mounted on wood backing with easel support, 29" diameter. **$26,250**

Sloans & Kenyon Auctioneers and Appraisers

English William IV wine cooler, shaped circular foot with oak leaf and acorn border waist acanthus leaf border, rim oak leaf and acorn border, RP GR, London, 1832, 20 oz., 9 3/4" high. **$2,250**

Sloans & Kenyon Auctioneers and Appraisers

English silver creamer, George III, faceted body, ribbed bandwork, basket weave rim, urn-form feet, by Charles Fox, London, 1810, 6 oz., 4 dwt. **$236**

David Rago Auctions, Inc.

Irish coffeepot, pear-shaped, repoussé gadrooning, marked with fire in basket, hallmarked CT, circa 1770, 37 oz., 12 3/4" x 4 1/2". **$4,700**

Sloans & Kenyon Auctioneers and Appraisers

Sheffield plate wine coasters, pair, George III, serpentine edges, turned treen bases, bosses with engraved armorials, circa 1810. **$355**

Sloans & Kenyon Auctioneers and Appraisers

Silver-plated chafing dish, covered, oval shape, four scrolling feet, stand with removable liner and plate, domed cover, acanthus handle, early 20th century, 17 1/4" long. **$445**

Skinner, Inc.

Sheffield, English, reticulated silver basket, George V, quatrefoil bowl pierced with foliate scrolls and four heart-shaped cartouches, beaded C-scroll and flower head rim, openwork shell and acanthus scroll feet, approximately 21 oz. troy, maker's mark "WS," 1913, 12 3/8" wide. **$590**

Pook & Pook, Inc.

Sheffield silver-plated hot water kettle, urn finial, lion mask handles, applied shield plaque, spout marked "TH," early 19th century, 13 1/2" high. **$380**

Pook & Pook, Inc.

English punch ladle with marks of William Gibson and John Langman, London, circa 1899, 13" long; English silver punch ladle, circa 1789, bearing mark of "T.S." (Thos. Shephard), 13 1/2" long. **$500**

Michaan's Auctions

Pair of Baroque-style sterling candlesticks, 28.25 oz. troy, 14" high. **$700**

Heritage Auctions, Inc.

Unger Brothers silver Indian head stamp box, Newark, New Jersey, circa 1905, hinged lid with Indian head decoration, marks: (UB intertwined), STERLING, FINE, 925, 1.7 oz. troy, 2 1/2" long. **$896**

Bonhams

Set of 12 Regency sterling silver dinner plates by Paul Storr, London, 1812, each with gadrooned border punctuated with shells and scrolling acanthus, engraved armorial of the first Earl of Onslow and motto "FESTINA LENTE," approximately 294 oz. troy, 10 1/2" diameter. **$15,000-25,000**

Woodbury Auctions

Continental silver three-piece tea set. **$2,706**

Woodbury Auctions

Four-piece sterling silver tea or coffee set. **$3,565**

Michaan's Auctions

Silver tea strainer with removable carved jadeite handle, matching box, 6 1/2" long.
$225

Michaan's Auctions

Fisher sterling kettle on stand with ivory fittings and hinged handle #2311, 52 oz. troy, 14" high.
$1,000

Michaan's Auctions

Continental silvered bronze jewelry casket with figural decoration, 2" x 4 1/8" x 2 3/8".
$110

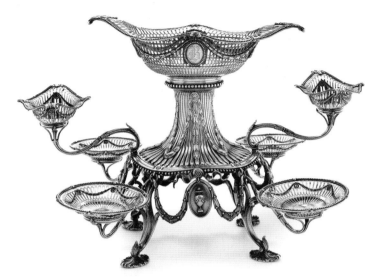

Bonhams

George III sterling silver seven-basket epergne by Thomas Pitts, London, 1775, central basket centering two oval cartouches, the first later engraved with Gothic style initial B, opposing cartouche engraved with script presentation inscription "Twenty-sixth/Anniversary/Dec. 25th/1949," 100 oz. troy, 14 1/4" high x 21 1/2" long x 17" wide. **$15,000**

Pook & Pook, Inc.

Sheffield silver-plated salver, gadrooned edge, ball and claw feet, early 19th century, 12" diameter. **$410**

Bonhams

Chinese Export silver floral repoussé decorated circular footed bowl by Wang Hing, Hong Kong, late 19th/early 20th century, decorated overall with blooming chrysanthemums, 36 oz. troy, 5" high, 10 1/4" diameter. **$3,750**

Michaan's Auctions

Danish sterling Modernist cocktail shaker designed by F. Hingelber Aarhos, 18 oz. troy, 9" high. **$1,700**

Bonhams

Italian sterling silver Neoclassical style nine-light candelabrum by Pampaloni, Florence, modern, fluted stem issuing acanthus-sheathed arms on circular base, 363 oz. troy, 30" high, 20 1/2" diameter. **$10,500**

Bonhams

Canadian Colonial silver oval tobacco box by Michael Arnoldi, Montreal, late 18th century, flat-hinged cover engraved with a ship under full sail within inscription "Success to the Everetta and the Fur Trade in all its Branches," 4 oz. troy, 1 3/8" high, 3 5/8" long. **$16,250**

Bonhams

German parcel-gilt and acid-etched silver beaker by Marx Burmeister, Nuremburg, circa 1631-1657, cylindrical, decorated with three medallions depicting infant Christ interspersed with trailing foliate clasps, inscriptions in Latin and High German, relief inscription to underside, raised on a foot, 3.5 oz. troy, 3" high, 2 3/4" diameter. **$25,830**

Bonhams

Italian sterling silver lobed oval footed bowl by Buccellati, Milan, mid-20th century, downswept feet, 21 oz. troy, 4" high, 10" long. **$2,000**

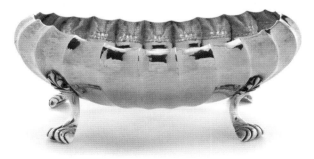

Bonhams

Danish hand-hammered sterling silver oval pedestal bowl by Georg Jensen Silversmithy, Copenhagen, circa 1926-1932, designed by Georg Jensen, #296 B, grape cluster pendants over similarly decorated base, 30 oz. troy, 4 1/4" high, 11" long. **$6,500**

Bonhams

Victorian silver-plated pierced oval center bowl/ jardinière, late 19th century, caryatid handles, liner replaced, 7 1/2" high, 19 1/2" long. **$1,625**

Bonhams

George III silver epergne with four arms and pendant baskets by Thomas Pitts I, London, 1765, four cast multi-scroll supports joined with cast floral garland raise a reticulated waisted hollow center column fitted with large oval basket, four inset cast leaf capped looped rising brackets with pin terminals securing hinged handles of circular reticulated baskets, 93 oz. troy, 17" high. **$8,125**

Bonhams

American sterling silver floral repoussé-decorated six-piece tea and coffee service manufactured and retailed by Bailey, Banks & Biddle, Philadelphia, circa 1874-1894, in Chinoiserie taste; teapot, coffee pot, hot water urn on lamp stand, cream jug, sugar bowl, waste bowl, all of square form chased with flowers and foliage, lids with seated Chinaman finials with matching two-handled silver-plated tray, 181 oz. troy, urn 15 1/4" high, tray 33 1/4" long. **$10,000**

Bonhams

American sterling silver mounted green overlay and cut glass pitcher by Gorham Manufacturing Company, Providence, Rhode Island, circa 1900, collar engraved with script "EAB" monogram, 12 1/2" high. **$3,500**

Bonhams

American coin silver floral repoussé and Chinoiserie scene decorated footed pitcher by Samuel Kirk, Baltimore, Maryland, circa 1840, navette form spout with squared ram's headed handle over tapering body decorated with floral clasps, scrolls and figures in exotic landscape and pagodas, with armorial for Moore family of Ireland, to central cartouche, 59 oz. troy, 17 1/2" high, 9 1/4" long. **$6,250**

Space Collectibles

BY NOAH FLEISHER

Human conquest of the cosmos has the ability to inspire humans like little else and, in the brief time we've been slipping these surly bonds, we've done remarkably well, all things considered. In the cosmic sense, this spans but a blink of a blink. We've walked on the moon, sent craft to mars to explore the surface, sent satellites hurtling headlong into the unknown of the Milky Way beyond our system and we've taken pictures of the beginning of time. These are but baby steps for which future generations will be grateful because they will enjoy the fruits of this early labor.

Noah Fleisher

Little wonder then that the pieces, parts, ephemera and personal memorabilia associated with America's space program – the men and women who, in large part, made science fiction a reality – have made collectors of all sorts sit up and take notice.

"The supply of the really important items is certainly finite," said Howard Weinberger, Senior Space Consultant for Heritage Auction Galleries in Dallas, and CEO of Asset Alternatives. "The old saying is that if you collected all the personal items from the six missions that landed on the moon, all of it would fit in a small suitcase."

Weinberger is talking about the cream of the crop, the things that the Apollo astronauts took special pains with to make sure they were on the lunar surface and spent time in the vacuum of space. The rest of the field – from souvenir patches, parts and models, autographs and well beyond – has as much room for variance of budget as a collector could wish and a plethora of material that – like the very subject it covers – can sometimes seem infinite.

Unlike so many categories of collecting, the market for space memorabilia is still being established. The subject has long been popular, but the ability to get the very best of The Right Stuff was not there until recently, as many of the astronauts themselves – or their families, if they've passed on – have realized the value, both historic and financial, of their accomplishments. The more that the remaining original astronauts release key pieces of their extra-terrestrial lives, the more established the market will become.

One of the most important things space collecting has going for it is its appeal, said Weinberger. The steady increase in prices at auction in the three years he's been working with Heritage shows just how broad this appeal is.

"I think it's a function of the fact that people are now aware that these items can be bought," said Weinberger, who is among the few with the connections to bring the choicest pieces to auction. "The genre is unique because the demographic, in my opinion, is among the top three to five potential demographics for collecting."

Meaning there's almost no soul on this planet who doesn't know about, and isn't at least peripherally fascinated by, space travel.

"Show a baseball card, a comic book or a regional American quilt to a woman in Asia," Weinberger said, "and it won't translate. If you go back to 1969, to Apollo 11 and the first moon landing, you have the entire planet watching. Everybody remembers where they were when

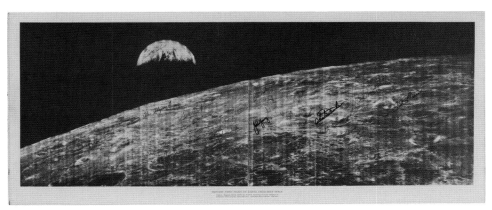

Heritage Auctions, Inc.

First photo of earth from deep space, black and white, mounted to heavy board, signed by all 29 Apollo astronauts with caption: "Taken August 23, 1966, by NASA - Boeing Lunar Orbiter I/ Distance from Earth 232,000 mi. - - Altitude above Moon - 730 Mi." Every astronaut who flew on one or more of the 11 Apollo missions has signed along the surface of moon or earth: Ken Mattingly, Ron Evans, Jack Swigert , Alan Shepard, Ed Mitchell, Wally Schirra, Charles Conrad Jr., Stuart A Roosa, Dave Scott, James Lovell, Harrison H Schmitt, Rusty Schweickart, Don Eisele, Buzz Aldrin, John Young, Al Worden, Neil Armstrong, Tom Stafford, Frank Borman, Charlie Duke, Jim Irwin, Walt Cunningham, Michael Collins, James A. McDivitt, Gene Cernan, Bill Anders, Dick Gordon, Fred Haise, and Alan Bean; 46" x 19" overall. **$38,837**

Neil Armstrong walked on the moon, or when Allan Sheppard went up with Mercury."

The broad scope of potential buyers is indeed as varied as the material, as a few minutes with the following pages will show. As the field sorts itself out, it is tough to break down into categories. The astronauts, and all the workers at NASA – from the men who walked on the moon to the guys who swept up at the end of the day – were all aware from the beginning of the historic nature of their pursuit – and it potential value.

This prospective worth, then, necessitates at least an attempt at breaking the hobby into categories. According to Weinberger, this is not something that should be done by item type, but rather by mission type and purpose.

"There's not a lot of the very best stuff, so there is a hierarchy of sorts that has evolved," he said. "The highest rung is for items that actually landed on the moon and went on the surface. Then it's something that landed on the moon but didn't leave the capsule. After that it's memorabilia that flew to the moon but only stayed in orbit. From there it's about things that flew in space, things that were strictly in earth orbit, and things that didn't fly in space but are of a personal nature belonging to the astronauts, or having their autographs."

Within these several categories, however, again there can be a striking difference in price depending on the name and the program it's associated with.

Whatever level a collector is looking at to get into the market for space memorabilia, the most important thing is authenticity, especially at the high end. In fact, Weinberger said, if it comes from an astronaut's personal collection, a signature and/or a letter of authentication is of paramount importance.

"No matter what it is, even if it's purchased personally from an astronaut, it has to be certified," he said. "The most desirable certification is having the signature on the item itself. If it has that, and a letter as well, then so much the better."

The most important thing to get started is not a broad general knowledge of what's out there, but to simply have a passion for it no matter how much cash you can put in. You can buy autographs, first-day covers or specially minted Robbins medals that flew on every Apollo mission. You can spend a few hundred or a few hundred thousand dollars; either way, it's an accessible market.

"You can start with something basic," Weinberger said. "The overall amount of memorabilia related to space is endless."

It's a good thing, then, that the enthusiasm of collectors, especially for something as inspiring as space travel, seems to be equally as endless.

NOAH FLEISHER received his Bachelor of Fine Arts degree from New York University and brings more than a decade of newspaper, magazine, book, antiques and art experience to his position as Public Relations Director of Heritage Auctions, one of the country's foremost auction houses. He is the former editor of Antique Trader, New England Antiques Journal and Northeast Antiques Journal, is the author of Warman's Modern Furniture, and has been a longtime contributor to Warman's Antiques & Collectibles.

Heritage Auctions, Inc.

Fourth largest piece of the moon ever offered for private acquisition, Dar Al Gani (DaG) 1058, determined by scientists to be lunar highland breccia from far side of moon, shaped like large slab, single largest surface area to mass ratio of any of largest lunar meteorites, composed primarily of mineral fragments, lithic clasts, and glassy matrix; 4 1/2" x 9.33" x 2 1/4", 3.92 lbs. **$330,000**

Heritage Auctions, Inc.

Gibeon meteorite, iron, fine octahedrite – IVA, Great Nama Land, Namibia – (25° 30'S, 18° 0'E), shape is product of manner in which Gibeon's chemical composition and octahedral crystalline structure interacted with geochemistry of Kalahari Desert, rich patina, custom armature, 9 1/2" x 9 1/2" x 3", 15.25 lbs. **$46,875**

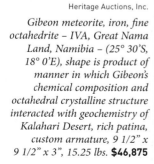

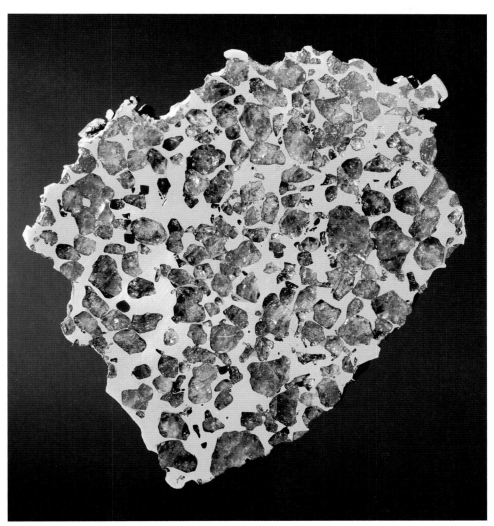

Heritage Auctions, Inc.

Imilac meteorite, end piece with space gems, Atacama Desert, Chile (24° 12' 12"S, 68° 48' 24"W). Pallasitic meteorites are the most sought-after meteorites and originate from boundary between stony mantle and molten iron core of a planetary body that broke apart during the formation of solar system. Olivine crystals are the result of small chunks of stony mantle suspended in molten nickel-iron, which slowly cooled and crystallized over a million years in outer space. Imilac occasionally contains gem-quality olivine or peridot. Olivine crystals from chartreuse to orange are scattered throughout, reverse is bathed in milk chocolate-hued patina with persimmon-colored crystals with voids and pockets where crystals had melted out of matrix during meteorite's descent to earth; 5 1/4" x 3 1/8" x 1/2", 0.9 lbs. **$16,250**

Heritage Auctions, Inc.

Photographs of Russian space dogs signed by cosmonauts including Yuri Gagarin, Gherman Titov, Pavel Popovich, Andriyan Nikolayev, Pavel Belyayev, Alexey Leonov, and Vladimir Komarov. Photographs picture Laika (the first animal in space), Strelka and Belka (orbited the earth and returned home on Sputnik 5), Chernuska and Zvedochka (orbited on Sputnik 9 and 10), and unidentified space dog. Various size images, largest 8" x 6 1/2". **$3,585**

Heritage Auctions, Inc.

Apollo 11 crew-signed color photo on mat with signatures from crew: Neil Armstrong, M. Collins, and Buzz Aldrin; above is printed dedication: "Presented to Bill and Eleanor from the Crew of Apollo XI." 13 3/4" x 10 3/4" photo, 20" x 16" mat, framed overall 20 1/2" x 16 1/2" (no glass). Provenance: From the personal collection of North American Aviation President William B. Bergen. **$4,481**

Heritage Auctions, Inc.

Apollo 14 lunar module-flown American cloth flag carried aboard lunar module Antares to surface of moon on Feb. 5, 1971, where it remained for more than 33 hours. Mission Lunar Module Pilot Dr. Edgar Mitchell has signed three lower white stripes: "Flown to the Lunar Surface aboard Antares - Feb 5, 1971 Edgar Mitchell Apollo 14 LMP"; 6" x 3 7/8". Provenance: From the personal collection of Dr. Edgar Mitchell, signed and certified, with signed letter of authenticity. **$65,725**

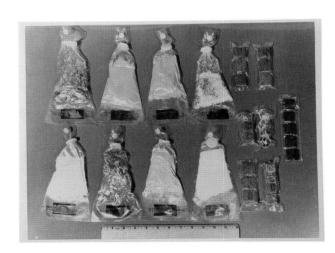

Heritage Auctions, Inc.

NASA 1963-era space triangular-shaped plastic food pouch, labeled: "Blended Juice, 6 oz. water; 2 minutes" (one of the earliest examples of food developed for long duration space flights of Gemini and Apollo), with 10" x 8" NASA glossy photo from 1963 showing several pouches with caption on verso explaining their development, 4 3/4" x 9" overall, including germicide tablet at top. **$298**

Heritage Auctions, Inc.

National Space Hall of Fame wooden plaque with text: "Edward H. White II having been duly nominated and elected is hereby presented National Space Hall of Fame Honor Award September 26, 1969 / A sculptured bronze plaque symbolizing this award is on permanent display in the National Space Hall of Fame, Lobby of Albert Thomas Convention Center, Houston, Texas," signed by hall of fame's president and executive vice president. White was one of the first 10 people inducted into hall of fame in Houston on this date (posthumously), along with Dr. Wernher von Braun, Dr. Kurt H. Debus, Dr. Hugh L. Dryden, Dr. Maxime A. Faget, Dr. Robert R. Gilruth, John H. Glenn Jr., Dr. Robert H. Goddard, Alan B. Shepard Jr., and U.S. Rep. Albert Thomas; 6" x 8" x 7/8". Provenance: From Ed White II's family's collection. **$597**

Heritage Auctions, Inc.

Apollo 17-flown sterling silver Robbins medallion, 35mm, one of 80 flown aboard Apollo 17, Dec. 7-19, 1972, with crewmembers Gene Cernan, Ron Evans, and Harrison Schmitt (300 were minted to commemorate sixth and final lunar landing of NASA program). Obverse features mission insignia depicting head of Greek god Apollo, U.S. flag and eagle, moon, and surnames of crewmembers; mission dates engraved on reverse with phrase, "The Beginning"; serial number and sterling and Robbins hallmarks on rim; eyelet added to top to allow it to be worn as a necklace. Rarest of all Apollo silver Robbins medallions, with original case. Provenance: From the personal collection of Mission Commander Gene Cernan, Serial Number 73, with signed letter of authenticity. **$38,837**

Heritage Auctions, Inc.

Apollo 10-flown sterling silver Robbins medallion, 29mm x 31mm, shield-shaped, one of 300 flown to moon aboard Apollo 10, May 18-26, 1969, with crewmembers Tom Stafford, Gene Cernan, and John Young. Obverse features mission insignia with Roman numeral "X" on moon with command and lunar modules preparing to rendezvous, earth visible in background; reverse has engraved mission dates along with serial number and sterling and Robbins hallmarks; original case with numbered sticker on bottom. Provenance: From the personal collection of astronaut Rusty Schweickart, Serial Number 70, with signed letter of authenticity. **$15,535**

Heritage Auctions, Inc.

Gemini 5 Mission Commander Gordon Cooper's flown space suit insignia patch, with signed and certified storage envelope, from record-breaking mission with Pete Conrad, Aug. 21-29, 1965. Cooper has written: "This is the Patch Flown on Cooper's Suit on Gemini V Gordon Cooper," as well as 8" x 10" black-and-white glossy photo of Cooper and Conrad in space suits on deck of recovery ship wearing their patches. Also included is early photocopy of memo, dated Aug. 18, 1965, sent from Deke Slayton in Flight Crew Operations to all astronauts spelling out the policy of personal items on space flights and mission badges. Provenance: From Gordon Cooper's personal collection. **$19,120**

Heritage Auctions, Inc.

NASA Snoopy customized HG-44/P-style flight helmet, PRK-37 helmet shell features PRU-36/P side-actuated dual visor (clear/tinted), Gentex MBU-12/P oxygen mask with AM-7067/A mask microphone, top front has NASA logo decal, on either side is decal of Snoopy on doghouse wearing space helmet; on back is decal of Snoopy in spacesuit, helmet, and red scarf, carrying life support system and doing "happy dance"; all around are stars and above is text: "Eyes on the Stars." **$3,585**

Heritage Auctions, Inc.

Russian Mir Space Station command control console and monitor used in training; command generation keys have mutual mechanical inhibits, keys used to issue activation and deactivation commands, two components mounted to 12" x 26" x 10" heavy black metal rack with metal plaque on base reading: "MIR Space Station Command Control Console and Monitor." Top piece is video monitor of 9 1/2" x 10 1/2" overall dimensions, beneath is mounted pushbutton panel of 10" x 7 1/2" with numerous pushbutton keys. **$5,526**

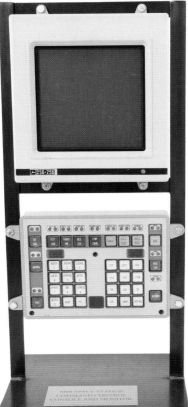

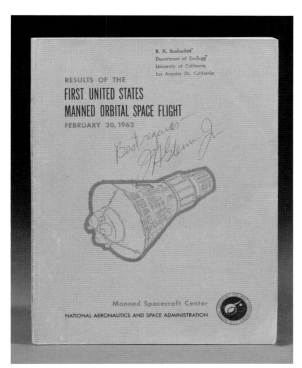

Skinner, Inc

John Glenn-signed copy of Results of the First United States Manned Orbital Space Flight, February 20, 1962, Washington: U.S. Government Printing Office, 1962, wraps, signed on cover, owner's stamp to cover, title page and spine. **$563**

Heritage Auctions, Inc.

Apollo Block II command module flight director attitude indicator, rare piece of equipment manufactured by Honeywell, original "indicator, attitude, flight director" metallic Honeywell sticker on side indicates manufacturer part number as DJG264E3 and manufacture date as "19 Sept 1966." Above that is metal modification identification plate with manufacturer part number of DGJ264E4 and acceptance date of "11 Apr 67." This FDAI or "8 Ball" was used to define relative position of spacecraft in three-dimensional space. Originally designed to be three different panel instruments, astronauts, many of whom were pilots, lobbied for an all-in-one device similar to "artificial horizon" indicator in airplanes. Overall 6 7/7" diameter x 10 3/4" deep, including electrical connector protruding from bottom. **$65,725**

Heritage Auctions, Inc.

Grumman Apollo Lunar Module Contractor's Model, manufactured for Grumman by Precise Models, Inc., prior to Apollo 11 moon landing, 10 1/4" black base with color logos of both Grumman and NASA with text "Lunar Module" only, two-piece LM is removable from base, made of injection-molded plastic, accurately separates into Ascent and Descent Stages and has numerous tiny projecting parts, approximately 6" high and 10" wide. **$2,151**

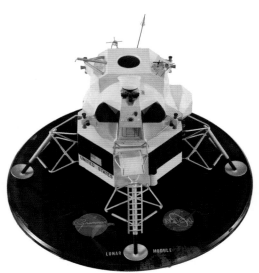

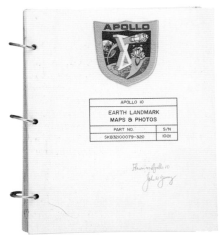

Heritage Auctions, Inc.

Apollo 10 Earth Landmark Maps & Photos book, 71 pages of color earth terrain photos, 207 color earth landmark maps, all on lightweight three hole-punched paper and each with plastic-coated tab; all bound with three binder rings between two cardstock covers. Front cover has Beta cloth Apollo 10 mission insignia laid down to it and lists part number as "SKB32100079-320" and serial number as "1001." Mission Command Module Pilot John Young signed front cover: "Flown on Apollo 10 John W. Young." Photos notated as to landmark and north compass point, all have various NASA photo numbers signifying that they were taken on a variety of flights during 1965 and 1966; each has a chart printed beneath giving latitude, longitude, elevation, and horizontal uncertainty calculations for each identified location. NASA Apollo earth landmark maps, printed by Army Map Service, are all on a scale of 1:1,000,000 and feature similar notations and calculations; 8 1/2" x 10 1/2". Provenance: From the personal collection of John Young, signed and certified. **$43,318**

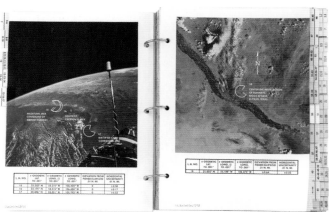

Heritage Auctions, Inc.

Astronaut Dr. Karl Henize's gold NASA flight suit originally from his personal collection, standard issue from late 1960s era, ID label at neck beneath Kings Point Mfg. Company tag, embroidered 2 3/4" diameter NASA "Meatball" patch sewn on right breast, 4 1/2" x 2" Skylab patch on left sleeve, Velcro strip sewn on left breast where nametag would be (not present), multiple zippers and pockets. **$776**

Sports

People have been saving sports-related equipment since the inception of sports. Some was passed down from generation to generation for reuse; the rest was stored in dark spaces in closets, attics, and basements.

Two key trends brought collectors' attention to sports collectibles. First, decorators began using old sports items, especially in restaurant décor. Second, collectors began to discover the thrill of owning the "real" thing.

Sports collectibles are more accessible than ever before because of online auctions and several auction houses that dedicate themselves to that segment of the hobby. Provenance is extremely important when investing in high-ticket sports collectibles. Being able to know the history of the object may greatly enhance the value, with a premium paid for items secured from the player or directly from their estate.

Some of the most popular golf collectibles are badges issued during the Masters tournament. Many collectors strive to get one from every year. The rarest of the bunch hail from the inaugural tournament, 1934. **$40,000**

The biggest story in baseball cards for the past year was the "Black Swamp Find" in Ohio. A family found a box of cards in an attic that belonged to a grandfather, which turned out to be the finest set of 1910 E98 in existence. The initial offering of the find was a "near set" – 27 of 30 cards. **$286,800**

From the same find, a Honus Wagner card – again, the finest in existence. **$239,000**

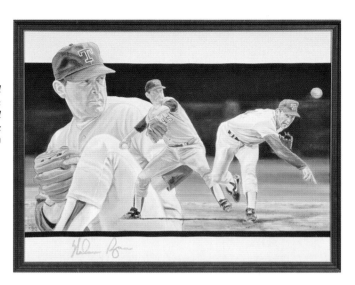

Nolan Ryan original painting on canvas by Tim Houle, signed by the Hall of Fame pitcher, 27 1/2" x 21 1/2". **$200**

World Series press pins, issued for each team participating in the Fall Classic, are collectible. Recent examples range in price from **$150-$250***; older examples can sell for much more. 1931 Philadelphia A's World Series pin.* **$4,000**

Items from athletes' personal collections are on the rise as players age. Sam Jones' 1958 200th Strikeout Trophy, awarded by the St. Louis Cardinals. **$3,286**

The recent sale of the Ted Williams
Collection by Hunt Auctions in
2012 added hundreds of signed
pieces by the Splendid Splinter to
the marketplace. Signed Hitters
Hall of Fame posters. **$200-$400**

A target of
baseball card
collectors are
unopened packs,
particularly packs
that have been
graded. 1973
Topps Baseball
wax pack, graded
PSA 8. **$200**

Mickey Mantle was a prolific signer, and one coveted by legions of New York Yankees
fans. Replica jersey signed by the slugger (authenticated by a third party). **$2,000**

Original photos, called Type 1 photos, are extremely popular. Even photos showcasing athletes when they are not in play are in high demand. 1910s photo of Ty Cobb. **$470**

Signed mini helmets are an affordable avenue for autograph collectors. Helmet signed by Dan Marino, one of the greatest quarterbacks ever to step on the field. **$100**

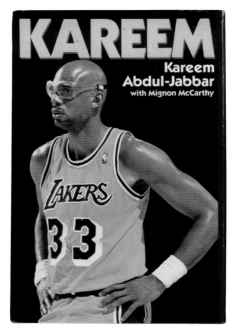

You never know what you might find at a thrift store. Many biographies signed by the authors slip through the cracks. A few dollars for a Kareem Abdul-Jabbar signed biography at a thrift store could result in a sizeable profit. **$25-$50**

Tobacco companies have a long association with baseball and baseball cards, which were inserted in packs of tobacco products as an enticement to buy, a practice that dates back to the late 1800s. These Waitt and Bond Yankees and Bayuk Phillies cigar boxes date to 1942 and 1935, respectively. **$85/pair**

Stadium giveaways are popular with collectors. This 1913 pinback celebrates Frank Chance Day at Comiskey Park on May 17, 1913. **$225**

Athletes hawking cigarettes was commonplace in the 1940s and 1950s. Baseball players featured in such advertising are in higher demand, but even golf stars command attention from collectors. 1949 Gene Sarazan and Lew Worsham Camel advertisement. **$15-$30**

White Sox Coca-Cola 8", 7 oz. bottle from Comiskey Park in 1932. The Chicago White Sox team was the only one with its own embossed bottle. **$500**

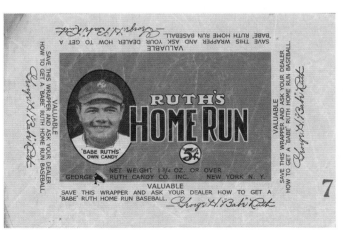

Most people wouldn't think to save a candy bar wrapper, much less one in 1928, but this example survived, probably because of the subject matter – Babe Ruth. Ruth's Home Run candy bar wrapper. **$200**

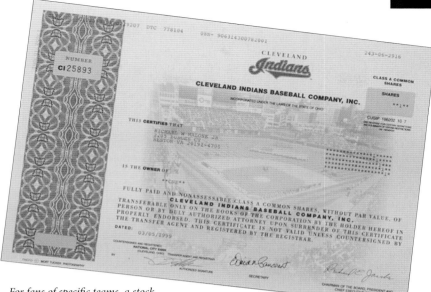

For fans of specific teams, a stock certificate is an interesting keepsake – and cheap! Cleveland Indians stock certificate from 1999 for one share. **$10**

Those looking for baseball collectibles not directly linked to the game will enjoy this circa 1888 Dark Town Battery Baseball mechanical bank by J & E Stevens, painted cast iron with figural pitcher, batter, and catcher, set above a rectangular coin-vault base; 9 1/2" x 2 3/4" x 7". **$4,150**

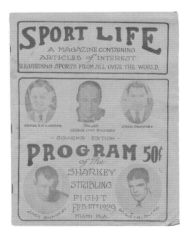

Prewar publications are coveted if they are in moderate or better condition. Completeness and minimal stains are key. 1929 Jack Sharkey vs. W.L. Stribling Official Program. **$180**

Vintage bobble heads from the 1950s and 1960s are extremely popular to this day. If the period piece depicts a famous slugger, like Willie Mays shown here, it can bring several hundred dollars depending on condition. White-base Mays bobble heads have his first name spelled wrong. **$350**

Toys

BY ERIC BRADLEY

Collectors of the best antique and vintage toys have been on the hunt for pristine examples from childhoods gone by. There seems to be no end to the number of record prices recorded across every major category, from dolls and clock-works to model trains and tin trucks. The phenomenon is primarily due to the number of large, well-curated collections coming to market, which is spurred no doubt by the number of toy-themed auction houses spread throughout the country.

Eric Bradley

The hobby has been punctuated by a few important milestones: When Part I of the Dick Claus collection of antique toy boats was auctioned by Bertoia Auctions in May 2012, collectors were astonished at the $1.8 million total for only 350 toys. The top lot, a Marklin "Providence," set a new world record for a nautical toy sold at auction, sailing away to the tune of $247,250.

Collectors of die-cast robots competed in September 2012 for items from Ed Sandford's collection of pristine Japanese examples. Most of the top-selling robots were made in the 1960s by companies whose designs are now very rare and collectible, e.g., Popy, Clover, Takara and Bandai. Fetching the highest price was Takara's Diaclone Big-Powered Convoy, a toy that inspired the later Transformer production known as Ultra Magnus. Estimated at $600-$1,000, it muscled its way to a winning bid of $10,800.

The October 2012 auction of Carter's Toy Museum of Zionsville, Indiana, released a dizzying variety of toys of all types to the market. Creator/collector Robert Carter was an inveterate buyer who rarely missed an auction or toy show in the Midwest. As a result, Carter's museum had a wonderfully eclectic look. Its walls, shelves and showcases were packed with colorful wind-up toys, pedal cars, pressed steel vehicles, railroadiana, BB guns and Western toys. Carter also had a fascination for pressed steel trucks from manufacturers such as Buddy 'L' and Keystone as well as pedal cars, toy trains and character toys, including classic pieces by Marx, Linemar and Lehmann.

Two renowned international doll museum collections were offered back-to-back by Theriault's in New Orleans in mid-2012. The two museums offered were the Spielzeugmuseum Prader of Davos, Switzerland, and the Dolls and Dreams Museum of Judene Hansen of Palm Beach, Florida. Surprisingly, a set of American dolls led the pricing battle in the end. A world record price for Madame Alexander was reached with wild bidding when a set of six dolls from the coveted and rare series known as the "Mystery Portrait Dolls" reached a top bid of $88,000. This price, while for a group, is also a world record for any American item in the doll genre.

ERIC BRADLEY *is public relations associate at Heritage Auctions, the world's third largest auction house. He is former editor of* Antique Trader *magazine and is the author of* Antique Trader 2013 Antiques and Collectibles Price Guide, *America's no. 1-selling guide to the antiques and collectibles market. An award-winning investigative journalist with a degree in economics, Bradley has written hundreds of articles about antiques and collectibles and has made several media appearances as an expert on the antiques market at MoneyShow San Francisco, on MSN Money, Nasdaq.com and on AdvisorOne.com. His work has received press from* The New York Times *and* The Philadelphia Inquirer.

Heritage Auctions, Inc.

Teddy Roosevelt on horseback, Steiff Toy Company. Leaping horse with glass eyes, Roosevelt sits atop an Appaloosa with Steiff button in its ear. Roosevelt is dressed in his Rough Rider military outfit with a composition painted head, complete with original gloves, boots and hat. Horse is 38" long with Roosevelt measuring approximately 27" tall, rare. **$7,170**

Hake's Americana & Collectibles Auctions

Girl in stroller, circa 1920, movable wheels, unmarked but most likely by Fisher, pictured in The Book of Penny Toys *by Pressland, page 96, 2 5/8" tall overall.* **$139**

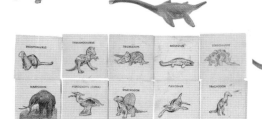

Hake's Americana & Collectibles Auctions

Ten metal dinosaur figures, SRG, circa 1950s, three marked "SRG" and five marked "SRGCO." Each is heavy cast metal with brass/antiqued green finish, sizes range from 2 7/8" to 4" long, each with individual 2" x 2" folder with image of dinosaur on front and text description on inside. Includes trachodon, pterodactyl, brontosaurus, plesiosaur, mosasaur, stegosaurus, tyrannosaurus, dimetrodon, triceratops, and mastodon. **$459**

Heritage Auctions, Inc.

Batman Ride-On Spring-Wound Batmobile, Marx Toys, 1966. One of four variations, car measures approximately 37" long, plastic, some losses, trunk opens, the steering wheel turns the wheels, and the spring mechanism appears to be in working order. Provenance: From the Ben Novack, Jr. Estate Collection. **$179**

Bertoia Auctions

Teddy bear, circa 1910-1920, possibly German, mohair, jointed arms and legs, glass eyes, recovered pads, 22" high. **$177**

Heritage Auctions, Inc.

Dennis the Menace doll and original box, Glad Toy Company, circa 1953, vinyl, head jointed at neck, hair is molded and painted, stationary glassine eyes, 17" tall. **$262**

Heritage Auctions, Inc.

GI Joe action soldier figure, Hasbro, 1964, No. 7500 in original box, excellent condition. Provenance: From the Jack and Julie Juka Collection. **$286**

Bertoia Auctions

Arcade 1932 Checker cab, rare cast iron example painted yellow overall, classic styling, nickel grille, rubber tires, does not contain the "Checkers" sign, 9" long; production was limited, making this model one of the most elusive of any toy auto known. **$8,850**

Hake's Americana & Collectibles Auctions

Pez Space Gun complete countertop display, circa 1950s, 9 1/2" x13 1/2" cardboard display with easel on back, images of a boy and girl using the space guns to fire Pez candy at each other, six hard plastic guns in four different colors, including rare and desirable silver plus yellow, green and three red. Each gun is 5" long with raised design on grips that includes rocketship and planets. **$2,300**

Little Audrey hopping toy, Linemar, Japan, from the Harvey comics list of characters, lithographed tin, key wind operated, bobbing head hopping toy, 4 1/4" high. **$ 324**

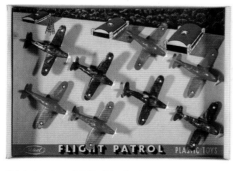

Hake's Americana & Collectibles Auctions

Flight Patrol eight-piece boxed set, Ideal, circa 1940s, 14" x 19 3/4" x 2" deep cardboard box has lid art with view from cockpit with pilot watching warplanes in action, contains eight plastic planes, each 4 1/4" long, replicating P-39 Airacobra with revolving props and wing decals. **$208**

Bertoia Auctions

Marklin live steam ocean liner "Rhein," Germany, circa 1920s, black and red hull, deck structure lifts to reveal steam boiler, upper deck features 16 lifeboats, eight of which are original, cabin and pilot's house simulated wood deck planking, dual propellers, 26" long. Provenance: Ingersoll Collection. **$27,140**

Bertoia Auctions

Bing Steam Vis-À-Vis, circa 1902, Germany, actually known as Bing's Dog Cart, rare steam-driven open auto has early paint scheme of green, yellow and orange with fully railed back rest, slant trap door, opening trap door, nickel head lamps, spoke wheels with rubber tires, seated hand-painted figure added to vehicle, front spring hangers with full running boards, 10" long. Provenance: Ingersoll Collection. **$18,880**

Bertoia Auctions

Hubley truk mixer, rare example, Mack cab with revolving cement drum body, nickeled water tank at top, "TRUK MIXER" embossed on elaborate drum frame, 7 1/2" long. **$14,160**

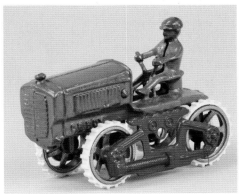

Bertoia Auctions

Kilgore "Oh Boy" tractor, circa 1931, cast iron, painted blue body, red wheel frame, white rubber tread tires, cast figure at driver's seat, embossed "OH BOY" on side of hood, 6" long. Provenance: Ex-Donald Kaufman Collection. **$3,835**

Bertoia Auctions

Kenton fire pumper, cast iron, painted in red overall, gold trimmed boiler cap, white rumble tires, 9" long. Provenance: Ex-Donald Kaufman Collection. **$88**

Bertoia Auctions

Arcade Allis Chalmers tractor, circa 1940, cast iron, painted in Persian orange, nickel driver, large black rubber tires with painted centers, "Allis Chalmers" decal on sides, 7" long. **$265**

Hake's Americana & Collectibles Auctions

"Santee Claus" boxed tin litho wind-up toy, Strauss Mechanical Toys, Ferdinand Strauss Corp., New York, 1921, 4" x 11 1/2" x 4" deep cardboard box has scenes on five sides, 11 1/4" long Santa in sleigh decorated with holly and mistletoe with originals string reins attached to two reindeer on front with metal bells under their noses. **$1,239**

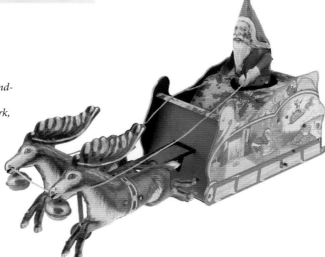

Hake's Americana & Collectibles Auctions

Krazy Kat character "Ignatz Mouse," Knickerbocker, 12" tall overall complete and all original including rubber tail and metal eyes, underside of left foot is stamped "Knickerbocker Toy Co. New York Ignatz Mouse © Intl. Features Service, Inc Trade Mark Des. Pat. Pend." Issued prior to Knickerbocker's production of Mickey Mouse dolls in 1934. **$1,645**

Theriault's

Madame Alexander set of six "Mystery Portrait Dolls," hard plastic, socket head, sleep eyes, closed mouth, five-piece body, with variations, each face hand-painted. Dolls are known by collectors as Champs-Elysee, Victorian Bride, Lady with Rhinestone Beauty Mark (or Judy), Deborah Ballerina, Pink Champagne (or Arlene Dahl) and Kathryn Grayson; only complete set of six known to exist intact from one original owner, each 21" high. **$88,000**

Heritage Auctions, Inc.

Mechanical paper mâché bulldog, electrified, circa 1940s, working condition, bulldog wags tail and moves head when plugged in; sits atop a homemade box covered with flocked fabric, body also flocked in dark brown with horse hair decorating collar, 21 1/2" high overall. **$1,195**

Vintage Fashion Accessories

The history of fashion is a mirror to the future. Nearly every style has already been done in some form and is reproduced with variations today. The popularity and demand for vintage pieces are growing because clothing and accessories are great collectibles that are also a good investment.

Many factors come into play when assessing value. When shopping vintage fashion, keep the following in mind:

Popularity: How well known the designer is affects the price.

Condition: Collectors tend to want the original design condition with no modifications or repairs.

Relevance: The piece should be a meaningful representation of a designer's work.

When you're hot you're hot: As a trend develops, it is shown in fashion magazines, and the original vintage pieces go up in value (and plummet when it goes out of favor).

Location: Prices fluctuate from one geographic region to another.

Value: The appeal of vintage fashion items has greatly increased over the last few years. Our rule of thumb is to buy quality.

For more information on vintage fashion, see *Warman's Handbags Field Guide* by Abigail Rutherford, *Vintage Fashion Accessories* by Stacy LoAlbo, and *Warman's Shoes Field Guide* by Caroline Ashleigh.

Leslie Hindman Auctioneers

Petit Point, French, early 20th century, 8" x 6". **$100-$200**

Handbags

Ritchies Auctioneers

Silk, Bakelite; second bag with faux turquoise, early 20th century, each 10" wide. **$75-$150 each**

Leslie Hindman Auctioneers

Sterling silver mesh bag, early 20th century, 4" x 7". **$200-$400**

Leslie Hindman Auctioneers

Silk, early 20th century, 6" x 6" (left) and 5" x 6". **$50-$100 each**

Leslie Hindman
Auctioneers

*Tiffany &
Company, beaded
purse, early 20th
century,
5" x 6".*
$300-$500

Julie Horvath

*Pearls and rhinestones 1930s
Art Deco-style purse, made in
France by Julie Petit.* **$155**

*Whiting and Davis 1920s black and
white enameled mesh purse (with
worn enameling).* **$195**

Kitsch 'n' Wear

Rose design 1950s vinyl plastic-covered cloth purse. **$65**

Kitsch 'n' Wear

Vinyl-covered embroidered cloth 1950s handbag. **$58**

Tiffany & Company, black silk, mid-20th century, 7" x 5 1/2". **$300-$500**

Roberta di Camerino, mid-20th century, 9" x 8". **$300-$500**

Plastic football purse, mid-20th century, 12" x 7". **$200-$400**

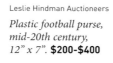

Snakeskin, mid-20th century, 9" x 7" (left) and 11" x 5". **$100-$200 each**

Scarves & Collars

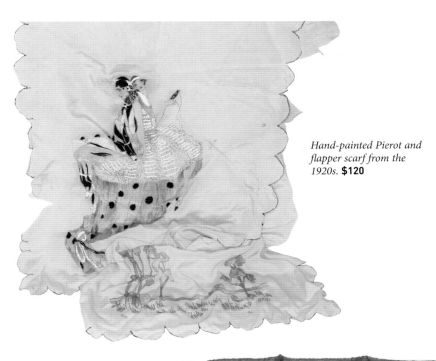

Hand-painted Pierot and flapper scarf from the 1920s. **$120**

Men's Art Deco printed silk 1940s hanky used mostly to decorate the breast pocket of a suit. **$38**

Deco all the way! Black and white silk scarf from the 1940s. **$45** Painted black on white leather gloves with clear glass buttons, from the 1920s. **$80**

Pearl beaded satin collar handmade in the 1940s. **$30**

Genuine leopard collar from the 1950s. **$45**

Silk ladies neck or hair tie in shades of pink and purple by Baar & Beards, circa 1950. **$38**

Shoes

Pair of 1930s brown shoes with beige and teal accents. **$110**

1920s T-strap leather heels with cut out details. **$175**

Late 1960s maroon suede pumps with black patent leather trim. **$68**

Incogneeto collection

Unique retro 1920s but from the 1980s woven Italian leather in antiqued gold by Pupi. **$85**

Sue Stani at Somerville Center Antiques collection

Woven black and white leather 1940s sandals. **$89**

Suede peep-toe heels with polka dot detailing, from the late 1940s. **$95**

Vintage with a Twist collection

Late 1940s metallic brocade pump in red and gold. **$185**

Lovely black beads and rhinestones adorn the pointy-toed vamp here, circa 1955. **$95**

Incogneeto collection

Two-tone leather 1940s resort shoes with an open toe and layered wedge heel. **$275**

Deep maroon reptile embossed leather pumps from the 1950s. **$75**

Lucite slingbacks from the 1950s have pink leather heels and decorations. **$125**

"I. Miller Beautiful Shoes" with pearls and steel-cut beading across the vamp, from the 1950s. **$165**

Vintage with a Twist collection

1960s Andrew Geller black silk pumps with unconventional metallic fish design. **$255**

Late 1950s/early 1960s points with multi layers of brown leather. **$75**

Men's Accessories

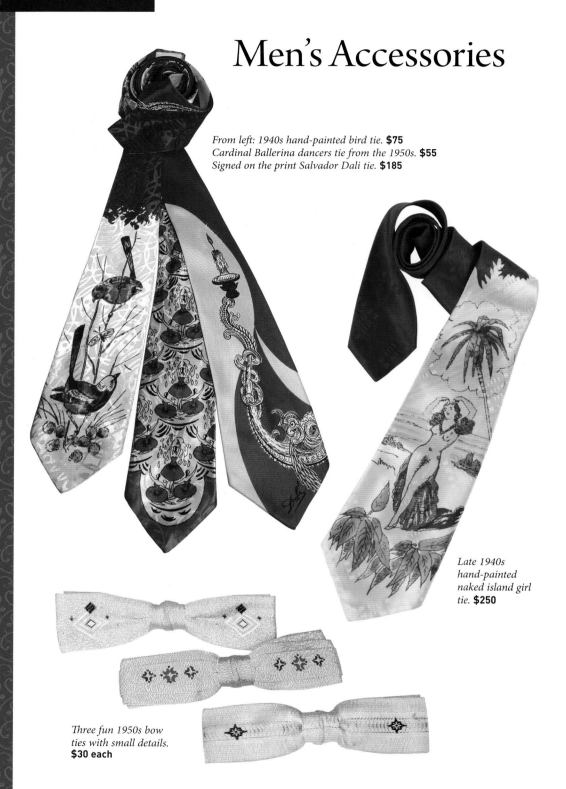

From left: 1940s hand-painted bird tie. **$75**
Cardinal Ballerina dancers tie from the 1950s. **$55**
Signed on the print Salvador Dali tie. **$185**

*Late 1940s
hand-painted
naked island girl
tie.* **$250**

*Three fun 1950s bow
ties with small details.*
$30 each

Early 1960s Bonds velour felt hat with braided band. **$78**

1940s Borsalino fur felt fedora, alongside a vintage store display for Dunlap hats, circa 1955. **$75 each**

The 1940s label states, "Hand Painted Design by Mark of California Pure Silk." **$65**
Hand-painted rayon cravat. **$55**
1950s Cardinal Fifth Ave with dancers. **$48**

From left: Never worn with tag Mercury tailor-made necktie from the 1930s, red and white stitching on brown silk. **$65**
1950s Far East-influenced tie, Palm Creation. **$30**
1960s painted on suede tie. **$55**
1930s "draped ribbon" design silk tie. **$65**

Late 1940s/early 1950s neckties: Oil rig design on a purple and lavender rayon tie. **$55**
Signed in the print Salvador Dali, titled "Inspiration." **$185**
Rayon Haband tie. **$45**

1940s hand-painted pheasant tie. **$75**
1950s hand-painted cowboys. **$60**
1950s rayon paisley and floral in wild colors. **$48**

The prestigious 100-year-old men's clothier of A. Sulka & Company made this all silk tie from the late 1920s. **$110**

Trio of 1950s small print bow ties in silk and rayon. **$28 each**

Late 1940s print on print with large flower design. **$40** "I Like Taft" hand-painted tie, reversible, 1950s. **$45**

1950s Royal Stetson Ivy League fedora. **$85**

1950s Royal Stetson Ivy League fedora. **$85**

Western

The popularity of Western collectibles isn't hard to understand. The Wild West brings to life the fascinating history, lore and culture of the great American frontier and the cowboys, Indians, and enterprising businessmen who helped shape the landscape. Many people have a fascination with the near-mythical gunslingers of the past, like Jesse James and Billy the Kid, whose 130-year-old photo fetched over $2 million at a 2011 auction. Some items associated with Native Americans of note also command high prices, such as an Ogala Sioux war shirt that also sold for over $2 million. (Please see "North American Indian Artifacts" section for more Native American items.)

Western guns such as Colts and Winchesters have long been of interest to collectors. A Colt revolver once wielded by Butch Cassidy, a bank robber and member of the outlaw gang, the Wild Bunch, drew $175,000 at a September 2012 auction, and a Colt once belonging to one of Cassidy's cohorts, Walter Putney, sold for $7,000 at a 2011 auction.

Prices have risen dramatically in the last decade, as collector interest has broadened to other collectibles, including saddles, spurs, badges, art, and items associated with TV and movie cowboys including Roy Rogers and John Wayne.

Sotheby's

Ogala Sioux beaded and fringed war shirt, classic design, composed of two tanned deerskin hides, seamed across top with transverse neck opening, painted with yellow and blue pigments, sinew sewn on front and back in numerous shades of tiny glass seed beads, radiant medallion, shoulders and sleeves with hide strips sinew sewn in red, blue, and two shades of green against a white ground, with linear motifs, the bibs, in similar colors, with a split-panel design, trimmed with quill-wrapped hair pendants and silk ribbon in mustard yellow and deep green, 51 1/2" long. **$2,658,500**

Brian Lebel's Old West Auction

Brian Lebel's Old West Auction

One-of-a-kind, special-order Edward H. Bohlin filigreed spurs, 14k, 18k and 22k gold and sterling silver, maker-marked Bohlinmade/Hollywood/Calif. Fully mounted sterling silver blanks and rose gold filigreed floral pattern heelbands, raised rose gold floral stylized straight shank, yellow gold rope edge, 2 1/8" two-piece 20 pt silver rowels with gold point inlays and 1" gold Indian head rowel covers. Solid silver dove wing spur straps with rose gold filigreed middle and yellow gold flowers along the perimeter inset with rubies. Straps attach to swinging buttons via 1 1/2" rose gold Indian head concho. Entire strap surrounded with twisted yellow rope edge. **$21,850**

G.S. Garcia No. 1 Pattern eagle bit originally designed for the Garcia Beauty, 1904 gold medal-winning saddle ensemble exhibited at the St. Louis World's Fair. Limited production half-breed bit is identical to the one featured on legendary Elko "prize" saddle, with its engraved silver overlay, perched eagle atop a Union shield and cheeks with 2 1/4" scalloped conchas and raised perimeter buttons plus mythical "fairy" horse heads (aka Pharaoh Horses), stylized spread eagle slobber bar, circa 1906-1912. **$3,910**

Brian Lebel's Old West Auction

A 130-year-old tintype photo, billed as the only authenticated picture of legendary outlaw Billy the Kid, who reportedly paid 25 cents to have the photo taken in Fort Sumner, New Mexico. **$2.3 million**

Heritage Auctions, Inc.

Stetson hat with ribbon trim in Annie Oakley's familiar style, purchased as a gift for her by brother-in-law William Butler in Douglas, Wyoming. **$17,295**

Heritage Auctions, Inc.

Carson City, Nevada, rare stage coach broadside, circa 1872, announcing service to "Lake Tahoe, The Gem of the Sierra" provided on J. M. Benton's Stage Line, in company with driver Hank Monk, best-known stage coach driver of the Old West; broadside 11" x 14". **$38,837**

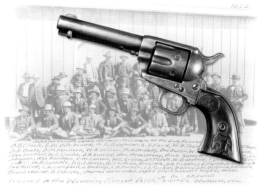

Brian Lebel's Old West Auction

Johnson County War revolver with impeccable provenance, Colt, serial number 11876, in list of "Arms and Accouterments of Major Wolcott's Party," May 8, 1892. Colt is .45 cal. with 4 3/4" barrel and hard rubber eagle grips with F.A. Meanea, Cheyenne, Wyoming holster with trimmed body. J.A. Garrett was only one of four men charged with murder in the first degree by the State of Wyoming (filed in Johnson County) for killing Rueben "Nick" Ray and his partner, Nate Champion, during the invasion of Johnson County and the siege of the K.C. Ranch. Garrett was a Texas gunfighter hired as a regulator by the big cattle ranchers, along with 21 other Texans. **$40,000**

Heritage Auctions, Inc.

Pair of hand-painted porcelain portrait vases of George Armstrong and Elizabeth Custer by photographer and portrait artist R. T. Lux, commissioned by Custer himself, vases of baluster form with bouquets of pink roses bound in blue ribbons, each dated "July 1865," signed "R.T. Lux, N.O.," 11" high. **$53,999**

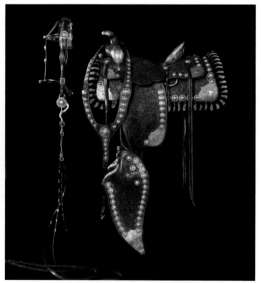

Brian Lebel's Old West Auction

D.E. Walker Visalia show saddle, brown with flower tooling and fixed corona, 24" tapaderos and matching martingale and bridle with Visalia show bit, 240 pieces of sterling silver, including the full cantle and swells, plus 16 gold horse heads. **$25,300**

Brian Lebel's Old West Auction

Colt 1878, serial #26673, 4 3/4" nickel in .38-40 caliber, once owned by Walter Putney, rancher, rustler, bank robber, and member of Hole in the Wall Gang. Frame retains 5 percent nickel, barrel and triggerguard have 80 percent nickel finish, frame in smooth gray with slight amount of blue on hammer in trigger. **$7,000**

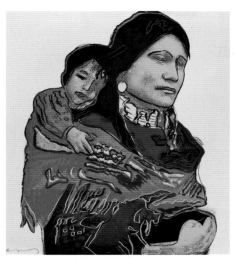

Brian Lebel's Old West Auction

Andy Warhol's Mother and Child Cowboys and Indians Series (1986) T.P. 18/36, serigraph, signed and numbered lower left, 36" x 36" image, framed to 51" x 51". **$16,000**

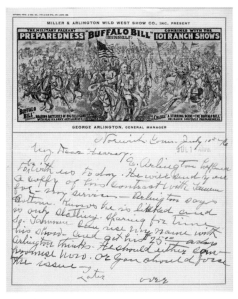

Sotheby's

Autograph letter signed "W.F. Cody," two pages, "Miller & Arlington Wild West Show Co." letterhead reproducing a famous advertising poster, Norwich, Connecticut, 10 July [19]16, to attorney Henry Hersey (here "Hearsy") discussing contracts and negotiations; half morocco and decorated cloth clamshell box, gilt stamped title label and leather fringe on spine, 11" x 8 1/4". **$2,000**

Heritage Auctions, Inc.

Rare cabinet photo of Martha "Calamity Jane" Canary, best remembered for her association with Wild Bill Hickok, with letter of transmittal from the Wyoming photographer; photo 4 1/8" x 6 3/8". **$26,290**

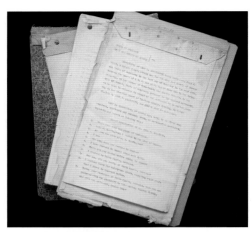

Brian Lebel's Old West Auction

Binders with original set of personal typed depositions in bitterly contested divorce between W.F. "Buffalo Bill" Cody, plaintiff, and Louisa Cody, defendant, circa1905. Papers include official depositions from Louisa, taken in Omaha (113 pages), Mary M. Harrington, taken in Denver (13 pages), Henry Blake, John W. Claire, Mrs. Boyer, Mr. Boyer, Mrs. May Bradford, C.P. Davis, Mrs. Elder, J. Evans, Dr. Gilliam, Miss Parker, and Mr. Parker, taken in Denver and Cheyenne (40 pages). Noted "Wilcox & Halligan" attorneys for Mrs. Cody. Provenance: Believed to be Louisa's own copies that she retained at her home at North Platte, Nebraska, as they are labeled as being from her attorneys. **$5,500**

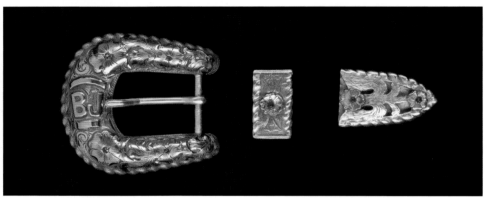

Brian Lebel's Old West Auction

Three-piece sterling and gold set, most likely made by the Srour Company in Los Angeles in late 1920s or early 1930s for mega cowboy movie star Buck Jones, quarter circle "BJ" bar brand on buckle in 10k gold. **$5,000**

Sotheby's

"The Last Drop" by Charles Schreyvogel, bronze, dark brown patina, inscribed "Copyrighted 1903 by Chas. Schreyvogel," with the Roman Bronze Works N-Y- foundry mark, numbered No 70 beneath the base, 12" high. **$56,250**

Brian Lebel's Old West Auction

"Headin' a Steer" watercolor by cowboy artist Edward Borein, signed lower left, 14 5/8" x 19 5/8" (under mat), framed to 31 1/2" x 28". **$120,000**

Sotheby's

Wild West diorama from Malcolm Forbes toy collection, circa 1920s-1960s, featuring Heyde buffalo hunt with cowboys and Indians, Elastolin stagecoach with various cowboys and Indians by Elastolin of Germany, Durso of Belgium, and other European makers; Elastolin wagon train being attacked by Indians; and various cowboy, Indian, U.S. Cavalry and Royal Canadian Mounties by Britains. **$8,750**

Brian Lebel's Old West Auction

Items that belonged to cowboy Chuck Ryan, the All-American Cowhand. Includes: belt and holster rig, revolvers, boots, buckle, spurs, photos, book. Belt and holster rig with a pair of Great Western single-action revolvers, consecutive serial numbers 22226 and 22227, 5 1/2" barrels, .38 special cal. Sterling buckle on belt marked Irvine and Jachens, belt tooled with steer head, initials CCR, eagles, oak leaves and stars. Large central silver conchos on each holster. Spurs are early Fleming marked with sterling overlay and tooled straps with conchos and sterling buckle sets. Custom Dago's Boots – N. Hollywood, Calif. fancy eagle boots with CCR stitched in tops. Trophy buckle is nickel silver and jewelers bronze: Commendation Presentation - The All American Cowhand - Cowboy Chuck Ryan - May 1960 - Courtesy of Secty of State - Presented by D.A.R. - for Patriotic Public Service. Book is number 42/50 of Chuck Ryan – Story of the Golden Voice of the Rangeland by Barbara Riley. **$4,500**

Wine

Not everyone drinks a bottle of wine right after they buy it. Many people collect it and put a cellar together for a variety of reasons, including for investment, whether for the love of certain wines, to make money, or both. If you want to invest because you are a connoisseur of fine wines, you can pick ones you enjoy, with an eye toward ideally selling it at an appreciated value in the future, although there is no guarantee values will go up.

Most investment grade wine is sold at auction, and some of the most popular types are Bordeaux, burgundy, cult wines from Europe and elsewhere, and vintage port. Heritage Auctions, Sotheby's, Christie's, Skinner, and Bonhams 1793 are among the auction houses that have various wine sales throughout the year, with many bottles selling for record prices and sales as a whole bringing in millions of dollars.

In 2011, Christie's sale of a Chateau Mouton-Rothschild collection of magnums, vintages 1945-2005, set a world-record price of $251,660 when it was sold to an Asian buyer. At a Sotheby's auction in Hong Kong, three bottles of Chateau Lafite's 1869 vintage each sold for a record price of $1.8 million ($230,000 in U.S. dollars). These two sales are examples of the large and growing Asian market, which has played an important role in the strong demand for the finest wines in the world over the last few years.

Before you decide to start collecting wine, it's important to have a place where it can be stored properly—a dark area with optimal temperature and humidity levels. A custom-built cellar or pre-made wine cabinet that keeps bottles around 55 to 58 degrees, with relative humidity of 60 to 75 percent, is suitable for wine. You can also buy a wine cabinet that's environmentally controlled, or space in wine-storage facilities common in larger cities.

Heritage Auctions, Inc.

Chateau Petrus red Bordeaux, Pomerol, 12 bottles, 2000. **$46,555**

Sotheby's

Three bottles of Echezeaux Henri Jayer, Cote de Nuits, Grand Cru, one capsule removed to reveal fully branded cork, capsules with French tax stamps, one nicked label, one nicked vintage neck label, 1993. **$17,355**

Sotheby's

Louis Roederer, Cristal Brut, packed in individual gift cartons, 12 bottles, 1990. **$7,573**

Sotheby's

Rare Nebuchadnezzar 15-liter bottle of Masseto 2007, one of only eight bottles ever produced by the Italian winery, Tenuta dell'Ornellaia. **$49,000**

Heritage Auctions, Inc.

Romanee Conti red burgundy, Domaine de la Romanee Conti, 2009. **$10,755**

Heritage Auctions, Inc.

Chateau Petrus red Bordeaux, Pomerol, 12 bottles, 1996. **$17,925**

Heritage Auctions, Inc.

La Tache red burgundy, Domaine de la Romanee Conti, three bottles, 2005. **$8,365**

Collection of wine from the "Wild Goose," 1970s. Eighteen bottles from the Windsor Vineyards in Healdsburg, California, various types including Cabernet Sauvignon, Pinot Noir, Petite Syrah, and Zinfandel among others, all with customized labels noting the wine was "Selected by John Wayne for Hospitality Aboard The Wild Goose"; other similar type labels, though all with slightly different verbiage, each bottle 12" high or shorter. **$4,780**

Heritage Auctions, Inc.

Domestic Syrah/ Grenache, Sine Qua Non Grenache, The Inaugural, six bottles, 2003. **$5,078**

Heritage Auctions, Inc.

Chateau Pavie red Bordeaux, St. Emilion, 24 half bottles, 2000. **$4,033**

Heritage Auctions, Inc.

Chateau d'Yquem white Bordeaux, Sauternes, 12 bottles, 2001. **$5,975**

Heritage Auctions, Inc.

Chateau Lafite Rothschild red Bordeaux, Pauillac, 12 bottles, 1982. **$50,787**

Heritage Auctions, Inc.

Meursault white burgundy, Les Perrieres, Coche-Dury, three bottles, 1992. **$4,780**

Heritage Auctions, Inc.

Domestic Cabernet Sauvignon/Meritage, Harlan Estate Cabernet Sauvignon, six bottles, 2007. **$4,481**

Heritage Auctions, Inc.

Chateau Haut Brion red Bordeaux, Pessac-Leognan, 1998. **$8,066**

Heritage Auctions, Inc.

Montrachet white burgundy, Domaine de la Romanee Conti, three bottles, 2004. **$8,365**

Heritage Auctions, Inc.

Richebourg red burgundy, H. Jayer, Martine's Wines integrated label, one bottle, 1978. **$10,157**

Heritage Auctions, Inc.

Chateau Latour red Bordeaux, Pauillac, Imperial, 1982. **$16,730**

Heritage Auctions, Inc.

Twenty-one bottles from Bond Winery, all red: two bottles of 2003 Matriarch; one bottle of 2004 Matriarch; three bottles of 2003 Melbury; two bottles of 2004 Melbury; three bottles of 2003 Pluribus; one bottle of 2004 Pluribus; four bottles of 2003 St. Eden; two bottles of 2004 St. Eden; two bottles of 2003 Vecina; and one bottle of 2004. **$3,585**

World War II Collectibles

In the 65 years since the end of World War II, veterans, collectors, and history buffs have eagerly bought, sold and traded the "spoils of war." Actually, souvenir collecting began as soon as troops set foot on foreign soil.

Soldiers from every nation involved in the greatest armed conflict mankind has known eagerly sought items that would remind them of their time in the service, validate their presence during the making of history, and potentially generate income when they returned home. Such items might also be bartered with fellow soldiers for highly prized or scarce goods. Helmets, medals, Lugers, field gear, daggers, and other pieces of war material filled parcels, which were mailed home or stuffed into the duffel bags of soldiers who gathered them.

As soon as hostilities ended in 1945, the populations of the defeated nations quickly realized that they could make money by selling souvenirs to their former enemies. This was particularly true in Germany and Japan, which hosted large contingents of occupying U.S. soldiers and troops from other Allied nations. The flow of war material increased. Values became well established. For instance, a Luger was worth several packs of cigarettes, a helmet, just one. A Japanese sword was worth two boxes of K-rations, and an Arisaka bayonet was worth a chocolate Hershey bar.

Over the years, these values have remained proportionally consistent. Today, that "two-pack" Luger might be worth $4,000 and that one-pack helmet $1,000. The Japanese sword might fetch $1,200 and the Arisaka bayonet $85. Though values have increased dramatically, demand has not slackened. In fact, World War II collecting is the largest segment of the militaria hobby.

For more information on World War II collectibles, see *Warman's World War II Collectibles Identification and Price Guide* by Michael E. Haskew.

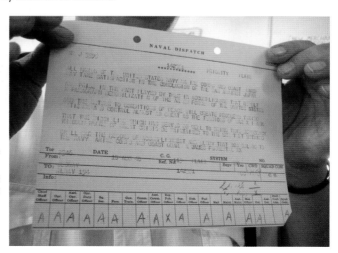

Kirk Williams/Col. Kirk's Auction Gallery

Rare naval dispatch heralding the end of hostilities with Japan, received aboard the USS Holland on Aug. 15, 1945, after the bombing of Hiroshima and Nagasaki. The 112-word dispatch, 8" x 6 1/2", from President Harry S. Truman's navy secretary said, in part: "All hands of the United States Navy, Marine Corps and Coast Guard may take satisfaction in the conclusion of the war against Japan." **$20,500**

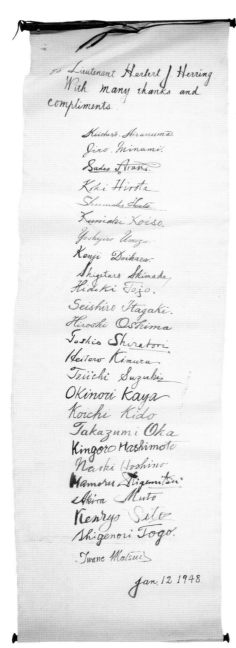

Heritage Auctions, Inc.

Original B-26 nose art painting "Gee Bee," by Sgt. Elwood Thompson, featuring cartoon bee stinging pained Adolf Hitler character over number "59," signed lower right "E. C. Thompson 44," in mat 10 1/2" x 13 3/4". **$2,270**

Heritage Auctions, Inc.

Japanese prisoners of war scroll, printed on cloth with wooden scroll bars, 25 prisoners tried in Tokyo Trials listed, scroll dedicated "To Lieutenant Herbert J. Herring/With many thanks and compliments," dated Jan. 12, 1948, three months before trial convened; 21 3/4" x 71 1/2". **$4,780**

Peter Suciu

Model 1928 Bersaglieri sun helmet. **$500-$750**

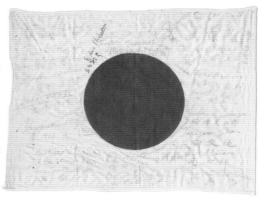

Heritage Auctions, Inc.

Japanese flag, cloth, autographed by 24 accused World War II criminals including Prime Minister Tojo, 13" x 10 1/2". **$16,100**

Mohawk Arms Inc. Militaria Auctions

Merit award, gilt chrysanthemum, green enameled cross. **$50**

Heritage Auctions, Inc.

American prisoner of war archive of Captain Craig D. Campbell, aide-de-camp to General Dwight D. Eisenhower. Covers all facets of Captain Campbell's military service from the issuance of his Selective Service card (included), training, and deployment to North Africa as a member of Eisenhower's staff, capture, captivity in German prisoner of war camp Oflag 64, liberation by Russian troops, return to service as an aide-de-camp to Eisenhower, and eventual discharge from the Army. Included: more than 100 letters and photographs from P.O.W. camp, original copies of camp newspaper, The Oflag 64 Item; inscribed and signed 7 1/2" x 9 3/4" photograph of Eisenhower that reads, "To Capt. Craig Campbell - My former aide - with best wishes, Dwight D. Eisenhower, Germany 1945"; period patch from Supreme Headquarters Allied Expeditionary Force; receipt to "General Eisenhower" from Simpson & Son (Livery Outfitters) of London for "4 sets of medal ribbons"; receipt to "General Dwight D. Eisenhower" from Peal and Co., boot makers, of London for "1 Pr. Brown Field Boots, well eased left bunion and cleaned / Own Trees, added bunion to left." **$2,151**

Heritage Auctions, Inc.

Propaganda poster by J. H. King, U.S. Government Printing Office, 1943, "We've Made a Monkey Out of You!" showing Hitler as organ grinder's monkey, begging for coins, as Uncle Sam grinds organ, making the monkey dance, and leaders of free world—John Bull from England, Joseph Stalin from Russia, and Chiang Kai-shek from China— laugh,15" x 20". **$836**

Heritage Auctions, Inc.

Joe Louis propaganda poster, 1942. During World War II, Louis went into the army and fought numerous exhibitions to raise troop morale and contributed the entirety of his boxing purses to the war effort. In 1942, the army had Louis pose for this now famous poster, which pictures him in army gear with bayonet and slogan, "…we'll win because we're on God's side," scarce, 18" x 25". **$334**

Rock Island Auction Co.

Miniature Japanese Katana in Tashe mounting, 15 1/2" blade. **$750-$1,200**

Heritage Auctions, Inc.

Three-sheet "The Memphis Belle" poster, Paramount, 1944, 41" x 81". In order to correctly document the last mission of the B-17 Flying Fortress nicknamed "Memphis Belle," director William Wyler flew along with the crew on several raids and did some filming himself at great personal risk. The result was one of the finest documentaries ever to come out of the offices of the War Activities Committee. **$334**

Heritage Auctions

American Volunteer Group Flying Tiger enameled pin and Chinese Air Force wing. Flying Tiger pin is 1", pin-back, with enamels and red stone mounted in flying tiger's mouth, back is stamped with Whitehead & Hoag company mark and "1/20-10KT Gold Filled"; gilt and enamel Chinese Army wing measures 3", with screw-back fasteners, stamped with Chinese characters and number "62949." **$1,195**

Heritage Auctions, Inc.

Large silver presentation punch bowl given to Admiral William "Bull" Halsey, who commanded the United States Navy's Third Fleet, engraved with diamond-shaped lozenge and inscription, "Presented to Admiral Bull Halsey From His Staff 1945," 16" diameter, 12 1/4" high. **$3,585**

Heritage Auctions, Inc.

Jack Kirby and Dick Ayers Sgt. Fury #2 "Weapons of War: Chatter Guns of World War II" page original art, Marvel, 1963. Details the array of machine guns Kirby himself had to face during his combat days, signed at lower right, 12 1/2" x 18 1/2". **$2,151**

Heritage Auctions, Inc.

Pair of John F. Kennedy's undershorts from his naval training at Melville, Rhode Island, in 1943. **$2,509**

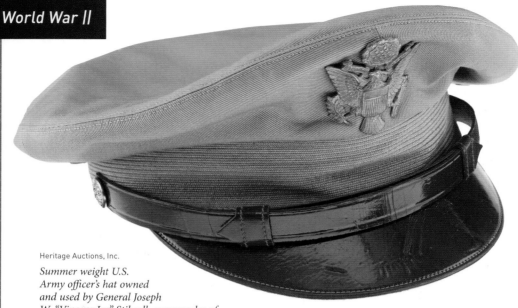

Heritage Auctions, Inc.

*Summer weight U.S.
Army officer's hat owned
and used by General Joseph
W. "Vinegar Joe" Stilwell, commander of
China/Burma/India Theater, period, high gloss brown patent
leather visor and chinstrap, original gilt brass eagle hat insignia.
Donated by Stilwell to an auction to help raise money for Navy
Relief Fund, accompanied by letter of provenance.* **$3,585**

Rock Island Auction Co.

*Mk. 1 John Inglis & Co.
pistol, Chinese contract
model.* **$950-$2,250**

Heritage Auctions, Inc.

*General Matthew B. Ridgway's overseas cap with two bullion stars and braid trim, size 7, with name of
English maker J. Collett Ltd. and 1944 date on inside leather band. Made for Ridgway in Britain awaiting
D-Day. His 82nd Airborne unit played a major role in the invasion. He succeeded Douglas MacArthur in
Korea and was Army Chief of Staff 1953-1955.* **$836**

Camp Ripley Museum

Overseas cap for enlisted parachute infantryman.
$85-$165

www.advanceguardmilitaria.com

Model 40 army helmet with gray camouflage. **$675-$850**

www.advanceguardmilitaria.com

MK IV gas mask and pouch. **$100-$125**

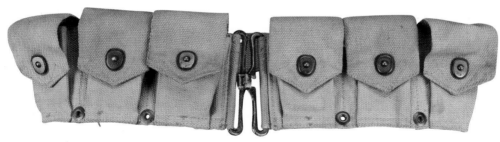

www.advanceguardmilitaria.com

Marines cartridge belt with large USMC stamp on interior. **$75-$95**

Rock Island Auction Co.

1940-dated Mauser code 42 Luger pistol with a number mismatched magazine. **$1,200-$1,600**

Index

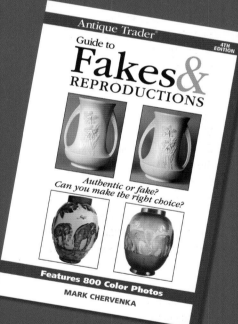

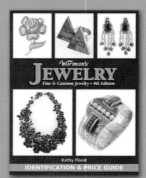
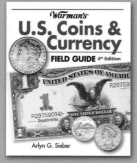
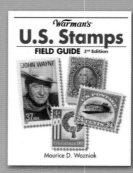

Pottery Appreciated

Pigeon Forge
ampbell
McCoy
ey Gonde
Teco **Owens** Dou
American Encaustic Tiling Con
urley Winter Motawi **Coors**
Zane Stangl **Grueby** Tren
Robinson Ransbottom Weatley Watt
Avon Faience Hull **Nicodemu** Alhar
rd **Weller** Van Briggle M
ch Art Pottery Com
Zanesville Majolica **Door** Hamilto
rk Brush McCoy **Pauline Pot**
Hartford Campbell
Roseville Katrich
Ford Kensington Art Tile Com
hardt Tiffany **Marblehead**
Mosaic Saturday Evening Gi
well Teco Moravian
er **Rookwood**
California Art Tile Com
Galloway **Cambridg**
ington Shawnee Niloak
Newcomb
& Reed **Camark Ephrain**
Grindley Pardee Wo
mmon Ground Clev
Unzicker Broth
Cowan Fa
Revere Pottery Pewabi
ce Fulper Clark Stoneware
Kensington M

Every Piece Counts

BELHORN
AUCTIONS

BelhornAuctions.com | (614) 921-9441

GURNEE ANTIQUE CENTER, L.L.C

The Gurnee Antique Center offers antiques and fine collectibles through the mid 20th century in a comfortable and spacious 24,000 sq. ft. building - a paradise for collectors, decorators, and casual shoppers.

Unlike many "antique" stores, we strive to sell true antiques and no reproductions. We have a 50+ years old rule, with very limited exceptions.

A large barn-like red structure visible from I-94, we're located in Gurnee near Six Flags Great America, & a short hop to the Naval Training Center, Great Lakes or the Gurnee Mills Outlets.

We're close to the Wisconsin Border, about an hour North of Chicago and ½ hour from O'Hare.

Now in our 14th successful year, we welcome antiquers & seekers of the rare, beautiful, and unusual.

Store-wide Sales occur 3 times a year: Labor Day and Memorial Day week-ends & mid-December. Call for dates.

5742 Northridge Dr., Gurnee, IL 60031

From I-94 Take Route 132 East. Turn right at Dilleys Road (1st stop light) follow Dilleys Road into Northridge Dr.

Closed only on Easter, Thanksgiving, and Christmas Day.

Gift Certificates Available.

(847) 782-9094

www.GurneeAntiqueCenter.com

19th - Mid 20th Century:
Baccarat
Belleek - Irish
Buffalo Pottery
Carnival Glass
Doulton - Royal Doulton
Ironstone China
Limoges
Majolica
Mary Gregory
Royal Dux
Royal Worcester
Satin Glass
Staffordshire
Wedgwood
Zsolnay
&
American Antiques

Antique Legacies
www.antiquelegacies.com
email: antique_legacies@comcast.net
www.facebook.com/Antique.Legacies

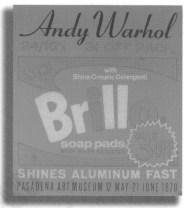